W9-DJC-703

Seattle

Debra Miller

LONELY PLANET PUBLICATIONS
Melbourne • Oakland • London • Paris

Seattle
2nd edition – November 2001
First published – September 1998

Published by
Lonely Planet Publications Pty Ltd ABN 36 005 607 983
90 Maribyrnong St, Footscray, Victoria 3011, Australia

Lonely Planet Offices
Australia Locked Bag 1, Footscray, Victoria 3011
USA 150 Linden St, Oakland, CA 94607
UK 10a Spring Place, London NW5 3BH
France 1 rue du Dahomey, 75011 Paris

Photographs
Many of the images in this guide are available for licensing from
Lonely Planet Images.
email: lpi@lonelyplanet.com.au

Front cover photograph
Fishermen's Terminal, Salmon Bay, Seattle (Richard Cummins)

Map section photograph
Space Needle, Seattle (Ann Cecil)

ISBN 1 86450 304 1

text & maps © Lonely Planet Publications Pty Ltd 2001
photos © photographers as indicated 2001

Printed by Colorcraft Ltd, Hong Kong

Contents

ACTIVITIES   119

PLACES TO STAY   129

PLACES TO EAT   137

ENTERTAINMENT   156

SHOPPING   169

EXCURSIONS   176

INDEX   206

MAP SECTION   217

The Author

Debra Miller

Deb was born in Halifax, Nova Scotia, and raised on the other side of Canada, in North Vancouver. After wandering the world and slinging cocktails at various bartending gigs, she finally got a writing degree from the University of Victoria. Deb worked as a reporter before joining Lonely Planet's Oakland office as an editor for Pisces Diving & Snorkeling guides. The magical Pacific Northwest keeps pulling her back – one can never tire of watching the Pacific waves or climbing through fir forests. In addition to *Seattle,* Deb has co-authored Lonely Planet's *British Columbia* and *Pacific Northwest.*

FROM THE AUTHOR

This book is dedicated to the memory of Maia Hansen (1966–2001), whose adventurous spirit and capacity for great laughter and love continue to inspire me daily. We miss you.

Many people helped me write this book, from the anonymous guy I shared a fish burger with at Pike Place Market to the many coffee and beer slingers I chatted up around town – I thank you all for sharing your local knowledge. More thanks go to: David Takami at Seattle Parks for his enthusiasm and assistance; Andrew Hanson-Krueger, whose knowledge of Pike Place Market is as incredible as the market itself; Amy Dodson for hooking us up at EMP; Dan Savage for his enlightened views on sex in the city; Sean Keller, who saved me from rainy days with pints of beer and good conversation; Richard I'Anson for the interesting chat at the Alibi Room; and Suki Gear and Sid and Brent Hayes for their helpful takes on the Seattle scene.

Big gratitude goes to Doug, Carol and Alex Miller for bestowing family love (and great sailing); to Rob Landau, and to my family and friends in Vancouver and California, thank you all for your patience, trust and understanding of my need to roam.

I thank David Zingarelli, Mariah Bear and everyone at LP for their incredible support when things got rough; my editor Paul Sheridan for his excellent sense of humor and careful eye; and Mary Hagemann, Patrick Huerta, Annette Olson and especially Tracey Croom for their cartography expertise. Thanks to Laura Harger for asking me to do this project in the first place and Carolyn Hubbard for the always-excellent advice.

Kudos to Bill McRae, who wrote the 1st edition, a sturdy framework that made my job writing this 2nd edition much easier.

Maia Hansen graciously updated the San Juan Islands and Eastside portions of this text. I can never thank Maia and Clark Yeomans enough for allowing me to share their Seattle home, their friends and their love of the Northwest outdoors. I'll never forget you, the laughs or the time we spent together, sharing cups of tea and your view of the Olympics at sunset.

This Book

The 1st edition of *Seattle* was written by Bill McRae.

FROM THE PUBLISHER

It never rains, but it pours. And to prove it, a deluge of people equally knowledgeable about travel and publishing pooled resources in the sunny Oakland, USA, office of Lonely Planet to swiftly transform the 2nd edition of Seattle from manuscript to book. Paul Sheridan edited the book, but wouldn't have been able to pull it all together without the expert guidance of senior editor David Zingarelli. Kathryn Ettinger edited the Excursions chapter. Proofing went smoothly along like a log down a skid road courtesy of Kevin Anglin, Pelin Thornhill and Wendy Taylor. Managing editor Kate Hoffman oversaw the whole process.

Now, we'd be nowhere without the maps. They were crafted by Lonely Planet cartographers Mary Hagemann and Patrick Huerta with the guidance of senior cartographer Tracey Croom. Justin Colgan, Tim Lohnes and Bart Wright also lent their expertise.

Think it looks good? It's all down to the design team of Wendy Yanagihara and Jenn Steffey, who laid out the book with the help of Gerilyn Attebery. Wendy also designed the colorwraps. Design manager Susan Rimerman kept the whole thing together and designed the fabulous cover to boot. And just to show imagination and talent go hand in hand, the original illustrations were drawn by our very own talented and good-humored illustrators Becca Lafore, Justin Marler and Jenn Steffey. Thanks also to Hugh D'Andrade, Shelley Firth, Hayden Foell, Beth Grundvig, Rini Keagy and Jim Swanson for their illustration legacies.

ACKNOWLEDGMENTS

Gratitude to King County Metro Transit for letting us reproduce its map of public transportation and to Seattle Public Library for allowing us to reproduce some of its historical photographs.

Foreword

ABOUT LONELY PLANET GUIDEBOOKS

The story begins with a classic travel adventure: Tony and Maureen Wheeler's 1972 journey across Europe and Asia to Australia. Useful information about the overland trail did not exist at that time, so Tony and Maureen published the first Lonely Planet guidebook to meet a growing need.

From a kitchen table, then from a tiny office in Melbourne (Australia), Lonely Planet has become the largest independent travel publisher in the world, an international company that has offices in Melbourne, Oakland (USA), London (UK) and Paris (France).

Today Lonely Planet guidebooks cover the globe. There is an ever-growing list of books, and there's information in a variety of forms and media. Some things haven't changed. The main aim is still to help make it possible for adventurous travelers to get out there – to explore and better understand the world.

At Lonely Planet we believe travelers can make a positive contribution to the countries they visit – if they respect their host communities and spend their money wisely. Since 1986 a percentage of the income from each book has been donated to aid projects and human-rights campaigns.

Updates Lonely Planet thoroughly updates each guidebook as often as possible. This usually means there are around two years between editions, although for more unusual or more stable destinations the gap can be longer. Check the imprint page (usually following the color map at the beginning of the book) for publication dates.

Between editions up-to-date information is available in two free newsletters – the paper *Planet Talk* and email *Comet* (to subscribe, contact any Lonely Planet office) – and on our Web site at www.lonelyplanet.com. The *Upgrades* section of the Web site covers a number of important and volatile destinations and is regularly updated by Lonely Planet authors. *Scoop* covers news and current affairs relevant to travelers. And, lastly, *the Thorn Tree* bulletin board and *Postcards* section of the site carry unverified, but fascinating, reports from travelers.

Correspondence The process of creating new editions begins with the letters, postcards and emails received from travelers. This correspondence often includes suggestions, criticisms and comments about the current editions. Interesting excerpts are immediately passed on via newsletters and the Web site, and everything goes to our authors to be verified when they're researching on the road. We're keen to get more feedback from organizations or individuals who represent communities visited by travelers.

> Lonely Planet gathers information for everyone who's curious about the planet – and especially for those who explore it first-hand. Through guidebooks, phrasebooks, activity guides, maps, literature, newsletters, image library, TV series and Web site we act as an information exchange for a worldwide community of travelers.

Research Authors aim to gather sufficient practical information to enable travelers to make informed choices and to make the mechanics of a journey run smoothly. They also research historical and cultural background to help enrich the travel experience and allow travelers to understand and respond appropriately to cultural and environmental issues.

Authors don't stay in every hotel because that would mean spending a couple of months in each medium-size city and, no, they don't eat at every restaurant because that would mean stretching belts beyond capacity. They do visit hotels and restaurants to check standards and prices, but feedback based on readers' direct experiences can be very helpful.

Many of our authors work undercover; others aren't so secretive. None of them accept freebies in exchange for positive write-ups. And none of our guidebooks contain any advertising.

Production Authors submit their raw manuscripts and maps to offices in Australia, the USA, the UK or France. Editors and cartographers – all experienced travelers themselves – then begin the process of assembling the pieces. When the book finally hits the shops, some things are already out of date, we start getting feedback from readers and the process begins again...

WARNING & REQUEST

Things change – prices go up, schedules change, good places go bad and bad places go bankrupt – nothing stays the same. So, if you find things better or worse, recently opened or long since closed, please tell us and help make the next edition even more accurate and useful. We genuinely value all the feedback we receive. A well-traveled team reads and acknowledges every letter, postcard and email and ensures that every morsel of information finds its way to the appropriate authors, editors and cartographers for verification.

Everyone who writes to us will find their name in the next edition of the appropriate guidebook. They will also receive the latest issue of *Planet Talk*, our quarterly printed newsletter, or *Comet*, our monthly email newsletter. Subscriptions to both newsletters are free. The very best contributions will be rewarded with a free guidebook.

Excerpts from your correspondence may appear in new editions of Lonely Planet guidebooks, the Lonely Planet Web site, *Planet Talk* or *Comet*, so please let us know if you *don't* want your letter published or your name acknowledged.

Send all correspondence to the Lonely Planet office closest to you:

Australia: Locked Bag 1, Footscray, Victoria 3011
USA: 150 Linden St, Oakland, CA 94607
UK: 10a Spring Place, London NW5 3BH
France: 1 rue du Dahomey, 75011 Paris

Or email us at: talk2us@lonelyplanet.com.au

For news, views and updates, see our Web site: www.lonelyplanet.com

HOW TO USE A LONELY PLANET GUIDEBOOK

The best way to use a Lonely Planet guidebook is any way you choose. At Lonely Planet, we believe the most memorable travel experiences are often those that are unexpected, and the finest discoveries are those you make yourself. Guidebooks are not intended to be used as if they provided a detailed set of infallible instructions!

Contents All Lonely Planet guidebooks follow roughly the same format. The Facts about the Destination chapters or sections give background information ranging from history to weather. Facts for the Visitor gives practical information on issues like visas and health. Getting There & Away gives a brief starting point for researching travel to and from the destination. Getting Around gives an overview of the transport options when you arrive.

The peculiar demands of each destination determine how subsequent chapters are broken up, but some things remain constant. We always start with background, then proceed to sights, places to stay, places to eat, entertainment, getting there and away, and getting around information – in that order.

Heading Hierarchy Lonely Planet headings are used in a strict hierarchical structure that can be visualized as a set of Russian dolls. Each heading (and its following text) is encompassed by any preceding heading that is higher on the hierarchical ladder.

Entry Points We do not assume guidebooks will be read from beginning to end, but that people will dip into them. The traditional entry points are the list of contents and the index. In addition, however, some books have a complete list of maps and an index map illustrating map coverage.

There may also be a color map that shows highlights. These highlights are dealt with in greater detail in the Facts for the Visitor chapter, along with planning questions and suggested itineraries. Each chapter covering a geographical region usually begins with a locator map and another list of highlights. Once you find something of interest in a list of highlights, turn to the index.

Maps Maps play a crucial role in Lonely Planet guidebooks and include a huge amount of information. A legend is printed on the back page. We seek to have complete consistency between maps and text and to have every important place in the text captured on a map. Map key numbers usually start in the top left corner.

> Although inclusion in a guidebook usually implies a recommendation, we cannot list every good place. Exclusion does not necessarily imply criticism. In fact there are a number of reasons why we might exclude a place – sometimes it is simply inappropriate to encourage an influx of travelers.

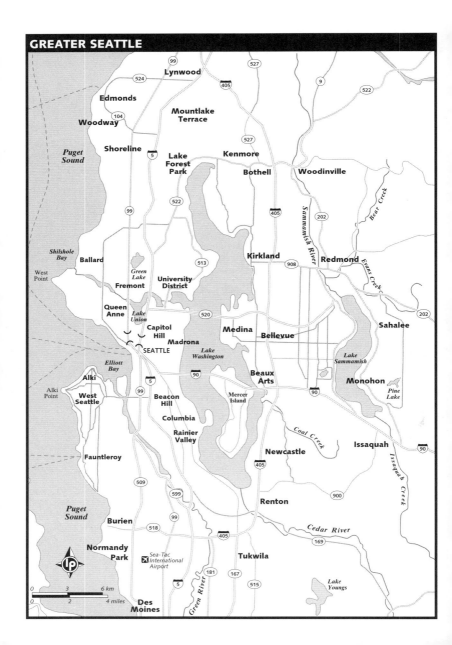

Introduction

Head out in a kayak on Lake Union at sunset, breathe in the fresh Northwest air, dock by a lakeside tavern and rejoice that you've earned your beer. Slip away on a ferry, saddle up to a smoky bar or lap up the rain on your face. Eat your heart out at the famous Pike Place Market, boogie down at a Capitol Hill club or flutter with the ballet at Benaroya Hall. This is the life, up here in the far northwest corner of the USA, a place not too long ago considered a backwater full of rednecks but today shining with the glory longtime residents know to their core. You don't just come to Seattle; rather, in no time at all the majestic mountains, lush forests and weaving waterways, well, they come to you.

The snow-capped Olympic Mountains rise out of the west across the deep blue waters of Puget Sound, as ships and ferries wind through scattered, green-clad islands. South and east of the city are the massive peaks of the Cascade volcanoes, with Mt Rainier, known in Seattle simply as 'the mountain,' taking up half the horizon. Lakes Union and Washington connect to Puget Sound, making it seem like water flows in every direction.

Until very recently, as late as the 1970s, Seattle was a fairly nondescript, midsize city peopled by frontier-stock families with progressive but hardly avant-garde ideas. Within one generation, however, Puget Sound's population more than doubled. The city's collective confidence grew and things started to change. In the '80s, with the advent of grunge music and the whirring sounds of espresso machines, Seattle started to get interesting as a cultural center when its locally born idealists, artists and writers stayed home instead of heading elsewhere to find success. Seattle was like an undiscovered gold mine and cultural prospectors started mining it in droves.

What's interesting is not just how Seattle arrived at the cultural table, but also what it brought. A town whose economics depended almost solely on Boeing's manufacturing plant, Seattle's financial outlook changed dramatically when high-tech companies, led by Microsoft, realized the pot of gold at the end of the rainbow sat brimming right here. The influx of technologically trained Californians and other out-of-state immigrants, who brought with them pop-culture instincts and media savvy, added significantly to the artistic brew.

The largest city in Washington, Seattle is the core of the USA's Pacific Northwest. Its busy port connects the rest of the nation with the Pacific Rim and its success as a trade and manufacturing center, mixed with its beautiful, big-as-all-outdoors setting, makes it one of the fastest growing cities in the USA. Young people especially find their way to this seaport in the upper-left corner of the country, in search of a city that offers economic opportunity, easy access to recreation and forward-looking politics and culture. In short, if you're looking for lifestyle, Seattle has it in spades.

Seattle almost single-handedly made coffee a national obsession. But for a city that spends 90% of its time jacked up on caffeine, Seattle maintains a fairly mellow and laid-back attitude. Fitness and outdoor recreation come naturally here, and whether you're climbing mountains or cycling through downtown traffic, there's a healthy respect for the outdoors you don't find in most big US cities. Yeah, sure it rains. OK, it rains a lot. But throw on the proper gear and readjust your attitude, and the rain becomes refreshing.

While many of Seattle's big-ticket attractions – the market, Pioneer Square, the Waterfront – are downtown, Seattle's outlying neighborhoods are distinct enclaves, getting more defined as time goes on. Fremont relishes in its quirkiness, Wallingford embraces the solid virtues of an old-fashioned neighborhood, Ballard toasts a pint to anyone who will listen and Capitol Hill lovingly embraces every and all forms of sexual orientation. Conversations in the University

District cover the gamut from Aldo Leopold's environmental philosophies to where to get a good tattoo. Queen Anne is just so damn good-looking, and Seattle Center keeps a carnival-like atmosphere all year long. Dim sum doesn't get any better than in the International District, and the Central District serves up the best fried chicken this side of the bayou. West Seattle, which juts its shiny nose into the sound, and neighborhoods along Lake Washington take full advantage of their natural paradise.

Seattle's restaurants give any big city a run for its money, its small fringe theater and dance troupes receive much national recognition and the experimental music scene beats in the warm, fuzzy glow of an ever-supportive local audience. The Seattle Mariners' Safeco Field is just about the best place in the world to watch the sunset and a baseball game, and the NFL Seattle Seahawks have grand plans for their new $450 million stadium.

These are fine times for the Pacific Northwest's Emerald City. The youthful millionaires the area's high-tech industry spat out like empty peanut shells are fueling money into the city's landscape, small businesses and arts. The flow of philanthropic and investment dollars has added a new element of sophistication and frivolousness to a town formerly rooted in its practical but staid ways.

Of course, all this growth and vitality comes at a cost. The rush to Seattle threatens the very features and values that made people move here in the first place. Crime rates are rising, traffic in many parts of the city is at gridlock much of the day and increased housing prices force anyone on a budget further to the city's edges. Urban sprawl is claiming more and more farmland and is converting outlying towns into suburbs.

But perhaps the best part of Seattle is its contradictions. As much as everyone hates the traffic and the one-way flood of people coming into the city, longtime residents are gratified that the rest of the world has finally noticed that the good life *is* Seattle.

Facts about Seattle

HISTORY

For a major US city, Seattle's civic history begins very late in the chronicle of the nation. While the rest of the country had established firm roots, most of today's Seattle was covered in deep forest that was perennially drenched in rain. Though native groups lived here since before the recognized dawn of time, colonialist settlement didn't reach Puget Sound until 1851.

Native Peoples of Puget Sound

When the accumulated ice of the great polar glaciers of the Pleistocene Epoch lowered sea levels throughout the world, the ancestors of American Indians migrated from Siberia to Alaska via a land bridge across the Bering Strait. By this reckoning, the present tribes of Puget Sound arrived here 11,000 or 12,000 years ago, before the glaciers receded.

Unlike the Plains Indians living further inland, who were primarily nomadic hunter-gatherers, the first inhabitants of the Pacific Northwest were intimately tied to the rivers, lakes and sea. The tribe living on the site of today's Seattle was called the Duwamish. While nearby Olympic Peninsula tribes like the Quinault, Quileute and Makah went to sea in pursuit of whales, the Duwamish and other tribal groups along Puget Sound – notably the Suquamish, Coast Salish and Chinook – depended on catching salmon, cod and shellfish. On land, they hunted deer and elk, more for their protective hides than for their flesh. Though each group had its own dialect, coastal natives communicated through a language called Lushootseed, which natives today struggle to keep from extinction.

Summer and fall were dedicated to harvesting the bounty of the sea and forest. Food was stored in massive quantities to

Potlatch ceremony, Seattle area tribes – 1912

carry the tribes through the long winter months, when the most important ancient legends and ceremonies were handed down to the younger generations. In terms of artistic, religious and cultural forms, the Northwest coastal Indians reached a pinnacle of sophistication unmatched by most Native American groups.

The coastal tribes were short in stature, with strong upper bodies, which they developed after generations of paddling the coastal waterways. Ornately carved cedar canoes served as transportation, and extensive trading networks evolved between the permanent settlements that stretched up and down the coast and along the river valleys.

Extended family groups lived in cedar longhouses, which were constructed over a central pitlike living area. The social structure in these self-sustaining villages was quite stratified, with wealth and power held by an aristocratic class of chiefs. Social and religious rituals were dominated by a strict clan system. Unlike native tribes in the north (what is now British Columbia), Puget Sound natives did not carve totem poles. Instead, wealth was measured in goods such as blankets, salmon and fish oil; these items were consumed and to some degree redistributed in ceremonial feasts in which great honor accrued to the person who gave away valued items.

Chief Sealth & the Duwamish

The Seattle area was originally the homeland of the Duwamish tribe, whose culture was deeply linked to the salmon that made seasonal runs on the Green and Duwamish Rivers. A notably peaceful tribe, the Duwamish initially welcomed members of the Denny party when they arrived in 1851. The white settlers received permission from the Duwamish to build their first structures on the site of a summer camp that the area's native inhabitants called Duwamps – the name that the settlers applied to their little town as well.

The Duwamish chief Sealth (1786–1866) urged peaceful coexistence between the people of his tribe and the whites, and he encouraged the Duwamish to work side by side with the settlers erecting houses, cutting trees and laying out streets. Relations with other tribes along Puget Sound were not as good. To address growing hostilities, the US government drew up a treaty in 1854 granting

area tribes $150,000 in goods and 2600 acres of reservation land in return for vacating two million acres of prime real estate in western Washington, including the present-day Seattle area. Distrust and anger soon broke out, and in 1855 warfare erupted between the natives and white settlers.

Chief Sealth managed to persuade the Duwamish not to become involved in the conflict; however, the settlement at Duwamps was besieged by a group of hostile Indians, forcing the settlers to take shelter in the town's small stockade. A visiting navy sloop, the *Decatur*, fired its cannons into the forest above the little town to frighten the Indians away. In retaliation, the Indians burned and looted nearly all of the settlements on Puget Sound. In the end, the settlers prevailed and one of the Indian rebel leaders, Leschi, was captured, tried and hanged for murder.

Chief Sealth

Puget Sound natives evolved complex cultural, social, and economic structures, which the invasion of Euro-American settlers in the mid-1800s almost erased. Today tribes struggle for survival, respect and renewal.

Early Exploration
Puget Sound and the Pacific Northwest in general were among the last areas of the Americas to be explored by Europeans. In fact, almost 300 years passed between the arrival of white explorers in America and their 'discovery' of Puget Sound.

The first white expedition to explore the Puget Sound area came in 1792, when the British sea captain George Vancouver sailed through the inland waterways of the Straits of Juan de Fuca and Georgia. In the same year, the USA entered the competition to claim the Northwest when Captain Robert Gray reached the mouth of the Columbia River. The Lewis and Clark Expedition (1804–06) made its way down the Columbia River to the Pacific, establishing a further US claim on the territory.

The major reason for European and American eagerness to claim this forested and well-watered corner of the map was its immense wealth in furs. The region's waterways were especially rich in beavers and otters, the pelts of which were a highly valued commodity in Europe and Asia and thus an important article of trade.

Chief Sealth & the Duwamish

The Duwamish were moved to the Port Madison Reservation in 1856, despite their peaceable history. In part to recognize Chief Sealth's aid and pacifist efforts, the settlers renamed their little town in the chief's honor (unable to pronounce the final glottal 'h,' whites had called him by his anglicized name, 'Seattle'). Apparently Chief Sealth was not exactly pleased with the honor: According to Duwamish beliefs, if someone utters a dead person's name, the soul of the deceased is denied everlasting peace.

Chief Sealth was a noted orator. His most famous speech was delivered at a gathering of natives and white settlers, which included territorial governor Isaac Stevens, who was attempting to purchase Puget Sound land from the area's native inhabitants. This 1855 address is considered one of the masterpieces of Native American oratory, although the standard text of the speech was penned 30 years later from notes by a literary-minded surgeon who attended the event. Now considered a canonical text of New Age environmental belief, the transcript of the speech reads in part as follows:

How can you buy or sell the sky, the warmth of the land? This idea is strange to us. If we do not own the freshness of the air and the sparkle of the water, how can you buy them? Every part of this earth is sacred to my people. Every shining pine needle, every sandy shore, every mist in the dark woods, every clearing and humming insect is holy in the memory and experience of my people....

But if we sell you our land, you must remember that the air is precious to us, that the air shares its spirit with all the life it supports. The wind that gave our grandparents their first breath also receives their last sigh. And the wind must also give our children the spirit of life. And if we sell you our land, you must keep it apart and sacred, as a place where even the white people can go to taste the wind that is sweetened by the meadow's flowers....All things are connected....

The earth does not belong to human beings; human beings belong to the earth. This we know. All things are connected like the blood that unites one family. All things are connected. Whatever befalls the earth befalls the sons and daughters of the earth....

Looks better on him – a furry sea otter

However, none of these exploration or trade expeditions led directly to a pioneer settlement or even a permanent trading post. This development awaited the arrival of the powerful fur-trading companies, especially the British Hudson's Bay Company (HBC). By 1824, the HBC had effective control of most of present-day British Columbia, Washington and Oregon from its Pacific Coast headquarters at Fort Vancouver, founded on the north banks of the Columbia River. The Puget Sound area was linked to this imposing fur-trading fort by the Cowlitz River, a short portage from the sound's southern shores.

The Politics of Settlement

From its toehold at Fort Vancouver, the HBC – and hence Britain – had control over all trade in the Pacific Northwest. Because of its strict code of conduct and protocol, the company had legal authority over the area's few whites, mostly French Canadian and Scottish trappers. The HBC also policed trade relationships between the whites and the region's native inhabitants.

The first US settlers straggled overland to the Pacific Northwest in the 1830s on the rough tracks that would become the Oregon Trail. The HBC chief factor, Dr John McLoughlin, sought to restrict American settlement to the region south of the Columbia River, in Oregon. In doing so, he kept the prime land along Puget Sound from settlement. McLoughlin sensed that one day the USA and Britain would divide the territory; if US settlement could be limited to the area south of the Columbia, then Britain would have a stronger claim to the land north of the river. Indeed, when the settlers in Oregon voted in 1843 to become a US territory, present-day Washington remained in British hands.

American settlers continued rolling into the Pacific Northwest. Between 1843 and 1860 some 53,000 settlers migrated across the 2000-mile-long Oregon Trail. The first US settlement in Washington was established at Tumwater in 1845, on the southern edge of Puget Sound.

As American settlement pushed northward into land controlled largely by the HBC, boundary disputes between the USA and Britain became increasingly antagonistic. The popular slogan of the 1844 US presidential campaign was 'Fifty-four Forty or Fight,' which urged citizens of the USA to occupy territory in the Northwest up to the present Alaskan border, including all of Washington State and British Columbia. Finally, in 1846, the British and the Americans agreed to the present US-Canadian border along the 49th parallel.

'By and By New York'

Arthur and David Denny were native New Yorkers who in 1851 led a group of settlers across the Oregon Trail with the intention of settling in the Willamette Valley. While en route, however, the Denny brothers heard stories of good land and deep water ports along Puget Sound. The Denny party arrived in Portland in the fall and decided to strike on northward to seek their fortunes. The settlers staked claims on Alki Point, in present-day West Seattle. The group named their encampment Alki-New York (the Chinookan word *Alki* means 'by and by,' which gives a good sense of the Dennys' aspirations). After a winter of wind and rain, the group determined that their fledgling city needed a deeper harbor and moved the settlement to the mudflats across Elliott Bay. The colony was renamed Seattle for the Duwamish chief Sealth (pronounced 'See-aalth' with a guttural 'th' being made up of a hard 't' and an 'h' that's almost a lisp off the end of the word), who was the friend of an early merchant.

The attitudes of Seattle's first settlers established it as a progressive, budding community. Traversing the Oregon Trail was an arduous and costly adventure. Those who chose to travel it had to be able to afford a wagon or two and sufficient foodstuffs for a six-month journey. The Pacific Northwest was not settled by penniless wanderers, but earnest young men and women, mostly in their twenties, who were determined to establish farms, businesses and communities.

Birth of the City
Early Seattle was hardly a boomtown. The heart of the young city beat in the area now known as Pioneer Square. Although there was a small but deep harbor at this point in Elliott Bay, much of the land immediately to the south was mudflats, ideal for oysters but not much else. The land to the north and east was steep and forested. However, the early settlers (whose names now ring as a compendium of street names and landmarks: Denny, Yesler, Bell, Boren) quickly cleared the land and established a sawmill, schools, churches and other civic institutions. From the start, the people who settled Seattle never doubted that they were founding a great city. The original homesteads were quickly platted into city streets, and trade, not farming or lumbering, became the goal of the little settlement.

Since it was a frontier town, the majority of Seattle's male settlers were bachelors. One of the town's founders (and sole professor at the newly established university), Asa Mercer, went back to the East Coast with the express purpose of inducing young unmarried women to venture to Seattle. On two different trips, a total of 57 women made the journey to Seattle and married into the frontier stock, in the process establishing a more civilized tone in the city (and inspiring the especially bad 1960s TV show *Here Come the Brides*).

Seattle's early economic growth came from shipping logs to San Francisco, a city booming with gold wealth. At the time, loggers had to go no farther than the bluffs above town, now First and Capitol Hills, to find hundreds of acres of old-growth fir forest. As the sawmill was located on the waterfront, the logs had to be transported down the steep hillside. A skid road was developed on which horses and mules pulled the logs down a chute of ever-present mud. This skid road later became Yesler Way, the prototype of the term 'skid road' – or skid row.

Because it was isolated from preexisting transport systems, Seattle had to develop many trades and industries for itself: If the early settlers wanted bread, they built flour mills; if they wanted leather shoes, they built a tannery. This sense of self-sufficiency and industry characterized the early growth of the city and gave young Seattle the strength to rise above its sister cities and competitors for trade on Puget Sound.

The Battle for Railroads
The Northwest's first rail link was the Northern Pacific Railroad, which linked Portland to Chicago in 1883. The young towns of Puget Sound – Seattle, Tacoma, Port Townsend and Bellingham – believed that their dreams of becoming major trade centers depended on luring a national rail line to link them to the East. Land speculators especially profited when railroads like the Northern Pacific and the Great Northern came shopping for a Puget Sound terminus. Seattle lost out to Tacoma when the Northern Pacific built its shipyards there in 1887; however, Seattle later became the terminus for the Great Northern Railroad (1893) and the Milwaukee Road (1903).

Seattle was perhaps fortunate in having to wait for its rail link to the East. The Northern Pacific's impact on Tacoma was immediate: the city's population grew considerably, but the lasting effect was to imprint the young city with a manufacturing base and to consign it to the vicissitudes of the forest products industry.

By the time the Great Northern crossed the Cascades and the Northern Pacific reached Seattle from Portland in 1893, the role of the railroads had changed. Federal homesteading policy had evolved, and the newer railroads saw their niche in bringing new immigrants to the West. Both railroads operated enlistment programs in Europe, promising free land and new opportunities to settlers in the western USA. Not only did the new rail lines give Seattle a chance to ship its products to the rest of the nation, but they brought vast numbers of industrious new citizens – and consumers – eager to make their new home in the Pacific Northwest an ideal community.

Anti-Chinese Riots of 1886

For a city whose birthright was only a few decades old, young Seattle's righteous indignation over nonwhite settlers is surprising. Because of the region's many railroad and mining companies – whose abundant opportunities for employment were deemed too lowly for most white settlers – and Seattle's position on the Pacific Rim, a large number of Chinese immigrants settled in the city. The fact that Asian laborers worked at jobs that most white Americans shunned didn't prevent the perception that these 'foreign' workers were taking jobs away from 'real Americans,' and, then as now, it didn't prevent episodes of ugly racism.

As anti-Chinese sentiment grew in outlying communities around the Pacific Northwest, more and more Chinese moved to Seattle, where they felt some community protection, and where the multitude of employment opportunities offered them continued security. The area south of Yesler Way was considered Chinatown, where most of the new arrivals made their homes; today it is known more euphemistically as the International District.

The first recorded incident between the Chinese minority and the white settlers came in 1885, when a Chinese immigrant was knifed to death. That same year, a group called the Anti-Chinese Congress began meeting in Seattle. They established, by more or less mob assent, a date by which all the Chinese would be forced to leave the Puget Sound area (it didn't matter to where: some were sent to Victoria, others to Portland, others to China). These dictatorial edicts did to some degree serve their intended purpose, and a majority of the Chinese, between 750 and 1000 workers, left the area. However, about 500 Chinese continued to live and work in Seattle. The Anti-Chinese Congress decided to act.

COURTESY OF SEATTLE PUBLIC LIBRARY

First passenger train between Seattle and Renton – 1877

In February of 1886, a mob entered Chinatown and evicted the remaining Chinese, forcing them onto ships. State and city officials tried to mediate the mob action, but violence erupted. In the end five people were shot; one white protester died from his wounds. Federal troops were called in to restore order. The Chinese population plummeted, especially in light of a law that prohibited Chinese men from sending for their wives in China.

The Great Fire & the Regrading of Seattle

Frontier Seattle was a thrown-together village of wooden storefronts, log homes and lumber mills. Tidewater lapped against present-day 1st Ave S, and many of the buildings and the streets that led to them were on stilts. No part of the original downtown was more than 4 feet above the bay at high tide, and the streets were frequently a quagmire.

On June 6, 1889, a fire started in a store basement on 1st Ave and quickly spread across the young city: The boardwalks provided an unstoppable conduit for the flames. By the end of the day, 30 blocks of the city had burned, gutting the core of downtown.

What might have seemed a catastrophe was in fact a blessing, as the city rebuilt immediately with handsome structures of brick, steel and stone. This time, however, the streets were regraded, and ravines and inlets filled in. This raised the new city about a dozen feet above the old; in some areas the regrading simply meant building on top of older ground-level buildings and streets (see 'A Town Underground' in the Things to See & Do chapter).

The sense of transformation inspired by the Great Fire also fueled another great rebuilding project. One of Seattle's original seven hills, Denny Hill, rose out of Elliott Bay just north of Pine St. Its very steep face limited commercial traffic, though some hotels and private homes were perched on the hilltop. City engineers determined that if Seattle's growth was to continue, then Denny Hill had to go. The regrading of Denny Hill took place between 1899 and 1912, though the finishing touches continued into the 1930s.

The regrade was accomplished by sluicing the hill into Elliott Bay: During the project, 20 million gallons of water were pumped daily from Lake Union and sprayed onto the rock and soil. Under great pressure, the water liquefied the clay and dislodged the rock, all of which was sluiced into flumes. Existing homes were simply undercut and then burned.

Engineered into a plain, the Denny Regrade, now better known as Belltown, became a rather lackluster area of light industry, warehouses and cheap hotels, and never the extension of downtown commercial property that the engineers envisioned (see 'The Thrill on Denny Hill' in the Things to See & Do chapter).

Klondike Gold Rush

Seattle's first real boom came when the ship *Portland* docked at the waterfront in 1897 with its now-famous cargo: two tons of gold newly gleaned from northern Yukon gold fields. The news spread quickly across the USA; within weeks, thousands of fortune seekers from all over the world converged on Seattle, the last stop before heading north. That summer and autumn, 74 ships left Seattle bound for Skagway, Alaska, and onto the goldfields in Dawson City, Yukon.

In all, more than 40,000 prospectors passed through Seattle. The Canadian government demanded that prospectors bring a year's worth of supplies, so they wouldn't freeze or starve to death midway. Outfitting the miners became big business in Seattle. The town became the banking center for the fortunes made in the Yukon. Bars, brothels, theaters and honky-tonks in Pioneer Square blossomed.

Many of Seattle's shopkeepers, tavern owners and restaurateurs made quick fortunes in the late 1890s – far more so than most of the prospectors. Many of the men who made fortunes in Alaska chose to stay in the Northwest, settling in the thriving port city on Puget Sound.

Seattle was growing very quickly. The Klondike Gold Rush provided great wealth, and the railroads brought in a steady stream of immigrants, mostly from Eastern Europe and Scandinavia. Seattle controlled most of the shipping trade with Alaska and increasingly with nations of the Pacific Rim. Company-controlled communities like Ballard sprang up, populated almost exclusively with Scandinavians who worked in massive sawmills. A new influx of Asian immigrants, this time from Japan, began streaming into Seattle, establishing fishing fleets and vegetable farms.

At the height of the gold rush in 1900, Seattle's population reached 80,000 – doubling the population figures from the 1890 census. By 1910, Seattle's population jumped to a quarter million. Seattle had become the preeminent city of the Pacific Northwest.

The War Years

Seattle's boom continued through WWI, when Northwest lumber was in great demand; the opening of the Panama Canal in 1914 brought increased trade to Pacific ports, which were free from wartime threats. Shipyards opened along Puget Sound, bringing the shipbuilding industry close to the forests of the Northwest.

One of the seminal events in Seattle history occurred in 1916 when William Boeing, a pioneer aviator, began his air transport empire by designing and producing a pontoon biplane. Boeing went on to establish an airline, Boeing Air Transport, which in 1927 operated the first commercial flight between Chicago and San Francisco. (Boeing Air Transport later became United Airlines.) But it was WWII that really started the engines at Boeing; the factory received contracts to produce the B-17 and B-29 bombers, which led in the US air war

against Axis nations. Huge defense contracts began to flow into Boeing and by extension into Seattle, fueling more rapid growth and prosperity.

WWII brought other, less positive developments to Seattle. About 6000 Japanese residents in Seattle were forcibly removed from their jobs and homes; most were sent to internment camps in Idaho, Montana and eastern Oregon, where they were detained under prison conditions for the duration of the war. This greatly depleted the Japanese community, which to this point had built a thriving existence farming and fishing in Puget Sound. In all, an estimated 110,000 Japanese across the country, two-thirds of whom were US citizens, were sent to internment camps. Needless to say, many did not return to the homes they had been forced to abandon.

Meanwhile, the boom in aircraft manufacturing and shipbuilding brought tens of thousands of new workers to the region. Because of Boeing and the shipyards at Bremerton, Puget Sound became a highly defended area, which led to the building of several military facilities in the region. These bases also brought in thousands of new residents. By the end of the war, Seattle had grown to nearly half a million people.

A Company Town

Boeing After the war, Boeing diversified its product line and began to develop civilian aircraft. In 1954, Boeing announced the 707, and the response was immediate and overwhelming. The world found itself at the beginning of an era of mass air travel, and Boeing produced the jets that led this revolution in transportation. The Korean War brought more defense contracts to Boeing, and the company continued to grow exponentially. By 1960, when the population of Seattle topped one million, one in 10 people worked for Boeing, and one in four people worked jobs directly affected by Boeing. Aircraft manufacture was the biggest and almost the only game in town.

The self-assured, forward-ho swagger of Seattle was perfectly captured in the spirit of the 1962 World's Fair, which attracted nearly

10 million visitors from around the world. Seattle, the home of high-tech jumbo jets, saw itself as the city of the future; the Space Needle and the Monorail are remnants of the fair's distinctive vision of tomorrow's world.

However, the fortunes of Boeing weren't always to soar. A combination of over-stretched capital (due to cost overruns in the development of the 747) and a cut in defense spending led to a severe financial crisis in the early 1970s. Boeing was forced to cut its work force by two-thirds; in one year, nearly 60,000 Seattleites lost their jobs. The local economy went into a tailspin for a number of years.

Recent history has been kinder to Boeing. Increased defense spending in the 1980s brought vigor back to aircraft production lines, and expanding trade relations with China and other Pacific Rim nations brought business to Boeing too; currently, one-half of all commercial aircraft made by Boeing is sold to Asia. Boeing remains an overwhelming force in the economy of Seattle, but the company's announcement in March 2001 to relocate its headquarters to Chicago left Seattleites stunned and more than just a little concerned about what the future holds. For more on Boeing's move, see the Economy section, later.

Microsoft Though Boeing never relinquished its position as the backbone of the Puget Sound economy, the mid-1970s and '80s brought a force that would also change Seattle forever. After tinkering around with a little notion called BASIC (a programming language for the world's first microcomputer), local boy Bill Gates joined up with his childhood chum Paul Allen (See 'Paul Allen: Seattle's Co-Owner' in the Things to See & Do chapter) to start Microsoft in 1975. Though the software giant, located in Redmond across Lake Washington, doesn't have quite the total control over Seattle economy that Boeing once had, it is increasingly hard to find someone who isn't a contractor, caterer or car dealer for the Microsoft crowd. More importantly, Microsoft attracted other high-tech companies like bees to honey. Eager techies

figured success was just a given in the fresh Northwest air.

Through the 1990s, computer-related start-ups – often financed by the young, affluent millionaires that Microsoft's early days spawned – sprouted like weeds and attracted a younger, more educated population than Seattle had ever seen. Though

Boing, Boing Boeing

Just a few days after Seattle was rattled by a mighty earthquake, the city received a blow that rocked it even more. Boeing head honcho Phil Condit announced in March 2001 that the world's largest airplane manufacturer, the company as synonymous with Seattle as rain, was blowing town. Boeing, he said, would relocate at least 50% of its headquarter staff to bigger and brighter digs in Chicago in September 2001. Seattleites were stunned, and amid the cries of surprise and panic, you could almost hear founder Bill Boeing rolling over in his grave. Boeing's move is as major as Disney leaving Disney World.

While jets still account for about 60% of Boeing's sales, the headquarters shift is part of Boeing's plan to diversify its corporate interests. Condit's reasoning? You can't be the life of the party if you don't mingle, or if you stay stuck in the north-west corner of the room. CEOs of the world's largest airplane manufacturer, it seems, are sick of flying.

And Seattleites aren't buying it. When Seattle became more popular to other companies, it became a headache for Boeing. Competition for skilled workers grew fierce, and the antagonistic relationship the company already had with its union workers only intensified. Though Boeing's 80,000 plant workers are staying put for now, everyone worries that the headquarters move is just the first in a series of big steps to relocate the company entirely.

Only time will tell just how much of a toll Boeing's departure will take. In the meanwhile, Seattle's economy will lean even harder on high-tech and biotech industries.

long-standing Seattleites grumble about soaring housing prices and too much city growth, defenders of this high-tech boom insist that the industry – and the money that comes with it – has fueled massive expansion of the arts, increased philanthropy and provided a boon to other local businesses.

Microsoft's heyday hit something of a capitalist brick wall in the late 1990s, when the federal government began a very long and politically hot suit against Microsoft. The Justice Department accused the company of monopolistic practices and alleged that it used – and abused – its prodigious market power to prevent any competition from getting in its way. Microsoft's reputation for bullying other players on the technological playfield was deemed, by the most capitalist nation on earth, to be legally unfair.

In April 2000, Judge Thomas Penfield Jackson ruled that Microsoft had violated antitrust laws by 'engaging in predatory tactics

Bill Gates: The Richest Guy on Earth

William Gates III, born October 28, 1955, grew up in Seattle's upper-class Laurelhurst neighborhood and began developing software in school at the ripe old age of 13. Gates went to Harvard, hung out in the computer lab and whipped up programming language for the world's first microcomputer. Occasionally he'd wave down the Harvard halls to Steve Ballmer, Microsoft's current CEO.

Gates dropped out of Harvard, hooked up with his buddy Paul Allen, and the two went on to develop DOS, soon followed up by the Windows operating systems. At the age of 37, Gates became the second-richest man in the US. A few years later, he became the richest man in the world, with a fortune estimated at a mind-numbing $48 billion.

As Bill Gates became a global household name, he also unwittingly became the object of resentment and antagonism. People who suffered a bad experience with a Microsoft product now had an individual, not just a company, to blame.

But Microsoft insiders say Bill's just a geeky guy who likes developing software and tries to do good in the world. Gates and his wife, Melinda, created the Bill and Melinda Gates Foundation, which has endowed some $21 billion to support such initiatives as health care and education in developing countries. Gates was quoted as saying 'Health care and literacy – not computers – are the most important way to help the world's four billion poorest people.' Gates and his Microsoft millionaires' club make a point of handing out philanthropic dollars, but skeptics say it's not enough; Gates should give away more.

In his spare time, Gates plays bridge, golfs and hangs out at his house. Few Bill Gates stories generate more tongue wagging than the saga of the Gates mansion in Medina, just west of Bellevue on Lake Washington. Built to represent the ultimate in high-tech living, this 48,000-sq-foot structure boasts such features as walls made of video monitors and music sensors that are electronically programmed to play your favorite tunes as you wander from room to room. The price tag? An estimated $40 million.

Mr Bulging Wallet, Bill Gates

that discourage technological competition.' The judge ruled that Microsoft needed to divest the company. Two or three Microsofts, the ruling seemed to suggest, are better than one. Of course, Microsoft launched a barrage of appeals, which are currently working their ways up the legal ladder to the US Supreme Court. While Microsoft opponents believe that Bill Gates shouldn't be allowed to play God, its supporters believe the Justice Department shouldn't be allowed to either.

GEOGRAPHY

Seattle's complex geography is defined by the towering peaks of the ruggedly forested Cascade Mountains to the east and the intruding channels of the Pacific Ocean, carved mostly by melting glaciers from an ice age 15,000 years ago. To the west looms another set of majestic mountains, the wild Olympic Range on the Olympic Peninsula, a land formation that juts like a thumb into the Pacific Ocean. Moist marine air rolls in off the ocean and hits these nearly 8000-foot peaks, dumping immense amounts of precipitation on Puget Sound, which lies like a valley between the Olympics and the Cascades.

Puget Sound and its connecting waterways – the Strait of Juan de Fuca, Hood Canal and many smaller bays and inlets – reach like tendrils far inland, where they meet up with the arms and creeks of the mighty Northwest rivers. Hundreds of isolated islands and peninsulas dot the sound and, protected by the mountains from the harsh Pacific winds, contain extremely fertile agricultural land. Farms, dairies, plant nurseries, orchards and vineyards thrive in the mild climate and rich soil.

Seattle is on an isthmus between Puget Sound and Lake Washington that wraps itself in a C-shaped hug around Elliott Bay. Water floods the heart and soul of Seattle, whose rivers, lakes, channels and deep-water harbor account for much of its prosperity.

The massive volcanoes of the Cascade Range march lengthways across Washington. These peaks, including Mt Baker (10,778 feet) to the north and Mt Rainier (14,411 feet) to the south, rise from the horizon as isolated, snow-clad cones. The Cascades cut Seattle off from the eastern side of the state, presenting both a physical and psychological barrier that's hard to ignore. Seattleites probably have more in common with people in Portland, Vancouver or even San Francisco than they do with other Washingtonians.

GEOLOGY

Seattle sits right alongside the Cascadia Subduction Zone, one of the earth's most active seismic regions. Beneath the Strait of Juan de Fuca, two tectonic plates – the North American Plate and the Juan de Fuca Plate – struggle against each other, grinding away as the North American Plate slides underneath, causing pressure to build and the earth to rumble. The most recent of these rumblings happened on February 28, 2001, when an earthquake measuring 6.8 on the Richter scale rocked the Seattle area. The quake caused only one death but rang up more than $2 billion in damages and caused some dramatic geological change. The earthquake narrowed the Duwamish River by a few inches, shifted Seattle about a fifth of an inch to the south-southwest and pushed the Eastside about a third of an inch farther east.

A snapshot of this area 60 million years ago would show a vista of jumbled offshore islands, low coastal mountains and marine marshlands invaded by the shallow Pacific. Plants and animals thrived in the tropical climate, which flowed inland unobstructed by mountains. Coastal sediments and offshore islands started wedging together, forming today's Olympic Range and setting the stage for three intense periods of volcanic activity, which would utterly change the face of the region. The line of volcanoes that shot up as the Cascade Range caused enormous explosions of lava, ash and mud. The region's most recent volcanic activity drew worldwide attention in 1980 when Mt St Helens, just 150 miles south of Seattle, blew her top, killing 55 people and spreading ash through five states and three Canadian provinces.

CLIMATE

Seattle's reputation for rain is somewhat undeserved. With 38 inches of precipitation a year, Seattle ranks behind many East Coast cities – including New York, Boston and Atlanta – for total precipitation. However, when it comes to damp and cold, there aren't many places like it. The city receives an average of only 55 days of unalloyed sunshine a year; the remaining 310 days see some form of fog, mist or cloud. This pervasive grayness can sometimes lend a bone-chilling effect to Seattle's otherwise moderate temperatures: Winter highs range between 40° and 50°F (5° and 10°C) and summer highs range between 75° and 85°F (25° and 30°C).

The majority of rain falls in the winter, between November and April. Snow is unusual, but when it comes it piles up – everyone in Seattle has a story about the last big snowfall. Because of moderate temperatures and quirky weather patterns, snow rarely lasts more than a few hours on the ground. Summer is very pleasant, though cool. Marine clouds often blanket the Seattle area in the morning but burn off completely by afternoon. Spring and fall are best described as transitional with rain and sun alternating several times a day.

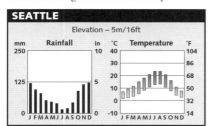

ECOLOGY & ENVIRONMENT

Environmental issues in many ways dominate life in the Pacific Northwest. Seattle was founded on resource-extractive industries; the city's first major employer was a sawmill, and the ability to export the area's wealth in timber was key in the city's development. Fishing Puget Sound and the area's rivers for salmon was also a major source of employment, especially for immigrant workers from Japan and Scandinavia. Today, endangered fish runs, especially of seagoing salmon, top the list of environmental concerns. While jet manufacturing and software dominate Seattle's present economy, the older resource-based industries continue to be an active feature of the city's economic and political landscape.

Environmental Issues

Logging Low-cost timber sales, unsustainable harvest levels and devastating logging practices have made logging one of the region's most contentious issues. Before high- and biotech industries moved in during the late 1980s and '90s, forestry was the dominant economic force in the smaller towns of the Olympic Peninsula and Puget Sound. Make no mistake: A *lot* of logging still goes on, especially on lands administered by the US Forest Service (USFS). A traveler in the mountains need not stray too far from Seattle before coming across a clear-cut, a series of hillsides logged flat and stripped of all vegetation. The most questionable and controversial logging practice, clear-cutting erodes hillsides, causing mudslides to choke streambeds with silt. Choked-up rivers destroy wildlife habitat up and down the food chain. Although the forests are regarded as an agricultural crop, which in theory can be planted and harvested indefinitely, they're being cut down much faster than they can grow back.

Environmental groups seeking to protect wildlife habitat made headway in the late 1980s and early '90s when their successful lawsuits against the USFS forced the organization to halt logging in federal forests. The endangered spotted owl became a political football in an emotional skirmish between environmentalists and timber communities. Once old trees were proved to be the birds' primary nesting habitat, courts ordered millions of acres of federal forests ripe with old-growth timber to be removed from sale. Mills closed, leaving embittered loggers and mill workers to spend their days screen-printing

T-shirts with anti–spotted owl slogans, such as 'I love spotted owl…fried.'

You won't drive far on rural roads before seeing hand-printed signs in front of homes stating, 'This family supported by timber dollars,' or 'Forestry feeds my family.' To ameliorate the economic loss to timber communities, the sale of national forest land is still permitted for 'salvage logging,' a practice at the center of ongoing forest battles. Muddied with environmental rhetoric, salvage logging asserts that forests that have been burned or are diseased by wood-boring insects should be logged to protect the rest of the forest. Thrown in with the charred and diseased logs, however, are stands of perfectly healthy trees, dubiously removed for 'thinning.' It wasn't long before the national forests were declared in a state of 'forest health emergency,' a concept more accurately described as a gigantic loophole through which the USFS reaped millions of dollars in timber sales.

Salmon While the major focus of concern for advocates of migrating salmon is the Columbia River, Seattle has its own twist on the salmon saga. Wild salmon once ran in great numbers from Puget Sound, through Lake Union and Lake Washington, and then up the Sammamish River – essentially right through the center of Seattle. When canals and locks replaced the streams, fish ladders were built at former creek mouths and at the Hiram M Chittenden Locks (also known as the Ballard Locks) to enable the fish to continue their ancient spawning cycles.

In an attempt to mimic the fishes' natural habitat, the fish ladders slow the progress of the salmon and seagoing steelhead trout. The delay causes fish to congregate at the mouth of the locks. The problem is, the crowd of fish looks a lot like dinner to local sea lions, who gather at the locks to munch on the fish in such numbers that they now threaten the stability of the Sammamish River's salmon and steelhead breeding population.

Just what to do about the troublesome sea lions proves to be a very thorny issue for Seattle-area fish and wildlife officials. At first, the problem sea lions (who are known collectively as Herschel) were captured and released thousands of miles south in California. It took only days for the same sea lions to return to the free lunch at the Ballard Locks. Scaring the sea lions away with loud noises, rubber bullets and other disturbances proved equally ineffective.

Then, as the sea lions constitute a real threat to the continued existence of the Sammamish River's anadromous fish population (they eat about 65% of the migrating

Trainload of logs at Yesler's Mill – 1893

steelhead), fish and wildlife officials unhappily offered the final solution: to kill the sea lions. This decision sparked an immediate and fierce debate within the ranks of environmentalists and animal-rights activists. Luckily, Florida's Sea World agreed to take three of the most notorious Herschels. Other Herschels remain, however, as does the problem. (See Hiram M Chittenden Locks under Ballard in the Things to See & Do chapter.)

Recycling

In keeping with its 'green' reputation, Seattle has one of most comprehensive curbside recycling programs in the USA. Depending on where Seattleites live, their recycling is picked up either weekly or monthly; the cost is included in the price of regular garbage collection. Recycling here is easy; as such, you won't find anyone chucking a tin can or ditching a plastic bottle. Coffee drinkers basically boycott styrofoam, and don't be surprised if somebody scolds you for littering.

Seattle's success at recycling is inspiring: Participation in the recycling program stands at over 90% of city households. The program is responsible for 40% fewer tons of residential garbage going to landfills. Even if you're just visiting and don't have access to curbside recycling, it's easy to find a place to recycle the cans, bottles and papers that accumulate as you travel. Most public areas and food courts will have separate recycling bins for various kinds of products. Call Friends of Recycling at ☎ 684-4685 if you have a lot of goods to recycle.

FLORA & FAUNA

The land on which Seattle now stands was once dense forest, and the waters of Puget Sound and the freshwater lakes that surround the city once teemed with wildlife. While metropolitan Seattle hardly accounts for a natural ecosystem, you don't have to go far from the center of the city to find vestiges of the wild Pacific Northwest. Flora & Fauna Books (☎ 623-4727), 121 1st Ave S near Pioneer Square, has an excellent collection of books on natural history, botany

and gardening, along with field guides to Northwest animals and plants.

Flora

Forests around Puget Sound are thick, fast-growing and, in established stands, the mix of trees is truly astounding. The dominant tree is the Douglas fir, a statuesque conifer that can grow to nearly 300 feet high, which makes it the prime target for foresters. Joining the Douglas fir in coastal forests are the trusty hemlock, towering Sitka spruce, western hemlock – Washington's state tree – and western red cedar, which is considered the Tree of Life by West Coast natives, who use it to make everything from clothing and baskets to dug-out canoes. Other common trees found throughout Seattle include maple, oak and, in the forests, yellow cedar.

The understory of an old forest is like the foundation of a building; without it everything would eventually tumble down. Common plants include countless numbers of brilliant green ferns and salal, an evergreen shrub whose berries are used for jam. Canadian dogwood produces small white

Western hemlock

flowers and bright red berries. Cascade huckleberries, more commonly known as blueberries, and red huckleberries make excellent trail snacks. Fall brings bright red and yellow leaves to vine maple and dark red salmonberries that burst out of their pink flowers. Thorny blackberry shrubs grab at clothing but provide sweet berries for eating, jam making or pie baking.

A number of Seattle parks provide a glimpse of the natural vegetative glory that once cloaked the land. Discovery and Seward Parks are both administered by the city and contain stands of old-growth forest as well as a network of maintained hiking trails. The Washington Park Arboretum has an excellent collection of Northwest shrubs, flowers, plants and trees. For more on Discovery and Seward Parks or the arboretum, see their respective sections in the Things to See & Do chapter.

Fauna

Seattle's maritime location brings even the most casual of visitors into contact with some of the region's wildlife. Seagulls are forever squawking overhead and will think nothing of swooping down and stealing your french fries. A sightseeing trip or a ferry ride provides even more opportunity to spot wildlife. Watch for sleek black cormorants, diving pelicans and various species of ducks and geese. Sea lions, porpoises and harbor seals are common visitors to fishing piers and boat docks; look for porpoises leaping in the ferry's wake. One of the most exciting sea mammals you'll ever encounter is undoubtedly the orca, or killer whale, which travels in pods throughout Puget Sound. The giant black-and-white orcas will sometimes delight ferry commuters – if you see one, you'll usually get a glimpse of the whole pod, as orcas rarely swim alone.

Crested, blue-bodied Steller's jays are boisterous and common in forests, as are enormous crows and ravens. Sharp eyes may spot rufous hummingbirds around flowers. Bird watchers will thrill at the region's many varieties of woodpecker. The large, red-crested pileated woodpecker is an especially worthy pursuit. Notable lake and streamside birds include elegant, prehistoric-looking great blue herons and belted kingfishers; also watch for handsome, black-necked loons. Canada geese are common in most parks. If they are flying overhead, take cover; they are not the least bit shy about pooping wherever they want. Good places for bird watching in Seattle are Foster Island in the Washington Park Arboretum, Montlake Cut (near the Arboretum) and Discovery Park.

Almost all seaward rivers and streams in Washington produce their own salmon runs, meaning essentially that each river has its own native species of salmon. Once salmon hatch they follow the water out to the ocean; when they are ready to spawn again, they follow the same, usually arduous route back upstream through rocks and rapids. Once they've finished spawning, most salmon species die, and their offspring start this incredible cycle of life all over again.

Northwestern waters are also rich in trout, especially the seagoing steelhead trout. While deer and coyotes occasionally visit Seattle suburbs, other mammals have adapted to city life. Don't be surprised when you come across a raccoon family or an opossum; these unlikely urban dwellers live in attics, garages and crawl spaces throughout the city.

Oh goodness, opossum!

GOVERNMENT & POLITICS

Seattle is governed by a mayor and a nine-person city council. All city council members are elected on an at-large basis, meaning that they are not assigned to a specific council district. Although all city posts are nonpartisan, politics in Seattle dependably veers to the left-leaning side of the Democratic Party. The current mayor, Paul Schell, was elected in 1997.

Seattle's recent spectacular economic and population growth has produced a bevy of

Rage Against the Machine

In December 1999, tear gas bombed through Seattle's normally placid streets, police with rubber bullets picked off protesters, and everywhere rocks went flying through glass windows while demonstrators rioted in the streets. It was a show of protest not seen since the 1960s, but it wasn't about free love or freeing Vietnam. It was about a much less alluring topic: free trade.

The business of the World Trade Organization (WTO) has traditionally garnered yawns from an ambivalent public. The organization's task is to administer and enforce the trade agreements made by its 135 member nations, ensuring a fair and unobstructed flow of goods and services. WTO decisions affect *everyone*, from factory workers in Indonesia to fishermen in Malaysia to brewers in Washington State. Tariffs and multilateral investment agreements hardly seem the stuff massive protests are made of, but when demonstrators descended on Seattle, they weren't objecting to free trade. Instead, they were protesting global corporations hiding behind the WTO's mandate (to keep free trade moving) in attempts to loosen labor laws, slip on environmental protections and forget about subsidizing developing countries.

Free trade, as enforced by the WTO, favors large global corporations that take advantage of cheap labor or lax regulation in one country to produce goods for affluent customers in another. Both inside the WTO talks and outside on Seattle streets, anti-US sentiment focused on what other nations deem the USA's double standards on free trade.

The riot chaos on Seattle's streets was aggravated by an overzealous police force that had never dealt with such an uproar in the city's passive history. The WTO debacle caused $20 million in damages to downtown, led to the firing of the Seattle police chief and caused major embarrassment for Mayor Paul Schell. But the protests woke Seattle – and the world – up to corporations' and the WTO's overwhelming power to determine everything from environmental standards to issues of human rights. And that, most Seattleites agree, was worth the damage.

concerns that play themselves out across the city's political landscape. Fueled by the explosive growth of Microsoft – and the sudden young millionaires its stock options created – Seattle faces new problems, such as outrageous real estate bidding wars and a glut of traffic.

In fact, one of Seattle's most thorny issues is transportation. With the Puget Sound area's population growing fast, the transportation infrastructure simply isn't holding up. Traffic is often horrendous, due in large part to topography, but also to the lack of effective planning for public transport. Voters continually swing back and forth in support of funding light rail commuter trains, but inevitably a glitch rears its ugly, and often political, head, keeping the construction at bay. Repeatedly voters have approved feasibility studies for expanding the World's Fair Monorail; however, few experts on public transport deem a costly new monorail system a viable response to transit problems. While everyone wants better public transport, no one wants the rails, roads, bridges or Monorail towers in their neighborhood. And so the gridlock, both physical and political, continues.

The skyrocketing cost of housing in Seattle is also a major political and social concern. Seattle is playing catch-up with urban growth and land-use planning; the city's rapid growth, especially on the Eastside, has turned thousands of acres of farmland into anonymous tract developments, and the suburbs are rolling up to the foothills of the Cascades. In the Bellevue suburb of Medina, where Bill Gates built his 48,000-sq-foot mansion, a limit is now enforced on how many 'mega houses' are allowed to be built.

Another political concern stemming from the city's growth is how to preserve the city's livability. Voters imposed a cap on building height in the early 1990s, seeking to prevent the downtown area from turning into an increasingly sterile enclave of towering business complexes. However, as high-tech towns across the country are realizing, when you've got a lot of people with a lot of

money to spend, you've got to keep building to accommodate them all.

However, present in all of these issues are two contradictory themes: The first preserves the environment, the community and civic virtue, while the other takes pride in building bigger and better, going beyond the backwater Seattle of yesteryear. The odd thing is that these polar themes are not as evident in the polls as they are, in varying degrees, in each citizen.

ECONOMY

More than many US cities, Seattle has been dependent on a modest number of very large companies for much of its economic history. While the economy has certainly diversified since the days when Boeing was the only game in town, a handful of large corporations still accounts for a significant portion of the local economy. Even though Boeing still employs more people than any other company, high-tech jobs represent the other pillar of the Seattle economy, and will likely take the brunt of the impact when Boeing splits town (see 'Boing, Boing Boeing'). Microsoft, the world's largest software manufacturer for personal computers, employs only 22,000 people at its growing 'campus' in Redmond on the Eastside, but its presence has encouraged many other high-tech firms, such as Amazon.com, Adobe, and RealNetworks, to call Seattle home. Biotechnology is also a key player in the Seattle economy.

The Port of Seattle is another big employer. Seattle ranks as the third-largest port on the US West Coast in total tonnage. Washington is the nation's fifth-largest exporting state, and one in four jobs depends to some degree on international trade. The University of Washington employs a large number of people, as do area hospitals and city and county governments. The federal government employs some 200,000 people, largely in the five military bases that ring Puget Sound.

Other corporations with Seattle-area headquarters are Nordstrom, the clothing retailer; Costco, the discount retail giant; Alaska Airlines, with a strong fleet flying up and down the West Coast; and Starbucks, the caffe latte king. Weyerhaeuser controls 2.7 million acres of timberland in the Northwest, and is one of the world's largest lumber companies. Seattle is also the financial center of the Northwest, and many banks are headquartered here.

POPULATION & PEOPLE

Seattle's population is 563,374, making it the 22nd largest city in the US. Seattle's population doesn't reflect the size of the city, whose greater area stretches from Tacoma north to Everett, and from the Kitsap Peninsula east to the Cascades. With a population of 3,056,800, the Seattle metro area is the 13th largest in the nation.

Ethnically, Seattle is exceedingly white, with whites comprising 75% of the population. Asian Americans are the largest minority group, representing 11.2% of the population. African Americans comprise only 10%. Hispanics (3.6%) and Native Americans (1%) are also represented.

The city's cultural demographics echo its history. Seattle's first settlers were mostly white colonialists who migrated west from towns along the US eastern seaboard. Later, Scandinavians came to work in the Ballard sawmill and used their seagoing skills to fish in Puget Sound.

The low number of Asians in Seattle is also explained by history. Chinese workers, who helped build pioneer Seattle, faced a forced mass exodus (see Anti-Chinese Riots of 1886, earlier). The Japanese population plummeted when most were forced into internment camps during WWII. The area now called the International District, where most of the Asian population lives, is constantly fighting against development that threatens its cultural livelihood (see International District in the Things to See & Do chapter).

During WWII, the demand for airplane manufacturing and shipbuilding brought tens of thousands of new workers to the region, especially African Americans. Today only 52,000 African Americans live in the Seattle area and the population is mostly focused on the Central District. Hispanics have been slow to move to Seattle, unlike other West Coast cities.

The largest group of Native Americans in urban Seattle continues to be the Duwamish, the tribe that originally lived on the shores of Elliott Bay. The Duwamish were given a land grant on the Kitsap Peninsula, but many have returned to their rightful homeland in present-day Seattle. Other Native Americans representing tribes throughout Washington have moved to Seattle for economic opportunity and education.

Nearly 38% of Seattle's population is between the ages of 25 and 44. Young people have poured into the city in droves in recent years, finding not only new music, fashion and attitude, but also very high-paying jobs. Software engineers right out of college can land jobs with salaries nearing six figures. This is most apparent when you see a guy in sneakers and a university sweatshirt dialing into his palm pilot to check on the NASDAQ. At a bar, you may be very surprised to find that the shabbily dressed, green-haired woman standing next to you is actually a software developer at Microsoft.

ARTS

Seattle is the cultural center of the Pacific Northwest, with a thriving music, theater and dance scene. The city's visual arts are especially dynamic, as its cultural strands – from Native American to Asian to contemporary American – meet and transfuse on canvas, in glass and in sculpture. Always known as a city of readers (with more bookstores per capita than any other US city), Seattle is increasingly home to a stable of internationally recognized writers. Musically, Seattle has become a hotbed of cutting-edge bands and music clubs. For more information on venues for the arts, see the Entertainment chapter.

Visual Arts

Seattle is the center of Washington's art and gallery scene. In addition to high-quality art galleries, a number of exhibition spaces are devoted to contemporary Native American carvings and paintings. Seattle is also home to the Seattle Art Museum, whose collection of native artifacts and folk art is especially impressive. A sizable Asian art collection is located at the Seattle Asian Art Museum in Volunteer Park. More experimental and conceptual art is displayed at the University of Washington's Henry Art Gallery.

A specialty of the Puget Sound area is glassblowing, led by a group of inventive and influential artisans known as the Pilchuck School. The most famous of these is Dale Chihuly, whose work is on display at the Benaroya Concert Hall and in a number of galleries. (See 'Glassmaster Dale Chihuly' in the Shopping chapter.)

Another characteristic of the Seattle art scene is Northwest native crafts and artwork. Wood carvings, weavings and jewelry are beautiful and strikingly simple in design.

Dance

Seattle is home to the nationally noted Pacific Northwest Ballet, which blushes at its acclaim as one of the nation's five best ballet companies. Seattle is a springboard for dancers. The modern dance pioneer Merce Cunningham was born and raised in nearby Centralia and was trained at Cornish College in Seattle. Choreographer Mark Morris, known for his fusion of classical and modern dance, is a Seattle native. He's worked everything from small opera houses to Broadway and now does most of his work in Europe. New York–based avant-garde dancer Trisha Brown is originally from Aberdeen, Washington, and classical ballet choreographer Robert Joffrey hails from Seattle.

The World Dance Series at UW's Meany Theater brings talent from all over the world, and smaller dance groups, such as On the Boards, which performs at the Behnke Center for Contemporary Performance, bring an exciting edge to the city's dance scene.

Theater

Seattle has one of the most dynamic theater scenes in the USA; there are apparently more equity theaters in Seattle than anywhere in the USA except New York City. This abundance of venues provides Seattle with a range

---

Seattle Public Art

A King County ordinance, established in 1973, stipulates that one percent of all municipal capital-improvement project funds be set aside for public art. This 'one percent for art' clause has imbued Seattle with an extensive collection of artworks ranging from monumental sculpture to landscape design to individualized sewer hole covers. Seattle's 1000-piece collection of public art enhances ordinarily bland civic structures and gives local artists a chance to display their talents.

All of the county's public artwork is commissioned through a public process. A panel of artists and project and city planners gets together and chooses an artist out of thousands of applicants. Keep your eyes open and your art radar on high; you'll find public art throughout Seattle, in the metro bus tunnels, in public parks, on building walls and embedded in the sidewalks.

---

of classical and modern dramatic theater. In addition to quality professional theater, the city offers a wide array of amateur and special-interest troupes, including both gay and lesbian theater groups, puppet theaters, children's theater troupes, cabarets and plenty of alternative theaters staging fringe plays by local playwrights. The excellent Seattle Fringe Festival, held in late February or early March, keeps theatergoers busy for the duration of the three-week festival.

Music

Rock & Alternative Pioneering Northwest rock bands like the Kingsmen, the Sonics and Seattle's own legendary Jimi Hendrix helped define rock 'n' roll in the '60s. Local groups like Heart and the Steve Miller Band made it big in the '70s. Blues musician Robert Cray and saxophonist Kenny G gained notoriety during the '80s. The media represented none of these artists as being Seattle musicians per say. Not until the city's grunge boom in the '90s did the rest of the world turn to Seattle as the origin of a unique sound.

Grunge is best described as a guitar and angst-driven derivative of the punk rock scene, but calmer. Grunge grew out of garage rock, where dudes with nothing else to do jammed in their garages because, before grunge, there were few places to rock out in Seattle.

All of the attention that Seattle harvested from the success of these bands led to an ongoing efflorescence of new alternative music groups. Despite the popularity of many of the original bands, the grunge image lost much of its appeal when impressionable suburban youth all over the country adopted its ratty, plaid-shirted style. Today grunge is simply passé in Seattle, but it endowed the city with some great venues and made Seattle a musical town. Seattle's music fans are very supportive of local talent, and going to see new or established groups has long been a favorite evening activity.

Classical Seattle offers a full array of classical music, including well-respected professional symphony and opera companies. The Seattle Symphony is regarded as a major regional orchestra and its downtown performance hall, the Benaroya Concert Hall, is as gorgeous as it is acoustically exquisite. The Northwest Chamber Orchestra is the Northwest's only orchestra that focuses on period chamber music; the group performs at various venues throughout the city.

The Seattle Opera is another major cultural focus in Seattle. For a regional company it isn't afraid to tackle weighty or nontraditional works; productions of Philip Glass and a summer *Wagner's Ring* cycle have given opera lovers a lot to mull over. However, the company is perhaps most noted for its unconventional stagings of the traditional repertoire. The Seattle Men's Chorus, a 180-member gay chorus, delights audiences with its 30 concerts each year (see Classical Music, Opera & Dance in the Entertainment chapter).

Literature

The pioneers of early Seattle had city building on their minds, and didn't exactly fill libraries with weighty tomes. Nonetheless, some of the city's first settlers took time to record chronicles of pioneer days. In 1888 Arthur Denny, one of the founders of Seattle, wrote *Pioneer Days on Puget Sound* (1908); James Swan wrote *The Northwest Coast* (1869) and *Indians of Cape Flattery* (1870) during the 1850s. *The Canoe and the Saddle* by Theodore Winthrop (1863) recounts a young man's trip across Washington on his way to Seattle in 1853.

One of the most prolific Seattle writers of the early 20th century was Archie Binns. Of his many novels, *The Land is Bright* (1939), the story of an Oregon Trail family, is still read today. A social and economic chronicle of Seattle, *The Northwest Gateway* (1941) provides a good if dated introduction to Seattle's attitudes toward itself. The quirky characters of pioneer Seattle come to life in Murray Morgan's *Skid Road: An Informal Portrait of Seattle* (1951).

In the 1960s and '70s, western Washington attracted a number of counterculture writers. The most famous of these is Tom Robbins, whose books, including *Another Roadside Attraction* (1971) and *Even Cowgirls Get the Blues* (1976), became the scripture of a generation. Poet Theodore Roethke taught for years at the University of Washington, and with Washington native Richard Hugo he cast a profound influence over Northwest poetry. Raymond Carver, the poet and short story master whose books include *Will You Please Be Quiet Please* (1976) and *Where I'm Calling From* (1988), lived near Seattle on the Olympic Peninsula. Carver's dark and quirky vision of working-class angst has profoundly affected other young writers of his time. Carver's wife Tess Gallagher is also a novelist and poet whose books include *At the Owl Woman Saloon* (1997).

Ivan Doig writes of his move to Seattle in *The Sea Runners* (1982). In *Winter Brothers* (1980), Doig examines the diaries of early Washington writer James Swan, who lived among the Makah Indians on the northern tip of the Olympic Peninsula. Noted travel writer Jonathan Raban, also a new immigrant to Seattle, has written such books as *Coasting* (1987), *Huntin' Mister Heartbreak* (1990) and *Badlands* (1996). Annie Dillard, essayist and novelist, wrote about the Northwest in *The Living* (1992).

Sherman Alexie writes from a Native American perspective. His book *The Lone Ranger and Tonto Fistfight in Heaven* (1993) is a collection of stories about reservation life; in 1996, he published to great critical acclaim *Indian Killer,* a chilling tale of ritual murder set in Seattle. David Guterson writes about the Puget Sound area and the internment of Japanese Americans during WWII in *Snow Falling on Cedars* (1994).

The misty environs of western Washington is a fecund habitat for mystery writers. Dashiell Hammett once lived in Seattle, while noted writers JA Jance, Earl Emerson and Frederick D Huebner currently make the Northwest home.

Another peculiar phenomenon is the number of cartoonists who live in the Seattle area. Lynda Barry *(Ernie Pook's Comeek)* and Matt Groening (creator of *The Simpsons)* were students together at Olympia's Evergreen State College. Gary Larson, whose *Far Side* animal antics have netted international fame and great fortune, lives in Seattle.

In *Stepping Westward* (1991), Sallie Tisdale tells her story of growing up in the Northwest, with insights into the region's culture. Timothy Egan's *The Good Rain*

The talented Mr Groening

(1990) is an insightful discussion of the Northwest and its people by the local *New York Times* correspondent. Seattle preacher Robert Fulghum made it big as an inspirational writer with *All I Really Need to Know I Learned in Kindergarten* (1988).

Film & TV

Seattle has come a long way as a movie mecca since the days when Elvis starred in the 1963 film *It Happened at the World's Fair,* a chestnut of civic boosterism. Films with Seattle as their backdrop include the 1930s *Tugboat Annie; Cinderella Liberty* (1974), a steamy romance with James Caan and Marsha Mason; and *The Parallax View* (1974) with Warren Beatty. Jessica Lange's movie *Frances,* about local Frances Farmer, was shot here in 1981. Debra Winger's hit *Black Widow* (1986) shows many scenes shot at UW, and Sly Stallone and Antonio Banderas starred in the flop *Assassins* (1995).

Fun-loving comedies and dramas shot in Seattle have done well. John Cusack starred in *Say Anything* (1989), Michelle Pfeiffer and Jeff Bridges did it up in *The Fabulous Baker Boys* (1989), and *Singles* (1992), with Campbell Scott, Kyra Sedgwick, Matt Dillon and Bridget Fonda, captured the Seattle vibe. Incidentally, both *Singles* and *Say Anything* were directed by Cameron Crowe. But no film shot in Seattle garnered as much attention as *Sleepless in Seattle,* the 1993 blockbuster starring Tom Hanks, Meg Ryan and, perhaps more importantly, Seattle's Lake Union houseboats.

Television's *Northern Exposure,* filmed in nearby Roslyn, Washington, and *Frasier* have both done a lot to create Seattle's current reputation as a hip and youthful place to live. The creepy, darker side of the Northwest was captured in the moody *Twin Peaks.*

Architecture

In terms of architecture, Seattle is as notable for what is missing as for what remains. Seattle's Great Fire of 1889 ravaged the old wooden storefronts of downtown, which were replaced by the stone and brick structures that still spread around the city's old center in Pioneer Square. Architect Elmer Fisher is responsible for more than 50 buildings erected immediately after the fire. Any Victorian homes and structures that escaped the Great Fire did not escape the Denny Regrade (1899–1912), which flattened a steep residential hill in order to make room for more downtown commercial properties.

Seattle's next big building phase came in the early decades of the 20th century. The beaux arts and art deco hospitals that fill the skyline on First and Beacon Hills are good examples of the civic buildings of that era. Smith Tower, near Pioneer Square, was built in 1914, and with 42 stories it was for many years the tallest building in the world outside of New York City. The campanile-like tower of white terra-cotta brick is still one of the city's beauties (see Pioneer Square in the Things to See & Do chapter). Also during this time, Capitol and Queen Anne Hills filled with homes of the popular Georgian, Federal, English and Arts and Crafts styles.

More recent additions to the downtown skyline include the West Coast's tallest building, the Bank of America Building (formerly the Columbia Seafirst Center), a black monolith possessing no other distinction than its 76-story shadow. Six other buildings rise above 50 stories, though only the Washington Mutual Building, with its plaidlike facade and turquoise glass, makes a pleasant impression.

As the architectural icon of Seattle, no other modern structure comes close to the Space Needle. Built for the 1962 World's Fair, its sleek but whimsical design has aged amazingly well. The newest and most controversial addition to Seattle architecture is the Frank O Gehry–designed Experience Music Project, whose curvy metallic design caused quite a commotion (see Seattle Center in the Things to See & Do chapter).

SOCIETY & CONDUCT

Though Seattle's population grew 10% between 1990 and 2000, the city is still racially segregated, where most whites and minorities live in distinct neighborhoods.

The segregation is particularly acute for African Americans, and bouts of class-tinged violence have erupted over everything from funding for schools to race discrimination in the workplace. The migration of a highly educated, generally white workforce to Seattle hasn't helped. Racial prejudices remain an unspoken undercurrent.

Seattle ranks second only to San Francisco for the smallest percentage of children in a large city. This is attributed to the influx of young professionals, who are waiting longer to start families and whose high earning capacity has helped drive Seattle housing prices up; families are now migrating to the suburbs in order to find affordable homes.

Despite its issues of cultural segregation and growth, Seattle remains a casual and laid-back city. Seattleites are friendly and unpretentious and, despite the rain, cherish Seattle's outdoorsy way of life.

RELIGION

Christianity is the dominant religion in Seattle, with Catholicism and Protestant sects roughly equal in the number of adherents. The Mormon church is prevalent throughout the Northwest, though more often in rural or suburban areas. Judaism, Islam and especially Buddhism are also represented in Seattle.

Nature religions also have a firm foothold in the Northwest, perhaps due to the Celtic gloom that presides here much of the year. Forms of Wicca (a pagan nature religion) and a myriad of other nature-based spiritual movements are practiced in western Washington.

LANGUAGE

English is by far the dominant language of Seattle, but many foreign tongues can be heard floating in the air. In the International District you'll hear a wide mix of Asian languages, including Japanese, Chinese, Korean, Vietnamese and Laotian, to name a few. In Ballard, it's common to hear Scandinavian languages spoken on the streets. Throughout town you'll hear bits of Spanish and Portuguese mixed in with Slavic languages.

Facts for the Visitor

WHEN TO GO

Most travelers choose to visit Seattle in the summer and fall, when the weather is pleasant and rainfall less frequent – the city receives 65% of its precipitation from November to March. September and October are often glorious months, as the Indian summer brings warm days and cool nights. The weather deteriorates after October and can be downright miserable in the dark, drizzly days of December, January and February. Come spring, the rain still drops, but skies lighten and temperatures slowly rise.

If your itinerary brings you to Seattle in winter, all is not lost. Hotel prices drop dramatically and many cultural events, including the symphony, opera and theater, are most active during winter months. Skiers can take advantage of great Northwestern skiing at nearby Snoqualmie Pass and Stevens Pass ski areas.

It's worth noting that Seattle can be very busy in summer and some of the popular sights and ferry trips can get oppressively overcrowded. Off-season travel has its advantages, even if it does mean you'll have to carry an umbrella.

WHAT TO BRING

For a big, urban city, Seattle is a very casual place, considered far more easygoing than most North American and European cities, so pack for comfort. Even if your trip will include dining out or attending formal events, there's no special need to wear formal clothes. People in Seattle do dress up; they just don't require it of others.

In summer it's usually warm but not humid, and evenings are often cool, so bring a jacket. In all seasons, it's a good idea to bring clothes that can stand a little rain. Layering is the key to dressing in the Pacific Northwest. Even if you come in winter, leave the heavy parka behind and bring three of four comfortable layers, including a light rain jacket. If you're inclined to lug along an umbrella, you'll probably use it,

though you'll notice many locals don't bother, opting instead to use their jacket hoods or nothing at all. This grin-and-bear-it method, however, takes some getting used to.

Winters in western Washington are usually chilly and wet but not extremely cold. Unless you're planning a trip that takes you over the mountains, heavy winter gear isn't usually necessary.

In all seasons, it's worth bringing along a pair of binoculars. You'll be glad to have them when you spot your first sea lion or orca whale. Likewise, consider bringing along or buying a good wildlife or wildflower guide. The rich diversity of animals and plants in the Northwest – even in Seattle's larger parks and along the waterfront – is astounding, and it's more fun if you can identify everything you see.

ORIENTATION

Seattle, Washington's largest city, sits on a slim isthmus between Puget Sound and Lake Washington. North of Seattle's downtown area is another freshwater lake, Lake Union. The lakes are linked to the Puget Sound by the canals and locks of the Lake Washington Ship Canal. Although Seattle is a major Pacific port, the ocean is 125 miles away, which seems a little confusing because there's water everywhere. It's a good idea to look at a map to get an understanding of how all the water bodies connect, and trace the long route that ships must sail from Seattle to the open seas.

As the size of the city proper is limited by water, most people and many businesses are beyond downtown in the greater Seattle and Puget Sound areas, making Seattle seem like a sprawling city. However, if you look at it in chunks you'll see that metropolitan Seattle is actually quite compact, and the neighborhoods pretty easy to figure out. Seattle's a city whose vibrancy depends on its interesting outlying communities. It probably evolved this way because, before bridges and ferries made navigating the canal and lakes easy, the disconnected terrain made it easier to stay close to home than to venture out across lakes and canals, resulting in the outlying neighborhoods being pretty isolated. Today getting around is easy, but the outlying areas are still pretty neighborhood-centric. (See the Getting There & Away chapter for travel options to Seattle.)

Neighborhoods

The downtown area butts up against Elliott Bay and encompasses the financial and shopping areas, First Hill, Pioneer Square, Pike Place Market, the Waterfront and Belltown. If you're trying to keep straight the street names in downtown Seattle, here's a handy mnemonic device: from Yesler Way up to Stewart, the streets proceed in alphabetic pairs – Jefferson and James, Cherry and Columbia, Marion and Madison, Spring and Seneca, University and Union, Pike and Pine. The tool for remembering the order is the old saw, learned by Seattle schoolchildren for years, that Jesus Christ Made Seattle Under Protest.

Seattle Center, with many of Seattle's cultural and sport facilities and attractions including the Space Needle, is just north of downtown. West of Seattle Center is funky Lower Queen Anne, which is connected to Upper Queen Anne by Seattle's steepest hill. East of Seattle Center is gritty Capitol Hill, the city's gay quarter and hub of youthful urban culture. Just north, a slim strip

---

Street Smarts

Because of Seattle's topographic stew of bays, islands, hills and peninsulas, nothing as sensible as a standard street grid system fits the city. Instead, Seattle's street system is an amalgam of several separate grids that sometimes overlap each other, leading to maximum confusion. That said, it's fairly easy to get a working understanding of the numbering system and the way all the areas of the city fit together.

Generally speaking, avenues run north and south, and streets run east and west. Yesler Way near Pioneer Square is the zero street for numbering addresses on downtown avenues; Western Ave is the zero street for addresses on streets. Usually Seattle's avenues have a directional suffix (6th Ave S), while its streets have directional prefixes (S Charles St); however, downtown streets and avenues have no directional affixes.

Addresses with a West affix are in the Queen Anne and Magnolia neighborhoods, directly northwest of downtown. A swathe of streets and avenues cutting north from Lake Union, taking in parts of Fremont, Wallingford, Green Lake and the eastern part of Queen Anne, take a simple North prefix (avenues with a North suffix, however, are north of downtown near Seattle Center). Loosely speaking, streets and avenues with a Northeast affix are east of I-5 and north of Lake Union in an area that takes in the University of Washington. To add to the confusion, many of the streets and avenues in this area are numbered. Streets and avenues with a Northwest affix are north of the shipping canal in and around Ballard. Addresses with a Southwest affix are in West Seattle. Streets and avenues south of Yesler Way are labeled South. Up on Capitol Hill, watch for the East affix on streets and avenues.

Clearly, Seattle street addresses are really confusing, and few people go to the trouble to figure out how the system fits together. Instead, people use neighborhoods to indicate where things are found. For instance, '10th Ave on Queen Anne' indicates which 10th Ave is being referred to; likewise '1st Ave in Wallingford' directs one to that particular 1st Ave. Therefore, it's important to arrive at a working knowledge of Seattle's neighborhoods. With so many numbering systems at odds with each other, it's the only way to easily make sense of the city.

along Lake Union's eastern side is aptly named Eastlake. The Central District, Madison Valley, Madison Park and Madrona are residential neighborhoods on the east side of the Seattle peninsula as it slopes down to Lake Washington.

Lake Union and the Lake Washington Ship Canal divide the city into northern and southern halves. The northern neighborhoods include the U District, named for the University of Washington campus, Wallingford, Fremont and Ballard. Each of these areas has a lively commercial center filled with restaurants, shops and bars. Just north of Fremont and Wallingford is Green Lake, the focal point of a large park area that also contains the city zoo.

It's worth noting that four bridges (besides the freeway bridges) cross the ship canal. The University and Montlake Bridges connect neighborhoods south of the canal with the U District. West of Lake Union, the Fremont Bridge crosses from Queen Anne to Fremont. The westernmost bridge, Ballard Bridge, links the neighborhood of Magnolia, west of Queen Anne, with Ballard.

To the west of Seattle, across Elliott Bay, is another peninsula, called West Seattle. This is where the original pioneer settlers founded Seattle.

The urban mass of Greater Seattle stretches south to north, from Tacoma up to Everett – a distance of 60 miles. To the south are Renton, Kent, Federal Way and Tacoma. East across Lake Washington, referred to as the 'Eastside', are Bellevue, Kirkland and Redmond. To the north lie Edmonds and Everett. Several islands in Puget Sound, notably Bainbridge and Vashon, also serve as suburbs whose commuters ride the ferries to work in Seattle.

MAPS

Seattle is a potentially challenging place to get around in, so it's a good idea to invest in a detailed map and to spend some time getting familiar with how the city is laid out before setting out, especially in a car. If you're not driving and only in town for a couple of days, the free maps given out by

the tourist office will help you enough to get around downtown.

An excellent source for maps in Seattle is Metsker Maps (Map 4, ☎ 623-8747), 702 1st Ave. Especially handy is *Streetwise Seattle,* a laminated map that fits easily in a pocket or bag. If you're serious about knowing your way around, consider the *Rand McNally's Seattle City Map* or the *Thomas Brothers Atlas* of King County. If you're going to be using public transit, you can pick up a free color map of Seattle's transportation system from the King County Metro Transit office (Map 4, ☎ 553-3000) at 201 S Jackson St. There is a Downtown Metro Transit map (Map 3) in the map section at the back of this book. You can also get transit information at the main public library on 4th Ave at Madison St (Map 2).

The American Automobile Association (AAA) office (Map 8, ☎ 448-5353), 330 6th Ave N, has maps and all sorts of travel information available for members. If you're planning to venture into the mountains, parks and recreation areas outside of Seattle, the book section upstairs at the REI store (Map 8, ☎ 223-1944), 222 Yale Ave N, has a good selection of topographic and regional maps.

TOURIST OFFICES

The Seattle/King County Convention & Visitors Bureau (Map 2, ☎ 461-5840), 800 Convention Place, is at the Washington State Convention & Trade Center on Pike St at 7th Ave. You can enter this four-story structure, built directly above I-5, from either Pike St or the Union St underpass. Here you can get everything from glossy brochures to maps and practical information from the knowledgeable staff. If you want to write to the Convention & Visitors Bureau for information, the mailing address is 520 Pike St, Suite 1300, Seattle, WA 98101. A market information kiosk (Map 5) just outside the Pike Place Market at 1st Ave at Pike St also dispenses maps and brochures. At Sea-Tac airport, the information center (☎ 433-5288) is on the baggage claim level and will help you with everything from booking hotels to getting transportation from the airport into the city.

For information about the rest of Washington State, contact the Washington State Department of Travel Counseling (☎ 360-586-2088).

TRAVEL AGENCIES

Council Travel specializes in round-the-world airplane tickets, student exchanges and arranging work abroad. It has two offices in Seattle: one on Capitol Hill (Map 8, ☎ 329-4567), 424 Broadway E; and another in the University District (Map 9, ☎ 632-2448), 4211½ University Way NE. Both offices are open 9 am to 5 pm weekdays and 10 am to 2 pm Saturday. STA Travel (☎ 633-5000), 4341 University Way NE, also specializes in student and low-budget travel.

DOCUMENTS
Passport & Visas

To enter the US, Canadians need only proper proof of Canadian citizenship, such as a birth certificate with photo ID or a passport. All other foreign visitors must have a valid passport and, unless they qualify under the reciprocal visa-waiver program, a US visa.

The reciprocal visa-waiver program allows citizens of certain countries to enter the USA for stays of 90 days or less without first obtaining a US visa. Currently, these 29 countries are: Andorra, Argentina, Australia, Austria, Belgium, Brunei, Denmark, Finland, France, Germany, Iceland, Ireland, Italy, Japan, Liechtenstein, Luxembourg, Monaco, the Netherlands, New Zealand, Norway, Portugal, San Marino, Singapore, Slovenia, Spain, Sweden, Switzerland, Uruguay and the UK. Under this program you must have a roundtrip ticket that is nonrefundable in the USA and proof of financial solvency, such as credit cards, a bank account with evidence of sufficient funds or employment in your home country. You will not be allowed to extend your stay beyond 90 days.

Other travelers will need to obtain a visa from a US consulate or embassy. In most countries the process can be done by mail or through a travel agent.

Your passport should be valid for at least six months longer than your intended stay in the USA, and you'll need to submit a recent photo 1½ inches square (37mm x 37mm) with the application. Documents of

HIV & Entering the USA

Anyone entering the USA who isn't a US citizen is subject to the authority of the Immigration & Naturalization Service (INS). The INS can exclude or deport anyone entering or staying in the USA. This is especially relevant to travelers with HIV (human immunodeficiency virus). Though being HIV-positive is not cause for deportation, it is a 'ground of exclusion' and the INS can invoke it to refuse admission.

Although the INS doesn't test people for HIV at immigration, it may try to exclude anyone who answers 'yes' to this question on the nonimmigrant visa application form: 'Have you ever been afflicted with a communicable disease of public health significance?' INS officials may also stop people if they seem sick, are carrying AIDS/HIV medicine or, sadly, if the officer happens to think the person 'looks gay,' though sexual orientation is not legally a ground of exclusion.

It's imperative that visitors know and assert their rights. Immigrants and visitors who may face exclusion should discuss their rights and options with a trained immigration advocate before applying for a visa. For legal immigration information and referrals to immigration advocates, contact the National Immigration Project of the National Lawyers Guild (☎ 617-227-9727), 14 Beacon St, Suite 506, Boston, MA 02108, USA; or Immigrant HIV Assistance Project, Bar Association of San Francisco (☎ 415-782-8995), 465 California St, Suite 1100, San Francisco, CA 94104, USA.

financial stability and/or guarantees from a US resident are sometimes required, particularly for those from developing countries.

Visa applicants may be required to 'demonstrate binding obligations' that will ensure their return back home. Because of this requirement, those planning to travel through other countries before arriving in the USA are generally better off applying for their US visa while they are still in their home country, rather than while on the road.

The most common visa is a nonimmigrant visitor's visa: B1 for business purposes, B2 for tourism or visiting friends and relatives. A visitor's visa is good for one or five years with multiple entries, and it specifically prohibits the visitor from taking paid employment in the USA. The validity period depends on what country you're from. The length of time you'll be allowed to stay in the USA is ultimately determined by US immigration authorities at the port of entry.

Visa Extensions & Re-Entry Tourists without visa waivers are usually granted a six-month stay on first arrival. If you extend that time, the first assumption will be that you are working illegally, so come prepared with concrete evidence that you've been traveling extensively and will continue to be a model tourist. A wad of traveler's checks looks much better than a solid and unmoving bank account. If you want, need or hope to stay in the USA longer than the date stamped on your passport, visit or call the local INS office (☎ 800-755-0777, or look in the local white pages telephone directory under US Government) *before* the stamped date.

Alternatively, cross the border into Mexico or Canada and apply for another period of entry when you come back. US officials don't usually collect the Departure Record cards from your passport when you leave at a land border, so they may not notice if you've overstayed by a couple of days. Returning to the USA, you go through the same procedure as when you entered the USA for the first time, so be ready with your proposed itinerary and evidence of sufficient funds. If you try this border hopping more than once, to get a third six-month period of entry, you may find the INS very strict. Generally, it seems that they are reluctant to let you stay more than a year.

Travel Insurance

No matter how you're traveling, make sure you take out travel insurance. This should cover you not only for medical expenses and luggage theft or loss but also for cancellations or delays in your travel arrangements. It should also cover the worst possible case, such as an accident that requires hospital treatment and a flight home. Coverage depends on your insurance and type of ticket, so ask both your insurer and your ticket-issuing agency to explain the finer points. Ticket loss is also covered by travel insurance. Make sure you have a separate record of all your ticket details – or, better still, a photocopy of your ticket. Also make a copy of your policy, in case the original is lost.

Buy travel insurance as early as possible. If you buy it the week before you fly, you may find, for instance, that you're not covered for delays to your flight caused by strikes or other industrial action that may have been in force before you took out the insurance.

Insurance may seem very expensive, but it's nowhere near the cost of a medical emergency in the USA. If you find yourself uninsured in Seattle, contact Council Travel (see Travel Agencies, earlier), which provides travel insurance to foreign nationals while they're on US soil. Be aware, however, that this insurance won't cover you as soon as you leave the USA (via air, ferry, bus etc), so you will have to get further insurance if you're planning on going to Mexico or Canada.

Driver's License & Permits

If you're intending to drive in the USA, you need an International or Inter-American Driving Permit to supplement your national or state driver's license, but US police are more likely to want to see your national, provincial or state driver's license. Canadian and Mexican drivers aren't expected to carry international driver's licenses.

Drivers of cars and motorcycles will need the vehicle's registration papers and liability insurance. Customs officials along the entry points between British Columbia and Washington can be strict and wary of foreigners, so it helps to have your paperwork in order. To avoid unnecessary conflicts, dress well and be cordial during the time it takes to cross the border. For information on renting a car, see the Getting Around chapter.

If you plan on doing a lot of driving in the USA, it would be beneficial to join your national automobile association. This allows you access to the benefits and free information of the American Automobile Association (AAA).

Other Documents

Seattle's excellent HI Seattle hostel is a member of Hostelling International-American Youth Hostels (HI-AYH), which is affiliated with the International Youth Hostel Federation (IYHF). If you're a member, bring your card. Alternatively you can purchase membership on the spot when checking in.

If you're a student, get an international student ID or bring along a school or university ID card to take advantage of the discounts available to students.

Anyone 65 or older gets discounts throughout the USA. All you need is ID with proof of age. There are organizations, such as AARP (see Senior Travelers, later), that offer membership cards for further discounts; coverage is extended to citizens of other countries.

Copies

All important documents (passport data page and visa page, credit cards, travel insurance policy, air/bus/train tickets, driver's license etc) should be photocopied before you leave home. Leave one copy with someone at home and keep another with you, separate from the originals.

It's also a good idea to store details of your vital travel documents in Lonely Planet's free online Travel Vault in case you lose the photocopies or can't be bothered with them. Your password-protected Travel Vault is accessible online anywhere in the world; you can create one by visiting www.ekno.lonelyplanet.com.

EMBASSIES & CONSULATES
US Embassies & Consulates Abroad

US diplomatic offices abroad include the following:

Australia (☎ 2-6214-5600) Moonah Place, Yarralumla ACT 2600
(☎ 2-9373-9200) MLC Centre, Level 59, 19-29 Martin Place, Sydney NSW 2000
(☎ 3-9526-5900) 553 St Kilda Rd, Melbourne VIC 3004

Austria (☎ 1-313-39) Boltzmanngasse 16, A-1090, Vienna

Belgium (☎ 2-508-21-11) Regentlaan 27 Blvd du Regent, B-1000, Brussels

Canada (☎ 613-238-5335) 490 Sussex Drive, Ottawa, Ontario K1N 1G8
(☎ 604-685-4311) 1095 W Pender St, Vancouver, BC V6E 2M6
(☎ 514-398-9695) 1155 rue St Alexandre, Montréal, Québec H2Z 1Z2

Denmark (☎ 35-55-31-44) Dag Hammarskjölds Allé 24, 2100 Copenhagen

Finland (☎ 9-171-931) Itäinen Puistotie 14 B, FIN-00140 Helsinki

France (☎ 1 43 12 22 22) 2, avenue Gabriel, 75008 Paris

Germany (☎ 30-8305-0) Neustädtische Kirchstr. 4-5, 10117 Berlin

Greece (☎ 1-721-2951) 91 Vassilissis Sophias Avenue, 101 60 Athens

India (☎ 11-419-8000) Shantipath, Chanakyapuri, New Delhi 110021

Indonesia (☎ 21-3435-9000) Jl. Merdeka Selatan 4-5, Jakarta 10110

Ireland (☎ 1 6688777) 42 Elgin Rd, Dublin 4

Israel (☎ 3-519-7575) 71 Hayarkon St, Tel Aviv

Italy (☎ 6-46-741) Via Vittorio Veneto 119/A, 00187 Rome

Japan (☎ 3-3224-5000) 1-10-5 Akasaka, Minato-ku, Tokyo 107-8420

Korea (☎ 2-397-4114) 82 Sejong-ro, Chongro-ku, Seoul 110-710

Malaysia (☎ 3-2168-5000) 376 Jalan Tun Razak, 50400 Kuala Lumpur

Mexico (☎ 5-209-9100) Paseo de la Reforma 305, Col. Cuauhtémoc, 06500 Mexico City

Netherlands (☎ 70-310-9209) Lange Voorhout 102, 2514 EJ The Hague
(☎ 20-575-5309) Museumplein 19, 1071 DJ Amsterdam

New Zealand (☎ 4-472-2068) 29 Fitzherbert Terrace, Thorndon, Wellington

Norway (☎ 22-44-85-50) Drammensveien 18, 0244 Oslo

Philippines (☎ 2-523-1001) 1201 Roxas Blvd, Ermita 1000, Manila

Russia (☎ 095-728-5000) Bolshoy Devyatinskiy Pereulok No 8, 121099 Moscow

Singapore (☎ 476-9100) 27 Napier Rd, Singapore 258508

South Africa (☎ 12-342-1048) 877 Pretorius St, Box 9536, Pretoria 0001

Spain (☎ 91587-2200) Serrano 75, 28006 Madrid

Sweden (☎ 8-783-5300) Dag Hammarskjölds Väg 31, SE-115 89 Stockholm

Switzerland (☎ 31-357-70 11) Jubiläumsstrasse 93, 3001 Bern

Thailand (☎ 2-205-4000) 120/22 Wireless Rd, Bangkok

UK (☎ 20-7499-9000) 24 Grosvenor Square, London W1A 1AE
(☎ 131-556-8315) 3 Regent Terrace, Edinburgh EH7 5BW
(☎ 28-9032-8239) Queen's House, 14 Queen St, Belfast BT1 6EQ

To find US embassies in other countries, visit the Web site http://usembassy.state.gov.

Consulates in Seattle

Check the yellow pages under 'Consulates' for diplomatic representation in Seattle. Consulates include:

Austria (☎ 624-9887) 1111 3rd Ave, Suite 2626

Belgium (☎ 728-5145) 2200 Alaskan Way

Canada (☎ 443-1372) Plaza 600, 600 Stewart St

Denmark (☎ 230-0888) 6204 E Mercer Way, Mercer Island

Estonia (☎ 467-6314) 500 Union St, Suite 930

France (☎ 256-6184) PO Box 1249

Germany (☎ 682-4312) 600 University St, Suite 2500

Guatemala (☎ 728-5920) 2001 6th Ave, Suite 3300

Italy (☎ 425-485-8626) 23732 Bthl-Evrt Hwy, Bothell

Japan (☎ 682-9107) 601 Union St

Korea (☎ 441-1011) 2033 6th Ave

Mexico (☎ 448-3526) 2132 3rd Ave

New Zealand (☎ 525-0271) PO Box 51059

Russia (☎ 728-1910) 2001 6th Ave, Westin Bldg, Suite 2323

Sweden (☎ 622-5640) 1215 4th Ave

UK (☎ 622-9255) 900 4th Ave

For directory assistance with embassies and consulates outside Seattle, call ☎ 202-555-1212 or visit the Web site www.polisci.com/web/embassies.htm.

Your Own Embassy

It's important to realize what your own embassy or consulate – the mission of the country of which you are a citizen – can and can't do to help you if you get into trouble. Generally speaking, it won't be much help in emergencies if the trouble you're in is remotely your own fault. Remember that you are bound by the laws of the country you are in. Your embassy will not be sympathetic if you end up in jail after committing a crime locally, even if such actions are legal in your own country.

In genuine emergencies, you might get some assistance, but only if other channels have been exhausted. If you need to get home urgently, a free ticket home is exceedingly unlikely – the embassy would expect you to have insurance. If all your money and documents are stolen, it might assist you with getting a new passport, but a loan for onward travel is out of the question.

Some embassies used to keep letters for travelers or have a small reading room with home newspapers, but these days most of the mail-holding services have been stopped and even newspapers tend to be out of date.

CUSTOMS

US customs allows each person over the age of 21 to bring one liter of liquor and 200 cigarettes duty free into the USA. Non-US citizens are allowed to bring in $100 worth of gifts from abroad; US citizens are allowed $400 worth.

US law permits you to bring in, or take out, as much as $10,000 in US or foreign cash, traveler's checks or money orders without formality. Larger amounts of any or all of the above – there are no limits – must be declared to customs.

For more information visit the Web site www.customs.gov/travel/travel.htm.

MONEY
Currency
The US dollar is divided into 100 cents (¢). Coins come in denominations of 1¢ (penny), 5¢ (nickel), 10¢ (dime), 25¢ (quarter) and the seldom seen 50¢ (half-dollar). Quarters are the most commonly used coins in vending machines and parking meters, so it's handy to have a stash of them. US dollar notes, usually called bills, can be confusing in that they are all the same color and size, so get used to checking the amounts. Dollar bills come in $1, $2, $5, $10, $20, $50 and $100 denominations – $2 bills are rare but perfectly legal. The government continually tries to bring $1 coins into mass circulation, but they have never proliferated in everyday commerce. You may get them as change

from ticket and stamp machines. Beware that they look similar to quarters.

Exchange Rates
Banks usually offer the best rates when it comes to changing money. At press time exchange rates were:

country	unit		dollar
Australia	A$1	=	$0.50
Canada	C$1	=	$0.66
European Union	€1	=	$0.85
Hong Kong	HK$10	=	$1.28
Japan	¥100	=	$0.80
United Kingdom	UK£1	=	$1.41

Exchanging Money
At the airport, there are two Thomas Cook currency exchange booths in the main terminal. The one behind the Delta Airlines booth is open 6 am to 8 pm; the one behind Alaska Airlines is open 6 am to 6 pm. Another branch in the South Satellite is open 8 am to 6 pm. For information, call ☎ 248-6960. Should your flight arrive after hours, you can get cash from the ATMs near the booths.

The Price of the Good Life in Seattle

parking ticket (expired meter etc)	$25
pint of Ballard Bitter	$3.50
grande caffe latte at Torrefazione Italia	$3.05
adult admission to the Egyptian Cinema	$7.75
rack of lamb at the Hunt Club, Sorrento Hotel	$38
king salmon at the Flying Fish in Belltown	$18
Monorail ticket	$1.50
eyebrow piercing at the Pink Zone	$30
taxi from the airport to the Pike Place Market	$30
adult ticket up the Space Needle	$11
fresh crab at Pike Place Market	$8/lb
dorm bed at the HI hostel	$17
pan-fried scallops and prawns at the Sea Garden	$11.25
one ticket to theater sports at the Market Theater	$10
bus fare between downtown sites	free
super burrito from Bimbo's Bitchin' Burrito Kitchen	$7
rosemary baguette from Grand Central Baking	$1.90
live music cover on Saturday night at the Crocodile Cafe	$7

There are a number of options for exchanging money in Seattle. Thomas Cook Foreign Exchange has a downtown office (Map 2, ☎ 682-4525), 1601 5th Ave, Suite 400, in the Westlake Center; and a Bellevue office (☎ 425-462-2817), 10630 NE 8th Ave. American Express (Map 2, ☎ 441-8622) is at 600 Stewart St at 6th Ave.

Traveler's Checks Traveler's checks offer good protection from theft or loss and are as good as cash in the USA; you do not have to go to a bank to cash traveler's checks, as most restaurants, hotels and stores will accept them just like cash. Only purchase traveler's checks in US dollars, as the savings you *might* make on exchange rates by carrying traveler's checks in a foreign currency don't make up for the hassle of exchanging them at banks. Don't bother getting traveler's checks in denominations less than US$100. Having to change smaller bills is inconvenient, and you may be nailed with service charges if you wind up having to cash them at banks.

Keeping a record of the check numbers and the checks you have used is vital when it comes to replacing lost checks. Keep this record separate from the checks themselves. For refunds or lost or stolen traveler's checks (not credit cards), call American Express (☎ 800-221-7282), MasterCard (☎ 800-223-9920), Thomas Cook (☎ 800-223-7373) or Visa (☎ 800-227-6811).

If you plan on heading out into rural areas in the Northwest, you may want to exchange your money in Seattle first.

ATMs Automated Teller Machines (ATMs) are a convenient way of obtaining cash from a bank account back home. They are common in most shopping areas, and many banks have them. Most of the machines are open 24 hours a day. There are various ATM networks and most banks are affiliated with several. Exchange, Accel, Plus and Cirrus are the predominant networks in Seattle. For a nominal service charge, you can withdraw cash from an ATM using a credit card, but using bankcards linked to your personal checking account is far cheaper. Check with your bank or credit card company for exact information.

Credit & Debit Cards Major credit cards are accepted at hotels, restaurants, gas stations, shops and car-rental agencies throughout the USA. In fact, you'll find it hard to perform certain transactions, such as renting a car or purchasing tickets to performances, without one.

Even if you loathe credit cards and prefer to rely on traveler's checks and ATMs, it's a good idea to carry one for emergencies. If you're planning to rely primarily upon credit cards, it would be wise to have a Visa or MasterCard in your wallet, since other cards aren't as widely accepted.

Places that accept Visa and MasterCard are also likely to accept debit cards. Unlike a credit card, a debit card deducts payment directly from the user's checking account. Instead of an interest rate, users are charged a minimal fee for the transaction. Debit cards from large commercial banks can often be used worldwide – be sure to check with your bank to confirm that your debit card will be accepted in other states or countries.

Carry copies of your credit card numbers separately from the cards. If you lose your credit cards or they get stolen, contact the company immediately. Following are toll-free numbers for the main credit card companies.

American Express	☎ 800-528-4800
Diners Club	☎ 800-234-6377
Discover	☎ 800-347-2683
MasterCard	☎ 800-826-2181
Visa	☎ 800-336-8472

Contact your bank if you lose your ATM card.

International Transfers If you run out of money, you can instruct your bank back home to send you a draft. Specify the bank and branch in Seattle to which you want your money directed, or ask your home bank to tell you where a suitable one is, and make sure you get the details right. The procedure is easier if you've authorized someone back home to access your account. Money sent by telegraphic transfer should reach you within a week; by mail allow at least two weeks. When it arrives, the money will most likely be converted into local currency; you can take it as cash or buy traveler's checks.

You can also transfer money by American Express, Thomas Cook or Western Union, though the latter has fewer international offices.

Security

Be cautious – but not paranoid – about carrying money. If your hotel or hostel has a safe, keep your valuables and excess cash in it. It's best not to display large amounts of cash in public. A money belt worn under your clothes is a good place to carry extra money when you're on the move or otherwise unable to lock it in a safe. Avoid wearing a wallet in the back pocket of your pants; it's a prime target for pickpockets. Also be sure to zip up pockets on handbags or knapsacks and, when you're sitting in restaurants, avoid slinging your bag over the back of a chair.

Costs

The cost of accommodations varies seasonally in Seattle, especially in tourist-oriented hotels and motels. Rates tend to be a lot higher in summer, between Memorial Day (last Monday in May) and Labor Day (first Monday in September). The cheapest hotel rates are in the $60 to $80 range, while a mid-priced room will begin at $80 and go upward steeply in high season. You can save money by staying at a hostel (where beds go for around $17 a night).

The occasional splurge for a spectacular meal at a first-rate restaurant can run you anywhere from $25 to $35, not to mention booze and add-ons. On the flip side, many places offer good meals for less than $10 – or even half that at lunchtime. If you purchase food at markets, you can get by even more cheaply.

Public transportation is relatively inexpensive; bus fares cost from $1.25 to $1.75, depending on the distance (free within downtown). Rental cars can cost as little as $40 a day, though if you're staying in the downtown core, parking costs will make you think twice about bothering.

Tipping

Tipping is expected in restaurants, bars and better hotels, and by taxi drivers, hairdressers and baggage carriers. In restaurants, waiters are paid minimal wages and rely upon tips for their livelihoods. Tip 15% unless the service is terrible (in which case a complaint to the manager is warranted) or up to 20% if the service is great. No need to tip in fast-food, take-out or buffet-style restaurants where you serve yourself. Tip bartenders around 10% to 15%.

Taxi drivers expect 10% and hairdressers get 15% if their service is satisfactory. Baggage carriers (skycaps in airports, attendants in hotels) get $1 per bag and 50¢ for each additional bag. In budget hotels (where there aren't attendants anyway), tips are not expected.

Taxes

Washington's base state sales tax is 6.5%; counties and cities can assess an additional few percent on top of this, so the rate of tax varies from community to community. Seattle's sales tax is 8.8%. This tax is not levied on food in grocery stores, but it does apply to food served in restaurants. In fact, Seattle's tax on restaurant food is now 9.3%, as an additional 0.5% tax has been levied on meals in order to pay for the Mariners' new sports stadium.

When inquiring about hotel or motel rates, be sure to ask whether taxes are included or not. The so-called 'bed tax' is added to the cost of accommodations in hotels, motels, lodges and B&Bs (the 15.6% tax is usually levied on all charges, including phone calls, parking fees and room service).

POST & COMMUNICATIONS
Mail

Seattle's main post office is at 301 Union St (Map 2); the zip, or postal, code is 98101. If you're near the university, go to the University post office at 4244 University Way NE (Map 9); zip code 98105. On Capitol Hill, go to the Broadway branch at 101 Broadway E (Map 8); zip code 98122. Post offices are usually open 8 am to 5 pm weekdays and 8 am to 3 pm Saturday, but it all depends on the branch. For more information call ☎ 800-275-8777.

Postal Rates Current rates for 1st-class mail within the USA are 34¢ for letters up to 1oz (21¢ for each additional ounce) and 20¢ for postcards.

International airmail rates (except to Canada and Mexico) for letters under 1oz are 80¢; 2oz letters $1.60. International postcards cost 70¢. Letters to Canada are 60¢; 50¢ for a postcard. Letters to Mexico are 85¢; 50¢ for a postcard. Aerogrammes cost 70¢.

Sending Mail If you have the correct postage, you can drop your mail into any blue mailbox. To send a package 16oz or larger, you must take it to a post office. If you need to buy stamps or weigh your mail, go to the nearest post office. For the address of the nearest one, call ☎ 800-275-8777 or visit the main post office (☎ 748-5417) at 301 Union St.

Receiving Mail You can have mail sent to you c/o General Delivery (poste restante) at any post office that has its own zip code. Mail is usually held for 10 days before it's returned to sender; you might ask your correspondents to write 'hold for arrival' on their letters. Alternatively, have mail sent to the local representative of American Express or Thomas Cook; both provide mail service for their customers.

Telephone

All phone numbers within the USA and Canada consist of a three-digit area code (Seattle's is ☎ 206) followed by a seven-digit local number. If you are calling within Seattle, just dial the seven-digit number. If you are calling long distance elsewhere in the USA or Canada, dial 1 + the three-digit area code + the seven-digit number.

The ☎ 800 or ☎ 888 area codes are designated toll-free numbers within the USA and sometimes from Canada. If you are

dialing locally, the toll-free number is not available; you have to use the regular local number (also free). Some ☎ 800 numbers are limited to specific regions; the number may work in Washington but not in Oregon. The ☎ 900 area code is designated for calls paid at a premium rate – phone sex, horoscopes, jokes and so on.

Due to a skyrocketing demand for phone numbers (for faxes, cellular phones and modems), the Puget Sound region now has multiple area codes.

Seattle proper ☎ 206

Eastside (Bellevue, Kirkland, Redmond) ☎ 425

South of Seattle (Kent, Federal Way, Tacoma) ☎ 253

Bainbridge and Vashon Islands ☎ 206

Western Washington ☎ 360 and ☎ 564

Eastern Washington ☎ 509

Calls to the Eastside and areas south of Seattle (excluding Tacoma, which is long-distance) remain local calls. For example, don't use ☎ 1 + 425 to call Bellevue from Seattle, just dial ☎ 425 plus the number.

International Calls If you're calling from abroad, the international country code for the USA and Canada is ☎ 1; follow this with the three-digit area code and then the seven-digit number.

To make an international call direct from Seattle, dial ☎ 011, then the country code, followed by the area code and the phone number. You may need to wait as long as 45 seconds for the ringing to start.

Rates Local calls usually cost 25¢ at pay phones. Long-distance rates vary, depending on the destination, time you call and which telephone company you use – call the operator (☎ 0) for rate information. Don't ask the operator to put your call through, however, because operator-assisted calls are much more expensive than direct-dial calls. Nights (11 pm to 8 am), all day Saturday and 8 am to 5 pm Sunday are generally the cheapest times to call. Evenings (5 to 11 pm Sunday to Friday) are mid-priced and daytime calls (8 am to 5 pm weekdays) are full-price calls within the USA.

Many hotels, especially the more expensive ones, add a service charge to each local call made from your room, and they have hefty surcharges for long-distance calls. Ask when you check in whether local calls are free. If not, the public pay phones found in most lobbies are always cheaper.

Directory Assistance For local directory assistance dial ☎ 411. For directory assistance to places further afield, dial ☎ 1 + the three-digit area code of the place you want to call + 555-1212. For example, to obtain directory assistance for a toll-free number, dial ☎ 1-800-555-1212. The cost for directory assistance is 80¢ to $2, and there's an additional charge if the call is put through by the operator. For operator assistance dial ☎ 0. For international operator assistance dial ☎ 00. Area codes and country codes are listed in telephone directories.

Phone Cards Phone debit cards allow you to pay in advance for long-distance calls. Usually in amounts of $10, $20 and $50, phone cards are sold throughout the city at Western Union, corner stores, supermarkets and machines.

There's a wide range of local and international phone cards. Lonely Planet's eKno Communication Card (see the insert at the back of this book) is aimed specifically at independent travelers and provides budget international calls, a range of messaging services, free email and travel information – for local calls, you're usually better off with a local card. You can join online at www.eKno.lonelyplanet.com or by phone from Seattle by dialing ☎ 1-800-707-0031. To use eKno from the USA once you have joined, dial ☎ 1-800-706-1333.

Check the eKno Web site for joining and access numbers from other countries and updates on super budget local access numbers and new features.

Fax
Fax machines are easy to find at shipping companies like Mail Boxes Etc, photocopy centers and hotel business service centers, but be prepared to pay high prices (over $1

a page to send or receive). Kinko's dominates downtown: There is a branch at the convention center (Map 2, ☎ 467-1767), 735 Pike St, as well as two locations open 24 hours – 816 3rd Ave (Map 2, ☎ 749-0206) and 1335 2nd Ave (Map 2, ☎ 292-9255). Copy and fax businesses line 'The Ave' (University Way) in the U District, and any Office Depot or Mail Boxes Etc has business services. Telegrams can be sent from Western Union (☎ 800-325-6000).

Email & Internet Access
Seattle's a high-tech town. Email and Internet access is as important to Seattleites as a good pair of shoes. As such, most business and top-end hotels offer high-speed modem connections, even in standard rooms. For those traveling without hardware, stop by one of Seattle's public libraries, all of which are equipped to allow Web browsing and access to chat groups. Coffeehouses throughout town have Internet terminals for public use. One of the best places to go is the Speakeasy Café (Map 6, ☎ 728-9770), 2304 2nd Ave, in Belltown. On Capitol Hill, try the comfortable CapitolHill.net (Map 8, ☎ 860-6858), 219 Broadway E, or Online Coffee Company (Map 8, ☎ 328-3713), 1720 Olive Way. In Wallingford, the Cyber Café (Map 10, ☎ 633-4826), 1401 N 45th St, is a technical place that can help you out if you're having computer or access problems.

DIGITAL RESOURCES
The Internet is a rich resource for travelers. You can research your trip, hunt down bargain airfares, book hotels, check on weather conditions or chat with locals and other travelers about the best places to visit (or avoid!).

Start your Web explorations on the Lonely Planet Web site (www.lonelyplanet.com). Here, you'll find succinct summaries on traveling to most places on earth; postcards from other travelers; and the Thorn Tree bulletin board, where you can ask questions of other travelers before you go or dispense advice when you get back. You will also find travel news and updates and the subWWWay section, with links to the most useful travel resources elsewhere on the Web.

Useful Seattle Web Sites
You can learn about Seattle through many Web sites and almost every business these days has its own. Here are a few Seattle-specific sites you might find helpful:

Seattle-King County Visitors Bureau
www.seeseattle.org

Official site of the City of Seattle Official site
www.cityofseattle.net

Northwest Source, excellent local information
www.nwsource.com

Official site of the daily *Seattle Post-Intelligencer*
www.seattlep-i.com

Official site of the daily *Seattle Times*
www.seattletimes.com

Official site of the weekly *Seattle Stranger*
www.thestranger.com

Good commercial site and joint effort of *Seattle Weekly* and Microsoft
www.seattle.sidewalk.com

BOOKS
Seattle is blessed with an abundance of new and used bookstores; see the Shopping chapter for information on general and specialty bookstores. See the Literature section under Arts in the Facts About Seattle chapter for a rundown of books written by Seattleites. Also see Libraries, later.

Most books are published in different editions by different publishers in different countries. As a result, a book might be a hardcover rarity in one country but readily available in paperback in another. Fortunately, bookstores and libraries can search by title or author, so your local bookstore or library is the best place to advise you on the availability of the following recommendations.

Guidebooks
The *Seattle Survival Guide* by Theresa Morrow is full of insider information about local services, businesses, schools, housing, cultural organizations and clubs, and it is a good resource for anyone putting roots down in Seattle. Another good relocation guide is *Newcomer's Handbook for Seattle.* Morton Beebe captures the spirit and history of two of the Pacific Northwest's most fascinating cities in *Cascadia: A Tale of Seattle and Vancouver, BC.*

If you're planning to explore beyond Seattle itself, grab a copy of Lonely Planet's *Pacific Northwest,* which covers Oregon, Washington, Vancouver and Vancouver Island. If you're heading north from Seattle, Lonely Planet's *British Columbia* covers the entire province and the Alberta Rockies.

Outdoorsy types should look for Stephen Whitney's *Nature Walks in and Around Seattle,* and visitors to the San Juan Islands should check out Marge and Ted Meuller's *The San Juan Islands Afoot and Afloat* for camping, trails and water activities on the San Juans. Travelers on bikes will want to pick up Lonely Planet's *Cycling West Coast USA* (published May 2002), and anyone trekking into the mountains should check out Lonely Planet's *Hiking USA.*

For books on travel with children, see Seattle for Children, later.

History
Oddly, there isn't one single book currently in print that does a decent job of detailing the history of the Northwest. History buffs are left to look for *The Great Northwest* by OO Winther (1955) in a used bookstore or library. It's about the best book on the area and very readable.

A good book on Seattle history is *Seattle Past to Present* by Roger Sale. *Exploring Washington's Past* by Ruth Kirk & Carmela Alexander is the single best traveler's guide to Washington's history. *Forging of a Black Community: Seattle's Central District from 1870 through the Civil Rights Era* by Quintard Taylor examines the city's African American heritage.

Park lovers will respect the fine gem of a book *Enjoying Seattle's Parks.* No other book gives such detailed history of each park and how the city's park system developed. It is, unfortunately, out of print, but it often turns up in Seattle's used bookstores.

If you would like to experience the flavor of pioneer Seattle, find a copy of *Pioneer*

Days on Puget Sound by Seattle founder Arthur Denny (available in many editions). Also *Skid Road: An Informal Portrait of Seattle* by Murray Morgan introduces some of the lesser-known characters and their colorful contributions to pioneer Seattle. Canadian Pierre Burton recounts the giddiness of the 1890s gold rush in *The Klondike Fever.*

Architecture & Walking Tours
The most comprehensive guide to Seattle's historic architecture is *National Trust Seattle: America's Guide for Architecture and the History Traveler* by Walt Crowley. To learn more about buildings and monuments, pick up a copy of *Seeing Seattle* by Roger Sale, which has walking tours outlining the history and architecture of different neighborhoods. The walking tours in *A Field Guide to Seattle's Public Art* put emphasis on Seattle's contemporary monuments. The colorful *Seattle City Walks* by Laura Karnlinsey features 20 walks around the Emerald City neighborhoods and introduces interesting city facts you don't read anywhere else. *Woman's Place: Guide to Seattle & King County History* by Mildred T Andrews offers 11 walking tours that highlight the role of women in Seattle's history. (Also see the 'Center of the Universe: Fremont Walking Tour' and 'Downtown Architecture Walking Tour' special sections in the Things to See & Do chapter.)

Culture
With a patchwork cultural identity sewn together with pieces of Boeing, Microsoft, coffee and grunge music, writers on Seattle are left to figure out what's what. Consequently, there is no shortage of topical histories and social commentaries.

Walt Crowley's *Rights of Passage* looks at the 1960s and early '70s as years of social and political change in Seattle. Douglas Coupland's *Microserfs* is a day-in-the-life novel about six Microsoft workers. The most comprehensive biography on Bill Gates, Seattle's rich uncle, is *Gates* by Stephen Manes & Paul Andrews.

Loser: The Real Seattle Music Story by Clark Humphrey charts the story of Seattle's music scene from the 1960s to the mid-1990s. Paul de Barros' *Jackson Street After Hours: The Roots of Jazz in Seattle* covers the Seattle jazz scene from the 1930s to the 1950s. Tina Oldknow's *Pilchuck: A Glass School* is an illustrated history of one of Seattle's most unique art forms.

NEWSPAPERS & MAGAZINES
The major newspapers are the morning *Seattle Post-Intelligencer* (usually called the *PI)* and the afternoon *Seattle Times.* A good source for entertainment listings is 'The Ticket,' the *Seattle Times'* entertainment supplement distributed on Thursday.

Seattle has a lively alternative publishing scene. The most interesting of the many papers that litter clubs and cafes is the *Stranger,* the voice of Seattle's trendy counterculture. It's a valuable source for film and music information and is a great guide to the clubs; it also features weird local cartoons and the mandatory 'Savage Love' column (see 'Savage Lovin' in Seattle' in the Entertainment chapter). The *Seattle Gay News,* referred to mostly as *SGN,* covers the gay and lesbian scene. The *Seattle Weekly* is the baby-boom generation's alternative news weekly, with full listings of arts and entertainment and investigative pieces exposing city hall's bad guys. Check the 'Cheap Thrills' section for free or inexpensive entertainment.

RADIO & TV
The University of Washington's news-oriented National Public Radio (NPR) affiliate is heard on KUOW at 94.9 FM (which also carries the BBC World Service). NPR news and jazz can be picked up on KPLU at 88.5 FM. You can pick up the CBC at 92.3 FM.

Seattle's favorite commercial radio stations are:

KIRO 710/1090 AM	news and talk
KJR 950 AM	sports
KPLU 88.5 FM	NPR
KCMU 90.3 FM	UW radio; new and alternative rock
KUBE 93.3 FM	hip-hop, top 40, R&B

KMPS 94.1 FM	country & western
KUOW 94.9 FM	UW's NPR affiliate
KBSG 97.3 FM	oldies
KING 98.1 FM	classical
KZOK 102.5 FM	classic rock
KMTT 103.7 FM	adult contemporary
KNDD 107.7 FM	alternative rock

All the major TV networks, including ABC, CBS, NBC, Fox and PBS (the noncommercial public channel), have affiliated stations in Seattle. Most hotels have cable. The following list will help you find the network of your choice:

KOMO-TV (ABC)	channel 4
KING-TV (NBC)	channel 5
KIRO-TV (CBS)	channel 7
KCTS-TV (PBS)	channel 9
KSTW-TV (UPN)	channel 11
KCPQ-TV (Fox)	channel 13
KTZZ-TV (WB)	channel 22

PHOTOGRAPHY & VIDEO
Film & Equipment
Print film is widely available at supermarkets and discount drugstores. Drugstores are also a good place to get your film processed cheaply; if you drop it off by noon, you can usually pick it up the next day. A roll of 100 ASA 35mm color film with 24 exposures will cost about $8 to get processed. If you want your pictures right away, you can find one-hour processing services in the yellow pages under 'Photo Processing.' The prices tend to creep up to around $12. See Cameras & Photo Supplies in the Shopping chapter.

Video Systems
Overseas visitors who are thinking of purchasing videotapes should remember that the USA and Canada use the National Television System Committee (NTSC) standard. Unless converted, NTSC is incompatible with other standards (Phase Alternative Line or PAL; Système Electronique Couleur avec Mémoire or SECAM) used in Africa, Asia, Australasia and Europe. It's best to keep those seemingly cheap movie purchases on hold until you get home.

Airport Security
All air passengers have to pass their luggage through x-ray machines. Technology today doesn't jeopardize lower speed film, so you shouldn't have to worry about cameras going through the machine. If you are carrying high-speed (1600 ASA and above) film, you may want to carry film and cameras with you and ask the x-ray inspector to check your film without running it through the x-ray.

TIME
Seattle is in the Pacific Standard Time zone, eight hours behind Greenwich Mean Time (GMT/UTC). It is three hours behind New York City and 17 hours ahead of Tokyo. Washington observes the switch to daylight saving time: Clocks go forward one hour on the first Sunday in April and back one hour on the last Sunday in October.

In the USA, dates are usually written with the month first, then the day, then the year.

ELECTRICITY
In the USA and Canada voltage is 110V, and the plugs have two (flat) or three (two flat, one round) pins. Plugs with three pins don't fit into a two-hole socket, but inexpensive adapters are widely available at drugstores, hardware stores and consumer electronics stores like Radio Shack.

WEIGHTS & MEASURES
In the USA, distances are in feet, yards and miles; dry weights are in ounces (oz), pounds (lb) and tons; and liquid measures are in fluid ounces (fl oz), pints, quarts and gallons. Gasoline is dispensed by the US gallon, which is about 20% less than the Imperial gallon. Pints and quarts are also 20% less than Imperial ones. Check out the metric conversion chart inside the back cover of this book.

LAUNDRY
Self-service, coin-operated laundry facilities are found all over Seattle. Washing a load

costs about $1.25 and drying it another $1.50. Some laundries have attendants who will wash, dry and fold your clothes for you for an additional charge. Fancier hotels will also do laundry for you, but it isn't cheap. To find a laundry, look under 'Laundries' or 'Laundries – Self-Service' in the yellow pages. Dry cleaners are also listed under 'Laundries' or 'Cleaners.'

Sit & Spin (Map 6, ☎ 441-9484), 2219 4th Ave in Belltown, is just about the grooviest place in town to wash your clothes. This café, art gallery, live-music venue *and laundry* leaves you no reason to do your wash anywhere else. On Capitol Hill, go to 12th Ave Laundry (Map 8, ☎ 328-4610), 1807 12th Ave E. North of downtown, go to University Maytag Laundry (Map 9, ☎ 526-8992), 4733 University Way NE.

HEALTH

There are no unexpected health dangers associated with travel in the USA. Excellent medical attention is readily available, and the only real health concern is that a collision with the medical system can cause severe injuries to your financial state. Health care, especially emergency care, is very expensive. You should carry traveler's health insurance or make certain that your native country's health system will reimburse you for medical services incurred in the USA.

In general, the principal health-care providers are private clinics and hospitals, which are more and more linked through insurance-dominated consortiums called HMOs (Health Maintenance Organizations). Publicly funded hospitals perform a certain amount of charity work as well as research. Both public and private hospitals have emergency rooms but are very expensive. Unless your condition is life threatening, take the extra time and visit the closest walk-in clinic (see below); most are open extended hours and the costs are far more manageable than a hospital emergency room.

Medical Services

Hospitals and medical centers, walk-in clinics and referral services are easily found throughout the area, especially around First Hill (Map 2), where the mass of hospitals has earned it the name 'Pill Hill.' In a serious emergency, call ☎ 911 for an ambulance to take you to the nearest hospital's emergency room, but again, this route is incredibly expensive.

Full-service medical care, including emergency services, is available at any of the following: Harborview Medical Center (☎ 731-3000 or emergency room ☎ 731-3074), 325 9th Ave; Swedish Medical Center (☎ 386-2573 or emergency room ☎ 386-2573), 747 Broadway; Virginia Mason Hospital (☎ 624-1144 or emergency room ☎ 583-6433), 925 Seneca St; UW Medical Center (☎ 548-3300 or emergency room ☎ 548-4000), 1959 NE Pacific St up at the university.

If your medical needs aren't grave, then one of the following walk-in clinics should be able to deal with most situations: Health South (☎ 682-7418), 11551 Denny Way at Stewart St, is open 8 am to 7 pm weekdays and 9 am to 5 pm Saturday. The Pike Place Market Medical Clinic (☎ 728-4143), 1930 Post Alley, is open 9 am to 5 pm weekdays, though closed between noon and 1 pm. In Wallingford, the 45th St Clinic (☎ 633-3350), 1629 N 45th St, offers medical and dental services. The clinic is open 8 am to 9 pm Monday, 8 am to 5:30 pm Tuesday to Friday and 10 am to 2 pm Saturday. If you have a dental emergency, Seattle/King County Dental Society (☎ 443-7607) can refer you to a low-cost clinic or nearby dentist.

Persons with AIDS/HIV needing medical or dental care should call AIDS/HIV Care Access Project (☎ 284-9277) for medical referrals, or contact the National AIDS/HIV Hotline (☎ 800-342-2437). Also, see 'HIV & Entering the USA,' earlier.

See the Women Travelers section below for information on organizations specializing in health care for women.

WOMEN TRAVELERS

Aradia Women's Health Center (Map 2, ☎ 323-9388), 1300 Spring St, is a women's health clinic run exclusively by women. They offer gynecological services for women, including sexually transmitted disease (STD) testing, PAP tests and abortions. This is not a walk-in clinic; you need to make an appointment. Planned Parenthood of Seattle/King County (☎ 328-7700), 2211 E Madison, provides health-care services for women, including pregnancy testing and birth-control counseling. Another resource is the Abortion-Birth Control Referral Service (☎ 522-0973). The local chapter of the National Organization for Women (NOW; ☎ 632-8547), 4649 Sunnyside Ave N, provides numerous resources and services for women, as does the YWCA of Seattle (Map 2, ☎ 461-4888), 1118 5th Ave. The YWCA also rents out inexpensive rooms to women only (see Downtown in the Places to Stay chapter).

The Community Info Line (☎ 461-3200) provides information on emergency and community services, from legal advice to housing services. Safe houses and women's shelters throughout Seattle offer everything from clothing and shelter to counseling services. For shelter referral during the day, call Noel House (☎ 441-3210); between 6 pm and 9:30 pm call the Evening Referral Center (☎ 770-0156). In cases of domestic violence, call the statewide hotline (☎ 800-562-6025), and you'll be provided with a list of confidential shelters. The 24-hour Seattle Rape Relief line (☎ 632-7273) can provide assistance in cases of sexual assault. If you need the police, call ☎ 911.

For advice on areas of the city women should avoid walking alone at night, see Dangers & Annoyances, later.

GAY & LESBIAN TRAVELERS

Although Seattle is liberal-minded and accepting of alternative lifestyles, much of the rural Northwest is far more conservative. Travelers should be aware of this if they're planning excursions to outlying areas.

Capitol Hill (Map 8), with its unmatched vitality and creativity, is Seattle's principal gay and lesbian neighborhood. Nightclubs and bars are found along Pine and Pike Sts and along Broadway. The *Seattle Gay News* (☎ 324-4297) covers the gay and lesbian scene and is available at most Capitol Hill bars and restaurants. Local guides to gay-friendly businesses include the *Lesbian & Gay Pink Pages* and the *GSBA Guide & Directory,* which you can pick up free at participating businesses or by contacting the Greater Seattle Business Association (☎ 363-9188). To get a listing of gay-friendly businesses, contact the Gay/Lesbian Business Association (☎ 363-9188).

Drop by either of Capitol Hill's queer-oriented bookstores for a good selection of books, along with excellent community information. Along the Pike/Pine Corridor is Beyond the Closet Bookstore (Map 8, ☎ 322-4609), 518 E Pike St at Belmont Ave. Up on Broadway you'll find Bailey/Coy Books (Map 8, ☎ 323-8842), 414 Broadway Ave E.

The Lesbian Resource Center (☎ 322-3953), 2214 S Jackson St, provides social, housing, employment and other support services. For more social services support, contact the Seattle Counseling Service for Sexual Minorities (☎ 323-1768). Helpful national numbers include the National Gay/Lesbian Task Force (☎ 202-332-6483) in Washington, DC, and Lambda Legal Defense Fund (☎ 212-995-8585 in New York City, 213-937-2728 in Los Angeles).

DISABLED TRAVELERS

All public buildings (including hotels, restaurants, theaters and museums) are required by law to provide wheelchair access and to have available restroom facilities. Telephone companies provide relay operators for the hearing impaired. Many banks provide ATM instructions in Braille. Dropped curbs are standard at intersections throughout the city.

Around 80% of Metro's buses are equipped with wheelchair lifts. Timetables marked with an 'L' indicate wheelchair accessibility. Be sure to let the driver know if you need your stop to be called and, if possible, pull the cord when you hear the call. Seeing-eye dogs are allowed on Metro buses. Disabled passengers qualify for a reduced fare but need to first contact Metro (☎ 553-3060, 684-2029 TTY) for a permit. See Map 3 for wheelchair-accessible stops and stations.

Larger private and chain hotels have suites for disabled guests. Many car-rental agencies offer hand-controlled models at no extra charge; just make sure you give at least two days' notice. All major airlines, Greyhound buses and Amtrak trains allow seeing-eye dogs to accompany passengers and often sell two-for-one packages when attendants of seriously disabled passengers are required. Airlines will also provide assistance for connecting, boarding and disembarking the flight – just ask for assistance when making your reservation.

The following organizations and tour providers specialize in the needs of disabled travelers:

Access-Able Travel Service maintains an informative Web site at www.access-able.com

Easter Seal Society of Washington (☎ 281-5700) publishes *The Accessibility Handbook,* a very thorough guide to accessible businesses and programs; it costs $50. 521 2nd Ave W, Seattle, WA 98119

Twin Peaks Press (☎ 360-694-2462, 800-637-2256) publishes a quarterly newsletter, directories and access guides. PO Box 129, Vancouver, WA 98666

Mobility International USA (☎ 541-343-1284, fax 541-343-6812) runs an educational exchange program and advises disabled travelers on mobility and housing issues. PO Box 10767, Eugene, OR 97440

Moss Rehabilitation Hospital's Travel Information Service (☎ 215-456-9600, TTY 215-456-9602) 1200 W Tabor Rd, Philadelphia, PA 19141-3099

Society for the Advancement of Travel for the Handicapped (SATH; ☎ 212-447-7284) 347 Fifth Ave No 610, New York, NY 10016

SENIOR TRAVELERS

Travelers from 50 years and up can expect to receive cut rates and benefits. Be sure to inquire about special seniors' rates at hotels, museums and restaurants across Seattle.

Outside the city, costs can be cut greatly by using the Golden Age Passport, a card that allows US citizens aged 62 and over (and those traveling in the same car) free admission to national parks and a 50% reduction at National Park Service (NPS)

campgrounds. You can apply in person for the Passport at any national park or regional office of the United States Forest Service (USFS) or NPS, or call Destinet at ☎ 800-365-2267 for information and ordering.

The American Association of Retired Persons (AARP; ☎ 800-424-3410), 601 E St NW, Washington, DC 20049, is an advocacy group for Americans 50 years and older and a good resource for travel bargains. Memberships are available to US and non-US residents for $10/27 for one/three years. More information is available on the AARP Web site at www.aarp.org.

Elderhostel (☎ 877-426-8056), 75 Federal St, Boston, MA 02110-1941, is a nonprofit organization that offers seniors the opportunity to attend academic college courses throughout the USA and Canada. The programs last one to three weeks and include meals and accommodations; they are open to people 55 years and older. Check out its Web site at www.elderhostel.org.

Grand Circle Travel (☎ 617-350-7500, fax 350-6206), 347 Congress St, Boston, MA 02210, offers escorted tours and travel information in a variety of formats and distributes a useful free booklet, *Going Abroad: 101 Tips for Mature Travelers.*

SEATTLE FOR CHILDREN

Children get a lot of mileage out of Seattle Center (Map 7), home to the Seattle Children's Theatre, the Children's Museum, the Space Needle, the Monorail, an amusement park and the Pacific Science Center. The Seattle Children's Theatre presents six mainstage productions a year between June and September. (See Seattle Center in the Things to See & Do chapter.) Kids also enjoy the Woodland Park Zoo (Map 10), where animals roam free in large enclosures that simulate their natural environments, and the Rosalie Whyel Museum of Doll Art in the Eastside (see Bellevue in the Excursions chapter). Ferry rides to and from Puget Sound islands are also a big hit with children.

Children less than five years old ride free on any Metro Transit bus. When making hotel reservations, inquire if there are special family discounts. Often hotels and motels let young children stay free.

If you're traveling with children, look out for Julie Fanselow's *The Unofficial Guide to the Pacific Northwest With Kids,* a lively and colorful book covering the fun things to do in Oregon, Washington and British Columbia. Another book for families is *Going Places: Family Getaways in the Pacific Northwest* by Ann Bergman and Rosi and Rose Williamson. For more general information on enjoying travel with young ones, read *Travel with Children* by Lonely Planet cofounder Maureen Wheeler.

LIBRARIES
The Seattle Public Library has 26 branches throughout the city; the main branch is at 1000 4th Ave (Map 2, ☎ 386-4636). In addition to books to read, the library also offers programs, readings, activities and access to the Internet. Visitors to Seattle can buy a temporary 'Quest Card' for $10. The card gives you access to library resources for three months.

Library branches in outlying neighborhoods include:

Fremont Library (☎ 684-4084), 731 N 35th St

Green Lake Library (☎ 684-7547), 7364 E Green Lake Dr N

Queen Anne Library (☎ 386-4227), 400 W Garfield St

University Library (☎ 684-4063), 5009 Roosevelt Way NE

Wallingford Library (☎ 684-4088), 1501 N 45th St

UNIVERSITIES
The University of Washington (Map 9, ☎ 543-2100) is the city's primary center for higher education. With nearly 35,000 students, the 'U Dub,' as it is often referred to, is a major cultural force in Seattle, with a strong impact on the city's style and vitality. The beautiful 700-acre campus sits along the shores of Lake Union. The campus bookstore is actually the second-largest university bookstore in the country.

Other Seattle-area universities include Seattle University (☎ 296-6000), a private Jesuit school, and Seattle Pacific University

(☎ 281-2000), a private college associated with the Free Methodist Church. Seattle Community College (☎ 587-4100) has three campuses throughout Seattle. On two Capitol Hill campuses, the Cornish College of the Arts (Map 8, ☎ 323-1400) provides college-level instruction in music, art, dance and drama. In Belltown, the Art Institute of Seattle (☎ 800-275-4268) has instructional programs in various arts including painting, silk-screening and sculpture.

DANGERS & ANNOYANCES
For a largely sedate and seemingly sensible city, Seattle has a high rate of crime. However, most crimes are property crimes (that is, car theft and house break-ins), and travelers needn't fear random violence. As a rule of thumb, don't walk around the Central District alone at night. Women should avoid walking alone at night around Belltown, Seattle Center, Pioneer Square and the International District, where public drunkenness and vagrancy can sometimes feel threatening. After dark, areas around Pike Place Market are more unsavory than dangerous. Crowds visiting sex shops along 1st Ave can be a little off-putting. During the day, pickpockets can be a problem around the Pike Place Market, along the Waterfront and wherever crowds of tourists assemble.

Outdoor parking spaces under the Alaskan Way viaduct tend to attract car thieves. If you park here, especially after dark, be sure to put valuables in the trunk or at least out of sight. Avoid walking alone through this area. Wherever you park, don't leave anything in the car that would remotely attract thieves, even if you're just leaving the car for a few minutes.

Always be aware of your surroundings and who may be watching you. Walk purposefully and avoid unnecessary displays of money or jewelry. Divide money and credit cards to avoid losing everything. Aim to use ATM machines only in well-trafficked areas. In hotels, don't leave valuables lying around your room. Use safe-deposit boxes or at least place valuables in a locked bag. Don't open your door to strangers – check the peephole, and call the front desk if unexpected guests try to enter.

In terms of real danger, Seattle's gang problems are largely isolated to outlying neighborhoods, such as Rainier Valley southeast of town and, to a lesser degree, the Central District. The average tourist has no reason to spend much time in these areas, especially at night.

Car Thefts

Seattle is notorious for automobile theft, with thieves ripping off approximately 18.6 cars per day. Visitors should take care when selecting parking spaces, especially at night. Although car thieves are attracted to expensive cars or stereo systems, most are joyriding mischief-makers who steal simply for cheap thrills. Concerned drivers may want to look into purchasing an antitheft mechanism such as 'The Club' that locks either the steering wheel or gear shift. Anything that makes ripping off the car a hassle will help save your car from theft. Secure parking garages are safer than street lots, though you'll pay considerably more to park.

If your car is missing, call the Police Auto Records Department (☎ 684-5444) to find out if it's been towed. If you have no luck there, you'll need to report a car theft by calling the Seattle Police nonemergency number (☎ 625-5011). Car thieves are rarely caught, but most cars are recovered. Typically, stolen cars turn up in several days.

Panhandlers & the Homeless

The USA has a lamentable record in dealing with its most unfortunate citizens, who often roam the streets of large cities in the daytime and sleep by storefronts, under freeways or in alleyways and abandoned buildings. Once upon a time guidebooks advised Americans venturing to developing countries how to cope with the culture shock of encountering beggars. Today, you're as likely to bump into beggars on the streets of Seattle as on the streets of Calcutta, except here they've been relabeled 'panhandlers.'

Seattle's downtown core has the city's highest concentration of homeless people.

Street people and panhandlers, most of whom are harmless, may approach you for money. A firm but polite 'No' usually does the trick, though some panhandlers are more persistent than others. If you're feeling threatened by someone hassling you for money, simply keep walking; the person will usually soon move on.

If you want to do something to help Seattle's homeless situation, you can donate to a good cause like homeless rehabilitation by buying *Real Change,* a legitimate mouthpiece for local homeless folks, many of whom sell the newspaper for a modest income. You can also call the Community Info Line (☎ 461-3200) to find out about organizations working to help people with low to no sources of income.

Guns

The USA has a reputation, partly true but also propagated and exaggerated by the media, as a dangerous place because of the availability of firearms. As in any big US city, people buy, sell and carry guns in Seattle, but shootings in the city are irregular and it's very unlikely you'll see anyone – other than police – carrying a gun. Residents of rural areas sometimes carry guns, but they most often target animals or isolated traffic signs, rather than humans. Be careful in the woods during the fall hunting season, when unsuccessful or drunken hunters may be less selective in their targets than one might hope.

EMERGENCIES

Dial ☎ 911 for all police, fire and medical emergencies of any sort; Spanish-speaking operators may be available, but other languages are less likely. This is a free call from any phone. The police can be contacted for nonurgent incidents at ☎ 625-5011; at Sea-Tac call ☎ 296-3311. For nonemergency police outside Seattle, contact King County Sheriff's Department (☎ 296-3311) or Washington State Patrol (☎ 425-649-4370). Both phone lines are open 24 hours a day.

For drug and alcohol emergencies, call the 24-hour hotline at ☎ 722-3700. In the event of sexual assault, call Seattle Rape

Relief at ☎ 632-7273 (for other women's emergency numbers see Women Travelers, earlier). The Seattle Community Info Line (☎ 461-3200) provides information on emergency and social services.

If you have something stolen, you'll need to make a police report, especially if you hope to claim the loss through your travel insurance policy. For stolen credit cards, cash cards or traveler's checks, notify your bank or the relevant company as soon as possible (see Money, earlier). If your passport and visa are stolen, call your embassy or consulate; see Embassies & Consulates, earlier, for a list of telephone numbers.

LEGAL MATTERS

For the most part, police in Seattle are friendly and helpful, and you shouldn't expect a run-in during your visit. Drinking outdoors is prohibited, though drinking beer or wine is often permissible at street fairs or other events where vendors have obtained permits. Police in Seattle are surprisingly strict about jaywalking. Bumbling around drunk in the street is another way to attract police attention, and if you're drunk and obnoxious you could find yourself 'sleeping it off' in jail.

If you are stopped by the police for any reason, bear in mind that under no circumstances do you need to pay fines on the spot. If you are arrested for serious offenses, it is your right to remain silent until you've obtained legal advice. You are not legally bound to speak to a police officer, but never walk away from an officer until given permission, or they'll assume you're looking for trouble. Anyone who gets arrested gets the right to make one phone call. If you don't have a lawyer or family member to help you, call your embassy (see Embassies & Consulates, earlier); the police will give you the number upon request.

The drinking age is 21 in the US, and you need an ID (identification with your photograph on it) to prove your age. Don't get caught driving under the influence of alcohol, or you'll get slammed with a DUI (Driving Under the Influence), which can result in stiff fines and jail time. A blood-alcohol reading of 0.08% or above is illegal, which loosely translates to about two drinks maximum in an average person. During festive holidays and special events, roadblocks are sometimes set up to deter drunk drivers.

BUSINESS HOURS

Businesses stay open 9 am to 5 pm, but there are certainly no hard and fast rules. A few supermarkets and restaurants are open 24 hours, as are some gas stations and convenience stores like 7-Eleven. Shops are usually open 9 or 10 am to 5 or 6 pm (often until 9 pm in shopping malls), except Sunday when hours are noon to 5 pm (often later in malls). Post offices are open 8 am to 4 or 5:30 pm weekdays, and some are open 8 am to 3 pm Saturday. Banks are usually open 9 or 10 am to 5 or 6 pm weekdays. A few banks are open on 9 am to 2 or 4 pm Saturday. Hours are decided by individual branches so if you need specifics, give the branch a call. Many art galleries are closed Monday, as are many finer restaurants.

PUBLIC HOLIDAYS

National public holidays are celebrated throughout the USA. On public holidays banks, schools and government offices (including post offices) are closed and public transportation follows a Sunday schedule. Holidays falling on a weekend are usually observed the following Monday (except Easter).

New Year's Day – January 1
Martin Luther King Jr Day – third Monday in January
Presidents' Day – third Monday in February
Easter Sunday – falls in March or April
Memorial Day – last Monday in May
Independence Day (Fourth of July) – July 4
Labor Day – first Monday in September
Columbus Day – second Monday in October
Veterans' Day – November 11
Thanksgiving Day – fourth Thursday in November
Christmas Day – December 25

SPECIAL EVENTS

Besides public holidays, Seattle celebrates a number of other events. The most widely observed ones are listed here.

January

Chinese New Year Beginning the end of January or start of February and lasting two weeks, the year's first big ethnic festival is held in the International District; call the Chinatown/International District Business Improvement Association (☎ 382-1197) for information. The first day is celebrated with parades, firecrackers, fireworks and lots of food.

February

Fat Tuesday The Pioneer Square district embraces its somewhat rowdy reputation on Mardi Gras, when the area is convulsed with celebration. Music and revelry in bars and restaurants obviously comprise the main events, although a special Seattle touch is lent by the annual Spam-Carving Contest.

Valentine's Day Held on the 14th; no one knows why St Valentine is associated with romance, but this is the day to celebrate with a loved one – or a prospective loved one.

March

Seattle Fringe Festival Usually in late February or early March. Various venues on Capitol Hill host hundreds of experimental stage performances. Call ☎ 526-1959 for details.

St Patrick's Day On the 17th the patron saint of Ireland is honored by all those who feel the Irish in their blood, and by those who want to feel Irish beer in their blood. Everyone wears green (otherwise you can get pinched). Irish bars like Kell's serve green beer and even bars that haven't an Irish trinket in sight get swamped. There's a parade from City Hall to Westlake Center along 4th Ave.

April

Passover Either in March or April, depending on the Jewish calendar, families get together to partake in the symbolic seder dinner, which commemorates the exodus of Jews from their slavery in Egypt.

Cherry Blossom & Japanese Cultural Festival A celebration of Japanese heritage with performances of music, dance and drama; held at Seattle Center. For information call ☎ 684-7200.

May

Cinco de Mayo The 5th is the day the Mexicans wiped out the French Army in 1862. Now it's the day all Americans get to eat lots of Mexican food and drink margaritas.

Opening Day of Yacht Season Held the first Saturday in May at various locations on Lakes Washington and Union, this Seattle original starts with a blessing of the fleet; it features scull racing and a boat parade through the canals.

Seattle International Childrens's Festival Held at Seattle Center in mid-May, this cultural extravaganza includes a wide variety of performances and activities for kids; call ☎ 684-7346 for information.

Northwest Folklife Festival This festival (☎ 684-7300) takes over Seattle Center during Memorial Day weekend. Over 5000 performers and artists from over 100 countries present music, dance, crafts, food and family activities. Admission is free.

Seattle International Film Festival Held in May and June, this festival brings nearly a month's worth of international premieres to Seattle. Screenings take place at several theaters; call ☎ 464-5830 for information.

June

Freedom Day Celebration Seattle's lesbian- and gay-pride event is usually held the last Sunday in June on Capitol Hill. The parade begins along Broadway and continues to Volunteer Park, where there are speeches, music and a rally.

Fremont Fair Fremont is Seattle's most party-oriented neighborhood, just the place you'd want to be for a street fair. The fair features live music, entertainment, food and crafts and is held adjacent to the ship canal. Call ☎ 633-4409 or check out the Web site at www.fremontfair.com.

July

Bite of Seattle This culinary celebration is held at Seattle Center, usually the second weekend in July. For a single entry fee, guests can sample foods from dozens of Seattle-area chefs and taste local beers and wines. The evening ends with live music. Call ☎ 232-2982 or check out the Web site at www.biteofseattle.com.

Seafair Held for three weeks in late July and August, Seafair is an extravagant civic celebration that began as a hydroplane race on Lake Washington. Old families in Seattle jealously maintain their moorages on Lake Washington in order to have the best possible views of these roaring jet boats. Today, however, all manner of festivities extend across all of Seattle and stretch the event to three weeks. Events include a torchlight parade, an airshow, lots of music, a carnival and even the arrival of the naval fleet. Lodging is in short supply in Seattle on Seafair weekends, so plan accordingly. Unless you want to watch the hydroplane races, avoid Seattle on the first weekend in August and don't plan to cross the I-90 or Hwy 520 bridges while the races are in progress. For more information, contact the festival office at ☎ 728-0123 or check out the Web site at www.seafair.com.

September

Bumbershoot Seattle's biggest arts and cultural event is held at Seattle Center on Labor Day weekend. In addition to a crafts street fair, there are hundreds of special theatrical and musical events playing on 25 stages. Check out Performing Arts in the Entertainment chapter for more information or call ☎ 281-8111. Up-to-date information is also available on the Web site at www.bumbershoot.com.

Northwest AIDS Walk This incredibly festive and friendly event, held the second weekend in September, grows every year. The 10km or 5km walk starts and finishes at Seattle Center. Contact the Lifelong AIDS Alliance at ☎ 329-6923 or check out the Web site at www.nwaids.org.

Western Washington Fair Puget Sound remembers its agricultural underpinnings at this fair held in mid-September in Puyallup, south of Seattle. The fair offers a bewildering array of livestock and agricultural displays, a carnival, a home and garden show and live entertainment.

October

Halloween On the 31st, kids and adults dress in scary costumes and, in safer neighborhoods, children go 'trick-or-treating' for candy. Gay and lesbian bars are especially wild places on Halloween.

Seattle Lesbian & Gay Film Festival Held in the third week of October, this film festival plays at various theaters around town. Call ☎ 323-4274 or go to the Web site at www.seattlequeerfilm.com.

November

Thanksgiving Established in the mid-19th century as a day for Americans to reflect upon and be thankful for their prosperity, Thanksgiving is observed the fourth Thursday of November. Families travel long distances to be together to watch televised parades and football games and to eat a huge turkey dinner. Plan ahead if you're traveling this week – flights are full, highways are jammed and restaurants and grocery stores close for the day.

December

Chanukah Also called the Feast of Lights, this eight-day Jewish holiday commemorates the victory of the Maccabees over the armies of Syria and the rededication of their temple in Jerusalem. Dates in December vary according to the Hebrew calendar.

Kwanzaa This African American celebration starts on December 26 and lasts to the 31st and is a time to give thanks for the harvest.

New Year's Eve The place to be on the 31st is Seattle Center, where festivities are focused on the Space Needle. Most people celebrate by dressing up and drinking champagne, or staying home and watching it all on TV. The following day people stay home to nurse their hangovers and watch college football.

WORK

Foreign visitors are not legally allowed to work in the USA without an appropriate working visa. Recent legislation was enacted to cut down on illegal immigrants, which is what you'll be if you work while on a tourist visa.

If you're not a US citizen, you need to apply for a work visa from the US embassy in your home country before you leave. The type of visa varies depending on how long you're staying and the kind of work you plan to do. Generally, you need either a J-1 visa, which you can obtain by joining a visitor-exchange program, or a H-2B visa, which you get when sponsored by a US employer. The former is issued mostly to students for work in summer camps; the latter is not easy to obtain, because the employer has to prove that no US citizen or permanent resident is available to do the job.

Getting There & Away

AIR

When flying to Seattle, you'll land at Seattle-Tacoma International Airport (☎ 431-4444), 13 miles south of Seattle. Known simply as Sea-Tac, it's the largest airport in the Pacific Northwest, with daily service to Europe and Asia. Sea-Tac is also a major hub for domestic and regional airlines, making it one of the nation's busiest airports; some 27 million people pass through it every year. See the Getting Around chapter for information on the airport and travel to/from the airport. You do not have to pay an airport departure tax before leaving Sea-Tac. That tax is included in the price of your ticket.

Air Passes & Special Fares

Visit USA Pass Most domestic carriers (including Continental, Delta, Northwest and American Airlines) offer Visit USA passes to non-US citizens. The pass is actually a book of coupons; each coupon equals a flight.

Warning

The information in this chapter is particularly vulnerable to change: Prices for international travel are volatile, routes are introduced and cancelled, schedules change, special deals come and go, and rules and visa requirements are amended. Airlines and governments seem to take a perverse pleasure in making price structures and regulations as complicated as possible. You should check directly with the airline or with a travel agent to make sure you understand how a fare (and a ticket you may buy) works. In addition, the travel industry is highly competitive, and there are many lurks and perks.

The upshot of this is that you should get opinions, quotes and advice from as many airlines and travel agents as possible before you part with your hard-earned cash. The details given in this chapter should be regarded as pointers and are not a substitute for your own careful, up-to-date research.

Typically, you have to buy a minimum of three coupons and a maximum of 10. Coupons must be purchased in conjunction with a flight on an international airline (excluding Canada and Mexico) and cost anywhere from $100 to $160 each, depending on how many you buy. Most airlines require you to plan your itinerary in advance and complete your flights within 60 days of arrival, but the rules can vary from one airline to another. A few allow you to use coupons on standby.

Round-the-World Tickets If you are coming from overseas, you may want to include Seattle on a round-the-world (RTW) itinerary. RTW tickets are wildly popular and are often real bargains. RTW tickets can work out to be no more expensive, and sometimes even cheaper, than an ordinary return ticket. Official airline RTW tickets are usually put together by a combination of two airlines, and they permit you to fly anywhere you want on their route systems, as long as you do not backtrack. Other restrictions and time limits often apply. An alternative type of RTW ticket is one put together by a travel agent using a combination of discounted tickets. The possibilities for RTW tickets are many, and it's worth checking them out. Your best bet is to find a travel agent that specializes in RTW tickets.

Circle Pacific Tickets Circle Pacific tickets use a combination of airlines to circle the Pacific, combining Australia, New Zealand, North America and Asia. Rather than simply flying from point A to point B, these tickets allow you to swing through much of the Pacific Rim and eastern Asia taking in a variety of destinations – as long as you keep traveling in the same circular direction. As with RTW tickets there are advance-purchase restrictions and limits on how many stopovers you can make (usually four – extra stops cost around US$50 each). These fares are likely to be around 15% cheaper than RTW tickets.

Other Parts of the USA & Canada

Sea-Tac is the major hub of the Northwest and a busy connecting point for flights along the Pacific Coast. Frequent, regularly scheduled flights connect Seattle with Portland, San Francisco, Los Angeles, Alaska and Vancouver, BC.

Alaska Airlines (☎ 800-252-7522), and its regional subsidiary Horizon Air (☎ 800-547-9308), offers the most frequent flights up and down the west coast of North America. Other airlines making frequent flights in and out of Sea-Tac include the generally low-cost Southwest Airlines (☎ 800-435-9792) and United Airlines (☎ 800-241-6522). Small

Air Travel Glossary

Alliances Many of the world's leading airlines are now intimately involved with each other, sharing everything from reservations systems and check-in to aircraft and frequent-flyer schemes. Opponents say that alliances restrict competition. Whatever the arguments, there is no doubt that big alliances are the way of the future.

Courier Fares Businesses often need to send urgent documents or freight securely and quickly. Courier companies hire people to accompany the package through customs and, in return, offer a discount ticket that is sometimes a bargain. However, you may have to surrender all your baggage allowance and take only carry-on luggage.

Fares Airlines traditionally offer 1st-class (coded F), business-class (coded J) and economy-class (coded Y) tickets. These days, there are so many promotional and discounted fares available that few passengers pay full fare.

Lost Tickets If you lose your airline ticket, an airline will usually treat it as a traveler's check and, after inquiries, issue you with another one. Legally, however, an airline is entitled to treat it as cash, so if you lose it, then it could be gone forever. Take very good care of your tickets.

Onward Tickets An entry requirement for many countries is that you have a ticket out of the country. If you're unsure of your next move, the easiest solution is to buy the cheapest onward ticket to a neighboring country or a ticket (from a reliable airline) that can later be refunded if you do not use it.

Open Tickets These are return tickets used to fly out to one place but return from another. If available, this can save you from having to backtrack to your arrival point.

Overbooking Since every flight has some passengers who fail to show up, airlines often book more passengers than they have seats. Usually excess passengers make up for the no-shows, but occasionally somebody gets 'bumped' onto the next available flight. Who is it most likely to be? The passengers who check in late. If you do get 'bumped,' you are normally offered some form of compensation.

Restrictions Discounted tickets often have various restrictions on them – such as mandatory advance payment and penalties for alterations or cancellations. Others have restrictions on the minimum and maximum period you must be away.

Round-the-World Tickets RTW tickets give you a limited period (usually a year) in which to circumnavigate the globe. You can go anywhere the carrying airlines go, as long as you don't backtrack. The number of stopovers or the total number of separate flights is decided before you set off, and these tickets usually cost a bit more than a basic return flight.

Ticketless Travel Airlines are waking up to the realization that paper tickets are unnecessary encumbrances. On simple one-way or return trips, reservation details can be held on computer, and the passengers merely show identification to claim their seats.

Transferred Tickets Airline tickets cannot be transferred from one person to another. Travelers sometimes try to sell the return half of their tickets, but officials can ask you to prove that you are the person named on the ticket. On an international flight, the name on the ticket is compared with the name on the passport.

commuter airlines fly to the San Juan Islands, Bellingham, Wenatchee, Yakima and Spokane. Air Canada (and its subsidiaries) is the primary carrier from/to Canadian cities, though smaller regional airlines serve the Vancouver/Victoria area as well.

Flights to elsewhere in the USA and Canada depart regularly, though be aware that airfares can vary tremendously depending on frequency of flights, season of travel and the whim of the industry. Both of Seattle's daily newspapers, the *Seattle Times* and *Seattle Post-Intelligencer,* have weekly travel sections where you can find flight deals and travel agents. Get good information and fares at Council Travel on Capitol Hill (Map 8, ☎ 329-4567), 424 Broadway E, or in the U District (Map 9, ☎ 632-2448), 4211½ University Way NE. STA Travel (Map 9, ☎ 633-5000), 4341 University Way NE, also offers competitive fares.

In the USA, Council Travel (☎ 800-226-8624), www.counciltravel.com, and STA Travel (☎ 800-781-4040), www.statravel.com, specialize in student travel and have offices

throughout the country. Look in the travel sections of major newspapers for deals on flights, hotels and package tours. Newspapers with good travel sections (usually in the weekend editions) include the *Los Angeles Times,* the *San Francisco Examiner* and the *New York Times.* Roundtrip fares between Seattle and New York City or other East Coast hubs will cost upwards of $600. Roundtrip flights to Chicago typically cost around $500. Flights along the West Coast can be inexpensive. With sufficient notice, you can usually fly from Seattle to Los Angeles or San Francisco for between $170 to $240 roundtrip.

In Canada, Travel CUTS (☎ 888-838-2887) is a chain of budget travel agencies with offices in major Canadian cities. You can also scan the *Vancouver Sun* and *Toronto Globe & Mail* newspapers for deals. A roundtrip jaunt from Vancouver averages C$230 (US$150). Typical roundtrip fares from other Canadian cities to Seattle are Calgary C$540 (US$350), Edmonton C$760 (US$500) and Toronto or Montréal C$1070 ($700). See the Excursions chapter for travel by seaplane or helicopter to Victoria, BC.

Airlines

Most major international and domestic carriers have a presence in Seattle. The following major airlines serve Seattle and offer toll-free telephone numbers:

Aeroflot	☎ 888-340-6400
Air Canada	☎ 888-247-2262
Alaska Airlines	☎ 800-252-7522
American Airlines	☎ 800-433-7300
British Airways	☎ 800-247-9297
Continental Airlines	☎ 800-523-3273
Delta Airlines	☎ 800-221-1212
EVA Air	☎ 800-695-1188
Hawaiian Airlines	☎ 800-367-5320
Japan Airlines (JAL)	☎ 800-525-3663
Northwest Airlines/KLM	☎ 800-225-2525
Reno Air	☎ 800-736-6247
Scandinavian Airlines (SAS)	☎ 800-221-2350
Southwest Airlines	☎ 800-435-9792
TWA	☎ 800-221-2000
United Airlines	☎ 800-241-6522
US Airways	☎ 800-428-4322

Australia & New Zealand

Because there are no direct flights between Australia or New Zealand and Seattle, service to/from Down Under requires a change of planes in Honolulu, San Francisco or Los Angeles.

The cheapest tickets have a 21-day advance-purchase requirement, a minimum stay of seven days and a maximum stay of 60 days. Qantas flies from Melbourne or Sydney to Los Angeles for roughly A$1549 (US$741) in the low season and A$2421 (US$1159) in the high season. Qantas flights from Cairns to Los Angeles cost A$1739 (US$832) in the low season and A$2611 (US$1250) in the high season. Roundtrip flights from Auckland to Los Angeles on Qantas cost NZ$2000 (US$850) in the low season and NZ$3985 (US$1700) in the high season. Flying with Air New Zealand is slightly cheaper. Both Qantas and Air New Zealand offer tickets with longer stays or stopovers, but you pay more. High season for Qantas and Air New Zealand is in

Australasia's summer (winter in North America).

In Australia and New Zealand, STA Travel and Flight Centres International are major dealers in cheap airfares; check the travel agents' ads in the yellow pages and in newspapers like the *Sydney Morning Herald* and the *Age* in Australia.

Europe

Scandinavian Airlines (SAS) flies nonstop to Seattle from Copenhagen, and Northwest Airlines flies direct from Amsterdam. Aeroflot offers direct service from Moscow. Fares fluctuate wildly, but are usually between €1140 (US$1000) and €1600 (US$1400) roundtrip between major European cities and Seattle during high season; off-season fares can drop as low as €797 (US$700) roundtrip.

Flying into Vancouver, BC, instead of Seattle is another option, as Vancouver International Airport has many more European links than Seattle, including direct flights to/from Amsterdam, Frankfurt, Glasgow, London, Paris and Zurich. Vancouver is three hours north of Seattle by car and ground transportation to Seattle is relatively inexpensive (see information on Amtrak and Greyhound later in this chapter).

The UK For budget ticket options, check the ads in magazines like *Time Out* and papers like the *Sunday Times* and London's *Evening Standard*. Also check the free magazines like *TNT* that are widely available in London – start by looking outside the main railway stations.

London is arguably the world's headquarters for bucket shops, which are well advertised and can usually beat published airline fares. Good, reliable agents for cheap tickets in the UK are:

Trailfinders (☎ 020-7937-5400) 194 Kensington High St, London W8 7RG

Council Travel (☎ 020-7437-7767) 28A Poland St, London W1

STA Travel (☎ 020-7581-4132) 86 Old Brompton Rd, London SW7 3LQ

An excellent information-sharing resource, the Globetrotters Club publishes a newsletter called *Globe* that covers obscure destinations and can help you find traveling companions. A one-year subscription costs £15 (€24/US$21). Subscribe on the Web site (www.globetrotters.co.uk), which also has an email newsletter and travel tips.

Continental Europe Other good European travel agents selling low-priced tickets are listed here. Most have branches nationwide; call for details.

France

USIT Connect Voyages (☎ 01 42 44 14 00) 14 rue de Vaugirard, 75006 Paris

OTU Voyages (☎ 01 40 29 12 12) 39 ave Georges-Bernanos, 75005 Paris; www.otu.fr

Voyageurs du Monde (☎ 01 42 86 16 00) 55 rue Ste-Anne, 75002 Paris

Nouvelles Frontières (nationwide ☎ 08 25 00 08 25, Paris ☎ 01 45 68 70 00) 87 blvd de Grenelle, 75015 Paris; www.nouvelles-frontieres.fr

Germany

STA Travel (☎ 030-311 0950) Goethesttrasse 73, 10625 Berlin

USIT Campus (nationwide ☎ 01805 788336, Köln ☎ 0221 923990) 2a Zuelpicher Strasse, 50674 Köln; www.usitcampus.de

Italy

CTS Viaggi (☎ 06-462 0431) 16 Via Genova, Roma

Passagi (☎ 06-474 0923) Stazione Termini FS, Galleria Di Tesla, Roma

The Netherlands

NBBS Reizen (☎ 020-620 5071) 66 Rokin, Amsterdam; www.nbbs.nl

Budget Air (☎ 020-627 1251) 34 Rokin, Amsterdam; www.nbbs.nl

Spain

USIT Unlimited (☎ 91-225 25 75) 3 Plaza de Callao, 28013 Madrid; www.unlimited.es

Barcelo Viajes (☎ 91-559 18 19) Princesa 3, 28008 Madrid

Nouvelles Frontières (☎ 91-547 42 00) Plaza de España 18, 28008 Madrid; www.nouvelles-frontieres.es

Switzerland

SSR (☎ 022-818 02 02) 8 rue de la Rive, Geneva; www.ssr.ch

Nouvelles Frontières (☎ 022-906 80 80) 10 rue Chante Poulet, Geneva

GETTING THERE & AWAY

Asia

Northwest Airlines has nonstop service from Tokyo and Osaka to Seattle, while American and United Airlines serve Seattle from Tokyo only. Both Korean Air and Japan Airlines (JAL) fly into Vancouver, BC. Though ticket prices vary widely, approximate roundtrip fares from Osaka and Tokyo to Seattle or Vancouver range from ¥170,000 (US$1375) to ¥212,000 (US$1713).

Aeroflot (through a link with Alaska Airlines) serves Seattle from several cities on the Russian Pacific, including Vladivostok. China Eastern Airlines serves Seattle from Beijing and Shanghai. Northwest and United have daily flights between Hong Kong and Seattle via Tokyo. Air Canada flies direct from Hong Kong to Vancouver, BC. High season roundtrip fares to Seattle or Vancouver from Hong Kong average HK$19,500 (US$2500). Ticket prices from Hong Kong fluctuate like crazy. You can often get much cheaper tickets if you book well in advance. EVA Airways offers direct flights to/from Taipei for around TW$50,200 (US$1500).

Northwest, Continental and United Airlines fly between Singapore and Seattle via Tokyo. Roundtrip fares from Singapore are around SG$2354 (US$1300). To reach Seattle from other parts of Southeast Asia, you'll need to make a connection, usually through Honolulu. Air Canada flies direct three times weekly between Delhi and Vancouver, BC, with a fueling stop in London.

Latin America

Most flights from Central and South America to Seattle are routed through Miami, Houston or Los Angeles. Most countries' international flag carriers – as well as US airlines like United and American – fly to these destinations with onward connections to Seattle. United and Continental have frequent flights to Seattle from cities throughout Mexico. Roundtrip fares from Cancún average 10,740 pesos (US$1200). From Mexico City, roundtrip fares to Seattle average 8950 pesos (US$1000). Continental, United and Northwest Airlines fly direct to Seattle from Guatemala City for around US$1000.

BUS
Greyhound

Greyhound (Map 2, ☎ 628-5561, 800-231-2222) is the only nationwide bus company operating in Seattle. Buses arrive at and depart from the Greyhound depot at 811 Stewart St. Buses travel I-5 between cities in California and Oregon and Vancouver, BC. They also travel east to Spokane and on through northern Idaho, Montana and Chicago to New York City.

Bus travel can be expensive when compared with bargain airfares or low-cost car rentals. Bus ticket prices fluctuate depending on the time of year. Summer is the high season, but if you purchase tickets more than seven days in advance you can save money, sometimes more than 50% of the original ticket cost. The trip durations listed below are average; some buses take longer than others.

Sample high-season, one-way fares from Seattle include:

destination	fare	duration
Vancouver, BC	$26	4 hours
Portland, OR	$32	4 hours
Spokane, WA	$43	6 hours
Banff, AB	$94	20 hours
San Francisco, CA	$108	22 hours
Los Angeles, CA	$119	29 hours
Chicago, IL	$139	54 hours
New York, NY	$159	72 hours

You can purchase tickets with a credit card over the phone or on Greyhound's Web site at www.greyhound.com.

North America Discovery Pass This Greyhound pass (referred to mostly as the 'Ameripass') permits you unlimited travel on Greyhound buses for up to 60 days. The pass allows you to travel throughout the USA for $185 (seven-day pass) to $509 (60-day pass), with unlimited stopovers. The North America Can/Am Pass gives you unlimited travel through the USA and Canada for $399 (15-day pass) to $639 (60-day pass). If you're sticking to the West Coast, the Western Can/Am Pass is $299 (15-day pass) to $399

(30-day pass). The North America Discovery Pass can be a good way to go if you know you want to move around but don't want to plan your itinerary ahead of time. Unlike the Visit USA Pass (see Air Passes & Special Fares earlier), anyone, including US citizens, can purchase an Ameripass.

Green Tortoise
Also serving the Pacific Northwest, the near-mythic Green Tortoise (Map 2, ☎ 415-956-7500, 800-867-8647) links San Francisco, Portland and Seattle via intervening hot springs and campfire cookouts. Green Tortoise buses, which have the atmosphere of a school bus-turned-lounge, are cheaper than Greyhound and *a lot* more interesting. Easy chairs replace bus seats, and food, drink, music and a carnival atmosphere prevail. In Seattle, the Green Tortoise leaves from 9th Ave at Stewart St, behind the Greyhound depot. Two buses a week make the trip back and forth between Seattle and San Francisco. Buses leave at 8 am on Sunday and Thursday and arrive in San Francisco at 9 am the next day. The one-way fare is $69; to Portland it's just $15.

Quick Shuttle
If you're coming to/from Vancouver, BC, consider using the Quick Shuttle (☎ 800-665-2122), which makes five daily express runs between Vancouver, downtown Seattle and Sea-Tac. The cost of an adult ticket from downtown to downtown is $29 one-way, $52 roundtrip. Reservations are requested.

TRAIN
Taking the train is somewhat slow but if you've got the time, it can be a comfortable and scenic way to travel. Amtrak (Map 4, ☎ 800-872-7245), 303 S Jackson St in the King St Station, offers train service south to/from Portland, San Francisco, Los Angeles and San Diego. Trains also chug north to Vancouver and east through Spokane, eventually reaching Chicago. Fares vary widely depending on advance purchase, season and availability. One-way fares to Vancouver (four hours) or Portland (3½ hours) range from $21 to $33. To Chicago (45 hours), the one-way fare

averages $240; San Francisco (23 hours) $100; and LA (35½ hours), around $110.

North America Rail Pass
The best value overall is Amtrak's North America Rail Pass, which allows you to ride trains throughout the USA and Canada. This costs $471/674 for low/high season. There are limitations, however. Travel must be completed in 30 days, and you are allowed up to three stopovers, or more if you want to pay extra. Your entire trip must be reserved in advance; the seats are limited, so book as far ahead as possible. If you want to travel in just the eastern, central or western parts of the USA, regional rail passes are available. Unlike the Visit USA Pass (see Air Passes & Special Events earlier), anyone, including US citizens, can purchase a North America Rail Pass. You can purchase tickets and get schedule information from Amtrak's Web site at www.amtrak.com.

CAR & MOTORCYCLE
Seattle is the hub of two major freeways. Interstate 5 (I-5) runs through the center of Seattle and links it with major cities south along the Pacific Coast, including Portland, San Francisco and Los Angeles. Northward I-5 goes to the Canadian border at Blaine (and continues into Canada as 99). I-90 joins I-5 just south of downtown, providing the main link to the Eastside and to eastern Washington as it cuts across the center of the state to Spokane.

Highway 520 links downtown with Kirkland and Bellevue via the 2-mile-long Evergreen Point Floating Bridge. I-405, known as the Eastside Freeway, cuts north-south through the suburbs east of Lake Washington.

Below are sample driving distances and approximate times for car travel between Seattle and nearby cities:

destination	distance	duration
Olympia, WA	60 miles	1½ hours
Vancouver, BC	142 miles	3 hours
Portland, OR	172 miles	3 hours
Spokane, WA	276 miles	5 hours
San Francisco, CA	840 miles	15 hours

See Documents in the Facts for the Visitor chapter for information on driver's licenses and permits.

Weather & Road Conditions

Seattle rarely sees snow, so heavy rain is generally the only weather-related driving condition to be concerned about. You'll need to be careful of hydroplaning, so remember to drive slowly and carefully, especially on the freeway when the spray from nearby trucks can make it seem as if you're driving underwater. Call ☎ 368-4499 for the local traffic report or ☎ 425-455-7700 for Washington State highway conditions. For the Seattle weather report call ☎ 442-2800, extension 2032.

HITCHHIKING

In general, hitchhiking anywhere in the USA is not recommended. Hitchhiking is never entirely safe in any country in the world, and it has a reputation for being much more dangerous in the USA than in Europe. Travelers who decide to hitchhike should understand that they are taking a small but potentially serious risk. People who do choose to hitchhike will be safer if they travel in pairs and let someone know where they are planning to go.

BOAT

Alaska State Ferries (☎ 800-642-0066) carries car traffic from Bellingham, about 85 miles north of Seattle, to Juneau, Skagway and other Alaskan ports. For information on traveling by ferry to/from Victoria, BC, see the Excursions chapter; for ferry trips around Puget Sound, see the Getting Around chapter.

Cruise ships serving the West Coast usually sail to the Caribbean (through the Panama Canal) or Alaska, grazing the Pacific Northwest with rare stops in Seattle. Vancouver, BC, is the main port of departure for pleasure cruises to Alaska.

Getting Around

The Space Needle dominates the Seattle skyline.

Seattle is a sprawling city with a complex topography, and getting around town – especially in a timely fashion – can be a real challenge (see 'Street Smarts' in the Facts for the Visitor chapter). If you're only in Seattle for a few days, you should think twice before renting a car. In many ways, the easiest means of getting around is to rely on a mix of public transport. Seattle's public transit system is very efficient, and it's easy to get to the major sights. When public transit doesn't suit your needs, it's likely that you can afford several taxi rides for the cost of a single parking ticket.

THE AIRPORT

Sea-Tac's main terminal has four concourses, plus north and south satellite terminals. International arrivals and departures jet in and out of the south satellite (see the Getting There & Away chapter for airlines). Both satellites are connected to the main terminal by an underground subway system, which can whisk you to and fro in just a few minutes. The airport, which opened for business in 1944, is undergoing a massive expansion project that will add a third runway to accommodate the demand for more flights. The runway is being built over 18 acres of wetlands west of the airport – a sore spot for local environmentalists concerned for the welfare of threatened wetland species, including Chinook salmon and bald eagles. The airport expansion will be completed in 2010.

Seattle-King County Visitors Bureau maintains an information booth in the center of the baggage claim level near baggage carousels eight and nine. There's a separate Japanese-language information booth near baggage carousel one. Traveler's Aid, on the ticketing level of the main terminal, provides assistance for children and elderly or disabled passengers weekdays 9:30 am to 9:30 pm and weekends 10 am to 6 pm. For lost property contact Lost and Found at ☎ 433-5312. For all other airport services, call the main Sea-Tac number at ☎ 431-4444.

63

Thomas Cook (☎ 248-6960) operates two currency exchange booths in the main terminal. The one behind the Delta Airlines booth is open 6 am to 8 pm; the one behind Alaska Airlines is open 6 am to 6 pm. Another branch in the South Satellite is open 8 am to 6 pm. Should your flight arrive after hours, you can get cash from the ATMs found throughout the airport.

TO/FROM THE AIRPORT

For information on ground transportation, call ☎ 431-5906, or visit the ground transportation booths at each end of the baggage claim area. By far the cheapest way to get to downtown is by taking a Metro Transit public bus. Pick up bus Nos 174 or 194 (express) on the lower roadway outside the baggage claim area, near the taxi stand. The trip will cost you a mere $2.

Gray Line runs the Airport Express (☎ 626-6088) every 15 minutes 5 am to 11 pm between Sea-Tac and downtown Seattle's major hotels. Shuttles leave from the north and south ends of the baggage claim area. The cost is $8.50 one-way or $14 roundtrip. Shuttle Express (☎ 622-1424, 800-487-7433) offers one-way, door-to-door service for $18 (from downtown) to $26 (from outlying neighborhoods). Call at least a day in advance to ensure availability. No reservations are necessary from the airport; simply stop by the service desk at the south end of baggage claim. Shuttles operate 24 hours a day.

If you're driving to the airport, be careful not to take the exit called 'Airport Way,' which takes you to Boeing Field, the private municipal airfield, not to Sea-Tac. On I-5, you want exit 154 from the north or exit 152 from the south. If the freeway is all jammed up coming from Seattle – which it frequently is – consider taking Hwy 509. To reach it, get on the Alaskan Way Viaduct (Hwy 99) southbound, which turns into Hwy 509 about 5 miles south of the city center. Coming from Sea-Tac, follow signs heading north to Hwy 509 (which will take you to Hwy 99 and into downtown) or to I-5. From I-5, take exits 165 or 166 for downtown.

Typical taxi fare to/from downtown is around $35, and you'll pay even more for a cab that gets stuck in traffic.

PUBLIC TRANSPORTATION
Bus (Map 3)

Seattle's excellent Metro Transit (☎ 553-3060) serves the greater Seattle area with more than 200 bus routes. The city has twice won awards for having the best public transit system in the country. It is so efficient that if you're staying downtown, you really don't need a car to get around.

Most of Seattle's buses run through downtown on 3rd Ave or through the Metro bus tunnel, which runs beneath Pine St and 3rd Ave and lets buses zip through the city without getting stuck in traffic. You can catch the bus inside the tunnel at one of five stations, including Convention Place, Westlake, University Street, Pioneer Square and International District. In the downtown core all bus rides are free between 6 am and 7 pm daily. This Ride Free Area includes the area between 6th Ave and the Waterfront, and between S Jackson St in Pioneer Square and Battery St. Note that Seattle Center is outside the Ride Free Area.

Regular bus fare costs $1.50 during peak hours (6 to 9 am and 3 to 6 pm) and $1.25 at other times (seniors and youths ages five to 17 pay 50¢ at all times). If you are catching a bus that's heading downtown, you buy your ticket when you get on; if you board a bus downtown and head elsewhere, you pay when you get off. You need exact change to board the bus, and if you plan on switching to a connecting route, you must ask for a transfer slip upon boarding – it's free. You can buy tickets in advance and pick up a free Metro bus map at the King County Metro Transit office at 201 S Jackson or at the Westlake Center bus tunnel station.

Metro's 24-hour Rider Information line (☎ 553-3000, 800-542-7876) can help you find the most efficient bus route from/to anywhere in the city. The phone lines are open 5 am to midnight weekdays, and 10 am to midnight weekends and holidays. Bus schedules are available at libraries, shopping centers and stores throughout Seattle.

Sunset courtesy of the Vashon Island ferry

A streetcar plies the Waterfront near Pier 54.

JAMES MARSHALL

DEBRA MILLER

ANN CECIL

JOHN ELK III

Sugar and spice and all things nice – Japanese maple trees, Chinese tea and herbs, Cambodian noodles

Waterfront Streetcar (Map 3)

Seattle's old trolley system was dismantled in the 1940s, but one section has been kept alive. It is especially handy for visitors, as it links the area near Seattle Center (from the base of Broad St) to the Waterfront and Pike Place Market, and on to Pioneer Square and the International District. The vintage trolley cars, imports from Australia, stop at nine stations; the most northerly is at the foot of Broad St at Alaskan Way, about a 10-minute walk from the Seattle Center. The system ends in the International District, across from Union Station. Fares and transfers are the same as the city buses (see earlier), but note that the streetcar is not included in the Ride Free Area. Tickets are good for 1½ hours after issuance. Buy tickets as you board.

Monorail (Map 3)

This 1½-mile experiment in mass transit was a signature piece at the 1962 World's Fair. The once-futuristic Monorail (☎ 441-6038) provides frequent transport between downtown's Westlake Center, Pine St at 4th Ave, and the Seattle Center. It runs through a purple slab of the Experience Music Project and stops at the Seattle Center depot near the base of the Space Needle. Children love this two-minute trip. Cars run about every 10 minutes; one-way tickets cost $1.25/50¢ for adults/seniors and children. It operates weekdays 7:30 am to 11 pm and weekends 9 am to 11 pm.

CAR & MOTORCYCLE

Some streets in Seattle are very steep, making standard-transmission cars a challenge. If your clutch foot's a little shaky, you might want to consider an automatic-transmission vehicle and save yourself some stress. One-way streets, lots of traffic and expensive parking are just a few more reasons why you might want to think twice

Traffic Blues in the Emerald City

No discussion of driving around Seattle can avoid mention of Seattle's sluggish traffic. In fact, studies show Seattle traffic is only marginally worse than traffic in Los Angeles, which has the most hellish traffic in the nation. The bottleneck on I-5 rarely ceases and no amount of jaw clenching or dashboard hammering will help; you simply have to wait your turn. The backup is due in part to traffic heading over the two bridges to the Eastside and to the Boeing workers' shift-changes, which begin at 2:30 pm. The average commuting speed in Seattle is 22mph and even when traffic is moving, heavy rains can make driving conditions nightmarish.

So you want to escape? Unless you are very familiar with Seattle streets, chances are that you'll spend more time getting lost than you'll gain with an untried shortcut. Relax, throw in a classical music tape, practice deep breathing or wave at angry commuters in the car next to you. Point is, if you're stuck in I-5 traffic, you're pretty much stuck.

However, if you know in advance that I-5 is completely jammed, then its time to look at a roadmap and get to know your best friend: Aurora Ave N (Hwy 99). Take Aurora if you want to get from downtown to Ballard, Fremont, Wallingford, the U District or anywhere north of the city. Likewise, if you're heading to downtown from north of the city, Aurora's your pal. If you're heading from the south, Alaska Way Viaduct (also Hwy 99) can save you from dealing with I-5 traffic.

about traveling around by car; if you can get by without one – and given Seattle's public transit options, you most likely can – you'll save yourself a lot of hassle. However, if you're traveling farther afield than metro Seattle, a car is helpful – if not necessary.

Speed limits are 65mph to 70mph on interstates and freeways unless otherwise posted; in urban areas, the freeway speed limit is 55mph. Seatbelts and motorcycle helmets are required by law. On some Seattle freeways, High-Occupancy Vehicle (HOV) lanes are set aside for vehicles carrying at least two or three people. Since most commuters drive alone, the carpool lane typically gets light usage and is therefore a handy way to escape a traffic jam. Don't be tempted to use the carpool lane illegally – the chances of getting fined are high. You must be at least 16 years of age and have a valid driver's license in order to drive in Washington state.

Parking

Parking is scarce and expensive in Seattle. Aside from availability, where you park also depends on how much you're willing to pay; $1 an hour for metered street parking or up to $20 a day for private-lot parking. Street parking or lots on the edge of downtown – especially in the International District or south of S Jackson St under the Alaskan Way Viaduct – are often cheaper, and public transportation can easily take you into the heart of the city. Unfortunately, these areas also have a bad reputation for car theft.

Metered street parking, available throughout most of downtown and surrounding neighborhoods, is the cheapest way to go, though meters are geared toward short-term parking needs and have designated time limits ranging from 10 minutes to three hours. Metered parking spaces are free on Sunday and public holidays and after business hours (8 am to 6 pm) Monday to Saturday. If you see a space but don't see a meter, look for 'no parking' signs or a colored curb. Red, yellow, white and blue paint on curbs indicates various parking restrictions. If there are no signs, and the curb is not painted, congratulations! You've just found a free parking spot. Parking fines range from $25 for an expired meter to $200 for parking in a zone designated for the disabled.

Attended parking garages are the most secure places to park but also the most expensive. City-owned public parking garages such as the one beneath Pike Place Market offer reasonable rates.

Many hotels charge $12 to $20 for parking in addition to the nightly room rate. Be sure to inquire about parking charges when making a reservation.

Rental

All of the major car rental agencies have offices in the Seattle area, along with a host of smaller or local operators. Rates go up and down like the stock market, and it's always worth phoning around to see what's available. Many rental agencies have bargain rates for weekend or weeklong rentals, especially outside the peak summer season or in conjunction with airline tickets. Booking ahead often ensures the best rates, and airport rates are usually better than those in the city.

Typically, a small car will cost you around $40 a day or $200 a week. Be sure to ask if the rate includes unlimited mileage; if a rate looks like a real bargain, there is likely a per-mile charge after a certain distance. Though the charge may seem negligible, it's surprising how quickly the miles add up. Basic liability insurance, which covers damage you may cause to another vehicle, is required by law and comes with the price of renting the car. You'll also be offered collision insurance, called a Liability Damage Waiver, which tacks on about $15 a day. Some credit cards cover collision insurance if you charge the full cost of rental to your card. If you opt to do that, you'll need to sign a waiver declining the coverage. Contact your credit card company to find out if it offers such a service and to determine the extent of the coverage.

To rent a car, you must have a valid driver's license (even if you also have an International Driving Permit), be at least 25 years of age and have a major credit card. Return the car with a full tank of fuel; if you let the operator fill it up, the gas price will be much higher.

Most national rental car firms have booths at the airport. The following also maintain offices in the downtown area:

Avis (☎ 448-1700, 800-831-2847) 1919 5th Ave

Budget (☎ 448-1940, 800-527-0700) 2001 Westlake Ave N

Dollar (☎ 682-1316, 800-800-4000) 710 Stewart St

Enterprise (☎ 382-1051, 800-736-8222) 2116 Westlake Ave N

EZ Rent-A-Car (☎ 770-0199, 800-356-8802) 2402 7th Ave

Hertz (☎ 903-6260, 800-654-3131) 720 Olive Way

National (☎ 448-7368, 800-227-7368) 2300 7th Ave

Rent A Wreck (☎ 800-876-4670) 2701 4th Ave S

Thrifty (☎ 625-1133, 800-847-4389) 801 Virginia St

TAXI

Probably due to the excellent transit system, Seattle's not the kind of city where you hop in a cab to get from A to B. Taxis aren't always easy to find in Seattle since they don't cruise the streets in the same way they do in New York. People in Seattle typically don't hail a taxi; when they want one they phone a cab company. It takes a while for a cab to show up, so be sure to order one at least 10 minutes before you want to leave. Taxis also wait for passengers outside large hotels, around Westlake Center (4th and 5th Aves at Pine St) and at the airport. Cab fare from the airport to downtown costs around $35 (see To/From the Airport, earlier). Drivers often expect a tip of about 10% of the fare. Call one of the following:

Farwest Taxi	☎ 622-1717
Graytop Cabs	☎ 282-8222
Stita Taxi	☎ 246-9980
Yellow Cabs	☎ 622-6500

Taxi fares are based on the following: The minimum drop charge is $1.80. After the first ninth of a mile, charges are either 20¢ a mile or 50¢ a minute if waiting. Extra passengers are 50¢ a person; children under 12 ride free.

BICYCLE

Despite its hilly terrain, a surprising number of people get around Seattle on bicycle,

including a division of the Seattle Police Department. Motorists are generally not courteous to cyclists, so cycling through the city takes a certain amount of bravado (some might say stupidity). For both recreationists and commuters, the popular Burke-Gilman Trail provides the safest, most scenic and efficient artery through the city. This fabulous, mostly flat path follows an old railway bed from Kenmore's Log Boom Park on the Eastside to Ballard. The route skirts the University of Washington and travels through Gas Works Park. Cyclists jump off the trail and take either the Fremont or Ballard Bridges to get to downtown (see 'Burke & Gilman's Railway' in the Activities chapter).

Helmets are not required in Seattle, but it's highly advisable to wear one anyway. The City of Seattle Transportation, Bicycle and Pedestrian Program (☎ 684-7583) publishes an excellent map of Seattle's bike routes on paths and city streets. All Metro buses are equipped with free bike racks; you just load your bike on before you get on the bus. Contact Metro Transit (☎ 553-3000) for instructions and bike-rack etiquette. Bicycles are also permitted on public ferries, although the number of bikes allowed per sailing is limited on passenger-only boats. Cyclists are usually loaded first and should wait for the ferry near the front of the loading area.

The quiet back roads of Bainbridge, Vashon and Mercer Islands are also popular places for bicycle outings. For more information on bike routes and rentals, see the Activities chapter.

FERRY

Washington State Ferries (☎ 464-6400, 800-808-7977 within Washington, 800-843-3779 automated information) operates an extensive network of ferries in the Puget Sound area. In all, 29 ferries link islands, peninsulas and the mainland. Popular routes from Seattle include trips to Bainbridge and Vashon Islands and to Bremerton on the Kitsap Peninsula.

Note that car-and-passenger and passenger-only ferries sail to most destinations. Most ferries are boarded on a first-come, first-served basis. On weekends and during the summer when tourist traffic increases, vehicle ferry lineups can become quite long, and the wait on the most popular routes can sometimes exceed three hours. It's a good idea to get into the ferry lineup well before the departure time. On weekdays, try to avoid traveling during peak commute hours (eastbound 5 to 9 am and westbound 3 to 7 pm). Pedestrians and cyclists rarely have to wait.

Vehicle ferries to Bainbridge Island and Bremerton board at the Washington State Ferries main terminal at Pier 52 (Map 4), on Alaskan Way at Marion St. Passenger-only ferries to Bremerton and Vashon Island leave Pier 50, just south of the main ferry terminal, on weekdays only. Car ferries also cross the sound from the Fauntleroy Dock in West Seattle to Vashon Island and Southworth. See the Puget Sound map in the Excursions chapter for ferry routes.

Ferries sail frequently every day. Schedules vary throughout the year. Stop by the ferry terminal or call the ferry information line for current schedules.

Washington State Ferries also serves the four main San Juan Islands (Lopez, Shaw, Orcas and San Juan) from Anacortes, approximately 85 miles north of Seattle. Anacortes is also the primary departure point for ferries to Victoria, BC. For more information on fares and ferry travel across Puget Sound and to the San Juans and Victoria, see the Excursions chapter. Also note that a full ferry map, route information and fares are available at www.wsdot.wa.gov/ferries.

WALKING
Of course you can walk around Seattle, and the city has enough density to make walking a pleasure. Walkers should bear in mind that maps of downtown don't reflect Seattle's hilly topography. Some hills are incredibly steep, and what may appear on a map as a short jaunt of a few blocks might turn into a strenuous climb. If your hoofs are hurting, remember that catching a bus in the downtown Ride Free Area is just that: free. For information on walking tours, see the Things to See & Do chapter .

Seattleites are somewhat famous for never crossing against the light, even if there's no traffic. Stringent urbanites find this annoying, but jaywalking (crossing on a red light or not using a pedestrian crossing) is illegal and, in Seattle, jaywalkers are still routinely fined.

ORGANIZED TOURS
A number of tour companies operate in Seattle. The following is a selection of the city's most popular tours.

Trolley Tours
Seattle Trolley Tours (☎ 626-5208) provides visitors with a great form of flexible downtown transport. Visitors are encouraged to get on and off these motorized trolley cars at leisure; tickets are good for the full day of operation. The 11 stops, indicated by bright yellow sandwich boards, are dotted throughout the city, including downtown, the Space Needle, Pike Place Market, Pioneer Square, the International District, Safeco Field, Seattle Art Museum and various points along the Waterfront. Information centers are at 1500 6th Ave or at the Gray Line ticket desk at the convention center at 800 Convention Place. The narrated ride runs from each stop every 30 minutes daily between May 1 and October 15. One-day tickets cost $15/10 adults/seniors and students and can be purchased either at the information centers or upon boarding.

Bus & Boat Tours
Gray Line of Seattle (☎ 626-5208, 800-426-7532) has a whole catalog of Seattle-area bus tours. Its six-hour Grand City Tour operates April to October; adult tickets cost $34, and children are half price. The City Sights Tour is an abbreviated version that runs year-round, lasts three hours and costs $29. Other Gray Line tours from Seattle include day trips to Mt Rainier for $50; two-day overnight trips for $160, including accommodations. The Hops and Grapes Tour ($27, 4¼ hours) takes you to the Eastside breweries and vineyards, and the Boeing Tour ($40, three hours) takes

you up to the Boeing plant in Everett. Gray Line also offers multiday package tours to the San Juan Islands and Victoria, BC. All trips depart from the Gray Line ticket desk at the convention center at 800 Convention Place. For more information, check out Gray Line's Web site at www.graylineofseattle.com.

A number of companies along the Waterfront offer boat sightseeing trips. One of the major operators is Argosy Cruises (Map 5, ☎ 623-1445, 800-642-7816), which has a number of different tours departing daily year-round from Pier 55. Its popular Seattle Harbor Tour is a one-hour narrated tour of Elliott Bay, the Waterfront and the Port of Seattle. Prices are $15/14/9 for adults/students and seniors/children ages five to 12 (kids under five cruise free). Its two-hour Lake Washington Cruise costs $24/21.50/12 and departs from the AGC Marina Dock at 1200 Westlake Ave N on Lake Union (Map 11). Argosy also offers tours of the Hiram M Chittenden locks, speedboat cruises and a fine-dining cruise. Check out its lineup at www.argosycruises.com.

Also departing from Pier 55, Tillicum Village Tours (☎ 443-1244) takes a trip to Blake Island, the birthplace of Seattle's namesake Chief Sealth. The four-hour trip includes a salmon bake, a native dance and a movie at an old Duwamish Indian village. The fare costs $65/59/25 adults/seniors/children five to 12. Check out details at www.tillicumvillage.com.

For an adventurous meal, join the *Spirit of Puget Sound* fine-dining cruise (☎ 674-3500). Departing at lunch and dinner from Pier 70, the luxury yacht can accommodate up to 600 passengers and provides excellent food and entertainment. The two-hour lunch cruise costs $35; the three-hour dinner cruise costs $65. Call for reservations or check it out at www.spiritofpugetsound.com.

Sailing in Seattle (☎ 289-0094), 2040 Westlake Ave, offers 2½-hour sunset sails around Lake Union on the 33-foot *Whoodat* every evening. A five-hour tour of Lake Washington swooshes past the university and affords views of Bill Gates' mansion. The Puget Sound Day Cruise includes a trip through the Hiram M Chittenden Locks and lasts from eight to 10 hours. The *Whoodat* accommodates up to six people and costs $100/hour (if six people sign up for the sunset cruise, for example, it would cost about $42 per person). Trips meet on Lake Union at Sailing in Seattle's dock behind the China Harbor Restaurant on Westlake Ave. Check out more information on its Web site at www.sailing-in-seattle.com.

Things to See & Do

Many visitors to Seattle stick close to downtown, the center of the city's most popular tourist areas, including Pioneer Square and Pike Place Market, and a variety of shopping opportunities. Seattle's first townsite at Pioneer Square is an enclave of handsome old buildings and shaded squares. The area is also full of restaurants and cafés and some of the best non-chain-store shopping in the city, with great bookstores, antique markets, art galleries and gift shops. At night, Pioneer Square pubs and clubs kick up an energetic party scene. The lively, always bustling Pike Place Market fills daily with the bounty of local farms, rivers and the sea. Add in arts and crafts, loads of restaurants and cafés and buskers and other performers, and you'll discover why this mazelike market is Seattle at its irrepressible best.

Seattle's excellent art museum is downtown, along with the aquarium and the tacky Waterfront, where you absolutely must go just to eat a bowl of clam chowder. Also nearby, the International District, Seattle's 'Chinatown,' clings to its multicultural roots. Here you can eat mouth-watering wontons or buy fish so fresh they're still twitching from the sea.

North of the downtown core, Belltown has grown out of its grungy flannel shirt and put on pressed trousers. This is Seattle's newest and hippest party zone, with plenty of good restaurants and bars to keep you busy.

Explore downtown, but do yourself a favor and realize that the city's cheeky, quirky and youthful culture really blossoms in some of its outlying neighborhoods. You haven't really experienced Seattle unless you spend part of a day in one of these islands of counterculture, whether it's exploring Capitol Hill – at once gay, flamboyant and gritty – or Fremont, with its peculiar urban art and studied irreverence. Seattle's excellent public transit system makes it quick and easy to get almost anywhere from downtown.

The sites and destinations in this chapter are arranged by neighborhood, beginning

with the downtown core, which sits on a long isthmus between Lake Washington and Elliott Bay.

See 'CityPass' under Seattle Center for a combination ticket to several Seattle attractions.

HIGHLIGHTS
If you find yourself with limited time in Seattle, here's a completely subjective list of the city's best sights and experiences:

Touring Around Pike Place Market
Bring your appetite and adventurous spirit to this wonderful market that's filled with fresh local produce and Seattle's most colorful citizenry. Take a tour of the market and learn more than longtime locals about the market's history, its precarious times and its best-hidden secrets.

Wandering Around Pioneer Square
The 19th-century heart of Seattle is filled with history, restaurants and excellent cafés, including Zeitgeist and Torrefazione Italia. Visit the remarkable Elliott Bay Books and pull out your Nikon for photos of the totem poles in Pioneer Square and Occidental Park.

Eating Dim Sum in the International District
Partake of Seattle's Asian heritage with a dim sum lunch in the old Chinatown and a visit to the modern Japanese supermarket, Uwajimaya. The food is great, and you'll find lots of small gifts for friends and family back home.

People Watching on Capitol Hill
One of Seattle's oldest and most prestigious neighborhoods, Capitol Hill is also the center of the city's gay life and is home to disaffected young hipsters sporting tattoos and piercings. In short, this is a wildly mixed

neighborhood. Pubs and cafés are ubiquitous and make good vantage points for people watching. If you get tired of the crowds, head to Volunteer Park for great views over the city and ample green space.

Spending an Afternoon at the Seattle Art Museum

Seattle's showcase art museum is unmistakable: It's the building with the giant black silhouette shaking tools at its entrance. If you're pressed for time, focus on the truly impressive collection of Pacific Northwest native artifacts; the carved masks, canoes and ceremonial objects give a glimpse of what life was like here just 200 years ago.

Waiting in Line for the Space Needle

Yes, the Space Needle is somewhat overrated and pricey and, on sunny summer days, yields long queues. But this symbol of Seattle is worth a look, if only for the stunning views over Puget Sound and downtown.

Experiencing the Experience Music Project

The $450 million 'EMP,' an over-the-top tribute to Jimi Hendrix and the major influences of rock 'n' roll, is housed in one of the most, um, er, interesting structures created by architect Frank O Gehry.

Admiring the View from Gas Works Park

Definitely Seattle's strangest attraction, the industrial Gas Works Park in southern Wallingford provides one of the best views of the Seattle skyline over Lake Union.

Frolicking in Fremont

The self-proclaimed 'Center of the Universe' is festooned in public art. Fremont's active community groups strive to keep the neighborhood as quirky and inviting as possible. Take the walking tour suggested in the Fremont section of this chapter.

Riding the Burke-Gilman Trail

Rent a bike and take a roll along this abandoned railroad corridor now converted into a wonderful 16½-mile recreation path. Start at Gas Works Park on the north side of Lake Union and cycle all the way to the far northern shores of Lake Washington. If you're ambitious, continue down the Sammamish River on 11 miles of bike trails extending to Marymoor Park, making this a 27½-mile one-way pedal through parks, forests and pleasant neighborhoods. See 'Burke & Gilman's Railway' in the Activities chapter.

Bothering with Ballard & the Locks

A true blue-collar neighborhood with greasy-spoon breakfast joints and gritty live-music venues, Ballard seems so removed from Seattle that many people don't bother. Well, bother. It's cool. Also home to the Hiram M Chittenden Locks at the mouth of the Lake Washington Ship Canal.

Ferrying to Bainbridge Island

Seattle is one of the most maritime cities in the USA, and you should get out on Puget Sound to fully appreciate the city's skyline and natural setting. There are plenty of package boat tours, but pretend you're a local and take the frequent and inexpensive car-and-passenger ferry across to Bainbridge Island. The views, the sting of the salt air and the realization that this is everyday life to thousands of Washingtonians make a ferry ride highly worthwhile.

WALKING TOURS

Organized walking tours are an excellent and educational way to learn about a city. In Seattle, you've got a few good options. Chinatown Discovery Tours (☎ 425-885-3085) leads travelers through the International District with stops at historic sites, a fortune cookie factory and various shops. The three-hour daytime tour, which includes a dim sum lunch, costs $39. You need to call ahead to reserve a time and meeting place.

See Seattle Walking Tours (☎ 425-226-7641) runs a variety of theme tours, from public-art walks to scavenger hunts. The tours meet at Westlake Center (Map 2) at 10 am Monday to Saturday. Tours cost $15 for four hours or $25 for six hours. More information is available on its Web site at www.see-seattle.com.

The Seattle Architectural Foundation (☎ 667-9186) offers Viewpoints, a series of theme tours that study historic architecture in downtown Seattle and surrounding neighborhoods. The tours, costing $8 for the lunchtime tours (lunch not included) and $18 for more in-depth, three-hour morning tours, sell out quickly so be sure to call well in advance. More information is available on the SAF Web site at www.seattlearchitectural .org/viewpoints. For a self-guided tour, see the 'Downtown Architecture Walking Tour' special section.

Another popular walking tour is Bill Speidel's Underground Tour (☎ 682-4646). Seattle's 'underground' consists of some rather ordinary-looking damp basements that date from the 1880s, before Seattle's fire and the rebuilding of the district elevated the city off the tide flats (see 'A Town Underground,' later). Tour guides tend to color the tour with whimsical tales of historic bordellos and corrupt politicians, both of which flourished in early Seattle. Long on hype and corny on content, this wildly popular tour takes 90 minutes. It starts daily from outside Doc Maynard's Public House (Map 6), a restored 1890s saloon in Pioneer Square; schedules vary seasonally, and reservations are recommended. Tickets cost $8/7 adults/ seniors and students ages 13 to 17, $4 for children ages six to 12; only cash is accepted.

Also see the self-guided 'Center of the Universe: Fremont Walking Tour' special section under Fremont, later.

DOWNTOWN (Map 2)

When the first residents arrived on Seattle's seemingly relentless rainy shores, doubt probably swept across their minds regularly. Was this really going to work? Can civilized people actually live amid giant forests and constant mud? Well, you could sit and mope or you could figure out a way to get out of the rain before you froze to death or slipped down a muddy creek back into Elliott Bay. Seattle's first homes were roughly hewn bungalows and simple craftsmen's houses –

utility construction that reflected the need to build quickly.

After the Great Fire in 1889, Seattle's pioneers knew they were going to stick it out and, come hell or high water (which they'd already lived through a few times over), they were going to prosper. Many post-fire buildings were built in the grand Romanesque Revival style already popular in Boston and Chicago, which to the pioneers was an indicator of wealth and prosperity. Plus, no one wanted to see his or her town go up in flames again and, let's face it, brick, stone and steel are a lot less likely to burn. The sense of transformation after the fire not only changed the architectural framework of Seattle, it also altered its geography. The dramatic regrading of Denny Hill, one of Seattle's original seven steep hills that rose sharply out of Elliott Bay (see 'The Thrill on Denny Hill,' later), opened up today's downtown.

Flanked to the south by Pioneer Square and to the north by Belltown (formerly called the Denny Regrade), today's city center is bordered to the east by First Hill, where Seattle's pioneer elite built elaborate mansions with views of downtown and Elliott Bay, and to the west by the historic Pike Place Market and the forever-bustling Waterfront. The jungle of high-rises teetering on Seattle's steep streets makes downtown look very imposing when viewed from a distance. The city seems especially daunting on the incoming ferry ride from Puget Sound or at the first glimpse of the city from I-5. The actual city center, however, is quite compact. No part of downtown is more than a brisk 20-minute walk from another, and the multiple transit options make it easy to get around.

It's worth remembering that Seattle has some *very* steep streets, a consideration for both drivers and pedestrians. In fact, if you're going to spend a significant chunk of time downtown, leave the car at home or parked in one of the outlying neighborhoods. Abrupt uphills, one-way streets and expensive parking make driving downtown a little hectic, especially when you consider that all buses in the downtown core are free. (For driving and public transportation options, see the Getting Around chapter.)

DOWNTOWN ARCHITECTURE WALKING TOUR

Arctic Building Start this walk on the south end of downtown at the Arctic Building, on Cherry St at 3rd Ave. This building, completed in 1917, is unique for its intricate terra-cotta ornamentation and 25 walrus heads peeking off the building's exterior. Though originally built with authentic ivory tusks, an earthquake in the 1940s shook a few tusks loose to the ground. To protect passersby from getting skewered by falling tusks, the ivory was later replaced with epoxy.
• Walk up Cherry St and take a left onto 4th Ave.

Bank of America Tower This tower, formerly the Columbia Seafirst Center, takes up the block between 4th and 5th Aves and Columbia and Cherry Sts. This is the tallest building on the West Coast, with 76 stories. The observation deck on the 73rd floor is open 8:30 am to 4:30 pm weekdays and costs $5/3 adults/children. There's a food court on the first level, with an abundance of fast-food venues and frazzled bankers.
• Follow 4th Ave to Madison St.

1001 Fourth Ave Plaza Built in 1969, this was one of the city's first real skyscrapers. At the time, 1001 Fourth Ave Plaza was a darling of the architectural world, though nowadays it looks incredibly dated. Many locals still refer to it as 'the box that the Space Needle came in.' In the plaza outside is the *Three Piece Sculpture: Vertebrae*, a sculpture by Henry Moore – a recipient of Seattle's 'one percent for art' clause. To further the pause on drab civic architecture, look across 4th Ave at the forlorn public library. The building itself is a pity, since it replaced a once-magnificent Carnegie library from 1906. The building is slated to be replaced in 2003.
• Continue north on 4th Ave to University St and take a left, walk half a block and look up.

Right: Seattle skyline view from the Bank of America Tower

LEE FOSTER

Seattle Tower Formerly the Northern Life Tower, this art deco skyscraper built in 1928 was designed to reflect the mountains of the Pacific Northwest. The brickwork on the exterior blends from dark to light, in the same way (supposedly) as mountains do when looking at them from bottom to top. Check out the 18-karat-gold relief map in the lobby.

• Continue down University St across 3rd Ave.

Washington Mutual Building The beauty of the Seattle skyline is the blue-and-cream Washington Mutual Building at 3rd Ave at Seneca St, which turns colors with the clouds and sunsets. Don't be shy; enter off 3rd Ave to explore the building's stunning interior.

• Cross University St.

Benaroya Concert Hall With a hefty bill of almost $120 million in construction costs, it's no wonder the Benaroya Concert Hall oozes with the feeling of luxury the minute you walk in. From the glass-enclosed lobby of the performance hall, symphony-goers can take in excellent views of Elliott Bay; on sunny days you might be lucky enough to see the snowy peaks of the Olympic Range far in the distance. Even if you're not attending the symphony, you can walk through the foyer and marvel at the 20-foot-long chandeliers, specially created by glassmaker Dale Chihuly.

• Walk back up University St, across 3rd Ave to the corner of 4th Ave.

Cobb Building Look up at the 1910 Cobb Building and see remnants of an older Seattle. Peering out from the building is the dour terra-cotta head of a Native American chief. Sixteen of these 800lb heads once decorated the exterior of the White-Henry-Stuart Building, one of the original structures near this site (it was torn down in 1976). If you like this highly ornamented terra-cotta style, also check out the **Alaska Building** at 2nd Ave at Cherry St, near Pioneer Square (Map 6).

• Continue on University St across 4th Ave.

Rainier Tower Taking up an entire block between 4th and 5th Aves and University and Union Sts you'll find Rainier Square, a shopping center connected to the top-heavy Rainier Tower. Built in 1979, this business tower looks as though a beaver started chipping away at its base. The architect, Seattle-born Minoru Yamasaki, also designed the World Trade Center in New York City.

• Cross University St.

Four Seasons Olympic Hotel One of the classiest remnants of Seattle's early-20th-century heyday is this fine hotel at 5th Ave at University St. This block-square building is sober and unrevealing on the

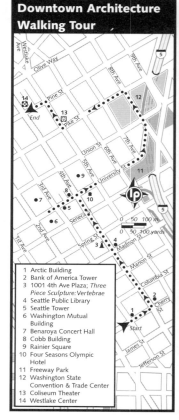

Downtown Architecture Walking Tour

1 Arctic Building
2 Bank of America Tower
3 1001 4th Ave Plaza; *Three Piece Sculpture: Vertebrae*
4 Seattle Public Library
5 Seattle Tower
6 Washington Mutual Building
7 Benaroya Concert Hall
8 Cobb Building
9 Rainier Square
10 Four Seasons Olympic Hotel
11 Freeway Park
12 Washington State Convention & Trade Center
13 Coliseum Theater
14 Westlake Center

outside, but journey through the revolving doors to discover a sumptuous lobby dominated by chandeliers, marble walls and exotic carpets – testimony to a distant, more glorious era. Peek into the Georgian Room to see a dining room right out of a stylish 1930s film. Interestingly, University St got its name because the original building of the University of Washington once stood on the location of the hotel. The university still owns 10 acres of land in the city center, part of a land donation made by Seattle founder Arthur Denny in 1860.

• Continue northeast on University St past 6th Ave; look ahead to the park.

Freeway Park This lone downtown island of greenery is in fact built right over I-5's ugly trench along the eastern edge of downtown. Built in a series of steps, the park escapes the growl of engines. The sound of traffic is masked by the roar of tumbling water from the waterfall, fountains and gurgling streams.

• Meander through Freeway Park then follow signs to the Washington State Convention & Trade Center, which is attached to the park.

Washington State Convention & Trade Center Pick up whatever brochures and maps you need at the Visitors Center inside the cavernous Washington State Convention & Trade Center building, whose front doors spill out at Pike St and 8th Ave. There's nothing much notable about the convention center itself – it's essentially a concrete gray bunker – but it solved two problems for city planners: where to put a major new conference center that was near to downtown hotels, yet far enough away from the roar of 1-5's 12 lanes of traffic. After much head-scratching, they came up with the ingenious idea to build the four-story structure *on top* of the freeway.

• Leave the Convention Center through its front doors on Pike St. Follow Pike south (you'll see Pike Place Market at the end of the street) to 5th Ave.

Coliseum Theater You won't be able to miss the imposing Banana Republic store at the corner of 5th Ave and Pike St, housed in the wonderful old terra-cotta-faced Coliseum Theater, a film palace dating back to 1916. In its heyday, the theater filled its 1700 seats with eager moviegoers. The theater suffered neglect over the years until it was saved by Banana Republic's multimillion-dollar rehabilitation project, which was completed in 1985.

• Take a right on 5th Ave to Pine St; turn left.

Westlake Center You can't miss the steel-and-glass vision of Westlake Center beckoning for your attention and pulsating with the frenzy of happy shoppers. What better way to finish up this tour than to stop by the Seattle's Best Coffee kiosk in front of Westlake Center and settle in for some people watching while you sip your brew. From here you have a couple of options: window shop at the upscale boutiques, go to the top of the mall and catch the Monorail to Seattle Center or head back south along 4th Ave to Cherry St where you started the tour.

For companies that offer guided tours, see Walking Tours, earlier in this chapter.

Downtown is anchored on 3rd, 4th and 5th Aves, between Olive Way and Cherry St. This area contains the vast majority of the city's major hotels, shopping venues and soaring business towers. It's easy to further divide this lengthy strip into two separate sections: the lively retail core to the north and the contemporary business district to the south.

Options for getting to, from and around downtown are excellent, and almost every bus in the city filters though at some point (see Map 3). Remember, all buses are free in the Ride Free Area between 6 am and 7 pm.

Retail District

From the corner of 5th Ave and Pike St, gaze two or three blocks in any direction and experience retail heaven, Seattle style. A block north, at 5th Ave at Pine St, is the flagship store of Nordstrom, the national clothing retailer that got its start in Seattle. Just to the west of Nordstrom is Westlake Center, the veritable pumping heart of the retail district. One of the Rowse Company developments found seemingly in every sizeable US city (notably Atlanta's Peach Tree Plaza, Boston's Faneuil Hall and Portland's Pioneer Place), Westlake Center is filled with national boutique chains and has a top-floor food court. It also contains the downtown stop of the Monorail from Seattle Center.

Across Pine St, a pedestrian plaza called Westlake Park is a popular people-watching haven and a great place to plop down on a bench and eat lunch or sip coffee on sunny days. Skateboarders and bike messengers careen through crowds of trench-coat-clad professionals and shoppers teetering under the weight of their bags. Buskers pipe out songs, entrepreneurs hawk T-shirts, and preachers bellow fire and brimstone. Don't miss artist Robert Maki's waterwall that you can walk through without getting wet.

If you're into the latest video games and virtual-reality interactive systems, then make a detour into Gameworks, at 7th Ave at Pike St, a vast new future-is-now entertainment center.

The entire retail area seems to be in a perpetual state of demolition and reconstruction. As the area's older hotels and red-brick warehouses fall to the wrecking ball, new shopping and parking structures go up in a feverish attempt to sustain all the boutiques and the growing number of consumers who throng to this area to ogle and buy. (See the Shopping chapter.)

Business District

Seattle's modern business district is south of the retail core, along 3rd, 4th and 5th Aves. Rather dull modern office towers dominate this area; however, some of the older art deco and terra-cotta-fronted buildings are charming – it's worth following the 'Downtown Architecture Walking Tour' for a closer look. This area explodes at noon when office workers are set free for lunch. Otherwise, in the evenings and on weekends, the area is practically devoid of life.

Tunnel Vision

One of the best places to get a sense of Seattle's quirky artistic vision is in any of the downtown area's five underground bus tunnel stations (Map 3; Convention Place, Westlake, University St, Pioneer Square and International District). Twenty-three artists were commissioned to decorate the spaces and to comprise part of the design team that worked with architects and construction crews. Completed in 1990, the result is a fairly wild assemblage of huge murals, ornamental gates and grates, painted tiles, sculpture and highly ornamental clocks. Because each tunnel had its own design team, each looks and feels completely different. If you're into urban art, it's definitely worth a wander down into one of the bus-tunnel entrances. On a nice day, the International District station, with its outdoor plaza decorated with postmodern trellises and pergolas, is especially pleasant. In terms of graphic art, the Westlake Center station is most notable with huge murals by artists like Fay Jones and Roger Shimomura. Check out the two light sculptures at the University Street station.

Seattle Art Museum (SAM)

West of the business and retail core of downtown Seattle is the Seattle Art Museum (☎ 654-3100), 100 University St at 1st Ave. Faced in limestone and ornamented terra-cotta, the postmodern structure makes the most of its hillside location; the spacious galleries step down the slope and are linked by immense staircases. This Robert Venturi–designed building has proven to be controversial, however, as only a third of its 145,000 sq feet is actually devoted to exhibition space.

The museum's collection, focusing on world art with an emphasis on Asian, African and Native American folk and tribal art, was greatly enhanced when the museum moved here in 1991 from its old digs in Volunteer Park. Especially good are the displays of masks, canoes and totems from Northwest coastal tribes. The permanent collection has a small but representational selection of paintings by European and American modern masters, but a rather thin and disappointing display of works by contemporary artists. Traveling shows are found in the Special Exhibits gallery; films and lectures take place in the 300-seat auditorium.

Welcoming visitors to the museum is Jonathan Borofsky's four-story action sculpture, *Hammering Man*. The towering figure waves tools at the museum's front door.

The museum is open 10 am to 5 pm Tuesday to Sunday; to 9 pm on Thursday. Admission costs $7/5 adults/seniors and students. On the first Thursday of every month, admission is free. Within one week of purchase, tickets are also valid at the Seattle Asian Art Museum in Volunteer Park (see Capitol Hill, later).

FIRST HILL (Map 2)

With its commanding position directly to the east and above downtown, First Hill became the foremost status neighborhood for early Seattleites. Throughout the area you'll still find traces of the early glory, including a few magnificent old mansions and some excellent examples of early Seattle architecture.

Over the decades, however, most mansions of the once mighty have long since been torn down and replaced by hospitals. Now known to many as 'Pill Hill,' First Hill is home to three major hospitals. With the accompanying research and support facilities, it can indeed seem that everything up here is related to the medical industry.

A few of the classic older structures remain, including the fantastic **Sorrento Hotel** at 900 Madison St. This grand working hotel is a fine example of Italian Renaissance–style architecture. Built in 1909 by a Seattle clothing merchant, the Sorrento was one of the first hotels built for the crowds of prospectors journeying through Seattle on their way to Alaska in search of gold. (See the Places to Stay chapter for more information on the hotel.)

One of the first homes on First Hill, the baronial **Stimson-Green Mansion** (☎ 624-0474), 1204 Minor Ave, is an English Tudor–style mansion completed in 1901 by lumber and real-estate developer CD Stimson. Built from brick, stucco and wood, this stately home is now owned by Stimson's granddaughter. The interior rooms are decorated to reflect the different design styles popular at the turn of the 20th century. Today the mansion is used for private catered events. The interior can be viewed by appointment only.

Bordered by downtown, the Pike/Pine Corridor and the International District, First Hill is liveliest at its fringes.

Frye Art Museum

This small museum (☎ 622-9250), 704 Terry Ave, preserves the collection of Charles and Emma Frye. The Fryes collected over 1000 paintings, mostly 19th- and early-20th-century European and American pieces, and a few Alaskan and Russian artworks. If this inspires a stifled yawn, think again. Since its expansion in 1997, the Frye has gained a hipness that was lacking before; music performances, poetry readings and interesting rotating exhibits, from travel painters to local printmakers, now make the museum a worthwhile stop. It's open 10 am to 5 pm Tuesday to Saturday; to 9 pm on Thursday. Sunday the museum is open noon to 5 pm. Admission is free.

Getting There & Away

You can catch bus No 2 on the west side of 3rd Ave downtown and get off at the Swedish Medical Center. Be aware, however, that First Hill is out of the Ride Free Area, so be prepared to pay up if you take the bus. On foot, First Hill is a short walk uphill from downtown. From Westlake Center, head over to University St and walk uphill through Freeway Park or, if you're in the business district, walk straight up Madison St to Terry Ave, and you'll be at the Sorrento Hotel.

PIONEER SQUARE (Map 4)

Browsing the Pioneer Square area is rather like visiting a movie set of early-20th-century Seattle, except that the food and the shopping are better. This is the birthplace of Seattle, and the redbrick district of historic buildings and totem-lined plazas is still a real crossroads of the modern city.

In the early days of Seattle, this area was a haphazard settlement made up of wooden storefronts, log homes and lumber mills. The Great Fire of 1889 (see History in the Facts About Seattle chapter) leveled most of the original town, but the city rapidly rebounded: Almost all of the buildings around Pioneer Square were constructed between 1890 and 1905. As many as 50 of these structures were designed by one architect, Elmer Fisher. As part of this massive rebuilding project, city streets were regraded, raising the new city about a dozen feet above the original settlement (see 'A Town Underground').

Pioneer Square was in decline for years until cheap rents and Historic Register status brought in art galleries, antique shops and interior design shops. Many Pioneer Square restaurants play up the frontier image while serving notably good food. Pioneer Square is also a major center for live music and nightlife. See the Places to Eat and Entertainment chapters for information.

Perhaps mirroring its early days when this was a rough-and-tumble frontier town, Pioneer Square still sees some rowdiness; often a juxtaposition of Seattle's homeless and drunken tourists out rambling around

the bar scene. Though the ruckus may seem a little unnerving, especially at night, there's little actual threat beyond the occasional instance of panhandling.

The Pioneer Square area is bounded roughly by Cherry and S King Sts to the north and south, and 1st and 3rd Aves S to the west and east.

Pioneer Square

Right at the corner of Cherry St and 1st Ave is the original Pioneer Square – a cobblestone triangular plaza where Henry Yesler's sawmill cut the giant trees that marked Seattle's first industry. Known officially as **Pioneer Square Park**, the plaza features a bust of Chief Sealth, an ornate pergola and a totem pole. Some wayward early Seattleites, so the story goes, stole the totem from the Tlingit natives in southeastern Alaska in 1890. An arsonist lit the pole aflame in 1938, burning it to the ground. When asked if they could carve a replacement pole, the Tlingit took the money offered, thanking the city for payment of the first totem, and waited for a better incentive to carve another one. The city coughed up $5000 and the Tlingit obliged with the pole you see today.

The decorative pergola was built in the early 1900s to serve as an entryway to an underground lavatory and to shelter those waiting for the cable car that went up and down Yesler Way. The reportedly elaborate restroom eventually closed due to serious plumbing problems at high tide. Today the pergola, outside Doc Maynard's Public House, is used as the meeting spot for the Underground Tour (see Walking Tours, above) and as a hangout for homeless people and weekend partiers, who seem to be turning the area back into a lavatory.

Incidentally, Yesler Way was the coining ground for the term 'skid road' – logs would 'skid' down the road linking a logging area above town to Henry Yesler's mill. With the decline of the area, the street became a haven for homeless people. Soon the nickname 'skid row' was being used for equally destitute areas around the country.

Facing Pioneer Square Park are several magnificent old structures. The **Pioneer**

Building, built in 1891, is one of the finest Victorian buildings left in Seattle; many mining companies had offices here during the Klondike Gold Rush years. It now in part houses **Doc Maynard's Public House**, a handsome old bar and restaurant, and the ticket office for the Underground Tour.

1st Avenue South

The main street in the Pioneer Square area is 1st Ave S. Join the crowds and wander down the avenue, past upscale stores, art galleries, trendy cafés and homeless missions. Even the most callous antishopper should stop at a couple of the old storefronts. The Grand Central Arcade, 214 1st Ave S between S Washington and S Main Sts, has a good bakery-café, plenty of tables, a cozy fire and staircases leading to the underground shopping arcade. You can walk straight through here to Occidental Park (see below).

Elliott Bay Book Company, on the corner of S Main St and 1st Ave S, is Seattle's premier bookstore and literary gathering place and the original home of the Globe Hotel, built in 1890. The place is made for

A Town Underground

The thought of a world left buried underground is so intriguing that every year tourists flock to buy tickets to join Bill Speidel's famous Underground Tour. Unfortunately, the tour is long on hype, short on content and gratifying only to people who snicker when someone uses the word 'brothel.'

While there's not much to see 'underground' except dirty passageways and decayed plumbing from the 1890s, the story of why it's there in the first place *is* pretty interesting. Despite its prime location on Elliott Bay, early Seattle wasn't exactly conducive to urban development. The area lacked any ideal foundation upon which to build; the land was either hilly and steep or shallow and wet. Many of the storefronts in the

Pioneer Square area were built upon soggy tideflats and actually dropped below sea level at high tide. When it rained hard (and it rained hard a lot), the streets bloated into a muddy soup, sewage backed up at high tide and things got pretty messy. As you can imagine, the smell wasn't so great either.

When an apprentice woodworker accidentally let a boiling pot of glue spill onto a pile of wood chips in a shop on 1st Ave and Madison St, he did Seattle a great favor. It was June 6, 1889 and the ensuing flames swept the town's wooden houses and storefronts up faster than a pioneer could swig a pint of beer. The Great Fire gutted the city and gave city planners a chance to lift the town out of its waterlogged foundation. They decided to regrade the streets first. Great piles of dirt were propped up with retaining walls, and streets were raised up to 10 feet higher than they originally were. People had to cross deep trenches to get from one side of the street to another. Buildings were constructed around the notion that the first floor or two would eventually be buried when the city got around to filling in the trenches. Storefronts from the old ramshackle town that were once at street level effectively became basements and, later, passageways for the Underground Tour. You can see bits of the underground by yourself in the Pioneer Square Antique Mall in the Pioneer Building and on the bottom floor of the Grand Central Arcade.

browsing, with its high ceilings, peculiar multilevels of bookshelves and funny niches and corners. Downstairs is a snug little café.

Occidental Park

A block east of 1st Ave S is Occidental Ave S, most of which is preserved as a park and a pedestrian mall. The nicest area around here is **Occidental Square**, between S Main and S Jackson Sts, with a cobblestone plaza flanked by unusually handsome Victorian buildings. Visit Glasshouse Art Glass to see local artists' impressive works of blown, cast and lampworked glass. If you need a shot of caffeine or a chance to catch your breath, detour to the original location of Torrefazione Italia, the best of the local coffee chains; you'll love their real Italian *faience* cups. Coffee junkies, poets or anyone wearing black will want to make the pilgrimage to Zeitgeist at the corner S Jackson St and 2nd Ave S. This groovy coffeehouse is a local haunt of artists and architects.

Along S Jackson St you'll find an excellent concentration of antique stores and some of the city's most prestigious galleries, including the Foster/White Gallery and the Northwest Gallery of Fine Woodworking, absolute must-stops for art lovers.

Across S Main St and the Waterfront Streetcar tracks is Occidental Park, another cobblestone plaza. Tourists vie with the homeless and pigeons for space in this otherwise lovely open space shaded by planetrees. Notable here are the totem poles carved by Duane Pasco, a nationally respected Chinookan carver and artist from Poulsbo on the Kitsap Peninsula. The totems depict the welcoming spirit of Kwakiutl, a totem bear, the tall Sun and Raven and a man riding on the tail of a whale. Also eye-catching is the Firefighters' Memorial, featuring life-size bronze sculptures of firefighters in action. Engraved on the granite slabs surrounding the sculpture are the names of Seattle firefighters who have been killed in the line of duty since the department's inception after the Great Fire. The artist is Hai Ying Wu, a University of Washington graduate.

From Occidental Park you can catch the Waterfront Streetcar east to the International District or west to the Waterfront. The fare costs $1.25 peak hours (6 to 9 am and 3 to 6 pm) and $1 at other times.

Smith Tower

You can't miss Seattle's first skyscraper, at 506 2nd Ave S at Yesler Way. The 42-story Smith Tower (☎ 622-4004) was well known as the tallest building west of Chicago for half a century after its construction in 1914. The distinctive tower was erected by LC Smith, a man who built his fortune on typewriters (Smith & Corona) and guns (Smith & Wesson). Smith died during the building's construction, so he never got to see the beauty that still bears his name. Walk into the onyx- and marble-paneled lobby, step aboard one of the brass-and-copper manually operated elevators and let it whisk you up to the 35th-floor observation deck for a great view of Seattle's Waterfront. The deck is open to the public 10 am to 4 pm daily May through October; $5/3 adults/seniors and children ages six to 12.

Waterfall Park

This unusual park, on the corner of S Main St and 2nd Ave S, is a lovely little urban oasis. It commemorates workers of the United Parcel Service (UPS), which began in a basement at this location in 1907. The artificial 22-foot waterfall that flows in this tiny open-air courtyard is flanked by tables and flowering plants. This is a perfect spot to eat a brown-bag lunch or to rest weary feet.

Klondike Gold Rush Park

Seattle's seminal position as the outfitting and transportation hub for the 1897 Alaskan and Yukon Gold Rush is recognized at Klondike Gold Rush Park (☎ 553-7220), 117 S Main St, one of the USA's few indoor national historical parks. Exhibits document the abundance of gear and food necessary to stake a claim in the Klondike, which brought a boom to Seattle merchants. Gold panning is demonstrated by park rangers, and you can sit down and view a slide presentation about the gold rush. The park is open 9 am to 5 pm daily; admission is free.

Totem Poles of the Northwest Coast

Totem poles are found along the Northwest Pacific Coast, roughly between northern Washington State and Alaska. Carved from a single cedar log by the Haida, Tlingit, Tsimshian and Kwakiutl tribes (Puget Sound tribes typically did not carve totems), totem poles identify a household's lineage in the same way a family crest might identify a group or clan in Europe, although the totem pole is more of a historical pictograph depicting the entire ancestry. Like a family crest, totem poles carry a sense of prestige and prosperity.

Totems serve a variety of functions: Freestanding poles welcome visitors to a waterfront or village; a memorial pole is often erected outside a deceased chief's home; mortuary poles are implanted with a box of the honored individual's decomposed remains. Incorporated into the design of a house, totem poles also appear as house posts and front doors. Shame poles, carved with upside-down figures denoting social or ritual transgressions, were temporary fixtures and are found only in museums today. Traditional poles vary greatly in height, though rarely exceed 60 feet. Modern poles can be much taller – the world's tallest totem pole at Alert Bay in British Columbia is 173 feet.

Despite the saying 'low man on the totem pole,' the most important figures are usually at eye level; figures at the bottom usually have an integral, grounding function that supports the rest of the pole. Figures can represent individuals, spirits, births, deaths, catastrophes or legends.

Unless you're an expert, it's not so easy to identify what's what on a totem. Here are a few rules of thumb: Birds are always identified with a pronounced beak – ravens have a straight, mid-size beak; eagles have a short, sharp, down-turned beak; hawks have a short, down-turned beak that curls inward. Bears usually have large, square teeth, while beavers have sharp incisors and a cross-stitched tail. A few animals appear as if viewed from overhead. For example, killer whales' fins protrude outward from the poles as if their heads face downward. Long-snouted wolves also face downward, as do frogs. Pointy-headed sharks (or dogfish), with grimacing mouths full of sharp teeth, face upward, as do humpback whales.

Though totem symbols are usually interconnected and complex, animals possess certain undeniable characteristics:

black bear a protector, guardian and spiritual link between humans and animals
beaver industriousness, wisdom and determined independence
eagle intelligence and power
frog adaptability; ability to live in both natural and supernatural worlds
hummingbird love, beauty and unity with nature
killer whale dignity and strength; often a reincarnated spirit of a great chief
raven mischievousness and cunning; the perennial trickster
salmon dependable sustenance, longevity and perseverance; a powerful symbol
shark ominous, fierce and solitary
thunderbird strong, supernatural; the wisdom of proud ancestors

Few old totem poles remain today, as most cedar logs begin to decay within 60 to 80 years, though totem poles at Ninstints and Skedans on the Queen Charlotte Islands in British Columbia are more than 100 years old. New totems are rarely constructed for tribal purposes and instead are more frequently carved for nontraditional use as public art. Modern totem poles commissioned for college campuses, museums and public buildings no longer recount the lineage of any one household, but instead stand to honor the first nations and their outstanding artistry.

Alaska-bound fortune hunters on the Seattle Waterfront – 1898

Kingdome Area Redevelopment

If you follow 1st or 2nd Aves south of Pioneer Square, you'll get an eyeful of what will be, for the next decade or so, Seattle's biggest urban redevelopment area. The Kingdome, long Seattle's biggest eyesore, was once the sports stadium that served as home field for the city's professional baseball and football franchises. Judged by the Mariners and the Seahawks to be too small for their expansionist fantasies, the Kingdome was demolished in 2000, after only 24 years as Seattle's big sports venue. The as-yet-unnamed 72,000-seat **Seahawks stadium** that will fill the hole the Kingdome left behind is slated to be ready in late summer 2002. (See 'Paul Allen: Seattle's Co-Owner,' later.)

Just south of the former Kingdome is the new **Washington State Exhibition Center**, a giant exhibit space for events like car and boat shows. Farther south still is the Mariners' new $517 million ballpark, **Safeco Field** (☎ 346-4241, 622-4487 ticket information), which opened in July 1999. This pricey new stadium, with its retractable roof, 46,621 seats and real grass, was funded

in part by taxpayers and tourists; more than half the money came from taxes on food sold in King County restaurants and bars and from taxes on rental cars. Money also came from profits on scratch lottery tickets. The Mariners coughed up most of the difference. You can go on an hour-long tour of Safeco Field. Tour times are 10:30 am and 12:20 and 2:30 pm on nongame days April to October. On game days there is no 2:30 pm tour; if the game is before 6 pm, there are no tours at all. From November to March, tour times are 12:30 and 2:30 pm Tuesday to Sunday. Tours cost $7/3 adults/children.

Another landmark building that benefited from the restoration fever is **Union Station**, the old Union Pacific Railroad depot, built in 1911. Until its recent renovation, Union Station sat unoccupied since 1971, when the last train left the station. The restoration project included preservation of the original tile floors, clocks and windows. More than 90 years of buildup was hand-scrubbed off the exterior brick. The Great Hall, half the size of a football field, is an impressive space.

While they are tearing up the neighborhood, city leaders have also decided to effect a renewal of the **King Street Station**, the old Great Northern Railroad depot that is now in use as the Amtrak station. This jewel of a train station has been blighted since the 1960s by a horrible ceiling-lowering revamping, but the fabulous old Italianate plasterwork and detailing are still there. The old depot's stately brick tower has long been an integral (though now dwarfed) piece of the downtown skyline. Renovation of the building will be dramatic, though costly; the Department of Transportation estimates the cost at around $42 million. Time ticks by while the state government figures out who's going to pay for it. Regardless, don't expect this area to be free of cranes and cement trucks till 2006 or so.

Getting There & Away

Pioneer Square is most easily reached by walking or by bus (it's in the Ride Free Area). If you're in the bus tunnel, get off at Pioneer Square. From the exit, Pioneer Square is immediately downhill. You can also take any of the aboveground buses that run along First Ave. For something more touristy and historic, take the Waterfront Streetcar from any of its stops along the Waterfront, which will put you smack-dab in the heart of Occidental Square.

If walking from Pike Place Market (about 10 minutes), take either Alaskan Way south along the Waterfront, or 1st Ave to pass by Seattle Art Museum's *Hammering Man* sculpture and some unusual shops.

INTERNATIONAL DISTRICT (Map 4)

East of Pioneer Square is the International District, Seattle's Chinatown, where Asian groceries and restaurants line the streets.

The Chinese were among the first settlers in Seattle in the late 1800s (the original Chinatown was north of pioneer downtown), followed by Japanese, Filipinos, Vietnamese, Laotians and others. Later immigrants settled just to the east of present-day Chinatown in an area known as Little Saigon.

Although 'International District' seems a pretty useful term for this mix of races and cultures, in fact it is a relatively recent and controversial moniker, fashioned at the start of political correctness in the early 1970s. The Chinese grew resentful when the renaming left 'Chinatown' a seemingly dirty word, but the other Asian groups welcomed representation. Scuffles about who the neighborhood belongs to continue as they have throughout the area's history. Many Seattleites still refer to the area as Chinatown or simply 'the ID.'

Asian immigrants had an important presence in Seattle pretty much from the beginning. The muscle behind this early Asian settlement was the Wa Chong Company, labor contractors who brought in Chinese workers for timber, mining and railroad jobs in the 1860s and 1870s. After the anti-Chinese riots of 1886 (see History in the Facts About Seattle chapter), the population of Chinatown dropped from an estimated 1500 to about 500, making room for the next wave of Asian immigrants, the Japanese.

Immigrants from Japan settled the area in the later 1800s and remained the largest minority group until WWII. From the 1920s to '40s, this was a very bustling place, thriving with Asian markets and other businesses that were built and patronized by the country's highest concentration of Japanese and Chinese Americans. African Americans and Filipinos also moved in around this time, but the area remained a veritable Japantown, with Japanese newspapers, schools, banks and restaurants.

The neighborhood took another massive, discriminating hit during WWII, when all inhabitants of Japanese descent were forcibly moved out and interned at labor camps in the US interior (see History in the Facts about Seattle chapter). The once-bustling shops were boarded up. When released, few chose to return here to their old homes; the ones that did, including the Moriguchis who founded the Uwajimaya store (see Chinatown, later), made quite an impact on the future development of the neighborhood.

When I-5 pushed through the heart of the district, destroying many blocks of housing, the area became even more blighted, its identity even more divided. The arrival of Vietnamese immigrants in the 1970s and '80s, and more recently, an influx of immigrants from Hong Kong and mainland China, have breathed new life into the city's Asian community.

The recent renovation of Union Station, new sports stadiums and nearby office and condo developments sprouting up like weeds around the International District have left neighborhood activists fearing homogeneity in a district already rife with boundary issues. Will the condos win out over low-income housing? Will they fill up with yuppies and open the door to more coffee shops, 24-hour gyms and the Gap? Throughout the USA, major cities boast Chinatowns, Japantowns and other neighborhoods that embody a specific ethnicity. In Seattle, they're all crowded into one small neighborhood whose boundaries get threatened every time a land-use application shows up at City Hall. Meanwhile, district activists strive to keep the area vital by stressing anticrime measures and by maintaining a strong community voice in housing and commercial development.

Chinatown

From Pioneer Square, walk eastward up S Jackson St past the outwardly handsome King Street Station. The main center of the district is between 5th and 7th Aves S and S Weller and S Jackson Sts. While this is definitely a Chinatown, it is nowhere near as large or as authentic as you'll find in San Francisco or Vancouver, BC. Only a few of the old markets and herbal-remedy shops remain, and if you look up, you can see a couple of Hong Kong-style balconies protruding rather oddly off the face of old redbrick storefronts. However, there's still some life left here, and if you're looking for Asian cuisine, you've come to the right place.

A good place to get a sense of Chinatown is S Weller St. Besides the many restaurants, there's Pacific Herb & Grocery (☎ 340-6411) at 610 S Weller St, between 6th and Maynard Aves S. The herbal-medicine specialists here can tell you all about the uses of different roots, bones, flowers and teas. The shop next door is a great place to buy tofu at low prices – you can even watch them make it on the premises.

Ironically, a Japanese store is the modern-day heart of Chinatown. **Uwajimaya** (☎ 624-6248), 519 6th Ave S, was founded by Fujimatsu Moriguchi, one of the few Japanese to return here from the WWII internment camps. At this large department and grocery store – a cornerstone of Seattle's Asian community – you'll find everything from fresh fish and exotic fruits and vegetables to cooking utensils, and you'll come face-to-face with those dim sum ingredients you've always wondered about. It's a great place to browse. Uwajimaya's owner (Moriguchi's grandson) has big expansionist plans, including a retail and residential complex that would take up a city block of Chinatown. Upstairs from Uwajimaya, the giant **Kinokuniya** bookstore has an excellent collection of books about Asia and by Asian writers.

At the corner of Maynard Ave S and S King St, **Hing Hay Park** lends a little green to this otherwise austere district. The traditional Chinese pavilion was a gift from the people of Taipei.

Little Saigon

Cross under I-5 along S Jackson St, and the pace changes considerably as you enter the International District's Vietnamese and Laotian areas. This is a genuine lived-in neighborhood that exists more for the locals and less for gawking tourists. The center of this area is a series of strip malls at 12th Ave S at S Jackson St, where you'll find all manner of Vietnamese businesses including barbershops, real-estate offices, dentists and a profusion of markets and restaurants.

A couple of markets in this area are worth exploring. Modern and bustling **Hau Hau Market**, 12th Ave S at S Jackson St, is the Vietnamese equivalent of Uwajimaya down the hill. The more authentic **Viet Hoa**,

7th Ave S at S Jackson St, has a greengrocer in one building and a fish and meat market in the other. Both display foods and cuts of meat you may have never seen before. The big tank of live turtles at the door and the buckets of fish that look like they're one splash away from coming back to life assure you that this market carries only the freshest ingredients.

Also up in this part of the International District is the **Danny Woo International District Community Gardens**. This 1½-acre plot is reserved for older and low-income International District residents, who use it to grow a profusion of vegetables and fruit trees; about 120 people have gardens here. Visitors can wander along the gravel paths and admire both the tidy gardens and the Seattle skyline and good views onto Elliott Bay. Unfortunately, while you take in the view you'll have about 17 lanes of I-5 traffic right at your back. To reach the gardens, walk up S Main St from 6th Ave S.

Wing Luke Asian Museum
This Pan-Asian museum (☎ 623-5124), 407 7th Ave S, is devoted solely to Asian and Pacific American culture, history and art. Named after the first Asian elected official in Seattle, the museum examines the often difficult and violent meeting of Asian and Western cultures in Seattle. Particularly good are the photos and displays on the Chinese settlement in the 1880s and the retelling of Japanese American internment during WWII. The museum is self-guided and open 11 am to 4:30 pm Tuesday to Friday; noon to 4 pm weekends. Admission costs $2.50/1.50 adults/seniors and students; 75¢ for children ages five to 12.

Getting There & Away
The International District has its own exit from the underground bus tunnel (see Map 3); take any bus southbound to this stop, the last in the tunnel. The International District is also the last (or the first) stop on the Waterfront Streetcar route. The best way to get to the International District on foot from Pioneer Square is to walk east up S Jackson St.

PIKE PLACE MARKET (Map 5)
Pike Place Market is one of Seattle's most popular tourist attractions, noted as much for its exuberant theatricality as for its vastly appealing fish and vegetable market. Pike Place Market features some of the most boisterous fishmongers in the world, whose daredevil antics with salmon merge gymnastics, theater and cuisine. Despite the tourist-tickling showiness, the market maintains a down-home authenticity; real people work and buy here. If you're heading to the market, don't eat first. This is one of the hotbeds of Seattle noshing and dining. You can get everything, from a freshly grown Washington apple to a pot sticker or a seven-course French meal. Some of Seattle's favorite watering holes are also tucked into unlikely corners of the market buildings. See the Places to Eat, Entertainment and Shopping chapters for suggestions

Busking in the Market
Looking to make a little extra dough on your trip to Seattle? Well, if you can sing a tune, play an instrument or be somehow entertaining, you can become a Pike Place Market busker. If it seems like the performers in the market seem unusually well behaved and strategically placed, well, they are. Notice the red music note painted on the floor beneath a performer's feet – that's an official market Performer Location, and you can't busk anywhere else. The number painted in the middle of the music note indicates the number of musicians allowed to play at that location at any one time, be it a one-man show or a four-piece band. Wannabe market buskers must buy a $15 permit from the market Preservation & Development Authority (PDA; ☎ 682-7452), whose office is behind the Main Arcade. The permit is good for an entire year (don't worry, you'll make lots more than that in an hour on any summer day). All of the 14 Performer Locations are first-come, first-dibs; you can strum for an hour or sing your heart out all day.

on dining, nightlife and shopping in the market area.

Pike Place Market is the oldest continuously operating market in the nation. It was established in 1907 to give local farmers a place to sell their fruit and vegetables and bypass the middleman. Soon, the greengrocers made room for fishmongers, bakers, ethnic groceries, butchers, cheese sellers and purveyors of the rest of the Northwest's agricultural bounty. The market wasn't exactly architecturally robust – from the beginning, it's just a throw-together series of sheds and stalls, haphazardly designed for utility – and was by no means an intentional tourist attraction. That came later.

An enthusiastic agricultural community spawned the market's heyday in the 1930s. Many of the first farmers were immigrants, a fact the market celebrates with annual themes acknowledging the contributions of various ethnic groups; past years have featured Japanese Americans, Italian Americans and Sephardic Jews.

By the 1960s, sales at the market were suffering from suburbanization, the growth of supermarkets and the move away from local, small-scale market gardening. Vast tracts of agricultural land were disappearing, being replaced by such ventures as the Northgate Mall and the Sea-Tac airport. The internment of Japanese American farmers during WWII had also taken its toll. The entire area became a bowery for the destitute and a center for prostitution and peep shows.

In the wake of the 1962 World's Fair, plans were drawn up to bulldoze the market and build high-rise office and apartment buildings on this piece of prime downtown real estate. Fortunately, public outcry prompted a voter's initiative to save the market. Subsequently, the space was cleaned up and restructured, and it has become once again the undeniable heart and soul of downtown; some 10 million people mill through the market each year. Thanks to unique management of the market, social services programs and low-income housing mix with the market commerce, giving it a gritty edge and preventing the area from ever sliding too upscale. A market law denies chain stores or franchises from opening up shop here and ensures all businesses are locally owned. The one exception is, of course, Starbucks, which gets away with it because its market location marks the coffee giant's first (it opened in 1971).

Helpful Market Facts

Summer weekends and Friday afternoons at the market can be a lesson in mob dynamics; visiting during these times is to be avoided unless you enjoy being stuck in human gridlock next to a stack of fresh crabs. The best bet for enjoying this wonderful market is to go on a weekday morning.

The Main Arcade has restrooms on the lower level. Market stalls are open 8 am to 6 pm. Most of the market remains open for access to restaurants and bars late into the night.

Parking is both limited and expensive in the area, with the exception of a couple of parking structures immediately below the market on Western Ave. To find them from 1st Ave, turn west (downhill) on Lenora St, turn south (left) on Western Ave. Continue on Western Ave until just past Victor Steinbrueck Park; the parking structures are immediately ahead.

Exploring the Market

Pike Place is made up of several buildings, covering about eight warrenlike blocks at the top of the bluff overlooking the Waterfront. It's easy to get lost here – in fact, experiencing a slight sense of mayhem and dislocation is part of the charm of your initial acquaintance with this leviathan of markets. Don't let the sometimes seedy nature of the neighborhood bother you; the streets around the market are still centers for sex shops and off-putting vagrancy, but there's very little real danger in the area. To help you find your way around, pick up a copy of 'Welcome to the Pike Place Market,' a brochure with a map and directory of market shops. It's available throughout the market and at the information booth (see below).

If you're coming from downtown, simply walk down Pike St toward the Waterfront; you can't miss the huge 'Public Market' sign etched against the horizon. Incidentally, the sign and clock, installed in 1927, constituted one of the first pieces of outdoor neon on the West Coast. From the top of Pike St and 1st Ave, stop and survey the bustle and vitality of the market: Buskers strum and sing, baguettes stick out of shoppers' backpacks, towers of artichokes loom in market stalls and bouquets of flowers bloom in the arms of passersby. Walk down the cobblestone street, past perennially gridlocked cars (don't even think of driving down to Pike Place) and, before walking into the market, stop and shake the bronze snout of Rachel the Market Pig, the de facto mascot and presiding spirit of the market. The life-size piggy bank, carved by Whidbey Island artist Georgia Gerber and named after a real pig, collects about $6000 dollars each year. The funds are pumped back into market social services. Nearby is the **market information booth**, which has maps of the market and information about Seattle in general. It also serves as a Ticket/Ticket booth, selling discount tickets to various shows throughout the city (see 'Ticket Services' in the Entertainment chapter).

The pig marks the main entrance to the **Main and North Arcades**, the thin shedlike structures that run along the edge of the hill and are the busiest of the market buildings. With banks of fresh produce carefully arranged in artful displays, and fresh fish, crab and other shellfish piled high on ice, this is the real heart of the market. Here you'll see fishmongers tossing salmon back and forth as if they were basketballs (many of these vendors will pack fish for overnight delivery). You'll also find cheese shops, butchers, tiny grocery stalls and most everything else needed to put together a meal. The end of the North Arcade is dedicated to local artisans and craftspeople – products must be handmade to be sold here.

Once a stable for merchants' horses, the **Economy Market Building** on the south side of the market entrance has a wonderful Italian grocery store, DeLaurenti's – a great place for an aficionado of Italian foods to browse and sample. There's also Tenzing Momo, one of the oldest apothecaries on the West Coast, where you can pick up herbal remedies, incense, oils and books. Tarot readings are available here on occasion. Look down at the Economy Market floor, and you'll see some of the 46,000 tiles that line the floor. The tiles were sold to the public in the 1980s for $35 apiece. If you bought a tile, you'd get your name on it and be proud that you helped save the market floor. Famous tile buyers include *Cat in the Hat* creator Dr Seuss and former US president Ronald Reagan.

If you continue past DeLaurenti's, you'll come into the **South Arcade**, the market's newest wing, which is home to upscale shops and a lively brewpub, Pike Place Pub & Brewery.

Across Pike Place from the Main Arcade is the **Corner Market Building** and the **Sanitary Market Building**. The latter was so named because it was the first of the market buildings in which live animals were prohibited. It's now a maze of ethnic groceries and great little eateries, including the Three Girls Bakery, with a sit-down area (it's always packed) and a take-out window with some of the best breads and sandwiches around. This is also the home of Sub Pop Mega Mart, the record label that gave birth to grunge rock, and Left Bank Books, an excellent source for all your socialist reading needs. All in a row in the **Triangle Building** are Mr D's Greek Deli, Mee Sum Pastries with great pork buns, a juice bar and Cinnamon Works – all great choices for a quick snack.

Between the Corner Market and the Triangle Building, tiny **Post Alley** is lined with more shops and restaurants. Extending north across Stewart St, Post Alley offers two of the area's best places for a drink: the Pink Door Ristorante, an Italian hideaway, and an Irish pub called Kell's Restaurant & Bar (see the Places to Eat and Entertainment chapters, respectively).

Farther down Pike Place gardeners shouldn't miss **Seattle Garden Center**, originally an egg market. It's now a wonderful nursery offering a huge selection of hard-to-find seeds and bulbs, as well as seasonal plant-starts and unusual houseplants. Pike Place continues past even more shops and stalls, including Sur La Table, a great cookware shop, Starbucks' flagship store and, near the end, Pike & Western Wine Shop, which has an excellent selection of regional wines (see the Shopping chapter).

As if this weren't enough, below the Main Arcade are three labyrinthine lower levels called the **Down Under**. Here, you'll find a fabulously eclectic mix of pocket-size shops, from Indian spice stalls to magicians' supply shops and military button booths.

When you've had enough of the market and its crowds, wander out the end of the North Arcade and cross Western Ave to **Victor Steinbrueck Park**, a grassy area with benches, a couple of totem poles designed by Quinault tribe member Marvin Oliver, a few shuffling vagrants and great views over the Waterfront and Elliott Bay.

Market Tours

To learn about the markets' many nooks and crannies, join one of the very worthwhile market tours. Tour leaders give colorful commentary on the market's history, its quirks, various personalities and shopping tips. Tours meet at the Market Heritage Center (☎ 682-7453), 1531 Western Ave, beneath the market parking garage. May through September, tours leave Wednesday through Saturday at 9 and 10 am and 2 pm; Sunday tours start at noon and at 2 pm. October through April departure times vary, so you'll need to check beforehand. The 1½-hour tours cost $7/5 adults/seniors and children.

Getting There & Away

Pike Place Market is on the western edge of downtown, off 1st Ave. Bus Nos 15, 18, 21, 22 and 56 (see Map 3) run up and down 1st Ave from Pioneer Square. You can also take any bus along 3rd Ave and get off at the University Street Station, then walk west, toward the water. Along the Waterfront Streetcar route, Pike St Station is the stop for Pike Place Market; from there you need

to climb the hill to the market itself. On foot, the market is just minutes from most downtown hotels. Walk down Pike, Pine or Stewart Sts toward the Waterfront and you're there. See 'Getting Up/Down to the Waterfront' for the most scenic and straightforward means of doing so.

THE WATERFRONT (Map 5)

Seattle's beginnings are indelibly tied to its waterfront area, where thousands of Klondike fortune hunters left on ships to Alaska in 1897 to seek gold, many returning with the wealth that served to boom the town into one of the foremost cities along the Pacific Rim (see History in the Facts About Seattle chapter). Seattle's Waterfront is still a busy place, although today tourist facilities far outnumber actual port activities. Most of Seattle's considerable traffic in containers and imports is handled at the port area south of the historic Waterfront.

The Waterfront is relatively cut off from the rest of downtown Seattle. The steep hillsides make access problematic; it can be as much as an eight-story descent down open stairways from 1st Ave to Alaskan Way. Also, when city planners elevated the Alaskan Way viaduct – essentially a freeway – between downtown and the Waterfront, they also created a psychological barrier that's hard to ignore. While it in no way infringes upon getting from one place to the other, it is incredibly noisy and the parking areas under the freeway can be a bit scary at night (see Dangers & Annoyances in the Facts for the Visitor chapter).

Exploring the Waterfront

Visitors can catch the flavor of a major seaport by walking along the Seattle Waterfront; they can also do a lot of eating and souvenir shopping in what is Seattle's tackiest tourist zone. Along the length of the Waterfront – amid the horse-drawn carriages, pedicabs and cotton-candy vendors – are a number of companies that offer harbor tours and boat excursions (see Organized Tours in the Getting Around chapter). Washington State Ferries operates transport to Bainbridge Island and Bremerton

Getting Up/Down to the Waterfront

A hint to those who plan to walk: This is one of the most precipitous parts of Seattle. There's an eight-story drop from Pike Place Market down to the Waterfront. This makes for great views, but it's an exhausting climb or descent for those on foot.

To give your feet a break when walking up from the Waterfront, take the elevator in the parking complex to the top, cross Western Ave and look for the sign with a pointing hand; the elevator to the market level is just below it, and you can take this up to the market. On the return journey, take the well-hidden elevator behind the fish markets in Pike Place to the bottom, then head into the parking structure across Western Ave and take the elevator down four stories to the Waterfront.

If you'd rather walk, you can take the Hillclimb Corridor up many steps from the aquarium at the Waterfront; it exits out the back of the market's Main Arcade. The good news is that the entire trajectory is flanked by shops, eateries and potted greenery. You can also take the Harbor Steps, a landscaped cascade of stairs that sweeps up to below the Seattle Art Museum. In the middle of it all is the rotating *Schubert's Sonata*, a sculpture by Mark di Suvero.

from the piers, while privately owned ferries travel to the San Juan Islands and Victoria, BC. For more information on ferry operators and routes, see the Getting Around and Excursions chapters.

First-time visitors to Seattle will want to make a pilgrimage to the Waterfront, though one trip ought to do it unless you're here to ride the ferries. Most of the piers are now enclosed with endless tourist shops and clam-chowder venues. If you're looking for that 'I ♥ Seattle' T-shirt, a souvenir coffee mug or a mass-produced trinket, then this is your kind of place. The main tourist areas of the Waterfront are between Piers 52 and 59. **Waterfront Park** is the name given to Pier 57; it's just a boardwalk on the pier, but at least you can get out onto the Sound and get a feeling for the area. It's also the best place to tote your corn dogs and fish-and-chips from the adjacent piers and take a seat on a waterside bench. Keep your eyes on your fries, however, as Waterfront seagulls can resemble a pack of hungry bears. Piers 54, 55 and 56 are devoted to **shops and restaurants**, including novelty venues like the 100-year-old Ye Olde Curiosity Shop, a bizarre cross between a museum and a souvenir shop.

During summer months, **outdoor concerts** by nationally known music acts are presented by Summer Nights at the Pier.

Open-air performances are held on Piers 63-64. Call Ticketmaster (☎ 628-0888) for tickets and concert schedule.

For the past few years, the Port of Seattle has been redeveloping much of the Waterfront area to the north of Seattle Aquarium. **Pier 66**, also known as the Bell Street Pier, is home to the Bell Harbor International Conference Center and new Odyssey Maritime Discovery Center (see later). This is also where you'll find Anthony's Pier 66, one of Seattle's best seafood restaurants. This area is a lot less touristy than the main Waterfront, though further expansion will likely change that.

Take a break from the carnival atmosphere of the Waterfront by walking north on Alaskan Way, past Pier 71, to **Myrtle Edwards Park**, a fringe of lawn and trees along Elliott Bay. The path is a favorite of joggers and power-walkers pursuing lunchtime fitness. In warm weather the park, with stupendous views over the Sound to the Olympic Mountains, is a good place for a picnic.

Seattle Aquarium

Probably the most interesting site in the Waterfront area, this well-designed aquarium (☎ 386-4320, 386-4300), 1483 Alaskan Way at Pier 59, offers a view into the underwater world of Puget Sound and the

Pacific Northwest coast. Exhibits include re-creations of ecosystems in Elliott Bay, Puget Sound and the Pacific Ocean, including tide pools, eelgrass beds, coral reefs and the seafloor. The centerpiece of the aquarium is a glass-domed room where sharks, octopi and other deepwater denizens lurk in the shadowy depths. The passages eventually lead outdoors to a salmon ladder and a pool where playful sea otters and northern fur and harbor seals await your attention.

One of the Aquarium's cute inhabitants

The Seattle Aquarium is open 10 am to 7 pm daily Memorial Day to Labor Day; 10 am to 5 pm the rest of the year. Admission costs $8.50 adults, $7.50 seniors and disabled visitors, $5.75 youths ages six to 18, and $3.75 children ages three to five; admission is free for children under three. Combination tickets with the Omnidome theater are available; see below. If you're tired of lugging all your Waterfront purchases around, you can rent a locker at the aquarium for 50¢.

Omnidome Film Experience

This 180° surround-screen theater (☎ 622-1868) is adjacent to the aquarium on Pier 59. Usually four shows are playing daily, though not all at once. The ongoing favorite is *The Eruption of Mt St Helens*, which features a helicopter ride over an exploding volcano (the film received an Academy Award nomination for best short documentary). Most features are 45 minutes long, and the first show begins at 10 am; call for

show times. Tickets cost $7/6.50/6.00 adults/seniors/youths ages six to 18; free for children five and under.

A combination ticket to the aquarium (see above) and the Omnidome Film Experience is available at $13/11.25/9.50/5.50 adults/seniors/youths ages six to 18/children ages three to five.

Odyssey Maritime Discovery Center

This unique museum (☎ 374-4001), 2205 Alaskan Way at Pier 66, is a haven for boat enthusiasts and a wonderful place for families to visit. With four galleries and more than 40 hands-on exhibits, it is interesting and interactive. Exhibits include a simulated kayak trip around Puget Sound, a chance to navigate a virtual ship through Elliott Bay and a visual journey of the cruise up the Inside Passage to southeast Alaska. You can find out about boat construction and high-tech contributions to boating, learn about oceanography and environmental issues and hear audio simulations of ocean animals. A section of the museum is devoted to fishing and another to ocean trade. Anyone with a nose for the nautical should check this place out. It is open 10 am to 5 pm Tuesday to Saturday and noon to 5 pm Sunday. Admission costs $6.50/4 adults/seniors, students and children. Its Web site is at www.ody.org.

Getting There & Away

The Waterfront Streetcar runs along Alaskan Way, the Waterfront's main thoroughfare. These trolleys are especially handy for visiting the Waterfront; they run from the area near Seattle Center (from the base of Broad St), along the Waterfront (including near Pike Place Market) and on to Pioneer Square and the International District. If you're anywhere downtown, it is an easy downhill walk westward to the Waterfront.

BELLTOWN (Map 6)

Belltown is immediately north of Pike Place Market, reaching from Virginia St to Denny Way and from the east side of Elliott Ave to 4th Ave. This is the area long known as the Denny Regrade, for the massive sluicing

THINGS TO SEE & DO

project that reduced Denny Hill to a more convenient flat (see 'The Thrill on Denny Hill'). Long a featureless area of warehouses and low-slung office buildings, this neighborhood was once dismissed by a writer in the 1970s as a 'chronically semi-blighted area,' as indeed it was. However, in ways mysterious to civic planners, seedy, low-rent neighborhoods tend to be spawning grounds for raw musical talent – and thereafter become cool. Much of the explosion of creative ferment that catapulted Seattle to international noteworthiness in the early 1990s took place here: Belltown gave birth to grunge music.

The clubs are still here, but the area has gone seriously upscale, making Belltown one of Seattle's hottest neighborhoods. Many people accuse Belltown of having sold its soul by succumbing to gentrification, but the nature of its soul was never that clear in the first place. While part of the neighborhood still clings to its grungy, punky roots, trying to preserve its once-irregular heartbeat, the other part marches onward, proudly, toward yuppiedom. The things that made Belltown cool – artists, musicians and the grungy edge – are now being smothered by the influx of people who want to be cool, too. This identity crisis is similar to that of a college grad who now makes too much money developing software. Not long ago he was scrounging coins for draft Budweiser and eating Kraft Dinner; now spends oodles on premium cocktails. Only in his morning hangover haze does he look at his credit card bill and remember where he came from. Like the college grad, Belltown still wakes up and remembers where it came from.

Signs of the old-and-new mix are everywhere. Some of the city's finest restaurants mingle with great cheap eateries (see the Places to Eat chapter), the warehouses are converting to lofts, and designer boutiques are now commonplace. Today, you're as likely to see businesspeople in three-piece suits as you are itinerant artists with multiple nose rings.

Getting There & Away

Bus Nos 15, 18, 21, 22 and 56 pass along 1st Ave. Traffic on 2nd Ave is one-way southbound; bus Nos 39 and 42 run along it. Routes on 3rd Ave include Nos 1, 2, 3, 4, 13 and 16, which link Belltown to downtown, Seattle Center and outlying neighborhoods. See the Downtown Metro Transit map

The Thrill on Denny Hill

Denny Hill used to dominate about 60 blocks of portions of today's downtown and Belltown. The steep and inconvenient knoll made carriage transport difficult and wasn't exactly conducive to massive construction; in short, the hill obstructed the city's view of itself as a sprawling metropolis. To solve this geographic conundrum, city engineer Reginald Thomson came up with the brainchild to simply remove the hill, thereby allowing downtown to extend northward. This concept dismayed some early residents but impressed others, who got excited at the sprawling possibility they thought the flatland would present.

The project began in 1899 and continued for over a decade. Landowners had to fund their own regrading, and since many opposed it in the first place, Denny Hill wound up looking like random studs on a dog collar. Streets were built around these lone mounds, called 'spite mounds,' due to the landowners' attempts to spite the city by not complying with the regrading. Eventually, however, landowners were forced to comply, and the hill flattening continued.

Today the leveling would seem a drastic and environmentally bad idea. The project involved pumping almost 20 million gallons of water *every day* out of Lake Union to help sluice the massive amount of dirt into Puget Sound. Besides, it didn't really work. Belltown never became a booming extension of downtown, becoming instead a neglected storage unit for downtown's stuff.

THINGS TO SEE & DO

Exploring Belltown

Most of Belltown's shops and fancy restaurants are along 1st Ave, while 2nd Ave has a string of bars and nightclubs. Activities in Belltown are fairly limited to shopping, eating and drinking. There's little mystery or need for extra guidance as you explore the area, and you can walk the whole thing in an hour.

Start wandering on the corner of 2nd Ave and Blanchard St, where you'll see the famed **Crocodile Cafe** (☎ 441-5611), 2200 2nd Ave, a popular diner and live-music venue where many an up-and-coming band has wooed or rocked the crowd. Even Nirvana played here in 1992, not even two years before Kurt Cobain's suicide (see 'The Life & Death of Grunge Music' in the Entertainment chapter).

Keep going north (away from downtown) and you'll come across the **Lava Lounge**, another groovy nightspot. Across Bell St you'll find the **Seattle Building Salvage** (☎ 448-3453), 202 Bell St, a unique store that collects and sells gems like old fixtures, hinges and knobs that have been salvaged from dilapidated buildings. A little farther down 2nd Ave is the **Speakeasy Café** (☎ 728-9770), 2304 2nd Ave, the best place in town to check your email. Head back a block up Bell St toward 3rd Ave to Regrade Park, where you'll usually find an unfortunate lot sleeping off the day's brown-bag beverage. Take a right on 4th Ave and you'll come to **Sit & Spin** (☎ 441-9484), 2219 4th Ave, one of the world's truly great laundries, where you can do a load, eat a burger, sip a latte and see a live band, all in the same spot.

Walk back down Bell St to 1st Ave, where the restaurants, shops and bars are generally more upscale. One definite exception is the **Frontier Room** (☎ 441-3377), 2203 1st Ave, a no-frills kind of tavern where you swig whiskey and ponder Kenny Rogers' 'The Gambler.' Fashionable stores and restaurants surround it on all sides. Walk along 1st Ave to Vine St, past the bars, bakeries and old-school Seattle restaurants, turn right and come back along 2nd Ave, and you will have completed a fairly thorough tour of Belltown. Now stop somewhere, order a beer and ponder one of Seattle's most seductive neighborhoods.

See the Places to Eat, Entertainment and Shopping chapters for more information on these and other Belltown venues.

(Map 3) at the back of the book to see where to catch your bus. Belltown is an easy walk from downtown hotels and lies just north of Pike Place Market.

SEATTLE CENTER (Map 7)

Seattle Center is bounded by Denny Way and Mercer St, and 1st and 5th Aves N. In the early 1960s, Seattle was confident and ready for company. And the 1962 World's Fair gave the city the perfect opportunity to display its self-assured, high-tech vision of itself and of the future. The fair, which was also known as 'Century 21 Exposition,' was a summer-long exhibition that brought in nearly 10 million visitors from around the world. A 74-acre warehouse area north of downtown was leveled, and a futuristic in-

ternational enclave of exhibition halls, arenas and public spaces sprang up. For today's visitor, the Seattle Center, as we now term the World's Fair grounds, evokes a distinctly 1960s notion of tomorrow's world; it generates more nostalgia for the Jetsons than thoughts of the future.

Probably no other building in Seattle epitomizes the city as well as the Space Needle, the 605-foot-high futuristic observation station and restaurant. The Monorail, a 1½-mile experiment in mass transit, was another signature piece of the 1962 fair. After the event, a number of the exhibition halls were converted to civic buildings, such as the Opera House (home of the Seattle Opera and Pacific Northwest Ballet) and the Bagley White, Intiman and Seattle Children's Theaters. Two sports complexes were also created, including the Key Arena, home of the Seattle Supersonics NBA franchise. Other public buildings include the Pacific Science Center and the Seattle Children's Museum. Various other museums and art spaces are also remnants of the World's Fair; the Fun Forest Amusement Park, near the Monorail stop, is replete with carnival rides.

Recent additions to Seattle Center include the Experience Music Project – the wildly expensive interactive music museum whose unique design is as controversial as it is interesting – a new skateboard park and a public basketball court.

Seattle Center also hosts many of the city's major annual events, including the popular Bumbershoot music festival, the Northwest Folklife Festival and the Seattle International Children's Festival (see Special Events in the Facts for the Visitor chapter). On a nice day, Seattle Center is a pleasant place to wander around, and no matter what season you're here, there's always lots going on.

Helpful Seattle Center Facts
Information booths, a number of fast-food venues, restrooms and other public facilities are in Center House near the Monorail Terminal. Some useful telephone numbers include ☎ 684-7200 for general information, ☎ 684-8582 for a recording of events and attractions and ☎ 233-3989 for parking and transportation information. Also helpful with links to all Seattle Center attractions is its Web site, at www.seattlecenter.com.

Parking can be limited around Seattle Center when more than one large event takes place. The biggest parking lots are on Mercer St, between 3rd and 4th Aves N, and on 5th Ave N between Mercer and Harrison Sts.

No admission is charged to enter the Seattle Center area.

Space Needle
Seattle's signature monument, the Space Needle (☎ 905-2100), 219 4th Ave N, takes advantage of its 520-foot-high observation deck with 360° views of Seattle and surrounding areas to bombard visitors with his-

torical information and interpretive displays. On clear days zip to the top on the elevators (43 seconds) for excellent views of downtown, Lake Union, Mt Rainier and the Olympic Range mountains way across Puget Sound; don't bother spending the cash on cloudy days. If you're coming up to take aerial photos, be forewarned that there's fencing around the observation deck's perimeter, making clear shots impossible. The trip up commands a charge of $11/9/5 adults/seniors/children ages five to 12.

Way back in 1962, the Space Needle surfed the wave of the future with its two revolving restaurants, and you had a choice between pricey and moderate dining. But today there's only one restaurant, Sky City (☎ 905-2100), which is, in line with the stellar views, astronomically expensive. Reservations in the dining room do, however, give you a free ride up the elevator (see the Places to Eat chapter).

Experience Music Project (EMP)
This much-anticipated and ambitious tribute to rock 'n' roll opened in June 2000. The pet project of Microsoft cofounder Paul Allen and his sister Jody Patton, the $450 million EMP (☎ 367-5483), 325 5th Ave N, houses some 80,000 artifacts of music memorabilia. No expense was spared in creating the collection, which features such items as handwritten lyrics by Nirvana's Kurt Cobain, Jimi Hendrix's signed contract to play at Woodstock, Janis Joplin's pink feather boa and the world's first steel guitar. Inspired by Allen's passion for Hendrix's music and initially intended as a tribute to only Hendrix, the project quickly blossomed into the gigantic display of excess you see today.

Likely to become as much a symbol of Seattle as the Space Needle, the exterior of the Frank O Gehry–designed EMP will have you rubbing your eyes and asking to be pinched – is this thing for real? Gehry, most notable for designing the famed Guggenheim Museum in Bilbao, Spain, reportedly went out and bought a bunch of Stratocaster guitars, smashed them up and used the resulting pile of guitar bits to inspire the building's design. More than 3000 panels of stainless steel and painted aluminum shingles cover the exterior in crazy shades of purple, red, blue, silver and gold, and there isn't a right angle in sight. The building has been fervently criticized and called everything from a 'pukish pile of sheet metal' to 'the ugliest building in Seattle.' It definitely

takes getting used to, but Seattleites are slowly coming around. Gehry has also been criticized for wasting space – of the building's 140,000 sq feet, only 35,000 constitute usable exhibit space.

Upon entering the museum, you'll get your own 'virtual companion' dubbed Meg

Paul Allen: Seattle's Co-Owner

On a national scale, Bill Gates' cofounder Paul Allen is the lesser-known Microsofty, but in the Pacific Northwest he is an increasingly dominant figure in professional sports, real estate, politics and music. Allen is the third richest man in the world, with a net worth somewhere in the $28 billion ballpark. Despite a lengthy history of philanthropy, Allen has also become an object of suspicion, at least for people who get in the way of his projects.

In 1982 Allen was diagnosed with Hodgkin's disease and shortly thereafter retired from Microsoft. He remains on the Microsoft board and is the company's second-largest stockholder. The reclusive Allen did not exactly retire from acquisitiveness. Indulging in a taste for professional sports, he bought the NBA Portland Trail Blazers, as well as the NFL Seattle Seahawks. In Portland, Allen managed to convince city leaders to build a new stadium, the Rose Quarter, to house his team.

Allen's role in the building of the Seahawks' new stadium was even more contentious. When the Seahawks' previous owner threatened to move the team out of Seattle, Allen agreed to buy the team, but only if the taxpayers would fund the construction of a new stadium. The legislature was wary of directly addressing the funding issues involved, so a unique solution was proposed: The funding bill would be referred directly to a public vote in a special statewide election paid for entirely by Paul Allen. Initial public opinion polls showed the referendum would easily go down in defeat, until Paul Allen's forces hired a high-profile public relations firm to make their case. In the end, this became the most expensive campaign in Washington State history, with Paul Allen and the pro-stadium contingent eking out a narrow victory at the ballot box. The election also made history as reportedly being the first special election paid for by a private citizen for the purpose of raising public taxes to finance a private moneymaking project.

Not all of Paul Allen's projects have caused such controversy. Allen built a beautiful new library at the University of Washington and is refurbishing Union Station, the old railroad depot. The Experience Music Project, another of Allen's endeavors, commemorates Seattle's role in rock music from Jimi Hendrix to the present; it seems that classic rock, like acquisition, is one of Allen's great passions (see Seattle Center in the Things to See & Do chapter).

Allen's future plans include redeveloping the area immediately south of Lake Union, which will add a new pier, park and $400 million in initial Allen developments. The plans don't stop there. Allen is acquiring so much city land that the public is left asking, 'Hey, who owns this town anyway?'

The inspiration for the EMP, Jimi Hendrix

(Museum Exhibit Guide), a rather clunky handheld computer that you strap over yourself and lug around, using it to access oral histories and exhibit descriptions. Staff train technophobes on how to use it. Though it's supposed to be easy and efficient, Meg is heavy and prone to technical difficulties, so you'll often see people walking around banging into each other because they're too busy fiddling with their Megs. Like many people before you, you'll learn less but might find it more enjoyable if you dump Meg altogether.

The **best exhibits** include the Hendrix Gallery, a major tribute to Jimi, the Northwest Passage, displaying everything from Ray Charles' debut album (recorded in Seattle) to Heart's stage apparel and the evolution of grunge. The Artist's Journey is a virtual roller coaster ride, complete with loud music and seats that roll as if you were on the real thing. Upstairs is the Sound Lab, a futuristic studio that lets you lay down vocal tracks and play guitars, drums and keyboards. The extensive exhibits will keep you – and the crowds – busy for a few hours. There is also a bar and a couple of live-music venues, including Sky Church (see the Entertainment chapter).

Despite the controversial building, the cost to both build and visit it, the technical difficulties and the fact that the museum gives little homage to rock's roots in folk and country music, the EMP is pretty darn cool.

EMP is open 9 am to 11 pm May to September; the rest of the year it's open 10 am to 6 pm daily, to 11 pm on Friday and Saturday. Admission costs $20/16 adults/seniors and students, and allows you in-and-out privileges for the day you go.

International Fountain

This is the place to be on sunny days. With 287 jets of water pumping in time to a computer-driven music system, the International Fountain at the heart of Seattle Center is a great place to rest your feet or eat lunch on sunny days. On summer nights, the computer kicks in with a free lighting-and-music show. Call ☎ 684-7200 for show times.

CityPass

If you're going to be in Seattle for a while and plan on seeing its premiere attractions, you might want to consider buying a CityPass. Good for nine days, the pass gets you entry into the Space Needle, Pacific Science Center, Seattle Art Museum, Seattle Aquarium, the Museum of Flight and the Woodland Park Zoo. You wind up saving 50% of admission costs and you never have to stand in line. A CityPass costs $28/24.25/16.50 for adults/seniors/children (ages 6-13). Buy one at whichever of the six venues you visit first.

Pacific Science Center

This interactive museum of science and industry (☎ 443-2001), 200 2nd Ave N, once housed the science pavilion of the World's Fair. Today, the center features virtual-reality exhibits, a tropical butterfly house, laser shows, holograms and other wonders of science, many with hands-on demonstrations. Also on the premises is the vaulted-screen **IMAX Theater** (☎ 443-4629), a laserium and a planetarium.

The Pacific Science Center is open 10 am to 5 pm weekdays, 10 am to 6 pm weekends. Admission to the exhibit space costs $8/5.50 adults/seniors and children ages six to 13; $4 for children ages two to five. Admission to the IMAX Theater and Laserium is $3 on top of the general admission or $6.75 for a theater-only ticket (all ages).

Children's Museum & Theatre

In the basement of Center House near the Monorail stop, the Children's Museum (☎ 441-1768) is a learning center that offers a number of imaginative activities and displays, many focusing on cross-cultural awareness and hands-on art sessions. The play area includes a child-size neighborhood, a play center and an area dedicated to blowing soap bubbles. The museum is open 10 am to 5 pm Tuesday to Sunday. During summer break, the museum also opens

10 am to 5 pm Monday and until 6 pm weekends in addition to normal hours. Admission costs $5/3 adults/children; infants under one year get in free.

Also in Seattle Center is the Seattle Children's Theatre (☎ 441-3322), a separate entity with summer performances in the Charlotte Martin and Eve Alvord Theaters.

Getting There & Away

Seattle Center is linked to downtown by a number of bus routes, including bus Nos 1, 2, 3, 4, 8, 13, 15, 16, 18, 19, 24, 33, 81 and 82; see the Downtown Metro Transit map (Map 3) at the back of the book to see where to catch your bus. Note that Seattle Center is outside the downtown Ride Free Area. Of course, the most entertaining way to get back and forth to Seattle Center is by the Monorail, which provides frequent transport between downtown's Westlake Center, at Pine St and 4th Ave, and Seattle Center; cars run about every 10 minutes (see the Getting Around chapter).

It's about a 10-minute walk from Seattle Center to the Waterfront Streetcar terminus at Broad St and Alaskan Way.

QUEEN ANNE (Map 7)

Rising above Seattle Center is Queen Anne – an old neighborhood of majestic redbrick houses and apartment buildings, sweeping lawns manicured to perfection and gorgeous views of the city and Elliott Bay. It has some of the most prestigious addresses in Seattle.

Queen Anne Hill was one of the original seven hills of Seattle. At 456 feet, it's also the steepest and highest, rising precipitously above Elliott Bay and Lake Union. Named for the prominent Queen Anne–style houses first built on the neighborhood's lower slopes, Queen Anne attracted affluent folks looking for views of the city. But unlike the First Hill neighborhood, whose residents dripped with money when they got here, Queen Anne was open to new wealth, too. As such, when walking around Queen Anne, you'll see a mix of architectural styles, reflecting the varying tastes and incomes of the neighborhood's first residents.

The Queen Anne neighborhood has two distinct sides. The funky Lower Queen Anne (or more interestingly, the Bottom of Queen Anne) flanks Seattle Center to the west and butts up against Belltown on the other side of Denny Way. Upper Queen Anne, on top of the hill, has excellent views of the city and some great restaurants. Between Upper and Lower Queen Anne runs Queen Anne Ave N, a very steep 18%-grade hill that'll give even avid hikers a workout. In the old days, trolley companies had to use counterbalances to pull the trolley cars up the hill.

Lower Queen Anne

Located at the bottom of Queen Anne Ave N, this part of Queen Anne has a pleasant, old-fashioned and lived-in quality despite its busy urban locale. The old redbrick apartment buildings house a generally youthful population that spends its time on Queen Anne Ave N between Mercer and W Harrison Sts. Favorite hangouts include the Uptown Espresso Bar (☎ 281-8669) and venerable old haunts like Sorry Charlies (☎ 283-3245), a sing-along piano bar that's too authentic to be kitsch. Larry's Market is also a big draw, providing enough gourmet ingredients to impress Martha Stewart. Also popular is the art deco Uptown Cinemas, an old theater converted into a movie triplex. Nearby, the Behnke Center for Contemporary Performance features excellent live theater. Because of their proximity to Seattle Center, bars and restaurants in Lower Queen Anne get quite a workout before and after home games at Key Arena or when there's a performance at the Opera House. (See the Places to Eat, Entertainment and Shopping chapters for more on the area.)

Upper Queen Anne

Way up on the hilltop, the neighborhood of Upper Queen Anne is much more establishment and old-money than Lower Queen Anne. Public ordinances decree that no one sit or lie down on public sidewalks, so if you're thinking about taking a load off, make sure there's a bench between you and

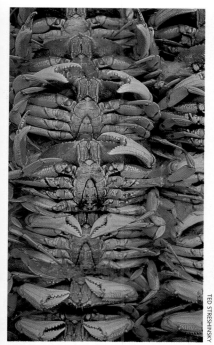

Welcome to seafood heaven, Pike Place Market

RICHARD CUMMINS

RICHARD I'ANSON

DEBRA MILLER

Signs around Pike Place Market

Rooms at Belltown's artsy Ace Hotel come complete with condoms.

The Fremont Troll chows down on a VW Beetle.

Kurt Cobain's former house from Viretta Park

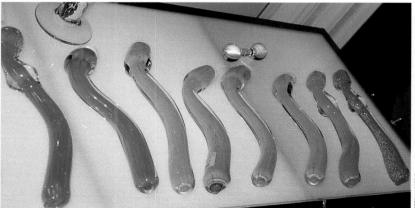

Looking for one careful owner – glass dildos at Toys in Babeland, Capitol Hill

Too much caffeine, Lake Washington

Washington Park Arboretum

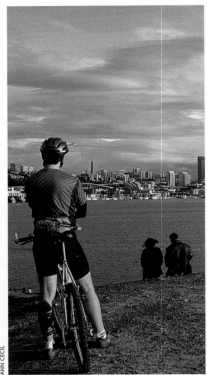
Pondering the city from Gas Works Park

With them in spirit – bench practice, Green Lake Park

the curb. Laws like this, combined with Upper Queen Anne's position as something of a destination neighborhood (you don't just stumble upon it), make the absence of panhandlers obvious.

Though it may sound like a snooty place, the shops and restaurants are patrician without seeming too pretentious. The main commercial strip is on Queen Anne Ave N between W Galer and W McGraw Sts. The Thriftway Market at Queen Anne Ave N and W Howe St is a popular neighborhood hangout. Forget about the bar scene; apparently the Thriftway is the best place in Queen Anne for young, professional singles to meet. Upper Queen Anne is quite a restaurant hub, especially for upscale ethnic food.

Other than to eat, the main reason to visit Upper Queen Anne is to check out the old mansions and spectacular views. For both views and architecture, take W Highland Drive, one of Seattle's most prestigious streets. You'll find it about halfway up Queen Anne Hill on the west side. Almost every tourist comes to get postcard-perfect photos of the Seattle skyline and the Space Needle from **Kerry Park**, near 3rd Ave W. It's one of the three best views in town; the other two are from Gas Works Park near Wallingford (Map 10) and Duwamish Head in West Seattle (Map 1). It's a magical vista, especially at night or sunset. A little farther along W Highland Dr will take you to the lesser-known **Betty Bowen Park**, an excellent spot for views across Puget Sound to the Olympic Mountains. Across the way, check out Parsons Garden, a public garden that's especially popular for summer weddings.

Bigelow Ave N, on the east side of Queen Anne Hill, offers more views and period architecture; Bigelow Ave and Highland Drive constitute part of 'the Boulevard,' a scenic ring of tree-lined streets that loops around the crest of Queen Anne Hill.

Getting There & Away
Bus Nos 2, 13 and 45 go up Queen Anne Ave N, passing the vista points on W Highland Drive. Though they take a more circuitous route, bus Nos 1, 3 and 4 also go up to Queen Anne; bus No 1 travels on the

Queen Anne Counterbalance

When logging inevitably began on Queen Anne Hill's thickly forested slopes in the late 1800s, the lure to build mansions on top of it soon followed. Who could resist the incredible views of the growing downtown with Mt Ranier perfectly situated behind it? Well, not many, so the question of how to get people up and down the hill soon followed. The tricky part was how to give a streetcar enough gumption to climb the hill, while giving it enough resistance to keep it from careening back down.

The solution, one that kept the streetcar running at 8mph for almost 40 years, was to attach an arm that reached from the streetcar to a flat railcar running on separate tracks beneath the road. You could see the slotted cable that propelled and slowed the railcar between the streetcar tracks. The railcars acted as counterweights; as the streetcars moved up the hill, the railcars moved down.

In 1940, the streetcars were retired and replaced by electric buses. The tunnels beneath the street, however, remain, and though hollow, empty and mostly forgotten, they preserve an integral part of Queen Anne's history.

west side of the hill along 10th Ave W, while Nos 3 and 4 go up Taylor Ave N on the east side. See the Downtown Metro Transit map (Map 3) at the back of the book to see where to catch your bus. If you're driving from downtown, travel north on 1st Ave, which turns into Queen Anne Ave N.

LAKE UNION (Map 7)
Even though Lake Union is known for having the largest houseboat population in the USA, it isn't really a neighborhood. The Y-shaped lake's waters lap against the shores of many traditional neighborhoods including Fremont, southern Wallingford, Eastlake and the eastern slopes of Queen Anne. What ties this area together is the number of restaurants, lodgings and recreational

facilities clustered around the lake. Lake Union is also a transport hub for flights by seaplane to the San Juan Islands or Victoria, BC (see the Excursions chapter).

If you're interested in the history and craft of wooden boats, then the **Center for Wooden Boats** (☎ 382-2628), 1010 Valley St, is for you. This museum and enthusiast's center features vintage and replica boats and offers sailing lessons and classes on subjects like sail repair and boat building. You can also rent sailboats and rowboats here. For information on boat and kayak rentals, see the Activities chapter.

Getting There & Away
The main arterials for access to Lake Union are Westlake and Eastlake Aves, which – unsurprisingly – follow the west and east shores of the lake. Westlake Ave N begins downtown near the intersection of Stewart St and 6th Ave; Eastlake Ave E is the continuation of Fairview Ave N, from Denny Way. Bus routes serving Westlake Ave are Nos 17, 26 and 28. Bus Nos 70, 71, 72 and 73 serve Eastlake Ave.

CAPITOL HILL (Map 8)
Northeast of downtown Seattle, Capitol Hill is probably Seattle's most diverse and lively neighborhood, owing to its distinct dual – some might say schizophrenic – personality. Long a counterculture oasis, there are probably more nose rings, tattoos and poetry readings on Capitol Hill's Broadway than anywhere else in the Pacific Northwest. Both trendy young students and urban homeless street kids share the sidewalks and café tables, although most people probably couldn't immediately spot the difference. East of Broadway, on 15th Ave E, you'll find a more subdued commercial area that serves some of the city's wealthiest residents, who live in the grand old mansions that line the treed streets. Add to these demographics Capitol Hill's thriving gay and lesbian community, and you have a very lively and colorful mix of residents.

When Capitol Hill was still thick forest, Seattle pioneer Arthur Denny claimed land here in the hopes that the area would be-come the Washington state capital. Though that hope was never realized (that honor went to Olympia, south of Seattle), Henry Yesler had already set to work logging the area, and soon people were building elaborate mansions on the slope that overlooks the east side of Lake Union. A streetcar route was installed up Broadway from Yesler Way to City Park, later renamed Volunteer Park (see below), and the area grew quickly. Some fantastic vestiges of the early architecture are well worth exploring.

Capitol Hill boasts three major commercial areas, each of which attracts a different kind of crowd. The main commercial street is Broadway. It is lined with coffeehouses, inexpensive restaurants, bars, trendy boutiques, bookstores and well-concealed supermarkets. This is where the crowds are thickest and the vitality most engaging. Running perpendicular to Broadway is the so-called Pike/Pine Corridor. With most of the city's gay and lesbian bars, dance and live-music clubs, all-night coffeehouses, an increasing number of restaurants and more than a few tattoo and piercing salons, this is nightlife central for Seattle. East of Broadway, the quieter business district along 15th Ave E has health-food stores, bookstores and ethnic restaurants.

Broadway
You get a hint that this isn't Kansas anymore when the brass inlaid dance steps along Broadway propel you into a rumba or a waltz. Actually, the dance-step diagrams set in the pavement are *The Broadway Dance Steps* public art, designed by Jack Mackie, and if you decide to attempt a tango on a street corner, you assuredly won't be the most unusual sight on Broadway.

In fact, a sense of spectacle is what Broadway is all about; people don't visit here for the food or the shopping (though you can indulge in both quite happily), it's the scene you come here for. You'll see any and every color of hair, semiclothed bodies with all manner of tattooing and piercing, men in both business suits and dresses, gray-haired widows carrying bags of groceries and homeless people walking their dogs.

Body Art & Accessories

The practices of tattooing and body piercing exploded in popularity nationwide in the late 1980s, and Seattle is still one of the leaders in this trend. If you feel inclined to join in or add to your collection of body embellishments, there are plenty of places throughout the city that would be happy to oblige you.

Before you go under the needles, however, you should check out the establishment carefully. Make sure it is licensed, that all equipment is autoclaved and that the general environment of the shop is clean. Though you never want to make hasty decisions when it comes to tattoos, you should know that most reputable parlors won't tattoo if you're drunk. Think about your preferred design and research the artists and their work. Don't be shy about consulting with an artist; if you aren't satisfied or don't like the vibe, go somewhere else. Finally, if you're wondering about tattoo removal, you shouldn't get one in the first place; the technology of tattoo removal is expensive, painful and not very effective.

Most tattoo prices vary according to the color, location and difficulty of the design, though for most of the following businesses, rates average about $100 to $120 an hour, with a minimum cost of $35 to $50. Piercings generally run $30 per hole for things like eyebrows and cheeks, and you'll need to choose jewelry, which typically runs $15 and up. The more intimate the body part, the more you're going to pay (possibly in more ways than one!).

Most shops are in Capitol Hill, Pike Place Market and the U District. The following list includes those with the best reputation among young Seattle hipsters.

Mind's Eye Tattoo At this U District shop (☎ 522-7954), 5206 University Way NE, co-owner Reverend Eric Eye performs a variety of services, such as weddings, baptisms and funerals – and tattoos. Open since 1992, this was the first tattoo shop in the U District and remains the most reputable. They do not do piercings. Mind's Eye is open 1 to 9 pm Monday to Saturday, and noon to 6 pm Sunday.

Anchor Tattoo This immaculately clean operation has two stores, one in Ballard (☎ 784-4051), 5317 Ballard Ave NW, and one in the U District (☎ 524-6466), 5006 University Way NE. They'll do a variety of tattoos but no piercings. Both stores are open noon to 8 pm daily; on Friday and Saturday, the Ballard location is open until 10 pm.

Pink Zone This shop (☎ 325-0050), 211 Broadway E in the heart of Capitol Hill, sells 'visible queer gear' in addition to performing body piercings. The friendly staff prides itself on cleanliness and attracts a diverse (but generally young) clientele. The store is open noon to 10 pm weekdays, noon to 9 pm Saturday and noon to 7 pm Sunday. For piercings, it's best to call for an appointment.

Rudy's Barber Shop Wildly popular with gay men and hip others for both piercings and tattoos, Rudy's (☎ 329-3008), 614 E Pine St on the Pike/Pine Corridor on Capitol Hill, is open 9 am to 9 pm Monday to Saturday and 11 am to 5 pm Sunday.

Superstar This groovy tattoo joint (☎ 324-6443), 1017 E Pike St, in the Pike/Pine Corridor on Capitol Hill, does piercings and tattoos. It's open noon to 6 pm daily.

Vyvyn Lazonga One of the foremost modern female tattoo artists, Vyvyn Lazonga has earned nationwide recognition. Her store (☎ 622-1535), 1516 Western Ave, in Pike Place Market, is open 11 am to 7 pm daily, but you must call ahead to book a tattoo appointment.

While the chances are good that you'll get panhandled by street kids or get an eyeful of pierced nipples, there's nothing particularly threatening about this in-your-face pageant. The slackers along Broadway manage to seem youthful and slightly menacing while never actually losing their decorum. It's all just part of the spectacle.

To find the center of street life on Capitol Hill, head to the junction of E Broadway and E John St (the continuation of Olive Way from downtown). The Broadway commercial strip extends to the north to E Roy St; just to the south is Seattle Central Community College. The best way to enjoy Broadway is to buy a cup of coffee, lounge along the street, poke around in the shops and watch the crowds.

Between E Harrison and E Republican Sts is Broadway Market, with two stories of shops, eateries and a cinema featuring more artsy flicks. Broadway Market used to be a farmers market before Fred Meyers remodeled the space and artfully tucked a supermarket behind it. Public restrooms are upstairs, along with a Ticket/Ticket booth, where you can buy discount tickets to live shows. Across the street, Dilettante Chocolates, decked in pink and umbrellas, is well known for confection truffles and 'adult' milkshakes. All along Broadway are good, inexpensive ethnic restaurants, many of which cater to a student or traveler's budget.

Broadway's commercial activity ends at E Roy St. Take a left on Roy and you'll see the Harvard Exit, an old brick movie theater. Across the street is the south campus of the ornamental Cornish College of the Arts. Built in 1921, the college survived many bouts of debt and is now a top-notch school for music, art, dance and drama. Continue north on Broadway – as the chaos turns to well-maintained houses with manicured lawns – until it turns into 10th Ave E, and you'll be within a block of Volunteer Park (see below). Near the corner of 10th Ave E and Galer St is **St Mark's Cathedral** (☎ 720-0217), 1245 10th Ave E, where a choir performs Gregorian chants at 9:30 pm Sunday. The performance is free and open to the public.

Pike/Pine Corridor

A stretch of aging brick warehouses and former 1950s car dealerships, the 'Corridor' doesn't look like much in the daylight. But after dark the area, roughly between Minor Ave and 16th Ave along E Pike and E Pine Sts, becomes Party Central (see the Entertainment chapter). While this is predominantly a gay- and lesbian-oriented area, it's not as categorically gay as San Francisco's Castro, and being straight here won't make you feel unwelcome.

There seem to be a few bars on every block, but there's more to do here than just drink and dance. For every after-hours bar, there's a late-night coffeehouse, many of which feature live music, poetry readings or pool tables. Here and there are antique stores and more unusual shops, including Toys in Babeland and Beyond the Closet Bookstore, with a good collection of gay, lesbian and transgender books (see the Shopping chapter). This area is also the center of the city's tattoo culture – what better way to capture the Seattle experience than to buy a double espresso and head into a body piercing salon?

Anchoring each end of the Pike/Pine Corridor are two of Seattle's best brewpubs: the Six Arms Pub & Brewery at E Pike St at Melrose Ave, and the Elysian Brewing Co at E Pike St at 13th Ave (see the Entertainment chapter).

15th Avenue East

The center of activity on 15th Ave E is the stretch between E Thomas and E Mercer Sts, with its center at E Republican St. The sense of urban disenfranchisement isn't nearly as strong here as on Broadway, and the crowds aren't as thick. Instead, with an organic grocery store and a couple of mellow bars as its anchors, 15th Ave E feels like an ex-hippie enclave and a real community. One of Seattle's favorite places for breakfast and brunch, Coastal Kitchen, is here (see the Places to Eat chapter). Hopscotch, an interesting bar and restaurant on 15th St between E Harrison and E Thomas Sts, features 60 different types of single-malt Scotch.

Volunteer Park

This stately 140-acre park above downtown Seattle on Capitol Hill began as pioneer Seattle's cemetery. However, as Seattle grew and the need for water became more pressing (particularly after the Great Fire of 1889), Volunteer Park, with its water tower and reservoir, was created. Originally called City Park, it was renamed in 1901 to honor volunteers in the Spanish-American War (1898-1902).

Roads and paths wind around the park, with green meadowlike lawns descending to the mansion-rich neighborhoods that flank the area. Because the park has existed in one form or another since 1876, the trees and landscaping here reflect a kind of maximum growth of the Seattle urban ecosystem. Keen seekers of views can climb the 107 steep steps to the top of the 75-foot **water tower** at 1400 E Prospect. Built in 1907, the tower provides wonderful vistas over the Space Needle and Elliott Bay.

For almost 60 years the Seattle Art Museum occupied a prestigious space in Volunteer Park. When it moved downtown in the early 1990s, the **Seattle Asian Art Museum** (☎ 654-3100) moved in. The museum now houses the extensive Asian art collection of Dr Richard Fuller, who donated this severe art moderne–style gallery to the city in 1932. The collection ranks among the top 10 Asian art collections outside Asia. Be sure to pick up a headset for the audio tour of the museum. Hours are 10 am to 5 pm Tuesday to Sunday; till 9 pm Thursday. Admission costs $3 for adults and is free to children under 12. Hang on to your ticket; it's good for $3 off admission to the Seattle Art Museum, if used within a week.

The park is also home to the **Volunteer Park Conservatory** (☎ 684-4743), 1400 E Galer St, a classic Victorian greenhouse built in 1912. Filled with palms, cacti and tropical plants, the conservatory features five galleries that represent different world environments. Its hours are 10 am to 7 pm daily in summer and 10 am to 4 pm the rest of the year. Admission is free.

One of Seattle's oldest cemeteries and the final resting place of many early settlers, **Lakeview Cemetery** borders Volunteer Park to the north. Arthur Denny and his family, Doc and Catherine Maynard, Thomas Mercer and Henry Yesler are all interred here. This is also the gravesite of Princess Angeline, the daughter of Duwamish Chief Sealth after whom Seattle was named. However, most people stop by to see the gravesite of martial arts film legends Bruce and Brandon Lee. Flowers from fans are usually scattered around Brandon's red and Bruce's black tombstones, which stand side by side in a tiny part of the cemetery. They're not so easy to find: Enter the cemetery at 15th Ave E and E Garfield St; follow the road in and turn left at the Terrace Hill Mausoleum. At the crest of the hill you'll see the large Denny family plot on your left. Look a little farther along the road, and you'll find the Lees. If you're not usually into graveyards, you'll at least enjoy the beautiful views.

Outside the Volunteer Park boundaries, at 15th Ave E at Garfield St, the **Louisa Boren Lookout** provides one of the best views over the university and Union Bay. The small park is named for the longest-surviving member of the party that founded Seattle in 1851.

Getting There & Away

Take bus Nos 7, 10 or 43 from Pike St downtown to get to Broadway E; the No 7 turns north and follows Broadway E, while the No 10 goes on to 15th Ave E and then turns north to follow that street. Bus No 43 continues on to the university via 24th Ave E.

If you're driving, the best streets up Capitol Hill from downtown are E Madison St, E Pike St or Olive Way. Be warned that parking is often difficult along Broadway, and many narrow side streets are zoned for residential parking only. The best bet is to park in the pay lot behind the Broadway Market (under the well-camouflaged Fred Meyer store) one block west of Broadway on Harvard Ave E. To reach Volunteer Park from 15th Ave E, travel north to E Galer St and turn west.

Graveyard Hopping

Most of Seattle's early pioneers were in their 20s when they arrived on Alki Point. These were visionaries and probably the last thing on their minds was where, when needed, they would bury their dead. It took a while for this problem to be laid to rest.

Seattle's first cemetery, on land near 2nd Ave and Stewart St in Belltown, was a casually operated affair where such nuisances as keeping records of burial plats were simply bypassed. However, when the body count reached 20, people began to worry a little. In 1860, the city asked Arthur Denny to donate the spot as an official cemetery, but Denny refused, saying he didn't want a bunch of corpses in the middle of Seattle's growing business district – that didn't quite fit with his vision. David Denny resolved the matter in 1884 by setting aside 5 acres for the official Seattle Cemetery, the spot that is now Denny Park. The bodies were dug up and moved to the new cemetery (well, most of them – workers later found two unidentified skulls had been left behind).

The better-organized Seattle Cemetery was divvied up into individual plots that sold for $10 apiece. Deaths were recorded, and careful markers on each grave kept track of who was where. People with no family or money were buried in the 'Potter's Field.' In 1882, however, a

small fire blew through and burned all the wooden markers. By then, the city had grown even more, and planners decided they didn't want a cemetery here either. Instead, they commissioned Denny Park as the first city park. But what about the dead people? A gravedigger was hired to dig up the bodies once again. However, because of the burnt markers and confusing records, a male corpse would turn up in a plot thought to be occupied by a woman, identities got mixed up, and no one knew what to do with the Potter's Field bodies. In all, 223 corpses were moved up to Capitol Hill. When that spot also turned into a park called City Park, today Volunteer Park, the bodies were moved *again,* this time to Lakeview Cemetery at the north end of Volunteer Park, where they finally got a chance to rest in peace.

THE U DISTRICT (Map 9)

The University of Washington (UW) campus sits at the edge of a busy commercial area known as the U District. The main streets here are University Way, also known as 'the Ave,' and NE 45th St. On these busy streets are innumerable cheap restaurants and cafés, student-oriented bars, second-hand clothing shops, cinemas and bookstores.

To get a sense of student life here, stroll through the lovely UW campus or wander up the Ave, grab a coffee and people watch.

Even though the campus is miles from downtown, the Ave is bustlingly urban. Down-and-outs mingle with students, giving the street a somewhat gritty feel.

The number of cheap places to eat, especially Indian and Asian, make the Ave the best place to find an inexpensive meal. Coffeehouses grow like weeds in this area, and owners are used to students buying one coffee and sitting around for three hours. The absolutely cavernous University Bookstore (☎ 634-3400), 4326 University Way

NE, takes up an entire city block. It has an excellent selection of general books and more scholarly tomes, along with a giant section of yellow and purple Huskies clothing. Also along the Ave is Wizards of the Coast, a popular high-tech game center with the latest video action and virtual-reality machines.

At the Ave and NE 50th St, the Grand Illusion Cinema, an excellent though tiny theater, shows foreign and art films. The coffee shop next door is a popular place to have a latte and settle into a novel.

Along NE 45th St east of the Ave are some of UW's sorority and frat houses. At 25th Ave NE you'll find the University Village, an upscale mall geared more toward the parents of the UW students than the students themselves.

University of Washington

Established in 1861, the University of Washington was first built downtown on the site of the present Four Seasons Olympic Hotel. There were originally 37 students, overseen by university president and carpenter Asa 'Here Come the Brides' Mercer (who in the 1860s masterminded the scheme to bring marriageable women to Seattle from the eastern USA).

The university moved to its present location along Lake Washington's Union Bay in 1895. Much of the 639-acre site constituted the grounds of the 1909 Alaska-Yukon-Pacific Exposition. Dozens of new buildings were constructed for this world's fair–like gathering and remained to landscape the campus.

Today, the university is the largest in the Northwest, with around 35,000 students, 211 buildings and 4000 faculty members. Noted programs include law and medicine; it's also highly regarded for computer science and liberal arts. 'U Dub,' as most people refer to the university, is also notable in that over half of its students are in graduate programs. The university publishes its own daily paper, aptly named *The Daily*. In it, you'll find out about whatever's causing the current campus angst, details about campus events and U-District classifieds.

The university is a lovely, lively place; it is definitely worth touring the campus, especially in spring when bulbs and azaleas paint the verdant campus with brilliant colors. Maps are available from the **Visitors Information Center** (☎ 543-9198) at 4014 University Way. The center also offers free 90-minute campus tours that start at its offices at 10:30 am weekdays.

The center of the campus is called **Central Plaza**, although everyone refers to it as 'Red Square' due to its base of red brick. To the east is **Suzzallo Library**, a fanciful Gothic Revival cathedral of books. Beyond the library is **The Quad**, an area that contains many of the original campus buildings. When the ivy turns red in the autumn, the effect is much more reminiscent of New England than the Northwest.

Just below Red Square is a wide promenade leading to lovely **Rainier Vista**, with spectacular views across Lake Washington to Mt Rainier. South of the vista is **Drumheller Fountain**, also known as 'Frosh Pond.' These two sites make up the principal remaining legacy of the 1909 exposition.

The collective name given to all the U Dub sports teams is the Huskies. They compete in 25 intercollegiate sports, most notably basketball and football, mostly playing at Husky Stadium and the Edmundson Pavilion, both on the east side of campus. To find out about athletic events and tickets, call ☎ 543-2200. The university's main arts venue is the 1200-seat Meany Hall. Live dance, theater and musical performances also take place at U Dub's other three theaters – The Penthouse, The Playhouse and The Studio. For information and tickets, call or stop by the UW Arts Ticket Office (☎ 543-4880), on the corner of University Way NE and NE 40th St, near the visitors center.

Burke Museum This museum of natural history and anthropology (☎ 543-5590) is on the UW campus near the junction of 16th Ave NE and NE 45th St. There's a good collection of dinosaur skeletons, but the real treasures here are the North Coast Indian artifacts, especially the collection of cedar canoes and totem poles. On the ground level of the museum is the pleasant Museum Cafe (☎ 543-9854).

The Burke Museum of Natural History & Culture is open 10 am to 5 pm daily; until 8 pm Thursday. Admission costs $5.50/4/2.50 adults/seniors/students and children.

Henry Art Gallery The university's newly expanded and renovated fine-art gallery, the Henry Art Gallery (☎ 543-2280), on campus near the corners of 15th Ave NE and NE 41st St, mounts some of the most intelligent exhibits and installations in Seattle. The focus is on 20th-century art and artists; there's a small permanent collection, but the changing shows – the Henry mounts 35 a year – are usually noteworthy. The gallery also has a café. The museum is open 11 am to 5 pm Tuesday to Sunday; 8 pm on Thursday. Admission costs $5/3.50 adults/seniors; UW students and all other college students with valid ID get in free. The Burke-Henry Dollar Deal lets you add $1 to the admission price at the Henry and is good for same-day admission to the Burke Museum.

Getting There & Away

Buses converge on the university from throughout the city. Nos 71, 72 and 73 offer the most direct routes to the university from the downtown bus tunnel. If you're driving, take I-5 north to the 45th St exit and travel east. A great way to explore campus is on a bicycle. The Burke-Gilman Trail follows the south side of campus, providing an excellent arterial for getting to and from the university.

WALLINGFORD (Map 10)

Wallingford has blossomed from an old working-class neighborhood into a pleasant district of interesting shops, bookstores and inexpensive eateries, all just across the I-5 freeway from the University of Washington. The neighborhood's west-east extent is from Stone Way N to roughly I-5, and you can walk its entire commercial district along N 45th St in less than an hour. The best thing about Wallingford is that it's not built

upon a gimmick or tourist draw. This is as real as a neighborhood gets; unlike other nearby communities, it's not so distant from its roots that it's become a parody of a real neighborhood. The people that hang out here live here; you can still find an old-fashioned hardware store and a locals' pub among the espresso shops.

Wallingford Center, a boutique and restaurant mall in the old Wallingford grade school at Wallingford Ave N at N 45th St, is the hub of the area. Out front, the *Wallingford Animal Storm Sculpture,* created by artist Ronald Petty, depicts wildlife found in and around the neighborhood.

Some excellent ethnic restaurants line N 45th St, along with some cool shops you don't want to miss. Be prepared to blush when you stop in at the Erotic Bakery (☎ 545-6969), 2323 N 45th St, where phallus-shaped desserts are made to order. Teahouse Kuan Yin is a great stop for a pot of exotic tea (see Wallingford in the Places to Eat chapter). Seattle's best travel bookstore is Wide World Books (☎ 634-3453), 4411 Wallingford Ave N. Another bookstore worth noting is Open Books (☎ 633-0811), 2414 N 45th St, devoted entirely to poetry; call to ask about readings and events. If you're not up for shopping, the Guild 45th St Theater (☎ 633-3353), 2215 N 45th St, shows mainstream and artsy flicks.

Gas Works Park

Urban reclamation has no greater monument in Seattle than Gas Works Park. On a grassy point on the north end of Lake Union, the former power station here produced gas for heating and lighting from 1906 to 1956. The gas works was thereafter understandably considered an eyesore and an environmental menace. However, the beautiful location of the park – with stellar views of downtown over Lake Union, while sailboats and yachts slide to and from the shipping canal – induced the city government to convert the former industrial site into a public park in 1975.

Rather than tear down the factory, however, landscape architects preserved much of the old plant. Painted black and

The alternatively aesthetic Gas Works Park

now highlighted with rather joyful graffiti, it looks like some odd remnant from a former civilization. A major drawback of this ode to industrial art is that the soil and groundwater beneath the park contain chemical contamination. Though this apparently poses no health risks to humans, state government and environmental agencies occasionally close the park to complete various cleanup and research projects. During the latest closure, from November 2000 to June 2001, a new soil cover and irrigation system was installed to avoid further contamination of Lake Union.

Despite all this contamination, Gas Works Park is still one of Seattle's best loved parks; people come here to fly kites, picnic near the lake and simply take in the view. And it *is* like nothing else you've ever seen. Be sure to climb the small hill to see the clever sundial at the top. This is one of the best places from which to photograph Seattle's skyline, especially at sunset, when you can see the sun glistening in the windows of downtown buildings.

Before the trail was extended to Fremont and Ballard, the Burke-Gilman Trail started in Gas Works Park. This is still a great spot to pick up the trail, which you can follow east to the University of Washington. See 'Burke & Gilman's Railway' in the Activities chapter.

Getting There & Away

Bus Nos 16 and 26 go to Wallingford from downtown 3rd and 4th Aves respectively; bus No 44 travels along N 45th St to and from the university. Gas Works Park is at the southern end of Meridian Ave at N Northlake Way. Take bus No 26 from downtown.

To reach Wallingford by car from downtown, take I-5 north; exit at 45th St and turn west. Alternately, take Aurora Ave N (Hwy 99), get off at the Stone Way exit and follow it east to N 45th St.

FREMONT (Map 10)

Probably the most fun-loving of the northern neighborhoods, Fremont is known for its unorthodox public sculpture, junk stores, summer outdoor film festivals and general high spirits. In the evenings, the pubs, restaurants and coffeehouses fill with a lively mix of old hippies, young professionals and gregarious students. Except for the odd glitch, chain stores stay away from Fremont. If there's any rule of thumb to the growth of the retail center here, it's this: 'I have this weird idea for a store/restaurant/coffeehouse/bar....' Unlike the flashy, urban disenfranchisement that gives Capitol Hill its spirit, life in Fremont is conducted with more humor and a sense of community well-being. Fremont's motto *'De Libertas Quirkas'* gives it the 'Freedom to be Peculiar,' and its residents happily live up to that proclamation.

Named by its first claim-holders after Fremont, Nebraska, the area was logged off by oxen in the late 1890s. Once a working-class town, filled with employees of the Stimson shingle mill in Ballard, Fremont didn't really flourish until the building of the Fremont Bridge in 1916. The Hiram M Chittenden Locks opened a year later, allowing boat traffic to travel from the lakes to Puget Sound via the ship canal (see Ballard, later). Fremont is located where Lake Union pours into the shipping canal. Anyone coming from downtown to the locks over the Fremont Bridge lands directly in the heart of Fremont. Consequently, the commercial hub of the neighborhood sits at the north end of the bridge at Fremont Ave N at N 35th St.

CENTER OF THE UNIVERSE: FREMONT WALKING TOUR

Exploring Fremont can take as much or as little time and energy as you want. This walk, if you do it at a leisurely pace, takes about an hour.

Fremont Rocket Start this walk on Evanston Ave N just up from N 36th St at the rather conspicuous Fremont Rocket. Fremont adopted this phallic and slightly zany-looking rocket as its community totem. Constructed in the 1950s for use in the Cold War, the rocket was plagued with difficulties and never actually went anywhere, leaving the engineering team with the unfortunate problem of 'not being able to get it up.' Before coming to Fremont, the rocket was affixed to an army surplus store in Belltown. When the store went out of business, the Fremont Business Association snapped it up. Look beneath the rocket and you'll find a coin box affixed to the building. Drop 50¢ in and the rocket will 'launch' by blowing a bunch of steam, but true to its underperformance nature, it won't go anywhere.

• Walk north (away from the water) up Evanston Ave N to N 36th St. Take a right onto Fremont Place N.

Statue of Lenin Right on the corner of N 36th St and Fremont Place N, you'll see the latest and most controversial addition to Fremont's collection of public art. This bronze, 16-foot statue of former communist leader Vladimir Lenin weighs 7 tons. It was brought to the USA from Slovakia by an American, Lewis Carpenter, who found the statue in a scrap pile after the 1989 revolution. Carpenter spent a fortune to bring it over, sure that some crazy American would want to buy it. Well, no one did, so here it stands biding its time in Fremont, still on sale for $150,000.

• Walk half a block east along Fremont Place N.

Deluxe Junk Stop in and look around one of Seattle's most kitschy secondhand shops. Located in a former funeral parlor, Deluxe Junk (☎ 634-2733), 3518 Fremont Place N, sells everything from retro sundresses and fluffy feather boas to housewares and furniture from the 1950s.

DEBRA MILLER

• Continue east along Fremont Place N, cross Fremont Ave N and go east on N 35th St.

Still Life in Fremont OK, it's coffee time. In Seattle, no walking tour is complete without a little caffeine. One of the city's best coffee shops, Still Life (☎ 547-9850), 705 N 35th St, is a haven on rainy days and one of the greatest places in town to curl up with a good book, a coffee and a bowl of homemade soup. The mismatched chairs, couches and tables, the large windows and friendly staff all invite you to spend hours if you want. But you're not lounging just now, so after sipping your coffee for a bit, get back on your feet. This is, after all, a *walking* tour.

Left: Greenbacks for a Red leader – Lenin for sale

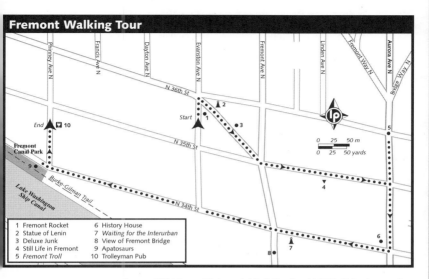

Fremont Walking Tour

1 Fremont Rocket
2 Statue of Lenin
3 Deluxe Junk
4 Still Life in Fremont
5 *Fremont Troll*
6 History House
7 *Waiting for the Interurban*
8 View of Fremont Bridge
9 Apatosaurs
10 Trolleyman Pub

• Leave Still Life and take a right, following N 35th St to Aurora Ave N. Here you'll be underneath the Aurora Bridge. Turn left and head for the dark, shadowy space where the bridge meets the ground.

Fremont Troll This incredible piece of public art is a must-see for anyone interested in the peculiar things in life. This 18-foot high, mammoth cement figure, constructed with two tons of ferro-cement, is in the process of consuming a whole (real) VW bug. Its creators – artists Steve Badanes, Will Martin, Donna Walter and Ross Whitehead – won a competition sponsored by the Fremont Arts Council in 1990. The team took seven weeks to complete the troll, whose menacing chrome eye keeps watch over Fremont.

• Head back down Aurora Ave N to N 34th St. Turn right.

History House On your right, you'll see the colorful metal fence of the History House. The fence, another piece of public art, built by blacksmith and welder Christopher Pauley, features colored houses with open doors that reflect Fremont's welcoming attitude. Inside, the History House (☎ 675-8875), 790 N 34th St, features rotating exhibits focused on the history of Seattle neighborhoods. It's a good place to see photos of early Seattle. It's open noon to 5 pm Wednesday to Sunday. Admission costs $1.

• Follow N 34th St west, toward the Fremont Bridge.

Waiting for the Interurban Seattle's most popular piece of public art, this lively sculpture in recycled aluminum depicts people waiting for a train that never comes. The train that once passed through Fremont stopped running in the 1930s, and Seattleites have been waiting for a new train – the Interurban – ever since. Finally, in 2001, Sound Transit trains started once again connecting Seattle with Everett, much like the original train did. The sculpture is prone to regular 'art attacks,' where locals lovingly decorate the people in outfits corresponding to a special event, the weather, someone's birthday, a Mariner win, whatever. Rarely do you see the sculpture 'undressed.' Take a look at the human-faced dog peeking out between the legs of the people. That face belongs to Armen Stepanian, one of the founders of today's Fremont and its excellent recycling system. Sculptor Richard Beyer and Stepanian had a disagreement about the design of the piece, which resulted in Beyer's spiteful yet humorous design of the dog's face.

Fremont Bridge Look across Fremont Ave N, and you'll see the Fremont Bridge, not exactly a spectacular structure or piece of art, but interesting nonetheless. The bridge was built in 1916 when construction of the Washington Ship Canal sliced a gully between Fremont and the northern reaches of Queen Anne. The bridge went up, providing a vital link across the canal. It was painted an industrial green; after all, this was long before Fremont became so colorful. When the neighborhood revitalization began in 1972, the bridge was to be repainted with the same shade of green. In the process, a coat of orange primer was painted on the bridge and a few people thought, 'Hey, that orange isn't bad!' Of course just as many people thought the orange was awful, but it won out and the bridge stayed orange until the mid-1980s, when it needed yet another repainting. The orange-haters were still adamant and what color to repaint the bridge was put to a vote. Orange wasn't even on the ballot, and an acceptable blue won. But the orange-lovers were still adamant too, and a group of Fremont rebels went out in the middle of the night and painted orange accents on the blue bridge. This orange and blue combination stuck and is now the official color scheme every time the bridge gets repainted.

• From the bridge, go west along N 34th St for two blocks until you get to Phinney Ave N.

Apatosaurs Along the banks of the ship canal, Fremont Canal Park extends west following the extension of the Burke-Gilman Trail. Right at the start of the park, at the bottom of Phinney Ave N, you'll see two giant, life-size apatosaurs. These are the world's largest known topiaries, given to Fremont by the Pacific Science Center.

Trolleyman Pub On the corner of Phinney Ave N and N 35th St is Redhook Brewery's Trolleyman Pub (☎ 634-4213). On the way to it, on the opposite corner to the apatosaurs, is the world headquarters and corporate offices of the Redhook Brewery. Redhook was started in nearby Ballard by Gordon Bowker and Paul Shipman (Bowker later went on to cofound Starbucks). The beer was brewed here in Fremont until 1997, when the brewery expanded to its current home in Woodinville (see the Excursions chapter). Though the beer is no longer brewed here, you can buy Redhook stuff at its little shop, and you can drink as much of it as you want at the Trolleyman. Yes, folks, it's beer time and the official end of your tour.

For companies that offer guided tours of Seattle, see Walking Tours, earlier in this chapter.

Fremont wasn't always cool and, like a child who lacks natural talent, had to work hard to get to where it is. The completion of the high-flying Aurora Bridge (officially known as the George Washington Memorial Bridge, a fact unknown even to most Seattleites) in the 1930s meant people didn't need to come through Fremont anymore, which sent its commercial district into a sharp decline. Through the 1950s and '60s, Fremont experienced a tragic architectural blight, when many of the old mill-workers' houses got converted into cookie-cutter duplexes and cheaply built apartment buildings. Through the 1960s, Fremont had more vacant stores than occupied ones; it lacked neighborhood necessities, such as a grocery store or pharmacy. The low-rent buildings attracted a rather dowdy and rowdy bunch who didn't have much energy for making Fremont a better place.

In the 1970s things started to change. The first Fremont Fair danced its way along the neighborhood streets in 1972; the Fremont Public Association (☎ 694-6700), today the envy of every neighborhood association, was created in 1974 to provide shelter, food and help to disadvantaged residents. The association did (and does) wonders for Fremont; its formation spawned a number of other thriving community associations, including the Fremont Arts Council (☎ 547-7440).

In 1994, Fremont citizens declared that they had seceded from Seattle, and the neighborhood was thenceforward the 'Republic of Fremont, Center of the Known Universe.' Public art, often wacky and unconventional, decorates neighborhood streets.

Fremont thrives today, but now it's got other problems. Like a teenager who suddenly becomes popular, everyone wants to hang out with it. Rents have skyrocketed here, stores and restaurants are pricier, and prime real estate is being sold to people who can afford it – generally not Fremont locals. The U-Park lot behind the Red Door Ale House long held the infamous Fremont Almost-Free Outdoor Cinema, where movies played on a building wall and filmgoers brought couches from home, sat back in the parking lot and watched movies. That lot was bulldozed in 2001. The ever-expanding Lake Union Center, which houses software giant Adobe among others, brought more than 500,000 sq feet of office space to the once building-free Fremont waterfront.

Fremont is still a great place to hang out, especially on Sunday at the **Fremont Sunday Market** (☎ 781-6776). The market features fresh fruits and vegetables and an incredible variety of artists and people getting rid of junk. The outdoor summer market is held in the parking lot at the corner of Stone Way and N 34th St and runs 10 am to 5 pm throughout summer. In winter, the market moves inside and is open 10 am to 4 pm. The original Fremont Almost-Free Outdoor Cinema is gone, but you can still watch movies outside at the **Fremont Outdoor Movies** (☎ 781-4230), shown in the parking lot behind the Redhook Brewery, 3400 Phinney Ave N at N 34th St. The movies start at dusk on Saturday nights. Admission is by a suggested $5 donation.

Another great Fremont must-attend is the **Fremont Fair** (☎ 633-4409), a colorful, musical and beer-filled event that takes place on the weekend nearest the summer solstice (in June). The fair kicks off with the Solstice Parade, where human-powered floats traipse through the neighborhood in a lively tribute to quirkiness. The fair's Web site, www.fremontfair.com, has information and a schedule of events. Another annual event, **Trolloween**, features a candlelight procession of costumed locals on Halloween night (October 31st), followed by a dance. Throw a costume on and join the fun. During either of these events, don't even think about parking in Fremont.

For a fun-loving tour of Lake Union and its houseboats, join the **Sunday Ice Cream Cruise** (☎ 889-0306) aboard the *Fremont Avenue*. Tours leave every hour between 11 am and 5 pm and cost $7/6/4 for adults/seniors/children ages 6-13. Catch the boat at the foot of Aurora Ave by the lower parking lot at Lake Union Center.

Getting There & Away
Bus Nos 26 and 28 go to Fremont from 4th Ave downtown. To drive to Fremont from downtown, take Westlake Ave N north along Lake Union and follow signs for the Fremont Bridge.

GREEN LAKE (Map 10)
Just north of Fremont and Wallingford is Green Lake, a small natural lake that's the hub of a large park complex and a pleasant low-key neighborhood. The lake is packed with crowds in summer, but it's even better in fall, when the leaves are changing, or on a rare rain-free day in winter. Anytime of the year, it's a great spot for a walk or a run or to sit back on a bench and watch the rowers on the water. If you want to get away from the lakefront crowds, the small but serviceable business district, just to the east along NE Ravenna Blvd, offers the requisite coffee shops and cheap restaurants.

Below Green Lake, the Woodland Park Zoo is a must-see. Phinney Ridge, the neighborhood north of the zoo along Phinney Ave N, also has some good restaurants (see the Places to Eat chapter).

Green Lake Park
One of the most popular spots in the city for recreationalists and sunbathers, scenic Green Lake Park surrounds **Green Lake**, a small natural lake created by a glacier during the last ice age. In the early 1900s, city planners lowered the lake's water level by 7 feet, increasing the shoreline to preserve parkland around the lake. After the lowering, however, Ravenna Creek, which fed the lake, no longer flowed through. Without any flush and flow, Green Lake became stagnant and filled with stinky green algae. Massive dredging efforts to keep Green Lake a lake (instead of a marshy wetland) continue today. The lake is still prone to massive alga blooms, which can cause an unpleasant condition called 'swimmer's itch' to anyone venturing into the water.

Two paths wind around the lake, but even these aren't enough to fill the needs of the hundreds of joggers, power-walkers, cyclists and in-line skaters who throng here daily. In fact, competition for space on the trails has led to altercations between speeding athletes; the city government now regulates traffic on the paths.

The **Bathhouse Theatre**, on the west side of the lake, is a 1928 bathing pavilion turned live-performance venue in 1970 .

A soccer field, bowling green, baseball diamond and basketball and tennis courts are some of the other recreational facilities available at the park. You can rent boats at the lake or rent in-line skates and bikes nearby (see the Activities chapter). Two sandy swimming beaches line the north end of the lake, but on sunny days the entire shoreline is massed with gleaming pale bodies.

Woodland Park Zoo
In Woodland Park, up the hill from Green Lake Park, the **Woodland Park Zoo** (☎ 684-4800), 5500 Phinney Ave N, one of Seattle's greatest tourist attractions, consistently rates as one of the top 10 zoos in the country. Seattle's zoo was one of the first in the nation to free animals from their restrictive cages in favor of ecosystem enclosures, where animals from similar environments share large spaces designed to replicate their natural surroundings. Feature exhibits include a tropical rain forest, two gorilla exhibits, an African savanna and an Asian elephant forest. In November 2000, the zoo celebrated the birth of its first baby elephant. Hunsa, which means 'supreme happiness,' was named by a seven-year-old Redmond girl in a statewide naming contest.

The zoo is open daily 9:30 am to dusk (roughly 6 pm from March 15 to October 14, and 4 pm at other times of the year). Admission costs $9/8.25/6.50/4.25 adults/seniors/youths ages six to 17/children ages three to five. Parking costs an additional $3.50.

The 2½-acre **Seattle Rose Garden**, near the entrance road to the zoo off N 50th St, contains 5000 plants. Varieties include heirloom roses and All-American Rose selections. Entrance is free.

Getting There & Away

To get to Green Lake, use bus Nos 16 or 358 going north on 3rd Ave. No 16 will drop you on the east side of the lake, by the restaurants and shops, while No 358 will take you to the west side, by the sports fields. Catch bus No 5 from downtown at 3rd Ave and Pine St (Westlake Station) to reach the zoo. If you're driving to Green Lake, use the N 45th St exit off I-5 north from downtown, head west through Wallingford and follow signs to the park; take the next exit at N 50th St for the zoo.

BALLARD (Map 11)

Northwest of downtown Seattle, west of Fremont and Green Lake, sits the ever-interesting, blue-collar Ballard. Once a seedy district where people spilled out of bars at 6 am only to puke on the sidewalk and go back in, Ballard has, in recent years, learned how to hold its own. Unlike other former lowbrow-turned-fashionable neighborhoods, such as Belltown or Fremont, Ballard still attracts folks looking for no-nonsense venues, where they can eat a greasy breakfast, drink $3 beers and listen to good down-home folk or rock 'n' roll. In fact, if you're at all snooty, you'll probably want to stay far away, as the locals are pretty protective of their seedy reputation.

Though just a bridge away, Ballard seems distant from urban Seattle. Settled principally by Swedes, Norwegians and Danes in the 1900s, Ballard has long been a Scandinavian enclave. Early Nordic settlers came to work sawmills (the Seattle area's largest was in Ballard) and to fish: These seafaring immigrants were instrumental in establishing Seattle's fishing fleet. Today, boats no longer leave Ballard to fish the high seas; they depart from Fishermen's Terminal, just across the shipping canal (see below).

Ballard still maintains a decidedly Nordic air, though only about a third of today's population is of Nordic descent. Along NW Market St, you can pop into Olsen's Scandinavian Foods and buy some fresh *lefsa,* or shop for trinkets at Norse Imports. The heart of old Ballard is centered along Ballard Ave NW, which seems to have hardly changed esthetically from the 1890s. Seven blocks here have been named a Historic Landmark District, but fortunately the buildings have not been thoughtlessly glamorized; the structures in this district are old, not 'olde.' Some are still hardware stores or meat markets, while others are brewpubs and bars; this is where you'll find Ballard's notable concentration of live music venues.

The 'Historic' designation helps protect Ballard from overcommercialization or other undesirable growth; any proposed development has to be approved by a board of locals, and the locals are pretty picky about who they'll let in. Ballard is fun and casual; here you can let your proverbial hair down, do shots with a fisherman, eat cheap food, get a tattoo or sit in a bar and get drunk all day (in Ballard, you won't be the only one).

Nonslackers will want to visit the Hiram M Chittenden Locks, also known as the Ballard Locks, just west of Ballard's core (see below). The **Shilshole Bay Marina**, about 2 miles west of the locks along Seaview Ave NW, offers nothing spectacular besides the usual tacky-touristy restaurants and shops that accompany harbors, but the boats are nice, as are the views across Puget Sound. Half a mile farther on is **Golden Gardens Park**, a beach park with pebbly shores and sandy beaches. There are picnic facilities, restrooms, basketball hoops, volleyball nets, gangs of Canada geese and plenty of space to get away from all the activity.

Nordic Heritage Museum

This museum (☎ 789-5707), 3014 NW 67th St, preserves the history of the northern Europeans who settled in Ballard and the Pacific Northwest. It's the only museum in the USA that commemorates the history of settlers from all five Scandinavian countries. A permanent exhibit features costumes, photographs and maritime equipment, while a second gallery is devoted to changing exhibitions. In addition to the two main exhibit areas, the museum offers Scandinavian language instruction, lectures and films. The museum is open 10 am to 4 pm Tuesday to Saturday and noon to 4 pm Sunday;

admission costs $4/3/2 adults/seniors and students/children. Kids under five enter free.

To get to the museum, take bus No 17 from downtown at 4th Ave and Union St. Get off on 32nd Ave NW and walk one block east on NW 67th St.

Hiram M Chittenden Locks

These locks, 3015 NW 54th St, also known as the Ballard Locks, are about a half mile west of Ballard off NW Market St. Watching boats traverse the two locks on the Lake Washington Ship Canal exerts a strange Zen-like attraction for locals and tourists alike. The process takes between 10 and 30 minutes, depending on tides and lake levels and on whether the large or the small lock is used. Walkways along the locks allow an intimate look at the workings of these water elevators and a chance to view the vessels that are coming and going from Puget Sound to Lakes Union and Washington.

On the southern side of the locks is a **fish ladder**, built in 1976 to allow salmon to fight their way to spawning grounds in the Cascade headwaters of the Sammamish River, which feeds Lake Washington. Visitors can watch the fish from underwater

glass-sided tanks or from above (nets are installed to keep salmon from over-leaping and stranding themselves on the pavement). Visitors can also watch sea lions munch on the salmon while the fish thrash around trying to figure out how to negotiate the ladder. Just what to do about the salmon-loving sea lions has stymied environmentalists, anglers and the local Fish & Wildlife Department (see Ecology & Environment in the Facts About Seattle chapter). The best time to see the salmon is during spawning season, from mid-June to September.

On the northern entrance to the lock area is the **Carl English Jr Botanical Gardens**, a charming, small arboretum and specimen garden. Trails wind through gardens filled with mature trees (with identifying labels) and flower gardens; plan on communing with imploring squirrels and haughty geese. The gardens are closed 9 pm to 7 am, although the locks remain open 24 hours.

Flanking the gardens is a small museum and **visitors center** (☎ 783-7059) documenting the history of the locks. The center is open 10 am to 7 pm daily June to September, and 11 am to 5 pm Thursday to Monday from October to May. Free tours of the locks are offered at 1 and 3 pm daily mid-May to mid-September, with an added tour at 11 am on weekends. The rest of the year, tours are offered at 2 pm Thursday to Monday.

Access to all areas at the locks is free. Get to them by taking bus No 17 from downtown at 4th Ave and Union St. The bus goes over the Ballard Bridge and takes you directly to the locks.

Fishermen's Terminal

Seattle's fishing fleet resides at Fishermen's Terminal, in a wide recess in the ship canal called Salmon Bay on the south side of the Ballard Bridge at 19th Ave and W Nickerson St. About 700 fishing boats dock here, making this the largest halibut and salmon fleet in the world. Fishermen's Terminal is a popular moorage spot because the facility is in freshwater, above the Chittenden Locks; freshwater is much less corrosive to boats than saltwater.

Lake Washington Ship Canal

Northwest of Seattle proper, the higher-elevation freshwater of Lake Washington and Lake Union meets the saltwater of Puget Sound in the 8-mile-long Lake Washington Ship Canal. The concept of linking the major lakes around Seattle to the Sound had been discussed since 1867, but it wasn't until 1911 that the Army Corps of Engineers, under the direction of Hiram Chittenden, began the unification of the waters. First, a channel was cut between Lake Washington and Lake Union, thereby lowering Lake Washington by 9 feet. Then the canal was cut through from Salmon Bay south of Ballard to Puget Sound, and two locks were installed in 1917. Today, 100,000 boats pass through the canal every year.

THINGS TO SEE & DO

It's great fun to wander the piers, watching crews unload their catch, clean boats and repair nets. Many of these fishing boats journey to Alaska in summer and return to dry dock while they wait out winter. Outdoor interpretive displays explain the history of Seattle's fishing fleet, starting with the Natives who first fished these waters in canoes, to the Slavs and Greeks, who dominating salmon fishing in the early 1900s. A statue, the bronze **Seattle Fisherman's Memorial** at the base of the piers, commemorates Seattle fishers lost at sea. This memorial is also the site of the ceremonial blessing of the fleet, held annually on the first Sunday in May.

In the two shedlike terminal buildings are a couple of good restaurants specializing in the freshest seafood in Seattle, a tobacconist, a ship chandler and a store devoted to navigational charts and nautical gifts. Stop at the Wild Salmon Fish Market (☎ 283-3366) to buy the freshest pick of the day's catch.

To get to Fishermen's Terminal from downtown, take Nos 15, 17 or 18 and get off on the south side of the Ballard Bridge. The terminal is just beneath the bridge.

Getting There & Away

Bus No 17 goes to Ballard from downtown at 4th Ave at Union. To drive to Ballard, you can take I-5 north to the 45th St exit and turn west, away from the university. Follow NW 45th St; it will become Shilshole Ave along the docks before it runs into NW Market St, which is the main commercial strip for Ballard. From downtown, you can also take Westlake Ave N toward Fremont, but continue west past Fremont Bridge on W Nickerson St to Ballard Bridge and over the ship canal.

DISCOVERY PARK (Map 11)

Discovery Park is 534 acres of urban wilderness northwest of downtown Seattle and just southwest of the mouth of Chittenden Locks. Locals love to come here to get away from the ever-present manicure of city gardens and get windswept along the park's many trails. For a $1 map of the

Chinook salmon

park's trail and road system, stop by the **visitors center** (☎ 386-4236) near the Government Way entrance; the center is open 8:30 am to 5:30 pm daily. The park runs educational programs including Saturday nature walks, day camps for children and bird watching tours.

The park was originally Fort Lawton, an army base established in 1897 to protect Seattle from unnamed enemies. Fort Lawton didn't see much activity until WWII, when it was used as barracks for troops bound for the Pacific. It held up to 1400 German and Italian prisoners of war. When the fort was declared surplus property in the 1960s, the City of Seattle decided to turn it into a park (although significant areas of the park are still used for military housing); the fort was finally proclaimed public parkland in 1972.

Later, in 1977, Native groups also laid claim to the land, and 17 acres of parkland were decreed Native land, on which now stands the **Daybreak Star Indian Cultural Center**, a community center for Seattle-area Native Americans. Except for a small art gallery, there are few facilities for outside visitors. The vista point in front of the center affords beautiful views of the sound, and several steep trails lead down through the forest to narrow, sandy beaches.

Discovery Park has over 7 miles of hiking trails, several of which lead to the Daybreak Star Center. A paved road makes an almost 3-mile loop of the park, with trails sprawling from there to lookouts. About a mile off from the loop, a trail skirts the water's edge all the way to the still functioning **West Point Lighthouse**, a great spot for panoramic views of the Sound and mountains to the west.

Sea and be seen. West Point Lighthouse

Getting There & Away

Simply take bus No 33 from downtown or Seattle Center. Though they take a more circuitous route, bus Nos 19 and 24 also come here from downtown (4th & Union). To reach Discovery Park by car from downtown, take Elliott Ave north, which will turn into 15th Ave W. Take the W Dravus St exit and turn left. Turn right onto 20th Ave W and proceed until it turns into Gilman Ave W, and eventually into W Government Way.

CENTRAL DISTRICT (Map 12)

Running down the east slope of First Hill to the upscale neighborhoods that flank Lake Washington, the Central District – often referred to as 'the CD' – represents the heart of Seattle's African American community. The principal commercial areas are along E Madison St from 12th to 18th Aves and along E Union St around 26th Ave. Few blacks lived in Seattle until WWII, when they moved to the area in large numbers to work in the shipyards and contribute to the war effort. Today the CD is overrun with empty storefronts, which is ironic considering the high price of real estate in nearby Capitol and First Hills. During the day it's a friendly place, where you can find some

great soul food and barbecue joints (see the Places to Eat chapter); you'll probably want to avoid walking alone in the CD at night.

One of the cornerstones of this neighborhood is **Mount Zion Baptist Church** (☎ 322-6500), 1634 19th Ave at E Madison St, a 2000-member congregation with a choir that has reached national acclaim through its gospel recordings. The church is over a century old.

To get to the Central District's main commercial area, take bus No 11 outbound on Madison St from downtown. From downtown or Pioneer Square, the best streets to walk along (about 20 blocks) are E Union or E Cherry.

WASHINGTON PARK ARBORETUM (Map 12)

This wild and lovely park (☎ 543-8800) offers a wide variety of gardens, a wetlands nature trail and 200 acres of mature forest threaded by paths. More than 5500 plant species grow within the arboretum's boundaries. In the spring **Azalea Way**, a jogger-free trail that winds through the arboretum, is lined with a giddy array of pink- and orange-flowered azaleas and rhododendrons. Trail guides to the plant collections are available at the **Graham Visitors Center & Gift Shop**, 2300 Arboretum Drive E; open 10 am to 4 pm daily. Free guided tours of the grounds are available at 1 pm weekends.

Japanese Garden
At the southern edge of the arboretum, this 3½-acre formal garden (☎ 684-4725) has koi pools, waterfalls, a teahouse and manicured plantings. The garden is open 10 am to 6 pm daily March to November, weather permitting. Entry costs $2.50/1.50 adults/seniors and youths ages 19 and under.

Foster Island Wetlands Trail
The northern edge of the arboretum includes this wonderful trail around Foster Island in Lake Washington's Union Bay. The waterfront trail winds through marshlands and over floating bridges to smaller islands and reedy shoals. Bird watching is popular here, as is swimming, fishing and kayaking (for kayak rentals see the Activities chapter). It's just too bad that busy, elevated Hwy 520 roars above the island. The nature trail is best accessed from the parking lot near the visitors center or from the museum parking lot (see below).

Museum of History & Industry
This museum (☎ 324-1126), 2700 24th Ave E, at the northwest corner of the arboretum, has an exhibition space that, despite its name, is probably best thought of as a museum of Seattle and Puget Sound history. Usually called by its acronym, MOHAI has a likeable collection of old planes, memorabilia from the Great Fire and artifacts and lore from Seattle's great seafaring era. The museum is open 10 am to 5 pm daily; entry costs $5.50/3 adults/seniors and students.

Getting There & Away
The Washington Park Arboretum is just south of the University of Washington across Union Bay. Public transport to the arboretum isn't great. The No 11 Madison St bus delivers you to the base of the park at Lake Washington Blvd, but there's still quite a walk (albeit through the park) to the visitors center. To MOHAI, it's proba-

bly better to catch one of the buses to the university and walk from there (see The U District, earlier).

To reach the visitors center and hiking trails at the north end of the park by car, take Hwy 520 east from I-5, and take the first exit (for Montlake/UW). This intersection can be confusing: Stay in the right lane and go straight through the first intersection. This lane becomes Lake Washington Blvd. Follow this street for about a quarter mile, and then turn onto Foster Island Rd (not 26th Ave E). Follow signs for the visitors center. If you're trying to get to MOHAI, follow the signs for Montlake and the university, but turn immediately left (east) on E Hamlin St or E Shelby St before crossing the Montlake Bridge.

Access from the south is somewhat less confusing. Follow Madison St from downtown until it intersects with Lake Washington Blvd E. Turn left at the junction. Take Arboretum Drive E to the visitors center.

MADISON VALLEY & MADISON PARK (Map 12)
If you follow Madison St from downtown (or take bus No 11), you're following the old trolley line that once served the east side of Capitol Hill and the amusement park and beach at Madison Park. Today these tranquil neighborhoods are quietly upscale, home to little commercial hubs lined with understated shops and good restaurants. When it gets hot in the summer – yes, Seattle can get hot – locals make the pilgrimage to Lake Washington to sprawl out on the small sandy-grassy beaches. Just driving or cycling around the area is a good respite – the houses along Lake Washington Blvd boast of old money or new corporate wealth.

The first neighborhood you come to is **Madison Valley**, where the biggest attractions are two notable restaurants: Rover's, often considered one of the best restaurants in Seattle, and Café Flora, a vegetarian's dream restaurant (see the Places to Eat chapter).

Continue toward Lake Washington to reach **Madison Park**, another neighborhood with the usual hub of trendy restaurants and cafés. In the 1890s, Madison Park proper comprised an amusement park, bathhouse, ballpark and racetrack. Ferries left from here to cross Lake Washington to Bellevue. Nowadays, Madison Park is a much quieter place, and very genteel. The park proper is the most northerly of the public parks and beaches along Lake Washington's western shore. In summer, the popular beach sees a sizeable gay male contingent mixed in with local families. The beach here is one of the more pleasant places to swim and sunbathe.

South of Madison Park toward the end of Lake Washington Blvd is **Denny Blaine Park**, found at the end of a looping tree-lined lane. This predominantly lesbian beach is surrounded by an old stone wall, which marked the shoreline before the lake level was dropped 9 feet during construction of the ship canal. Just a little farther south on your right-hand side, you'll find the two-tiered **Viretta Park**, from which you can see the mansion once owned by Nirvana's Kurt Cobain and Courtney Love (it's the house on the north, or left, side of the benches if you're facing the water). Seattle sweetheart Cobain took his life with a shotgun in the mansion's greenhouse in April 1994. The greenhouse is long gone and Love no longer owns the house, but Nirvana fans still make the pilgrimage to this small park to give tribute to the angst-ridden king of grunge. (See 'The Life & Death of Grunge Music' in the Entertainment chapter). On a pair of benches on the lower part of the park, fans have scribbled many variations of 'I love you, Kurt' and such tributes as 'Oh well, whatever, never mind.'

Just south of Viretta Park is a small beachfront called **Howell Park**. It is usually less crowded due to the park's lack of parking. If you're on foot, look for a small sign and trailhead that leads to the beach.

MADRONA (Map 12)

Madrona is one of Seattle's more ethnically diverse neighborhoods, blending elements of the Central District's African American community to the west with the predomi-

nantly white neighborhoods that ring Lake Washington proper. Once a relatively unheard-of neighborhood, Madrona now draws many to eat at one of the most popular brunch places in the city, the Hi Spot Cafe (see the Places to Eat chapter). The small business district is on 34th Ave, between E Pike and E Spring Sts. **Madrona Park Beach**, just down from the business district in Madrona Park, is one of the nicest along the lake; in clear weather, views of Mt Rainier are fantastic.

Farther south, past the yacht moorage, is **Leschi Park**, a grassy green space with a children's play area. Continue south along the boulevard through a very upscale neighborhood, and you'll end up at **Colman Park** (Map 1). The entire lakefront stretch between here and Seward Park (see later) is parkland. This is an especially good area for bike riding; on the weekends the boulevard is closed to cars.

Getting There & Away

Take bus No 2 outbound on Spring St from downtown to get to Madrona. No bus routes serve the whole length of Lake Washington Blvd, though you can get to Madrona Park by bus No 2. By car, follow Union or Cherry Sts from downtown to get to Madrona. Access to parks and beaches along the western shores of Lake Washington is primarily along Lake Washington Blvd, which isn't exactly easy to get to. From the north or downtown, it's easiest to follow Madison St out to the Washington Park Arboretum (see earlier). Lake Washington Blvd E intersects E Madison St before descending onto the lakeshore.

MERCER ISLAND

Mercer Island (see the Greater Seattle map at the beginning of this book) is linked to Bellevue and Seattle by busy, usually congested I-90. Mercer Island is almost completely residential and has few facilities to attract the casual tourist. However, its relatively quiet pace and isolation make it popular with cyclists, who make a loop out of E and W Mercer Way, a 14-mile pedal that passes by some lovely parks and magnificent homes. **Luther Burbank Park**, on the northeast corner of the island, is a popular swimming beach; if you know where to look from here, you can see Bill Gates' house across the lake in Medina.

To get to Mercer Island by bus, take No 550 eastbound from any of the downtown bus-tunnel stops.

SOUTH SEATTLE (Map 1)
Seward Park

For something wild, as in wilderness, go to Seward Park, dominating the 277-acre Bailey Peninsula, which juts into Lake Washington like a hitchhiking thumb. The park preserves about the only old-growth forest anywhere in the vicinity of Seattle and is known for its wildlife, including a nesting pair of bald eagles. Hikers and bikers will be interested in the 2½-mile paved **lakeside trail**; other trails lead to a fish hatchery, beach access and several picnic areas. On the weekends the lakefront boulevard between here and Colman Park (see Madrona, earlier) is closed to cars and makes an especially good area for bike riding. Seward Park can be dangerous after dark, so be attentive.

To get to Seward Park by bus, take route No 39 from 2nd Ave downtown. To reach the park by car, take I-5 south to I-90 (exit 164).

Once on I-90, take exit 1 for Rainier Ave S. Stay on Rainier Ave S until it intersects with S Orcas St after about 2 miles. Turn left (east) and follow the signs to the park.

Museum of Flight

In many ways, aviation and aircraft manufacturing have been integral to the growth of modern Seattle; unfortunately that fact alone doesn't justify this rather gratuitous paean to Boeing. While this vast museum (☎ 764-5720), 9494 E Marginal Way S on Boeing Field, about 10 miles south of downtown, has no formal ties to the aircraft giant, the local boosterism is implicit. Aviation buffs wholeheartedly enjoy the Museum of Flight, while others traipse through suppressing yawns, so be choosy about who you come with.

The museum presents the entire history of flight, from da Vinci to the Wright Brothers to the NASA space program. Over 50 historic aircraft are on display. The restored 1909 Red Barn, where Boeing had its beginnings, contains exhibits and displays. The six-story glass Great Gallery has 20 airplanes suspended from its ceiling. Vintage fliers reside on the grounds outside the buildings. There's also a hands-on area where visitors get to work the controls and sit in the driver's seat. Films about flight and

---

Boeing Factory Tours

Most of Boeing's wide-bodied jets – the 747, 767 and 777 – are produced north of Seattle, just south of the city of Everett. A 90-minute tour takes you through Boeing's Main Airplane Assembly Building, which at some 300 million cubic feet is the largest building in the world. Tours include a video about Boeing, a bus trip through the cavernous assembly building where gigantic airplanes look tiny, and out to the flight deck, where the shiny new airplanes get ready to serve the world. Anyone who's ever flown in a plane – not just aviation junkies – will enjoy the tour. Six tours are offered on weekdays only. Times change seasonally; call ahead to confirm at ☎ 544-1264 or 800-464-1476. Tours are offered on a first-come, first-served basis and are quite popular, so plan to get to the plant with plenty of lead time. Admission costs $5/3 adults/seniors and children. No photography is allowed in the facility.

To get to the Boeing factory by bus, you can catch Sound Transit bus Nos 510 or 512 from downtown at 4th Ave and Union St. These buses will take you to downtown Everett, where you'll need to catch Everett Transit bus No 2 southbound to the Boeing visitors center. By car, follow I-5 north of Seattle to exit 189; turn west and drive 3 miles on Hwy 526.

aircraft history are shown in the small theater, and there's also a gift shop and café.

The museum is open 10 am to 5 pm daily; until 9 pm Thursday. Admission costs $9.50/8.50/5 adults/seniors/youths ages five to 17; it's free for kids under five everyday, and for everyone 5 pm to 9 pm the first Thursday of every month.

From downtown, take Bus No 174 direct to the museum. Catch it southbound on 2nd Ave. Bus No 174 also stops at the museum on its way from the airport. By car, take I-5 south from downtown to exit 158, turn west and follow East Marginal Way north.

WEST SEATTLE (Map 1)

West Seattle is the nose of land across Elliott Bay to the west of downtown Seattle, beyond the Port of Seattle and Harbor Island. West Seattle hasn't succumbed to gentrification and still feels working class. Although access to downtown is good, it feels removed from the rest of the city. From here, views can be stellar – both of the city center and of the islands to the west.

Alki Point, the westernmost point of the peninsula, attracted the Denny party, who landed in the schooner *Exact* in 1851, establishing the village that would grow to become Seattle. Although the settlers only spent one winter here before moving across the bay to what is now Seattle proper, there's a monument to the pioneers on the beach; for some reason, there's a chip of Plymouth Rock imbedded in its base.

The main reason to visit West Seattle, especially in good weather, is to go to **Alki Beach Park**. The sober and purposeful settlers who landed here wouldn't recognize the place today. This 2-mile stretch of sandy beach is a madhouse in summer, when in emulation of southern California, the volleyball nets go up, mass sunbathing occupies the strand and teens in souped-up cars prowl the streets. Still, it's Seattle's only real beach scene, and the views of Seattle from **Duwamish Head**, at the northern end of the beach, are spectacular. You might want to avoid Alki on summer weekends, but good beachside cafés, quaint fish-and-chips joints, the miniature replica of the Statue of Liberty on the beach and the Alki Point Lighthouse make this area a nice getaway most other times.

The main commercial strip on West Seattle is along California Ave SW, centering at the junction of SW Alaska St. There's nothing particularly compelling about the shops here, except that they seem at least a generation and 200 miles removed from the rest of Seattle. Old five-and-dime stores slumber next to old diners, neither having changed much since the 1950s.

If you're interested in a **ferry** ride, follow Fauntleroy Way SW down through West Seattle to Fauntleroy Ferry Terminal at Henderson St SW, south of Lincoln Park. Here you can take a half-hour ferry ride to Vashon Island, a semirural island that also serves as a bedroom community to Seattle.

Getting There & Away

To get to Alki Beach by public transportation, catch bus Nos 37 or 56 heading southbound from anywhere along 1st Ave downtown. Route Nos 54, 116, 118 and 119 go to the Vashon Ferry departure point at Fauntleroy Ferry Terminal. Catch Nos 116, 118 or 119 from any of the designated stops along 2nd Ave downtown. Catch No 54 westbound on Union St, or southbound on 1st Ave.

By car, take Hwy 99 or I-5 south from Seattle to the West Seattle Freeway; for Alki Beach, take the exit for Harbor Ave SW and travel north (it later changes its name to Alki Ave SW and then Beach Drive SW on its way around the promontory). For the Vashon Ferry, follow the signs for Fauntleroy Way SW.

Activities

For a city that, at least in the popular mind, is perennially drenched in rain, Seattle is a very outdoorsy community. Of course, with the Olympic and North Cascade mountains and Mt Rainier National Park just out the backdoor, and the fingers of Puget Sound protruding everywhere, you won't have to drive far to find pristine wilderness or calm waters. But Seattle is rather unique for a large city in that many forms of outdoor recreation – hiking, kayaking, biking and windsurfing – are available within the city itself. (For spectator sports, see the Entertainment chapter.)

When it comes to finding out where to go, what to do or where to rent equipment, a couple of places deserve special notice. **REI**, or Recreational Equipment Inc, (Map 7, ☎ 223-1944), 222 Yale Ave N, is a Seattle native and is one of the largest sporting and recreational gear and equipment outfitters in the nation. Gearheads go giddy at this flagship store, a wild paean to the outdoor spirit, with a mock mountain-bike trail, a rock gym, simulated hiking trail (to test boots) and more tents, canoes and rucksacks than you've probably ever seen in one place. The eager staff is very knowledgeable about area recreation, and there are several bulletin boards with information on talks, gatherings, outings, clubs and courses. REI's good selection of books and maps on regional recreation is helpful, especially the topographic maps of area mountains. The rental department can rent you most kinds of equipment or tell you where to go to do so. REI Adventures (☎ 800-622-2236) organizes trips.

Upstairs at REI, the **Forest Service/National Park Service** runs an Outdoor Recreation Center (☎ 470-4060), and its staff can tell you anything you need to know about nearby national parks.

Another excellent Seattle-based travel resource, **The Mountaineers** (Map 7, ☎ 284-6310), 300 3rd Ave in Lower Queen Anne, specializes in Northwest recreation. The organization offers courses in hiking, mountaineering, kayaking, every type of snow sport and other outdoor skills, such as First Aid and backcountry travel. Events such as film and slide shows are enough to tickle anyone's adventurous spirit, and The Mountaineers bookstore boasts an unbeatable collection of outdoor books, maps and videos, many of which are available to borrow through The Mountaineers library.

BICYCLING

Despite frequent rain and hilly terrain, bicycling is still a major form of both transportation and recreation in the Seattle area. Both bicycle touring and mountain biking are widespread, so whether you're a clipless mudhound or a casual cruiser, you'll find plenty of places to ride.

In the city, commuter bike lanes continue to get painted on city streets, city trails are well maintained and the friendly and enthusiastic biking community is happy to share the road. The wildly popular 16½-mile **Burke-Gilman Trail** winds from Ballard to Log Boom Park in Kenmore on Seattle's

Burke & Gilman's Railway

In the hope of establishing Seattle as a viable city for transportation and trade, a bunch of guys, including Judge Thomas Burke and Daniel Gilman, set out in 1885 to build a Seattle-based railroad. Their big vision was a railway crossing Washington State, heading north and connecting with the Canadian Transcontinental line. The *Seattle, Lake Shore and Eastern Railroad* never got past Arlington, Washington, but the route became a major regional line serving Puget Sound logging areas. The line was later acquired by Northern Pacific, which merged with the Great Northern and Burlington lines in 1970, becoming the Burlington Northern Railroad. This new company quickly made plans to abandon the line, finally putting to rest Burke and Gilman's plan for a cross-state railroad.

Seattle citizens quickly recognized the recreation potential in the railroad line and petitioned for a public biking and walking trail. Despite what now seem like crazy objections from nearby residents, the City of Seattle, the University of Washington and King County co-developed the route. On August 19, 1978 the 12.1-mile paved recreation trail connecting Gas Works Park to Kenmore on the Eastside was born. Today, the 16½-mile trail extends west through Fremont to 8th Ave NW in Ballard. At twilight, when the evening light dances off the leaves along the tree-lined trail, you can sometimes see ole Burke and Gilman riding along on a tandem bike, happy at what their vision became.

Eastside. There, it connects with the 11-mile long **Sammamish River Trail**, which winds past the Chateau Ste Michelle winery in Woodinville before terminating at Redmond's Marymoor Park. Marymoor Park boasts the only **velodrome** (☎ 675-1424) in the Pacific Northwest. You'll need to be a trained velodrome rider before you can get on the track, but the untrained can watch the exciting races, which are held at 7 pm Wednesday and Friday mid-May to September. Admission to the amateur races is free Monday and Wednesday; when the pros hit the track on Friday, admission costs $3.

More cyclists than you can imagine peddle the loop around **Green Lake**, making it downright congested on sunny days. Closer to downtown, the scenic 2½-mile **Elliott Bay Trail** runs along the waterfront through Myrtle Edwards and Elliott Bay Parks. The 8-mile **Alki Trail** in West Seattle makes a pretty ride as it follows Alki Beach before connecting up with the 11-mile **Duwamish Trail** that heads south along W Marginal Way SW.

Though they are not specified trails, the tree-lined roads winding through the **Washington Park Arboretum** and along **Lake Washington Blvd** make for lovely road rides. The bike trail around **Seward Park** gives cyclists the sensation of looping a forested island. The 14-mile **Mercer Island Loop** is another residential ride along E and W Mercer Way around the perimeter of the island. (See the Things to See & Do chapter for more on these places.)

Bainbridge and Vashon Islands are popular with cyclists and are just a ferry ride away, offering near-rural isolation on rolling country back roads. Bike shops and the usually friendly folks who work there are always gushing fountains of good information. Most shops stock cycling publications and can point you in the right direction for public rides, trails and places to avoid. Anyone planning on cycling in Seattle should pick up a copy of the *Seattle Bicycling Map*, published by the City of Seattle's Transportation Bicycle and Pedestrian Program (☎ 684-7583) and available at bike shops. Alternatively you can order the map free of charge over the telephone or online at www.ci.seattle.wa.us/td/brmform.asp.

Cycling Clubs

Seattle's active biking community thrives because of organized clubs. With more than 5500 members, the Cascade Bicycle Club

(☎ 522-2453) is the largest cycling club in the USA. The club holds organized rides daily as well as various special events, such as races and long-distance rides. It publishes the *Cascade Corner,* a newsletter that describes what's happening in the bike world. Check out more information at its Web site at www.cascade.org.

Fat tire riders will want to contact Backcountry Bicycle Trails Club (☎ 293-2995), which organizes mountain-biking trail rides and offers bike repair and technical-riding courses. Check it out at www.bbtc.org.

Rentals
Rent a bike from Gregg's Greenlake Cycle (Map 10, ☎ 523-1822), 7007 Woodlawn Ave NE, near Green Lake. Convenient to the University of Washington and the Burke-Gilman Trail, Al Young Bike and Ski (Map 9, ☎ 524-2642), 3615 NE 45th St and Ti Cycles (Map 9, ☎ 522-7602), 2943 Blakely St NE, rent bikes and do repairs. On the Waterfront, Blazing Saddles (☎ 341-9994), 1230 Western Ave, rents higher-end mountain bikes. The average rental is about $20 for a half day, and up to $35 for a full day. (See What to Buy in the Shopping chapter for other bicycle shops.)

HIKING
In Seattle, it's possible to hike wilderness trails without ever leaving the city. **Seward Park** offers several miles of trails in a remnant of the area's old-growth forest, and an even more extensive network of trails is available in 534-acre **Discovery Park**, northwest of downtown. At the northern edge of Washington Park Arboretum, **Foster Island** offers a 20-minute nature walk along a wetlands trail winding through marshlands born upon the opening of the Lake Washington Ship Canal. This is a great place for bird watching, fishing and swimming. The trail begins at the bottom of the Museum of History and Industry (MOHAI) parking lot. (See the Things to See & Do chapter for more on these places.)

Outside the city, the hiking opportunities are practically endless in the Olympic Range, the north, central and south Cascades and in the Issaquah Alps. For specific trail information, contact REI, The Mountaineers (see the beginning of the chapter for both) or the Washington Trails Association (☎ 625-1367), a nonprofit group that organizes hiking trips, conservation efforts and trail-building jaunts into local mountains. Check out its Web site at www.wta.org.

The Cascade chapter of the Sierra Club (☎ 523-2019), 8511 15th Ave NE, is a busy and active group. Its extremely diverse offerings range from beachcombing and botany walks at Alki to weekend day-hiking and car-camping trips along the Pacific Crest Trail. Call for a recording of future events. Most day trips are free; longer trips may have minimal fees.

RUNNING
With its many parks, Seattle offers a number of good trails for runners. If you're in the downtown area, the trails along **Myrtle Edwards Park** – just north of the Waterfront along Elliott Bay – make for a nice run, with views over the sound and of the downtown skyline. **Green Lake** has two paths, the 2.8-mile paved path immediately surrounding the lake and a less-crowded, unpaved path on the perimeter of the park. The **Washington Park Arboretum** is another good choice, as the trails lead through beautiful trees and flower gardens. Trails in the arboretum connect to the Lake Washington Blvd trail system, which extends all the way south to Seward Park, just in case you are training for a marathon. Most of the bicycling routes listed earlier are also good running routes.

Running Clubs
Runners looking to hook up with running mates can contact a number of Seattle's running clubs, most of which offer organized runs that usually turn into social events. Active clubs include the Puget Sound Hash Harriers (☎ 528-2050), Seattle Frontrunners (☎ 322-7769) and the West Seattle Runners (☎ 938-2416). Super Jock n' Jills trains runners of all levels and maintains a running hotline at ☎ 524-7867. Also, check running and sports stores for *Northwest*

The Birth of Seattle's Parks

Some 15,000 years ago most of Seattle lay under blankets of ice so thick that landmarks as tall as the Space Needle would only measure a chink in the ice surface. When glaciers slowly melted away, they left the sculpted channels and elongated hills that decorate the city today. Thick forests grew up around the waterways and surrounding hills, making the land lush, fertile and mostly impenetrable. When settlers first started clear-cutting the land, the notion of setting aside areas for parkland seemed ludicrous – after all, wasn't the whole thing essentially parkland anyway?

When Mary and David Denny donated five acres of land for a cemetery in 1884 when Seattle was only 19 years old, the city's first park – Denny Park – was born. By 1890 Seattle was starting to thrive. More forests were logged to make way for more city streets, more houses and more roads. That's when a few visionaries began talking seriously about preserving parkland. Early Seattleites didn't take well to this nonsense and protested heartily when the city paid Guy Phinney $100,000 for his Woodland Park estate. In 1892 Parks Superintendent EO Schwagerl proposed the first comprehensive plan for a park system, which was later augmented by city engineer George Cotterill's elaborate plans for bicycle paths throughout the city. Seattle's growth happened quickly and without much design. Gold had been discovered in Alaska and the Seattle area produced and shipped out mass amounts of timber; to keep up foresters had to pluck trees as fast as they could, with little regard for what was left behind.

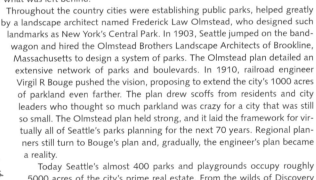

Throughout the country cities were establishing public parks, helped greatly by a landscape architect named Frederick Law Olmstead, who designed such landmarks as New York's Central Park. In 1903, Seattle jumped on the bandwagon and hired the Olmstead Brothers Landscape Architects of Brookline, Massachusetts to design a system of parks. The Olmstead plan detailed an extensive network of parks and boulevards. In 1910, railroad engineer Virgil R Bouge pushed the vision, proposing to extend the city's 1000 acres of parkland even farther. The plan drew scoffs from residents and city leaders who thought so much parkland was crazy for a city that was still so small. The Olmstead plan held strong, and it laid the framework for virtually all of Seattle's parks planning for the next 70 years. Regional planners still turn to Bouge's plan and, gradually, the engineer's plan became a reality.

Today Seattle's almost 400 parks and playgrounds occupy roughly 5000 acres of the city's prime real estate. From the wilds of Discovery and Seward Parks, to recreational gems like Green Lake and Madrona Park, to the bold utility of Gas Works Park, Seattle's park system is a true testament to the idea that a vision can change people's lives.

Runners, a monthly publication and a good resource for running-related information.

IN-LINE SKATING

Call 'em in-line skaters, rollerbladers or just kickbacks from the disco era, but skaters swoosh by everywhere, wearing everything from Nike's latest trends to groovy pink legwarmers. Seattle's paved paths are perfect except when it rains, which is why you should beware the skating storm on sunny days. Popular skating spots include the Burke-Gilman Trail, around Green Lake, Alki Point, Lake Washington Blvd and the Sammamish River Trail on the Eastside. Gregg's Greenlake Cycle (see Bicycling, earlier) rents in-line skates for $5/hour.

WATERSPORTS

Rumor has it that one in three Seattleites owns a boat of some sort. It could be a rubber dinghy, a crusty kayak or a salty sailboat, but regardless, the locals here love to play in the water. Whether you learn to windsurf on Green Lake, kayak past the houseboats on Lake Union or hoist the sails on Lake Washington, plenty of organizations are geared toward having fun on the water. For organized boat trips, see Organized Tours in the Getting Around chapter.

Kayaking

Sea kayaking can soothe your soul or wake up your adventurous spirit and, if you don't know how, it's one of the easiest sports to pick up. Seattle's many waterways are ideal for kayak exploration, and it doesn't take long before controlling your paddle is as natural as waving your arm. White-water kayaking on area rivers is also popular, though a little more challenging to pick up. But have no fear, many organizations offer excellent lessons. The Northwest Outdoor Center (Map 7, ☎ 281-9694), 2100 Westlake Ave N on Lake Union, offers a vast selection of rentals, guided tours and instruction in sea and white-water kayaking. Check out more at its Web site at www.nwoc.com. The Moss Bay Rowing & Kayak Center (Map 7, ☎ 682-2031), 1001 Fairview N, also offers rentals, extensive lessons and tours on Lake Union. Its Web site is at www.mossbay.net. The busy Washington Kayak Club (☎ 433-1983) offers white-water and sea kayaking courses, along with instruction in conservation and safety awareness.

On Bainbridge and Vashon Islands, the active Puget Sound Kayak Company (☎ 933-3008) offers classes, clinics and guided trips, including the popular Harbor Moonlight Paddle in Vashon's Quartermaster or Bainbridge's Eagle Harbors.

Rentals In addition to the above, rentals are available at the following. On Portage Bay, near the university and Washington Park Arboretum, rent kayaks from Agua Verde Paddle Club (Map 9, ☎ 545-8570),

1303 NE Boat St, where you can hop in a single kayak for $10/45 per hour/day or a double kayak for $15/60. It is open 10 am to dusk daily March to October; until 6 pm Sunday. (When you get back from your paddle, be sure the visit the cafe upstairs for the best fish tacos in town.)

Another good way to explore the waters surrounding the Arboretum is to rent a canoe or rowboat for $6.50 an hour from the UW Waterfront Activities Center (☎ 543-9433). You need to have a current driver's license or passport. The center is open 10 am to around 6:30 or 7:30 pm and is in the southeast corner of the Husky Stadium parking lot.

Green Lake's still waters help keep beginner kayakers calm, though the crowds might also keep you waiting. Green Lake Small Craft Center (Map 10, ☎ 527-0171), 7351 E Green Lake Dr, run by Seattle Parks & Recreation Department, rents kayaks, canoes, rowboats and paddleboats from March to October.

Sailing

Despite the flood of water in Seattle, the sailing isn't that great; in fact, you're lucky if the calm summer days cough up enough of a breeze to keep you moving bow-ward. However, in the spring, fall and winter a soft wind exhales over the sound, and sailing becomes a spectacular way to be outside. But even when the calm days keep the motor running, sailing offers views and perspectives you can only get on the water. More adventurous sailors head out on Puget Sound and along its inland waterways, or all the way up the coast to British Columbia.

Instruction & Rentals Sailing in Seattle (Map 7, ☎ 289-0094), 2040 Westlake Ave, offers sailing lessons for $100/hour. On Friday evenings it holds races on Lakes Washington and Union. Anyone can come join a racing crew and, though you should be somewhat fit, no experience is necessary; they'll show you what to do. Visit its Web site at www.sailing-in-seattle.com. For information on hiring Sailing in Seattle's 33-foot *Whoodat* see Organized Tours in the Getting Around chapter.

The Center for Wooden Boats (Map 7, ☎ 382-2628), 1010 Valley St, offers sailboat lessons and rentals on Lake Union. At least one person in your party needs to know how to sail and must do a checkout before you'll be permitted to rent. The checkout is pretty straightforward; you need to demonstrate tacking, jibing and docking. Weekday rentals cost $16/23.50 for small/large sailboats; $25/37.50 on the busy weekends. Nonsailors can rent rowboats for $12.50/18.75 weekdays; $20/30 weekends. The Center also offers sailing lessons, including an excellent beginner course for $250, which gives you as many lessons as it takes in a four-month period (usually eight to 12 lessons). Seasoned sailors who are a little rusty can take a one-on-one lesson for $30/hour. For more information check out the Center's Web site at www.cwb.org.

Windsurfing

Windsurfing is a big sport in Seattle; it's part of that quintessential Seattle mix of being in a band, having a job at an espresso stand and putting your sail up on the lake. As such, windsurfing draws more locals than tourists. Lake Washington is the most popular place to sail; it's big enough to accommodate traffic and out-of-control windsurfers. The warm waters of Green Lake are good for beginners, but it can get pretty congested in summer. Green Lake Small Craft Center (Map 10, ☎ 527-0171), 7351 E Green Lake Dr, offers lessons and rentals.

Between the sailboats, floatplanes and motor boat traffic, Lake Union is not good for anyone but expert windsurfers with full control. Usual launch spots are Magnuson and Mount Baker Parks. In summer, the calm waters of Puget Sound are good for experienced windsurfers; try setting out from Alki Beach in West Seattle, or from Golden Gardens northwest of Ballard.

Scuba Diving

Some people shy away from the chilly waters surrounding Seattle, but local divers will tell you that the marine biodiversity in the Northwest beats any tropical clime. Sure, you're not likely to see colorful tropical fish, but dive sites in Puget Sound and along the Northwest coast offer year-round diving and regular sightings of octopus, huge ling cod, cabezon, cathedral-like white anemones and giant sea stars.

Most of Seattle's best dive sites are actually out of Seattle, in sheltered coves and bays up and down the coast. Popular spots include Alki Cove, on the eastside of Alki Point, Saltwater State Park, south of Seattle in Des Moins, and Edmonds Underwater Park near the Edmonds Ferry Dock north of Seattle. Other popular spots include Port Angeles, Keystone and the San Juan Islands. For more information on area dive sites, pick up Lonely Planet's *Pisces Diving & Snorkeling Pacific Northwest* or look for *Northwest Shore Dives,* by Stephen Fischnaller, a helpful guide – considered the dive site bible by locals – to nearby sites.

Seattle dive shops offering **instruction and rentals** include Starfish Enterprise (Map 11, ☎ 286-6596), 600 W Nickerson St, on the south side of the Washington Ship Canal in northern Queen Anne. It offers rentals and instruction for all levels. Underwater Sports (☎ 362-3310), 10545 Aurora Ave, is the best place to go for gear repair, and it also offers courses in its on-site pool.

SWIMMING

Swimming is a great way to keep in shape. The following pools offer a variety of open swim sessions, lessons and lap swimming. Many pools host swim clubs or masters programs. Public pools include Evans Pool at Green Lake (Map, 10, ☎ 684-4961), 7201 E Green Lake Drive N; Queen Anne Pool (Map 7, ☎ 386-4282), 1920 1st Ave W; and Medgar Evers Aquatic Center (Map 12, ☎ 684-4766), 500 23rd Ave in the Central District. Drop-in fees are about $3. For information on other pools, contact Seattle Parks and Recreation at ☎ 684-4075.

When summer temperatures rise, there's no more popular place to be than on one of Seattle's **beaches**. One of the most popular is Alki Beach in West Seattle, a real scene with beach volleyball, acres of flesh and teenagers cruising in their cars. Green Lake Park has two lakefront swimming and sunbathing beaches, as do several parks along the western shores of Lake Washington, including Madison Park, Madrona Park, Seward Park, Magnuson Park and Mt Baker Park. Lifeguards are on duty at public beaches between 11 am and 8 pm mid-June to Labor Day at the beginning of September.

SKIING & SNOWBOARDING

When the winter rains make you squint in Seattle, you can bet that fluffy, blessed snow is kissing – make that making love to – the alpine peaks on the nearby Cascade mountains. Ski trips out of Seattle require driving from 90 minutes to a few hours, depending on which resort you want to go to. A couple of the ski resorts offer a shuttle from downtown, which is a convenient way to dodge

driving the snowy roads on high-elevation mountain passes. If you are taking a car, be sure to call ☎ 425-368-1944 for a report on current road conditions. If you're heading into the backcountry, contact the Northwest Avalanche Information Hotline (☎ 526-6677) and be absolutely certain you have a good understanding of trails and backcountry wilderness first aid. Contact The Mountaineers for training and advice before heading deep into the mountains. Also call the Cascade Ski Report (☎ 634-0200) for the latest on all local mountains.

The Summit at Snoqualmie

This ski and snowboard resort (☎ 425-434-7669, 236-1600 snow report), about 40 miles east of Seattle on I-90, encompasses four different ski areas: Alpental, Summit West, Summit Central and Summit East. The four areas vary greatly in difficulty and somewhat in conditions. Alpental is generally considered the most difficult, with steep slopes and a vertical drop of 2200 feet. Alpental also offers access to the backcountry. Summit West boasts one of the best snowboarding half-pipes in the Northwest, along with good terrain for beginner and intermediate skiers. Summit Central's lower slopes cater to families and beginner skiers, while its upper reaches offer treed runs and moguls. Summit East has a Nordic Center, with miles of trails for snowshoers and cross-country skiers.

Full rental and ski instruction options are available, and night skiing until 10 pm is offered daily except Sunday. One lift ticket is good at all four ski areas; free buses link the runs, as do trails on the slopes. All day weekend and holiday lift tickets cost $40/26/7 adult/seniors and youth/children six and under. Midweek, prices drop to $32/22/7. If you want to ski at night only (4 pm to 10 pm), lift tickets are $22/18/7. Rental equipment costs $25 for a ski package (boots, poles and skis) and $30 for a snowboard package (boots and board). Look for more information online at www.summit-at-snoqualmie.com.

Crystal Mountain Resort

One of the largest and most popular ski areas in Washington, Crystal Mountain Resort (☎ 360-663-2265, 888-754-6199 snow report), about 75 miles southeast of Seattle near Mt Rainier, offers year-round recreational activities.

Downhill skiers give Crystal Mountain high marks for its variety of terrain, which includes some very steep chutes and remote, unpatrolled backcountry trails for advanced skiers. Its summit (Silver King) tops out at 7012 feet; the vertical drop is 3120 feet. Crystal has 2300 acres of skiable terrain and 50 named runs, more than 50% of which are rated intermediate. The slopes are served by 10 lifts, including four high-speed chairs. Snowboarding in the deep bowls is also popular here. There's night skiing until 8 pm Friday to Sunday.

A variety of lessons is available, including a three-lesson package for just $150. All-day lift tickets cost $40/35/10 adults/youths 11 to 17/seniors. Children 10 and under ski

Northern Slopes

The skiing and snowboarding at British Columbia's mountain resorts draws snow enthusiasts from around the world, many of whom fly into Sea-Tac and drive to the wintry bliss. The following BC ski resorts are accessible by car or plane from Seattle.

Apex Mountain Resort If you're looking for no chair-lift line-ups and lots of technical skiing, Apex is the place to go.
Nearest town/city: Penticton, BC
Driving time from Seattle: seven hours
Information: ☎ 250-292-8222, 877-777-2739
Web site: www.apexresort.com

Big White Ski Resort One of the highest peaks in the Monashee Mountains, Big White has a mild climate, more than 100 marked trails and 8 sq km of terrain.
Nearest town/city: Kelowna, BC
Driving time from Seattle: 8½ hours
Information: ☎ 250-765-3101, 800-663-2772
Web site: www.bigwhite.com

Cypress Bowl Ski Area Just 20 minutes from downtown Vancouver, the wide, snow-filled Cypress bowl sits between Strachan and Black Mountains in the heart of Cypress Provincial Park.
Nearest town/city: West Vancouver, BC

Driving time from Seattle: 3½ hours
Information: ☎ 604-926-5612, 604-419-7669
Web site: www.cypressbowl.com

Fernie Alpine Resort Vast investment dollars transformed Fernie from a well-kept local secret to a fast-growing resort that could become the province's next Whistler.
Nearest town/city: Fernie, BC
Driving time from Seattle: 11 hours
Information: ☎ 250-423-4655, 800-258-7669
Web site: www.skifernie.com

Grouse Mountain Resort A 20-minute drive from downtown Vancouver, Grouse Mountain is a favorite for its easy access, night skiing and cheap lift tickets (compared to Whistler). An aerial tram whisks you to the mountaintop, offering incredible views along the way.
Nearest town/city: North Vancouver, BC
Driving time from Seattle: 3½ hours
Information: ☎ 604-984-0661
Web site: www.grousemountain.com

free. Rentals include ski packages ($33), telemark ski packages ($25) and snowboard packages ($32). More information is available on Crystal Mountain's Web site at www.skicrystal.com.

Stevens Pass

About 75 miles east of Seattle on Hwy 2, Stevens Pass (☎ 360-973-2441, 360-663-7711 snow report), with 37 runs, 11 lifts and a vertical drop of 1774 feet, is the state's second-largest downhill venue. Seasoned skiers love the dry snow, run variety and stellar views over the Cascades. Snowboarders cut trails through the powder and swoop around on the half-pipe. There's night skiing 4 pm to 10 pm daily.

All-day lift tickets cost $41/29/26/5 for adult/senior/youth/children under six. Night skiing only costs $26/24/22/5. Rentals include ski packages ($27) and snowboard packages ($32).

Just 5 miles east of the downhill resort is the Stevens Pass Nordic Center, which maintains 25 miles of groomed cross-country ski trails, a rental center and a restaurant. More information is available at www.stevenspass.com.

ROCK CLIMBING

There's plenty of climbing and mountaineering to be had in the Olympics and the Cascades, but even if your travel plans don't allow time for an excursion to the mountains, you can keep in shape by clambering up the faces at Seattle-area rock walls. REI's Pinnacle climbing wall is a 65-foot rock pinnacle to the side of the store's entryway (see the beginning of the chapter for REI's details). The wall is open for

ACTIVITIES

Northern Slopes

Kimberley Alpine Resort This resort is like an actress getting her first big break in the movies. Over the next few years, investment dollars will transform her from a small, humble mountain into a flashy, ever-expanding resort.
Nearest town/city: Kimberley, BC
Driving time from Seattle: 10 hours
Information: ☎ 250-427-4881, 800-258-7669
Web site: www.skikimberley.com

Mount Seymour Another local Vancouver area mountain (just 15 minutes from downtown Vancouver), Seymour is a haven for boarders, who come to rip it up in Seymour's three snowboard parks.
Nearest town/city: North Vancouver, BC
Driving time from Seattle: 3½ hours
Information: ☎ 604-986-2261
Web site: www.mountseymour.com

Red Mountain Ski Resort A breeding ground for Canadian Olympic skiers, 'Red' accesses two mountains – Red and Granite – and offers some of the province's best black-diamond runs.

Nearest town/city: Rossland, BC
Driving time from Seattle: eight hours
Information: ☎ 250-362-7384, 800-663-0105
Web site: www.ski-red.com

Sun Peaks Resort When there's no snow on Vancouver's mountains, locals head four hours northeast to Sun Peaks' Tod Mountain, where the snow falls early.
Nearest town/city: Kamloops, BC
Driving time from Seattle: five hours
Information: ☎ 250-578-7842, 800-807-3257
Web site: www.sunpeaksresort.com

Whistler/Blackcomb This world-famous, dual-mountain paradise can accommodate up to 54,000 skiers and snowboarders each day. With 5278 vertical feet, 11 sq miles of bowls, glades and steeps, the exploration seems endless. You could stay here for an entire season – and plenty of people do – and still not explore it all.
Nearest town/city: Whistler, BC
Driving Time from Seattle: 4½ hours
Information: ☎ 604-932-3434, 800-766-0449
Web site: www.whistler-blackcomb.com

scrambling at various times daily except Tuesday, when it's reserved for private groups. You can climb free of charge, but be prepared to wait your turn. In Ballard, Stone Gardens: The Climbers Gym (Map 11, ☎ 781-9828), 2839 NW Market St, is a full climbing gym with 14,000 sq feet of climbing surface on more than 100 routes. The gym also has weights, lockers and showers. Courses, from beginner climber to anchoring, are also offered. The drop-in rate is $12. If the weather is good, head to Marymoor Park in Redmond (on the Eastside), where there's a 45-foot outdoor climbing structure for all levels of climbers.

ULTIMATE FRISBEE

Ultimate is hugely popular in the Northwest and the many co-ed leagues offer games for players of every level. Disc Northwest runs a summer and winter league and is the primary resource for ultimate in the Seattle Area. It maintains the Disc NW Hotline (☎ 781-5840) and an up-to-date Web site at www.discnw.com, both of which give updates on league and pick-up games. Long-running pick-up games include 1 pm Saturday and 6 pm Wednesday at Dahl Field at 25th Ave NE and NE 77th St, above Ravenna Park and the U District. Pick-up games are also played noon Sunday at Sand Point in Magnuson Park, and 1 pm Saturday at Discovery Park. For directions to ultimate games, check the map section of the Web site.

The Potlatch tournament, held annually in Redmond in July, attracts the West Coast's top players.

TENNIS

Many of Seattle's public parks have tennis courts and unlike in other major cities, you usually don't have to wait long to play. The giant Seattle Tennis Center (☎ 684-4764), 2000 Martin Luther King Jr Way, in the Central District has the city's only indoor courts. You can play on one of the 10 courts for $15 for a singles game ($7.50 each) or $20 for a doubles game ($5 each). Seattle Parks and Recreation (☎ 684-4075) maintains a number of courts in parks throughout the city, and most are on a first-come, first-served basis. Play tennis on four courts in Volunteer Park on Capitol Hill, 10 courts in lower Woodland Park, adjacent to Green Lake, or on the four courts in Magnolia Playfield on 34th Ave W and W Smith St. For a full listing of public tennis courts contact Seattle Parks and Recreation.

GOLF

Seattle's Parks & Recreation Department (☎ 684-4075) runs three public golf courses in Seattle, along with a short course at Green Lake. The most popular municipal course is Jackson Park Golf Course (Map 1, ☎ 363-4747), 1000 NE 135th St, on the far northern edge of Seattle. This 18-hole course is best on weekdays, when there are fewer lines at the first tee. Another convenient tee spot is Jefferson Park Golf Course (Map 1, ☎ 762-4513), 4101 Beacon Ave S, an 18-hole course with short fairways and lots of lovely and mature – but sometimes troublesome – trees and bushes. The West Seattle Municipal Golf Course (Map 1, ☎ 935-5187), 4470 35th Ave SW, with 18 holes, is one of the area's best public courses, with superior views across Elliott Bay. Green fees for city courses are $25 per person on weekdays and $28 on weekends. When they are not booked, the courses offer reduced rates in the evenings.

The nine-hole course at Green Lake (☎ 632-2280), 5701 W Green Lake Way N, is a fun spot if you're just learning or lack the patience for a full course.

Every pigeon's favorite totem pole, Pioneer Square

And sometimes it rains. Occidental Square area

Signs and art around the city

RICHARD CUMMINS

The man himself, Chief Sealth, Pioneer Square

LEE FOSTER

Pioneer Square historic district

JOHN ELK III

The ornate pergola in Pioneer Square

Mailboxes for boat owners, Seattle Marina

Red sky at night, sailor's delight – Bell Harbor Marina

Places to Stay

It pays to plan ahead when you're booking a room in Seattle. Lodging can get tight in the popular summer months, specifically in July, August and September; during other times of the year, large conventions or special events can make finding a room difficult, especially if you want to stay in central Seattle.

Hotel prices soar in summer: Mid-range hotels run $80 to $170 a night; classier hotels easily double that. Thankfully, a few older hotels yet to be infused with renovation dollars offer cheap accommodations right in town. A few hostels, including Hostelling International's Seattle location near Pike Place Market, offer good values, but be prepared to book in advance in summer. Rates mentioned below are what you can expect to pay in peak season, though beware they can vary wildly depending on occupancy.

Options for out-of-season travelers are excellent. From mid-November through March 31, most downtown hotels offer Seattle Super Saver Packages. These rates are generally 50% off the rack rates, and they come with a coupon book good for savings on dining, shopping and attractions. To obtain the Super Saver Packages, or to get help finding a hotel when Seattle is all booked up, call the *Seattle Hotel Hotline* (☎ *461-5882, 800-535-7071*). You can also get information or make reservations on the Web site at www.seattlesupersaver.com.

The *Seattle B&B Association* (SBBA; ☎ *547-1020, PO Box 31772, Seattle, WA 98103-1772*) offers a brochure listing the association's member B&Bs.

Camping

Campers intending to visit downtown Seattle face lengthy commutes, with one exception. *Camp Long* (☎ *684-7434, 5200 35th Ave SW*) in West Seattle (Map 1) offers a unique semirustic option. This city park features 10 1930s wood cabins, 65 acres of forest, trails and a climbing rock. A nature center runs naturalist programs throughout

the summer. Each cabin has three double bunk beds (sleeping up to 12 people) and electric lights, but no heat or inside cooking facilities. Cabins are available Tuesday to Saturday and cost $35 a night. You must put down a refundable $50 damage deposit. Beware that this is not Party Central; the park gate closes at 10 pm and you must be inside by then. To get to Camp Long, take the West Seattle bridge exit from I-5 or Hwy 99. Follow signs to Fauntleroy Way SW. Take a left onto 35th Ave SW and another left onto Dawson St, where you'll find the Camp Long Nature Center.

Other options take you a little farther out of town to suburban campgrounds. In Bellevue, RVers should head to *Trailers Inn* (☎ *747-9181, 800-659-4684, 15531 SE 37th St*), which offers showers, an indoor pool, playground and laundry, but no tent facilities (see the Eastside map in the Excursions chapter). Sites range from $17 to $30, depending on the size of your rig. To reach the campground, take I-90 exit 11, turn south to the frontage road and follow the signs for five blocks.

Tent campers are pretty much limited to *Saltwater State Park* (☎ *800-233-0231, Washington State Parks*), a busy but pleasant beachfront park on Puget Sound, south of Seattle. Amenities include flush toilets, coin-operated showers (bring quarters), barbecues, hiking trails and a volleyball court. The 53 tent sites cost $14 and are on a first-come, first-served basis. To reach the park, take I-5 exit 149 west toward Des Moines. At the junction of Hwy 99 (also called Pacific Hwy), turn south and drive to 240th St. Turn west and follow signs to the park.

DOWNTOWN (Map 2)

Most of the following downtown motels offer some kind of parking program with in-and-out privileges, but you'll pay handsomely for it, usually between $12 and $20 a day. If you have a car, you'll need to factor the parking fees into the cost of staying downtown or else stay out at Seattle Center, where most lodgings offer free parking.

Hostels

Seattle's central YMCA no longer lets rooms, but the **YWCA of Seattle** (☎ 461-4888, 1118 5th Ave) rents rooms to women only; singles/doubles with private or shared bathroom start at $50/60. A few rooms without a bathroom or sink cost $33/44.

The **Green Tortoise Backpackers' Guesthouse** (☎ 340-1222, 888-424-6783, 1525 2nd Ave) charges $17 a night for a dorm bed and shared bathroom. It also has private rooms with a bathroom for $40 for one or two people. The hostel will arrange free pickup at the ferry terminal or bus and train stations and breakfast is included. Reservations are recommended, as this place fills fast with travelers from the Green Tortoise bus trips.

Hotels

Budget Just beyond the downtown core along the Monorail track, the **King's Inn** (☎ 441-8833, 800-546-4760, 2106 5th Ave) is a classic older motel that has somehow managed to resist the gentrification all around it. Rooms are incredibly basic with dated decor but are clean and a great deal, especially if you factor in the free parking. Standard rooms start at $65/75 single/double. See Belltown for two other budget hotels near downtown.

Mid-Range At the **Hotel Seattle** (☎ 623-5110, 800-426-2439, 315 Seneca St), basic but cozy rooms run $86/96 single/double. The **Pacific Plaza Hotel** (☎ 623-3900, 800-426-1165, 400 Spring St) is centrally located, just a block from the Four Seasons Olympic Hotel. Though small, the nicely remodeled rooms come with a big breakfast and range from $110 to $135. There's no air-conditioning, so it's not a good choice in summer.

Long one of Seattle's landmarks, the **Camlin Hotel** (☎ 682-0100, 800-426-0670, 1619 9th Ave) is worth a look for its beautiful lobby, which once again sparkles from recent renovation. Or stop by for a cocktail at the swanky Cloud Room on the top floor

(see the Entertainment chapter). Rooms here start at $100/110 single/double. The Camlin has been on the brink of a major renovation project for years. Though plans are still tentative, the hotel will close for a year, so call ahead to make sure it's open.

The **WestCoast Vance Hotel** (☎ 441-4200, 800-426-0670, 620 Stewart St) is another nicely restored older hotel in a classic European style. The hotel's 165 rooms aren't the largest in Seattle, but they're well appointed and comfortable. Rates range from $120 to $150. In winter, both the Camlin and the Vance offer special reduced B&B rates that include a free breakfast.

There's no old-fashioned glamour at the **Sixth Avenue Inn** (☎ 441-8300, 800-648-6440, 2000 6th Ave), a motor inn just five minutes north of the downtown shopping frenzy. Though the decor won't win any awards, it's clean, the price is right and there's free parking. High season rates range between $80 and $125 single, $110 and $140 double.

Nearby, and for a bit more money, the **Claremont Hotel** (☎ 448-8600, 800-448-8601, 2000 4th Ave) is an older hotel that didn't lose its comforting vibe or gain snobbery through its restoration. The location is good, close to both Pike Place Market and the downtown boutique malls. Its suites are spacious and worth the money if you're traveling with friends or family. Standard rooms range from $145 to $170, suites cost $190 to $220.

North of downtown toward Seattle Center, the no-fuss, no-muss **Days Inn Town Center** (☎ 448-3434, 800-225-7169, 2205 7th Ave) has rooms starting at $125/135, including parking. **Loyal Inn Best Western** (☎ 682-0200, 2301 8th Ave) has a whirlpool and sauna, complimentary continental breakfast and parking. Rooms cost $106 to $149. The newly renovated **Hawthorne Inn & Suites** (☎ 624-6820, 800-437-4867 in Washington, 2224 8th Ave) has the same amenities as the Loyal Inn, plus complimentary dinner every Wednesday. Rooms start at $140/150. **Travelodge Seattle City Center** (☎ 624-6300, 800-578-7878, 2213 8th Ave) also has free breakfast and parking, with basic rooms starting at $105/120.

Top End Most large hotel chains have facilities in Seattle, offering business travelers and convention-goers modern rooms with a wide range of facilities. The best of these is the *Sheraton Seattle Hotel & Towers* (☎ 621-9000, 800-325-3535, 1400 6th Ave); room prices range from $190 to $405. The *Westin Hotel Seattle* (☎ 728-1000, 800-228-3000, 1900 5th Ave) is another luxury business hotel with almost 900 rooms starting at $250. The *Renaissance Madison Hotel* (☎ 583-0300, 800-468-3571, 515 Madison St), in the former Stouffer Madison, is one of the city's nicest hotels, with rooms starting at $160/180 single/double.

Ramada Inn Downtown (☎ 441-9785, 800-272-6232, 2200 5th Ave) is within the Ride Free Area, on the Monorail route and about equidistant from downtown and Seattle Center. The rooms here cater to the business crowd; they are basic, featureless and seem overpriced, starting at $170/180.

For a unique Northwestern experience, stay at one of Seattle's local luxury hotels or one of the many historic grand hotels, many of which have been remodeled and retooled; both options offer gracious comforts of another era. The prices listed are peak rates; at most hotels, weekend packages and off-season deals will lower the prices considerably.

If you're coming to Seattle to shop, then the *Mayflower Park Hotel* (☎ 623-8700, 800-426-5100, 405 Olive Way) is for you. Immediately next door to the Westlake Center, this is also a good choice if you're going to take the Monorail out to Seattle Center for an event. The Mayflower was one of the first older downtown hotels to renovate, and its furnishings now don't quite seem of the class of the more recent luxury renovations at other vintage Seattle hotels. Still, it's a very comfortable place and a relatively good value for its location. Standard rooms start at $190 and suites range from $220 to $400.

The *Alexis Hotel* (☎ 624-4844, 800-426-7033, 1007 1st Ave), near Madison St, is a modern hotel tucked inside an old architectural exoskeleton. This is a hotel that emphasizes quiet, high-quality service and amenities, where the emphasis is on elegance rather than dramatic views or ostentatious glamour. Room prices range from $250 for a basic room up to $460 for a fireplace suite. Two-bedroom suites can reach up to $725. The cool thing about the Alexis is that you can bring your dog for an extra $25; the staff will even walk Rover for you.

The exceedingly artistic and hip *Hotel Monaco Seattle* (☎ 621-1770, 800-945-2240, 1101 4th Ave) is housed in the old Seattle Phone Building, which sat vacant before the Kimpton group from San Francisco recently converted it. The spacious suite-style rooms, all of which are individually decorated and colorfully furnished, begin at $240 to $395. Other Kimpton hotels include the Alexis and the *Hotel Vintage Park* (☎ 624-8000, 800-624-4433, 1100 5th Ave). Rooms here are a little smaller and get a bit more noise from I-5, but it's a very pleasant place to stay, especially if you get a west-facing room. Rooms start at $255 to $300, suites from $525. Again, prices for all these hotels sink in winter.

Although it doesn't look the part, *The Paramount Hotel* (☎ 292-9500, 800-426-0670, 724 Pine St) is a new hotel. Built with the elegant lines of a vintage historic structure, the hotel's 146 rooms are large and exquisitely furnished. The downstairs bar and lobby alone are worthy of a visit. Rooms start at $230.

There's no question that Seattle's doyen of old money and elegance is the *Four Seasons Olympic Hotel* (☎ 621-1700, 800-821-8106 in Washington, 800-332-3442 elsewhere, 411 University St). Imposing and luxurious, the Olympic was built in 1924, and subsequent remodels have worked to maintain the period glamour of its architecture. This 450-room hotel drips with opulence as bellhops, maids and concierges jump to your service. You'll feel like you've walked onto a set in an extra-suave Cary Grant picture. It's worth walking around the hotel even if you can't cough up the cash to stay here. Summer rates start at $395/405 and get steeper the more deluxe you get.

PLACES TO STAY

FIRST HILL (Map 2)

The *Inn at Virginia Mason* (☎ *583-6453, 800-283-6453, 1006 Spring St)* is on First Hill, just above downtown near a complex of hospitals. This nicely maintained older hotel caters to families needing to stay near the medical facilities, but it also offers quiet rooms to other visitors and has a nice rooftop garden overlooking the city. Rates begin at $120 for both singles and doubles, up to $240 for king suites; there are discounts if you are staying at the hotel for family medical reasons.

The *Sorrento Hotel* (☎ *622-6400, 800-426-1265, 900 Madison St)* was Seattle's finest hotel when it was built in 1909 for the Alaska-Yukon-Pacific Exposition. After substantial and continual refurbishing, this beautiful hotel in Italian Renaissance style, bejeweled with chandeliers and lined with mahogany, is again one of Seattle's best. Rooms for two people start at $235, and suites go from $280.

PIONEER SQUARE (Map 4)

Options are limited for accommodations in Pioneer Square, with one exception: The *Best Western Pioneer Square Hotel* (☎ *340-1234, 77 Yesler Way)* is in the historic heart of Seattle. This recently refurbished older hotel has some nicely appointed rooms at $160/180. Nightlife, restaurants and shopping are just steps from the door.

PIKE PLACE MARKET & THE WATERFRONT (Map 5)
Hostels

Housed in a former US immigration station, *Hostelling International – Seattle* (☎ *622-5443, reserve@hiseattle.org, 84 Union St)* is in a prime location at the south end of Post Alley, near the Pike Place Market and just above the waterfront. This bustling hostel offers 199 beds in 23 different rooms, including family and private rooms. A large common area with a TV, kitchen and laundry facilities are provided, along with information on Seattle events, attractions and excursions. Dorm bed rates are $17/20 for HI members/nonmembers. Four-bed rooms cost $19/23. Reservations are essential in summer. Check out the hostel's Web site at www.hiseattle.org.

Hotels

In a town with few cheap hotels and hardly any B&Bs right downtown, *Pensione Nichols* (☎ *441-7125, 1923 1st Ave)*, at Stewart St, is somewhat of a treat. Right in the urban thick of things between Pike Place Market and Belltown, this charmingly remodeled older hotel has ten rooms that share four bathrooms and a large common area that overlooks the market. Rooms cost $75/95 and they come with a complete and tasty breakfast.

Only one Seattle hotel actually faces directly onto Elliott Bay, and that's on the Waterfront at Pier 67. *Hotel Edgewater* (☎ *728-7000, 800-624-0670, 2411 Alaskan Way)* boasts excellent views over Puget Sound. When this hotel was first built, people paid a premium to stay in the rooms so they could literally hang over the bay and fish from the windows. Times have changed, and fishing is no longer allowed, but if you came to Seattle to experience the tang of sea air, this might be the hotel for you. Prices are steep and range quite a bit, depending on your proximity to saltwater. Peak-season rooms off the water start at $325; a waterfront suite can set you back as much as $450. Needless to say, during the rainy winters, room rates drop significantly.

Right in the thick of things at Pike Place, the *Inn at the Market* (☎ *443-3600, 800-446-4484, 86 Pine St)* is an elegant and architecturally interesting hotel and the only lodging in the venerable Pike Place Market. This 70-room boutique hotel has large rooms, many of which enjoy grand views onto market activity and Puget Sound. Room prices range from $190 to $380.

BELLTOWN (Map 6)

Considering that Belltown is one of Seattle's hippest areas, it's surprising that this is where you'll find some of the best hotel deals. Two large but modest older hotels offer inexpensive lodgings central to downtown, Pike Place Market and Belltown; the rooms are best described as no-frills, but there's nothing scary about them, and you can't argue with the rates. In fact, you can afford a suite here for the price of a closet at a remodeled hotel.

The cavernous *Commodore Hotel* (☎ 448-8868, 800-714-8868, 2013 2nd Ave) offers a mix of options, including $20 hostel rooms, rooms with bathroom down the hall ($49/59 single/double) and rooms with two beds and bathroom ($87). The hotel has a deal with two nearby city parking garages, so you only pay $3 a day when you stay at the hotel, a big plus in this part of Seattle. The once grand *Moore Hotel* (☎ 448-4851, 800-421-5508, 1926 2nd Ave) offers 135 bedrooms with shared bathrooms for $35/45 or with private bathrooms for $60/70.

Two of Seattle's most unique lodgings are found – characteristically – in Belltown. Right in the heart of all the dining and nightlife is the *Wall Street Inn* (☎ 448-0125, 800-624-1117, 2507 1st Ave), which follows neighborhood tradition as a converted space. The building used to be a residence for sailors in the merchant marine; however, the space has been updated into 20 large guestrooms, some with period details (including some original Murphy beds), others with kitchens or killer views out the back onto Elliott Bay. Robes and slippers come in the rooms, and breakfast is included. This family-run inn offers a cozy and cheery respite from the bustle of Belltown. Furnishings are sleek and modern; no rickety antiques here. Prices range from $120/135 for a room with a Murphy bed and kitchenette, or $140/155 for a queen-bed luxury room.

If you're looking for the absolutely coolest place and best value in town, you've found it at the *Ace Hotel* (☎ 448-4721, 2423 1st Ave), above Cyclops at 1st and Wall St in the heart of Belltown. Each of the Ace's 34 immaculate, artsy rooms is unique and so fashionable you quickly get the feeling you're the star of a film noir masterpiece. Rooms also come stocked with free condoms and a copy of the *Kama Sutra*. Rooms range from European-style with shared bathrooms ($65 to $85), to deluxe rooms ($130 to $175) that come with private bathrooms, CD players and enough mirrors to make you feel like a movie star.

SEATTLE CENTER (Map 7)

Staying around Seattle Center makes sense for a number of reasons: It's only five minutes from downtown on the Monorail or bus, and room prices are usually lower than those downtown (except when big concerts or festivals are on at Seattle Center). You can also park your vehicle free of charge at most hotels, and that's no small matter in Seattle.

None of the following is more than five minutes from the action at the Space Needle. Most of the hotels around here are fairly anonymous, motor-court type lodgings from the 1960s, but they are in good repair and offer no negative surprises. Many also cater to business travelers, so they are efficient, but devoid of much character.

At the *Vagabond Inn* (☎ 441-0400, 800-522-1555, 325 Aurora Ave N), youths 18 and under can stay free when accompanied by their parents, which is especially great when you're trying to scrounge enough dough to send your herd up the Space Needle. Rooms start at $94/105. The slightly rundown *Seattle Inn* (☎ 728-7666, 800-255-7932, 225 Aurora Ave N) has an indoor pool, exercise room and spa and a children's play area. It offers rooms for $79 for one or two people. Be warned that both of these hotels are on Aurora Ave N where the roar of traffic rarely ceases. Ask for rooms on the west side of the hotels.

The *Travelodge by the Space Needle* (☎ 441-7878, 800-578-7878, 200 6th Ave N) is much quieter. Amenities include a year-round Jacuzzi, a seasonal pool, coffeemakers, complimentary continental breakfast and parking. Rooms start at $109/119. Also in the shadow of the Space Needle, the *Best Western Executive Inn* (☎ 448-9444, 800-351-9444, 200 Taylor Ave N) has an exercise spa and a complimentary shuttle to downtown. Rooms start at $111/126. Across Aurora Ave N, the gigantic *Holiday Inn Express* (☎ 441-7222, 226 Aurora Ave N) has 195 rooms, an indoor pool, weight room, free continental breakfast and parking. Standard rooms start at $129; one-bedroom suites go up from $159, and two-bedroom suites start at $200.

PLACES TO STAY

QUEEN ANNE (Map 7)

A couple of blocks north of Seattle Center, the *Hampton Inn* (☎ 282-7700, 700 5th Ave N) has 198 rooms, most of which have balconies. There's a wide variety of rooms, ranging from the comfortable standard for $179/189 single/double to one-bedroom suites for $209 and two-bedroom suites with a fireplace for $289.

Immediately to the west of Seattle Center is Lower Queen Anne, essentially an extension of Seattle Center. It's only a five-minute walk from here to the opera house or Key Arena and a 10-minute walk to the Space Needle. The *Inn at Queen Anne* (☎ 282-7357, 800-952-5043, 505 1st Ave N) is a 1929 apartment building turned hotel. Rooms come with kitchenettes and continental breakfast, or you can grab a complimentary apple from the bowl in the lobby. Standard rooms cost $99; deluxe rooms cost $109. The only difference is that the deluxe rooms have air-conditioning.

Another old (1918) apartment building, the recently converted *MarQueen Hotel* (☎ 282-7407, 888-445-3076, 600 Queen Anne Ave N) has hardwood floors throughout and a variety of rooms, most of which have kitchenettes leftover from their days as apartments. Standard rooms cost $150/160, deluxe rooms with king-size beds cost $175/185 and suites start at $195.

On Queen Anne Hill, just north of Lower Queen Anne and Seattle Center, a clutch of nice older homes now serve as B&Bs. One of the best in the city is *Queen Anne Hill B&B* (☎ 284-9779, 1835 7th Ave W), on the west side of Queen Anne. It boasts majestic views of the Olympic Mountains over Puget Sound. Common areas include a sundeck, sun porch and a nice garden. There are four guestrooms decorated with Pacific Northwest art and antiques; three of the rooms have private bathrooms. Rooms range from $99 to $109.

LAKE UNION (Map 7)
B&Bs

If you think you know what life on a tugboat is like, then get ready to be surprised by *Tugboat Challenger Bunk & Breakfast* (☎ 340-1201, 1001 Fairview Ave N). The tugboat's eight rooms are small but perfectly charming. It has a common area with a fireplace, and the excellent breakfast included in the rates make this a good place to meet people and start your day. Rooms cost $55/85 single/double; up to $185 for the Admiral Suite. Get to the tugboat by taking Fairview Ave N to the Yale St Landing; it's directly behind the TGI Friday's restaurant.

Hotels

The modest *Eastlake Inn* (☎ 322-7726, 2215 Eastlake Ave E), on the east side of Lake Union, is one of the least expensive places to stay in central Seattle. Looking more like a motor inn, the Eastlake is nothing fancy, but it's close to everything in Lake Union, parking is included, and some rooms have kitchens. Rates are $75/85 for the first floor/second floor (with a view over Lake Union).

The new *Silver Cloud Inn Lake Union* (☎ 447-9500, 800-330-5812, 1150 Fairview Ave N) has 184 rooms, some of which have stunning views of Lake Union. The hotel has a gym, indoor and outdoor pool, laundry facilities, free parking and breakfast. It also provides a free shuttle service to downtown, a handy amenity in this area. Nonview rooms range from $150 to $185, while rooms with views start at $170 to $220.

If you're in Seattle for any length of time and price isn't an object, consider the appealing all-suite *Marriott Residence Inn* (☎ 624-6000, 800-331-3131, 800 Fairview Ave N). A lap pool, exercise room and spa let you work off all those excellent Seattle meals. All rooms have kitchens, and there's complimentary breakfast and evening desserts in the lobby; rooms on the west have good views of Lake Union. Again, rates here vary depending on whether you get a view or not. Studio suites start at $200, one-bedroom suites begin at $220 and two-bedroom suites start at $230.

Over on the southwest side of Lake Union, the *Courtyard Marriott* (☎ 213-0100, 800-321-2211, 925 Westlake Ave N) has all the big hotel amenities, including an indoor pool and restaurant. Rooms start at $190/200 for nonview/view.

CAPITOL HILL (Map 8)

Capitol Hill used to have a couple of hostels that gave budget travelers a choice for cheap digs on the Hill. They've both since shut down, and now inexpensive accommodations are hard to come by. However, some of Capitol Hill's lovely old homes have converted into beautiful B&Bs and, once you consider the free breakfast, location and cozy rooms, you'll see that you get a lot for your money. Seattle's unique B&Bs are dwindling fast; as housing prices skyrocket, many homeowners find it more viable to sell. Soon, the B&Bs could become a thing of the past.

The **Bacon Mansion B&B** (☎ 329-1864, 800-240-1864, 959 Broadway E), a couple blocks north of all the action on Broadway, offers 11 unique guestrooms, nine with private bathrooms. Rates at this 1909 Tudor-style mansion range from $94 to $154. Rooms include TVs and voicemail. **Mildred's B&B** (☎ 325-6072, 1202 15th Ave E) is a Victorian home across the street from Volunteer Park. The four guestrooms, each with private bathroom, range from $135 to $150. **Salisbury House B&B** (☎ 328-8682, 750 16th Ave E) is also near the park. The five guestrooms at this 1904 home range from $95 to $149. All rooms have private bathrooms and include a delicious vegetarian breakfast. On a much larger scale the **Gaslight Inn B&B** (☎ 325-3654, 1727 15th Ave E) has 15 rooms available in two neighboring homes, 12 of which have private bathrooms. In summer, it's refreshing to dive into the outdoor pool. Rooms range from $78 to $178. The **Hill House B&B** (☎ 720-7161, 800-720-7161, 1113 E John St), close to the hub of Capitol Hill, has seven guestrooms in a restored 1903 home. Five of the rooms have private bathrooms, and all the rooms come with queen beds and down comforters. Fresh flowers add a nice touch. Rates range from $80 to $105 for a room with shared bathroom, while private rooms range from $95 to $160.

Cozy **Capitol Hill Inn B&B** (☎ 323-1955, 1713 Belmont Ave), on the west side of Capitol Hill, is a 1903 Victorian home with seven rooms ranging from $120 to $170. One of Capitol Hill's most fantastic homes, the **Shafer Baillie Mansion** (☎ 322-4654, 800-922-4654, 907 14th Ave E) has 11 rooms, three of which have a shared bathroom. Most rooms have great views. This is the kind of grand old house that was built with a ballroom. Rooms with shared bathroom start at $79, and private rooms go up to $145.

THE U DISTRICT (Map 9)
B&Bs

The 1915 Georgian-style **Chambered Nautilus B&B Inn** (☎ 522-2536, 800-545-8459, 5005 22nd Ave NE) has six guestrooms decorated with authentic British antiques. The communal living room has a welcoming fireplace, and the full gourmet breakfast is reason enough to stay here. One of Seattle's first B&Bs, it's still one of the best. Its location – between the university and Ravenna Park – can't be beat. Rooms come with down comforters, bathrobes and voicemail. Rates are $99 with a detached bathroom or $104 to $129 with a private bathroom.

Hotels

Budget The closest thing the U District has to a hostel, the **College Inn** (☎ 633-4441, 4000 University Way NE) is a great inexpensive option. The building, built for the 1909 Alaska-Yukon-Pacific Exposition, has 25 European-style guestrooms, where the rooms have a sink, but the bathrooms are shared. This is a friendly, no-frills place that's a perfect spot to hang your hat while visiting UW. The cheapest rooms start at $45 and go up to $85 for two people. South-facing rooms get the most light. Rates include a continental breakfast served in the communal lounge. Stair-phobes should be aware that the old building lacks elevators, and you have to climb four flights up a narrow stairway.

Mid-Range Off I-5 exit 169, a number of moderately priced motels near the university and only a few miles from downtown cater to the U crowd and people visiting the Wallingford or Green Lake areas. The 135-room **University Plaza Hotel** (☎ 634-0100, 800-343-7040, 400 NE 45th St) is on the west side of the freeway, not far from campus. There's a heated swimming pool, gym, restaurant and an antique Steinway player piano in the lobby. Standard rooms cost $99/109 single/double. One of the best values in town, the *University Inn* (☎ 632-5055, 800-733-3855, 4140 Roosevelt Way NE), three blocks from campus on the north side of the University Bridge, has 102 rooms. Rooms are ironically reminiscent of university dorm rooms, which gives this friendly place a university-like bustle, and you'll more than likely join an interesting conversation in the lobby. Other features include a whirlpool, outdoor pool, laundry facilities and dataports on the phones. There's also a free continental breakfast. Standard rooms cost $105/115, deluxe rooms cost $117/127 and suites start at $139.

Just east of the university near the University Village mall, *Seattle University Travelodge* (☎ 525-4612, 800-578-7878, 4725 25th Ave NE) is close to the university, Husky Stadium and the Children's Hospital. Amenities include an outdoor pool and a year-round hot tub. Rooms start at $96/106. Nearby, the *Silver Cloud Inn* (☎ 526-5200, 800-205-6940, 5036 25th Ave NE) is a tastefully decorated hotel with large, clean rooms ranging from $110 to $125.

The art deco *Best Western University Tower* (☎ 634-2000, 800-899-0251, 4507 Brooklyn Ave NE), in the former Meany Tower Hotel, is one of the classiest places to stay in the U District. The same architect who designed the Old Faithful Lodge in Yellowstone National Park built this hotel in 1931. Recent renovations have given it a face-lift, modernizing the hotel's 155 comfortable rooms while keeping them decidedly unfussy. Rooms come with dataport phones, mini fridges and microwaves. There's a gym, a pub and free continental breakfast. Most rooms have good views and range from $89 to $179.

NEAR THE AIRPORT

If you're flying in to Sea-Tac late at night or out early in the morning, you might want to stay near the airport. The following hotels all offer complimentary airport shuttles and do a good job of getting you to and from the airport on time. The no-frills *Airport Plaza Hotel* (☎ 433-0400, 18601 Pacific Hwy S) has basic rooms for $50/55. The *Days Inn at Sea-Tac Airport* (☎ 244-3600, 800-325-2525, 19015 International Blvd S) has 86 rooms, a small gym and free continental breakfast. Rooms here start at $87/91. If you're looking for something fancier, the *Radisson Hotel Seattle Airport* (☎ 244-6000, 800-333-3333, 17001 Pacific Hwy S) has 308 rooms, a restaurant, lounge, outdoor pool, gym and sauna. The free shuttle will also take you to nearby restaurants or car rental agencies. Standard rooms here start at $109, suites start at $199.

Places to Eat

Seattle's restaurant scene offers a bewildering array of inexpensive eateries, where you can get everything from a thick burrito to a savory bowl of Thai noodles for less than $8. Alternately, way at the other end of the spectrum are some of Seattle's fine dining establishments, where you can max out your credit card on a seafood dinner. Some of the most expensive restaurants in the Northwest show up in Seattle, and the caliber is only getting better. Not long ago, you only had a few well-worn restaurants to choose from when it came to splurging on dinner, but today's bistros, seafood houses and ethnic choices excite even the most discerning palates.

In this book, restaurants are broken down into budget, mid-range and top end. In general, budget indicates a café or restaurant where you can get a meal for less than $10. Mid-range restaurants serve main dishes that cost from $10 to $18. Top-end restaurants serve meals that cost more than $18. Most restaurants have a bar or lounge, where you can order a drink and an appetizer if you don't want to have a whole meal. This is a great way to tour the restaurant scene without totally blowing your budget.

Seattle is a casual place that often seems underdressed compared to most other North American or European cities. This means there are few places where 'casual dress' is inappropriate.

Self-Catering

Between restaurant hopping, it's always good to know where a good supermarket is, and Seattle's got plenty. The following local groceries pay special attention to high-quality produce and products often hard to find at regular groceries. Thriftway Market has a few locations including Queen Anne (Map 7, ☎ 284-2530), 1908 Queen Ave N, and West Seattle (Map 1, ☎ 937-0551), 2320 42nd Ave SW. In Lower Queen Anne, higher-end and hard-to-find gourmet ingredients can be found at Larry's Market (Map 7, ☎ 213-0778), 100 Mercer St, which also has a good fresh seafood department.

On Capitol Hill, Madison Market (Map 8, ☎ 329-1545), 1600 E Madison St, has a great deli with food to go, along with a good selection of wines at reasonable prices. Get a shot of wheatgrass juice at Rainbow Natural Grocery (Map 8, ☎ 329-8440), 417 15th Ave E, along with a good selection of vitamins and natural foods.

The place to go in the U District is City Greens Market (Map 9, ☎ 675-1221), 1120 NE 45th St. At Pike Place Market, Louie's on the Pike (☎ 443-1025), 1926 Pike Place, is always bustling. See Market Stalls under Pike Place Market, later, for more market options.

DOWNTOWN (Map 2)
Budget
You could eat your heart – or wallet – out in the central downtown area, where a majority of the restaurants are designed with business meetings and expense accounts in mind. If you're on a budget and just want some grub, you'd be much better off finding cheap eats in Pike Place Market, in Belltown or in and around Pioneer Square, which are all within walking distance from the downtown core. If you're already downtown and want cheap food, go to the food court in Westlake Center at 4th Ave and Pine St.

For a pub scene with good food, try the *Rock Bottom Brewery* (☎ 623-3070) in Ranier Square at 5th Ave between Union and University Sts. This brewpub, open until 2 am daily, brews five of its own beers, including the tasty Flying Salmon Stout. The grub is good and reasonably priced. Try the Salmon BLT ($9) or the veggie enchilada ($8).

Mid-Range
When people think about Northwest food, visions of old-fashioned oyster bars and cavernous chophouses filled with rowdy yeomen come to mind. While local purveyors try to

Northwest Cuisine

With a long seacoast, fertile valleys of fields and orchards and miles of grassland devoted to live-stock, the Pacific Northwest grows an abundance of high-quality food products. Local chefs appreciate this natural bounty and prepare indigenous foods with simple elegance, along with an attitude that eating great food ought to be great fun.

Besides the high quality of the raw materials, what distinguishes Northwest cuisine from standard US food is the influence of Asian cooking traditions. Pan-Asian cooking, often referred to as Pacific Rim cuisine or fusion food, is the blending of American or European standards with ingredients from Asia. It results in some unusual combinations – don't be surprised if you get wasabi on your French fries.

Seafood is a cornerstone of Northwest cuisine. Restaurants vie for recognition of having the best fish-and-chips or the best clam chowder (which, in the Northwest style, is cream based). Crab, often Dungeness fresh from the boat, is available almost everywhere – you'll see stacks and stacks of crabs at Pike Place Market. In restaurants, crab is usually served in salad or with garlic butter, but you can also get crab cakes, crab bisque or even crab burgers.

The chilly waters of the Pacific produce sweet-tasting, delicately tangy oysters, causing oyster farms to spring up all along the coast. In good restaurants, discerning diners can choose which Northwestern bay their oysters on the half shell hail from. Clams, usually steamed in broth or seawater, are common as an appetizer. The elongated, delicately flavored razor clam, in particular, gets nobility status on the West Coast. Mussels, which cover practically every rock along the Pacific Coast, are also catching favor as harvestable seafood. Beware if you're out looking for oysters, clams or mussels on your own: Red tides often poison bivalves, making them unsafe to eat. Also fishing laws limit the amount – and season – you can harvest them.

Locally caught fish include red snapper, flounder, sole, tuna, halibut and cod. Shrimp is another major catch. Salmon, still a menu staple, is as likely to be from Alaska as from the Northwest. Local trout is also found in fish markets and on menus: Watch for vibrantly yellow golden trout.

The Northwest offers an incredibly rich diversity of **fruit**. Blueberries thrive in the acidic soil, and they appear in pies, breads, muffins and scones. The mild climate is also good for strawberries and raspberries. Washington is the nation's largest producer of apples, and other notable orchard crops include pears, cherries and peaches.

The thick forests also provide a bounty of fruit. Blackberry brambles snag clothing and grab at the legs of hikers. They're a great annoyance until late summer and early fall, when they produce a heady abundance of purple-black fruit. Delicate, light-orange salmonberries make a good hiker's snack or, if you can gather enough, a beautiful pastel jelly. A favorite of black bears, wild huckleberries are found high up in mountain meadows. Washington State is also a major producer of tart, bright-red cranberries, which appear in a bewildering array of local dishes.

Wild forest **mushrooms** garner a great deal of interest; especially noteworthy are the expensive varieties favored in French, Italian and Japanese cuisine. Mushrooms indigenous to Northwest forests include the chanterelle, oyster, morel, porcini and shiitake mushrooms, which are shipped worldwide.

No discussion of food from the Northwest would be complete without mentioning **nuts**. Filberts, or hazelnuts, grow profusely here, as do walnuts. For that special Northwest touch, look for hazelnut gift packs (some jazzed up in smokehouse- or jalapeno-style) or hazelnuts served in baked goods or with meat.

expunge this stereotype and the frontier yeoman get replaced with stockbrokers and bankers, the turn-of-the-20th-century steak and fish house still reigns at a few entertaining Seattle restaurants.

McCormick's Fish House & Bar (☎ 682-3900, 722 4th Ave) offers daily fresh fish specials, mostly grilled with zesty sauces, a fine selection of local oysters, chops and steak. The restaurant is a series of wood-lined, brass-outfitted chambers that gives off the aura of a bustling Victorian men's club. With similar mahogany boy's club decor, the handsome and atmospheric *Metropolitan Grill* (☎ 624-3287, 820 2nd Ave) is a favorite of stock analysts and bankers who pour out of nearby office towers. But broker types aren't the only ones who enjoy this venerable and historic bar and steakhouse; the Met popularity extends to anyone, especially those with a corporate credit card. Though you can get fish or even Beluga caviar, beef's the big thing here; many consider this the top chophouse in the city. A steak dinner – at both McCormick's and the Met – averages around $22. Both places are open weekdays for lunch and daily for dinner.

One of downtown's most stylish see-and-be-seen scenes is *Palomino Euro-Bistro* (☎ 623-1300, 1420 5th Ave), on the top floor of the City Centre Mall. The dining room is saturated with color and is always filled with gregarious, well-dressed diners, all of whom seem to know one another, or at least pretend they do. It's open for lunch and dinner. The divine *Dragonfish Asian Café* (☎ 467-7777, 722 Pine St), in the Paramount Hotel, is known for its exceptional cocktails, but the food here is pretty good too. Come here during its daily happy hours (4 to 6 pm and 10 pm to 1 am), where pot stickers, duck spring rolls and caramel-ginger chicken appetizers are just $3. This is a great spot for dinner, too, with entrées ranging from $12 to $22. Atmosphere is everything at the hipster-attended *icon Grill* (☎ 441-6330, 1933 5th Ave). It is decorated with elaborate multilamped chandeliers, enormous glass baubles and pink-orange lighting that makes you relax, like viewing life through rose-colored glasses. The lunch menu presents such things as ahi stir-fry ($12) and a cold meatloaf sandwich ($8). At dinner, entrées average $18. The *Palace Kitchen* (☎ 448-2001, 2030 5th Ave) is an excellent spot for an appetizer and cocktail in the bar, or stick around for a meal. Daily dinner specials present such wonders at spaetzl stuffed pumpkin ($18) or traditional pork loin ($21). The best thing about this place is that it's open until 2 am daily; this is by far the best choice for post-bar or aprés-movie munchies.

Top End

If Seattle is in fact home to a school of cuisine (as many here fervently presume), then the following restaurants are among the best practitioners. The *Dahlia Lounge* (☎ 682-4142, 2001 4th Ave) usually gets credit for having created the idea and the reality of Northwest cuisine. Its owners, Tom Douglas and Jackie Cross, started fusing flavors at this Seattle institution in the late 1980s and single-handedly made Seattleites more sophisticated. The duo also owns Etta's Seafood (see Pike Place Market, later) and the Palace Kitchen mentioned above. The *Painted Table* (☎ 624-3646, 92 Madison St) is an unpretentious, pretty restaurant in the Alexis Hotel also known for its pairing of local ingredients with Pacific Rim flair. Like the Dahlia, it's open weekdays for lunch and daily for dinner. If you're fond of standing in line to eat, join everyone else at *Wild Ginger* (☎ 623-4450, 1403 3rd Ave) Asian restaurant and satay bar . This wildly popular restaurant features the fiery cuisine of Indochina. Though it recently moved from its more intimate location near Pike Place Market, this swanky spot still packs 'em to the rafters, despite the staff's snobbish tendencies.

The city's best old-school restaurants specialize in swank service and elegance that you just don't find at newer restaurants. The waiters are professionals, the cocktails honest and the food downright elegant. *Fullers* (☎ 447-5544, 1400 6th Ave), at the Sheraton Seattle Hotel & Towers, is one of those places. A longtime favorite spot to splurge, Fullers has inventive cuisine, impeccable service and an extremely fine dining room. It's only open for dinner Tuesday to Saturday. A treat above treats, the *Georgian Room* (☎ 621-7889, 411 University St), at the Four Seasons Olympic Hotel, is one of the most imposing restaurants in the city. The high ceilings and dripping chandeliers, shiny silver and gilt details will have you spinning. The food is equally eye-catching and stylistically inspired by regional ingredients. The Georgian is open for lunch and dinner. Lunch entrées range from $13 to $20, and dinners average $20 to $35.

Nikko (☎ 322-4641, 1900 5th Ave), in the Westin Hotel Seattle, is the city's most attractive Japanese restaurant, with a giant sushi bar, robata bar with many grilled goodies and inventive variations on Japanese standards. It's open for dinner only Monday to Saturday. For a refined Italian dining experience, try *Tulio Ristorante* (☎ 624-5500, 1100 5th Ave), at the Hotel Vintage Park. The cuisine in this intimate brass-and-dark-wood dining room is classic Italian, with great grilled meats and hearty pasta dishes. Lunches, such as the delicious ravioli stuffed with salmon, fetch $13; meat dinners average about $25.

FIRST HILL (Map 2)

First Hill is not known for it's food, especially with so much competition in nearby downtown, but there are a couple of places worth checking out. The *Bean Collection/ Caffé Pacifica* (☎ 626-6476, 1000 Madison St) is the place to go for a coffee and hearty sandwich or bowl of soup. Avoid it at noon, when doctors and nurses from the nearby hospitals flock here for lunch.

Across the street, *The Hunt Club* (☎ 343-6156, 900 Madison St), inside the Sorrento Hotel, ought to be on the short list if you're looking for a special occasion, top-end restaurant. The setting is absolutely beautiful: an intimate mahogany-paneled dining room shimmering with candles and decked with flowers. The food is equally stellar, featuring local lamb, fish and steaks accentuated with inventive sauces. It's open daily for lunch and dinner.

PIONEER SQUARE (Map 4)
Coffeehouses

The original *Torrefazione Italia* (☎ 624-5847, 320 Occidental Ave S) is along the cobblestone walk in Occidental Square. When this shop opened in the late 1980s, the strong but flavorful coffee was a revelation that made Starbucks seem institutional (the real Italian *baristas* that staffed the coffee shop in the early days were also a major draw for both male and female fans). The lovely Italian faience cups and saucers are a classy touch. Another very pleasant place for a cup of coffee and a quiet conversation is *Zeitgeist* (☎ 583-0497, 171 S Jackson), a dimly lit and moody place that's instantly comfortable.

Restaurants

Budget Seattle's best bakery is *Grand Central Baking Co* (☎ 622-3644, 214 1st Ave S) in the Grand Central Arcade. It creates peasant-style loaves and baguettes and offers lunchtime salads and focaccia sandwiches. The *Elliott Bay Café* (☎ 682-6664, 101 S Main St), downstairs at the Elliott Bay Book Co, is a cozy place for soup, salad and sandwiches.

You can get inexpensive burgers and sandwiches at a number of Pioneer Square taverns, but for the same money you can also enjoy good ethnic food. For great burgers, you can't do better than the *J&M Cafe* (☎ 624-1670, 201 1st Ave S). For the best $5 falafel and humus in town, visit *Zaina* (☎ 624-5687, 108 Cherry St). Nearby, *Bakeman's* (☎ 622-3375, 122 Cherry St) is an old-fashioned diner with great American standards like meatloaf sandwiches ($3.50), chili ($2) and hot apple pie ($2).

Mae Pim Thai Restaurant (☎ 624-2979, 94 Columbia St) attracts a lively lunchtime crowd who come for the $4.60 lunches, including the irresistible garlic tofu. *Cafe Hue* (☎ 625-9833, 312 2nd Ave S), not far from Occidental Square, doesn't look like much on the outside, but the inside is decorated with tableaus of mother-of-pearl inlaid in black lacquer. You can taste the colonial French influences in the yummy Vietnamese food.

Mid-Range Purportedly the oldest operating restaurant on the West Coast, the friendly *Merchants Cafe (☎ 624-1515, 109 Yesler Way),* established in 1890, serves a wide assortment of salads and hot sandwiches ($7) and steak, seafood and chicken entrées ($10 to $14). The café is open for breakfast (omelets are the specialty), lunch and dinner and has a very reasonable beer and wine list. It's a good place to get a bite to eat or a drink, if only to check out the historical idiosyncrasies of the place, such as the stand-up bar, all 30 feet of it, that came from the East Coast on a schooner.

If you've got a hankering for Italian, you're in luck in Pioneer Square. *Trattoria Mitchelli (☎ 623-3883, 84 Yesler Way)* serves good pasta, pizza and calzones, all of which are about $9 and come with salad. The main attraction here, however, is that it stays open until 4 am Tuesday to Saturday to feed all those barhoppers hungry from prowling the local music clubs.

More authentic, dignified and, of course, expensive, *al Boccalino Ristorante (☎ 622-7688, 1 Yesler Way)* offers excellent pasta dishes but really delivers with innovative grilled fish and seafood dishes. Dinners average $20.

You can't come to Seattle without stopping by *FX McRory's Steak, Chop & Oyster House (☎ 623-4800, 419 Occidental Ave S),* if only to drink a beer on any day the Seahawks or Mariners play. This vast Pioneer Square landmark across from the sports stadiums is always full of jocks and can get completely out of hand after home games. It claims to have the largest selection of bourbon in the world; add 18 Northwest beers on tap and a stand-up oyster bar and you've got quite a party. At mellower times (when there's not a home game), diners can admire the lovely architecture and enjoy well-prepared New York steak ($24) in the restaurant. You can get less-pricey food in the bar, including burgers for $9.

Top End Often mentioned in discussions of Seattle's best restaurants, the very upscale *Il Terrazzo Carmine (☎ 467-7797, 411 1st Ave S)* is a showcase of European luxury that serves succulent multicourse Italian meals. A small fountain and the rustling of green ferns serenade the almost-hidden terrace out back. This is a wonderful spot in summer. If you come for a leisurely dinner, be prepared to spend at least $60 per person. If you want to check it out but don't want to stay for dinner, you could have an appetizer and drink in the lounge while checking out Seattle's elite.

INTERNATIONAL DISTRICT (Map 4)

The ID is another great neighborhood for cheap eats. The many Vietnamese, Thai and Chinese restaurants that line Jackson St between 6th and 12th Aves give you plenty of options. In many of these restaurants, you'll have trouble spending more than $7 on lunch or $10 at dinner. In the ID, there are places where the tourists go and places where everyone else goes. The following suggestions emphasize local favorites over those with lines and, consequently, higher prices.

If you're looking for a snack, stop by the *Sun Bakery (☎ 622-9288, 658 S Jackson St)* for a yummy Chinese pastry fresh out of the oven. The bakery specializes in ultra-fancy wedding cakes, which seems odd in this part of town. Anyone will tell you that the best bowl of phô in town is served up at the crazily popular *Pho Hoa (☎ 624-7189, 618 S Weller St).* The large bowl of noodles, broth and meat is only $5, and it's almost enough for two. It's open until 10 pm daily. For a cheap snack or meal, visit the *House of Dumplings (☎ 340-0774, 512 S King St),* across from Uwajimaya. Eight very good vegetable dumplings cost $5.

Hing Loon (☎ 682-2828, 628 S Weller St) specializes in Cantonese seafood dishes. The steamed prawns with garlic or the seafood tofu hot pot cost $9.25. The place is clean, the service fast. A bit pricier but with higher quality is *Sea Garden (☎ 623-2100, 509 7th Ave S).* Hot pots cost $9 to $14; huge bowls of noodle soup cost between $5 and $9. The menu at *Shanghai Garden (☎ 625-1689, 524 6th Ave S)* travels all over China, making this one of the best Chinese restaurants in the neighborhood. This popular restaurant presents an interesting selection of dishes that thankfully strays far from the usual sweet-and-sours and foo yungs.

Enjoying a leisurely dim sum stands as perhaps one of the best ways to spend a Sunday morning. In the ID, you can get excellent dim sum any day of the week. The following have regular menus too, but they are especially noted for their dim sum. *China Gate* (☎ 624-1730, 516 7th Ave S) is arguably the best place in town for dim sum. The Hong Kong–style menu offers a couple hundred choices. Dim sum is served twice daily; 10:30 am to 3 pm and 9:30 pm to 2 am. A close contender if you want to deal with huge crowds of locals, *Top Gun* (☎ 623-6606, 668 S King St) serves up good dim sum with such an authentic menu, you need to trust that what you're ordering won't kill you. *Sun Ya Seafood* (☎ 623-1670, 605 7th Ave S) is another excellent spot. If your hankering for dim sum hits in the middle of the day, head to *House of Hong* (☎ 622-7997, 409 8th Ave S). Dim sum is served 10 am to 5 pm daily.

East of 8th Ave S and I-5, Little Saigon takes over and the flavor becomes decidedly Vietnamese. In Asian Plaza on the corner of S Jackson St and 12th Ave, *Thanh Vi* (☎ 329-0208, 1046 S Jackson St) offers up authentic Vietnamese cuisine at very reasonable prices. Check out the charbroiled pork chop ($6) or salted fried squid ($6.50) with a bottle of Vietnamese beer. *Saigon Bistro* (☎ 329-4939, 1032 S Jackson St) is a favorite for its filling soups and special 'dry' noodles. This place also serves up a killer Kung Pao chicken.

PIKE PLACE MARKET (Map 5)

For a wide selection of fresh produce, bakery products, deli items and takeout ethnic foods, head to Pike Place Market. Explore the market on an empty stomach and commit to a few hours of snacking; you'll be full by the time you leave, and it doesn't have to cost you much. However, if you're looking for serious dining, you can find it here, too; some of Seattle's favorite restaurants are tucked in mysterious corners in the market district. For a full directory and map

of everything in the market, be sure to pick up a copy of *Welcome to the Pike Place Market*. Get it from the market information booth on 1st Ave at Pike St, in front of the main entrance.

Market Stalls

The market offers endless choices for quick snacks to munch on the run. *DeLaurenti's* (☎ 622-0141), in the Economy Market Building, has a takeout window on 1st Ave for freshly baked pizza.

Jack's Fish Spot (☎ 467-0514), in the Sanitary Market Building, sells fresh fish and offers fried fish-and-chips at the counter hidden behind the tanks and refrigerator cases. Next door, *Three Girls Bakery* (☎ 622-1045) is *the* place in the market for cookies, bread and other baked goods. You can also buy sandwiches from the takeout window. *Sisters Café* (☎ 623-6723), right up the alley, is a more traditional deli with giant sandwiches served on focaccia bread.

In the Triangle Building, at Pike Place and Stewart St, *Mr D's Greek Deli* (☎ 622-4881) is the place for takeout *spanakopita* and gyro sandwiches. Next door, *Mee Sum Pastries* (☎ 682-6780) is famed for its *hum baos,* meat- or vegetable-filled buns (kind of like a pot sticker).

In the Main Arcade, stop by the *Market Grill* (☎ 682-2654) for a killer salmon, prawn, halibut or cod sandwich with rosemary mayonnaise for $7, including coleslaw. Across the way, stop by *Uli's Famous Sausage* for a free sample of their delicious spicy sausage.

Coffeehouses

Coffee shops are thick down around the market, offering solace to harried shoppers and affording venues of vantage for people watchers. You can get espresso from many of the shops and bakeries in the market, but the following coffee shops warrant a stop. *SBC (Seattle's Best Coffee)* (☎ 467-7700), in the Post Alley Market, is a lively place with outdoor seating in fair weather. The original *Starbucks* (☎ 448-8762), on Pike Place between Stewart and Virginia Sts in the Soames Dunn Building, started steaming here in 1971. Even if you resent its mass franchising, you've got to make a pilgrimage because – admit it – Starbucks got you addicted.

Restaurants

Budget If you want a sit-down meal but nothing fancy, some of the market cafés offer delicious, inexpensive food. Both of the following Main Arcade eateries are as old as the market itself; they are well loved by shoppers, businesspeople and fellow market operators. *Lowell's Restaurant* (☎ 622-2036) serves up classic eye-opening breakfasts and cheap-and-cheerful lunches. Though the name implies Greek food, the *Athenian Inn* (☎ 624-7166) is actually the place for good American standards and fresh seafood, including excellent calamari.

If for some reason you've been hankering for Bolivian cuisine, hanker no more. *Copacabana Cafe* (☎ 622-6359), in the Triangle Building, offers delicious heaping Andean dishes like *pollo saltado* (braised chicken with green peppers and tomatoes) for $11.25. Good looks aside, perhaps the best reason to explore South American cuisine may be this convivial restaurant's great views over Pike Place Market.

You don't have to pay a handful to sample good Northwestern seafood, and *Emmett Watson's Oyster Bar* (☎ 448-7721), in the Soames Dunn building, is here to prove it. The uninspired decor is at least authentic, but the selection of oysters, chowder and grilled fish is excellent.

World Class Chili (☎ 623-3678) is a restaurant devoted to the many faces and strengths of chili soup. World Class Chili is on the lower level of the Economy Market Building, below DeLaurenti's – enter from 1st Ave. Another option in the market is the *Pike Place Pub & Brewery* (☎ 622-6044, 1415 1st Ave), with burgers and better-than-average pub grub to accompany a pint of ale. The pub also gets good views over Elliott Bay.

Mid-Range The *Pike Place Bar & Grill* (☎ 624-1365), in the Corner Market Building, is a relatively simple and unaffected place for a drink and good American standards from the grill. Upstairs, in an intentionally small and hard-to-find spot, *Matt's in the Market* (☎ 487-7908) is a gem, which locals protect fiercely. If you're lucky enough to get a seat in this tiny place, sip some wine, have a snack (all food, while delicious, is cooked on camping stoves) and admire the view over the bay.

A Seattle institution, the *Pink Door Ristorante* (☎ 443-3241, 1919 Post Alley), between Stewart and Virginia Sts, titillates first-time visitors by posting no sign. Just head for the pink door with the amazing Italian aromas wafting out, and *eccolo!* Lunch is mostly pasta dishes ($8) and a soul-stirring cioppino ($12); at dinner, á la carte entrées start at $14. *Café Campagne* (☎ 728-2233, 1600 Post Alley) is the casual younger sibling of upscale Campagne (see later), and the quality of the French-style cooking is what you'd expect from this talented kitchen. Unlike at its older sister, however, the prices here are manageable, and you don't have to dress up for dinner. *Place Pigalle* (☎ 624-1756, 81 Pike St) sits at the back of the market behind the Main Arcade, with great views over the sound. Oddly (given its name), the restaurant isn't French; instead, it serves up well-prepared seafood (it gets fresh salmon daily) and a variety of meats, including duck and rabbit.

In the street below the market, *Typhoon!* (☎ 262-9797, 1400 Western Ave) now occupies the former home of Wild Ginger, which gave up this space for a bigger and less attractive one downtown (see Downtown, earlier). Though it had big shoes to fill, Typhoon! fits them better than Cinderella. Creative, colorful Thai food fills the menu, and you are left with the taste of artwork in your mouth. Lunches come in two sizes for $7 or $9. Dinners average $12. If you're not up for the full meal, slink on up to the satay bar for a beer and a sampler of grilled lemongrass pork ($2.50) or portobello mushroom ($2).

Also outside the market, but still part of the scene, *Wolfgang Puck Café* (☎ 621-9653, 1225 1st Ave) is the California food guru's casual, eye-poppingly decorated bistro. Pizza, salads and pasta are the building blocks of the very international and well-priced menu. A few blocks north,

PLACES TO EAT

past Stewart St, *Le Pichet* (☎ 256-1499, *1933 1st Ave*) is a tiny French bistro and wine bar that could easily fill with dull, snooty types, but it doesn't. It's elegant and tasteful, but there's always an interesting conversation to overhear or contribute to. The reasonably priced menu features traditional French cuisine but without the aorta-clogging heaviness often found in French food.

Top End At *Il Bistro* (☎ 682-3049), in lower Post Alley, the best and freshest of the market is incorporated into daily Italian-influenced specials. Its red lighting gives it a gangster-movie atmosphere; even the Godfather would enjoy the roasted chicken ($20) or the herb-crusted pork loin ($27), with some pasta and red wine, of course. For the ultimate splurge, *Campagne* (☎ 728-2800, 86 Pine St), in the Inn at the Market, is Seattle's best traditional French restaurant, with an emphasis on the foods of Gascony. Try the pan-roasted sea scallops ($26) or the free-range beef tenderloin ($33). *Chez Shea* (☎ 467-9990), upstairs in the Corner Market Building, is another treasure hidden in one of the market's many corners. Great views over the sound combine with Mediterranean-influenced prix-fixe menus (four courses for $40) to make this one of the city's most romantic restaurants. You can also forego dinner and have a snack at the bar. *Maximilien-in-the-Market* (☎ 682-7270) hangs off the back of the Main Arcade and offers French bistro-style food in a warm and welcoming atmosphere; views are great.

Just north of the market along Western Ave are two excellent spots for seafood. *Etta's Seafood* (☎ 443-6000, 2020 Western Ave) is famous for its brunch served 9 am to 3 pm daily, with such mouth-waterers as poached eggs with Dungeness crab and chipotle hollandaise ($13). If you don't eat fish or meat, the dinner menu offers few choices, but the king salmon ($24) is almost enough to convert even ardent vegetarians. Across the street, *Cutter's Bayhouse* (☎ 448-4884, 2001 Western Ave) draws locals and tourists alike for its fresh Asian-influenced seafood and excellent views across Elliott Bay.

THE WATERFRONT (Map 5)

You can't eat all that well along the Waterfront, but you can eat a lot. The entire area is one fast-food gauntlet, but before you settle for a corndog, go to one of the following for a better class of snack.

For inexpensive fish-and-chips or clam chowder, stop at one of the *Steamer's Seafood Cafe* locations; one at the aquarium (☎ 624-0312), the other at Pier 56 (☎ 623-2066). As evident by the total domination of *Ivar's Acres of Clams* (☎ 624-6852, 1001 Alaskan Way), at Pier 54, Ivar Haglund was a local character and relentless self-promoter. He did, however, know how to fry clams and fish-and-chips. A meal here won't be your quintessential Seattle meal, but it's a tradition, and the outdoor seating on the wharf is lovely in nice weather. Much the same can be said for the pricier *Elliott's Oyster House* (☎ 623-4340, 1203 Alaskan Way), at Pier 56, except you have a choice of local oysters on the half shell as well as fried fish.

Over on at the Bell St Pier (Pier 66) at the Bell Harbor Conference Center, you'll find *Anthony's Pier 66* (☎ 448-6688, 2201 Alaskan Way). This branch of a local seafood chain fits perfectly in its Waterfront digs. It's pleasantly upscale, and the traditional seafood gives a pleasant nod to the Pacific Rim. Dinners average $22. Views are spectacular; this is also a great place for a drink. Below, the restaurant's offspring *Bell Street Diner* is a less formal version of Anthony's.

At the northern end of the waterfront, the *Old Spaghetti Factory* (☎ 441-7724, 2801 Elliott Ave) serves up well-prepared, well-priced pasta and is always popular with families or large groups.

BELLTOWN (Map 6)

This hip neighborhood flanking downtown is the uncontested center of fine dining in Seattle. Yes, you can eat well here, but you don't need to empty your wallet to do it. The beauty of Belltown is that you can

Grungy Belltown's going seriously upscale.

spend a little or spend a lot and still get a fabulous meal. Thankfully, an abundance of delis, inexpensive pubs and low-budget hangouts frequented by arty musicians and starving students are still found throughout the neighborhood.

Budget

The *Lux Coffee House* (☎ 443-0962, 2226 1st Ave) is the place to pick up your requisite cuppa joe. For baked goods or panini sandwiches, head to *Macrina* (☎ 448-4032, 2408 1st Ave), an artsy bakery that makes some of the best bread in town. If you've got a craving for matzoh balls or a sub sandwich with Italian meat, stop on by the New York–style *The Buffalo Deli* (☎ 728-8759, 2123 1st Ave). Join the hipsters at *Counter Culture Cafe* (☎ 441-8075, 2219 2nd Ave), where a decent-size soup and sandwich costs $6. The relaxing *Cherry Street Coffee House* (☎ 441-7176, 2121 1st Ave) serves up smoothies, salads and sandwiches.

Walk into *Belltown Pizza* (☎ 441-2653, 2422 1st Ave) and just try to resist. You can't. These guys know how to make pizza and the price is right. A large – enough to feed four hungry people – costs $15. You can also get salads, pasta and sandwiches.

Though you'd more likely go to *Crocodile Cafe* (☎ 448-2114, 2200 2nd Ave) to hear live music, the Croc has a decent diner-style menu, with big breakfasts, lunches and dinners for less than $8. The wildly popular, California-style *Mama's Mexican Kitchen* (☎ 728-6262, 2234 2nd Ave) is always packed. But that's no surprise for a place that serves $6 burritos, huge combination plates and, from 4 to 6 pm Monday to Saturday, $2.75 margaritas; it's filled with Mexican kitsch artifacts. Every stop in Seattle must include a visit to the *Noodle Ranch* (☎ 728-0463, 2228 2nd Ave). It is a hip diner with delicious Pan-Asian noodle dishes, such as the red curry with yams ($8). Vegetarians will be in noodle heaven here.

The venerable (and nonsmoking) *Two Bells Tavern* (☎ 441-3050, 2313 4th Ave) serves one of Seattle's best burgers and a couple of dozen regional draft beers.

Mid-Range

The best place in town for excellent and well-priced sushi is *Shiro's Sushi Restaurant* (☎ 443-9844, 2401 2nd Ave). Sushi master Shiro Kashiba uses only the freshest ingredients and takes his sushi very seriously. For Japanese noodles and soup try *Saito's Japanese Café & Bar* (☎ 728-1333, 2122 2nd Ave).

The easygoing, nonsmoking *Belltown Pub* (☎ 728-4311, 2322 1st Ave) is a great place for a beer. The excellent menu transcends usual pub fare. For the ultimate in groovy, stop by *Cyclops* (☎ 441-1677, 2421 1st Ave), where the decor is dominated by red vinyl and trippy art. Cyclops is a bar on one side and a restaurant on the other; after the dinner hour the two seem to merge. Leisurely weekend breakfasts here are a must. It is open for dinner daily and for breakfast on weekends only. For a different vibe entirely, the handsomely austere *Queen City Grill* (☎ 443-0975, 2201 1st Ave) offers great seafood from its daily menu and a solid selection of meats and chicken from its seasonal menu. The goat cheese appetizer ($9) and the grilled ahi ($22) are divine.

PLACES TO EAT

Sushi heaven at Shiro's in Belltown

Way at the north end of Belltown at the corner of 1st Ave and Denny Way, almost in Lower Queen Anne, *Caffe Minnie's* (☎ 448-6263, 101 Denny Way) is a 1950s-style diner open 24 hours – a blessing if you've got the munchies at 2 am.

Top End

Locals agree *Flying Fish* (☎ 728-8595, 2234 1st Ave) serves up the best seafood in town. This exciting restaurant specializes in using delicate spices and a little joie de vivre to transform an ordinary piece of salmon or tuna into something truly magical. The dining room is bustling and energetic, the service friendly and top-notch. A fresh sheet daily means you'll never painstakingly choose from the same menu twice. Dinners here average around $20 and are well worth it. Another good seafood stop in Belltown, *Falling Waters Seafood Restaurant* (☎ 374-3707, 2020 2nd Ave) infuses its seafood with Asian flavors. You'll see such menu items as swordfish and scallops over crab-filled pot stickers ($25) or amaretto prawns ($21). Both of these places are open for dinner only.

Owned by chef Christine Keff, who also owns Flying Fish, *Fandango* (☎ 441-1188, 2313 1st Ave) blasted onto the Seattle scene with gusto. Offering up Latin American food and a lively atmosphere, Fandango will be around for a while.

A contender for the title of Seattle's best formal Italian restaurant, *Lampreia* (☎ 443-3301, 2400 1st Ave) specializes in grilled meat and poultry and is known for its excellent wine list. Dinners, served Tuesday to Saturday, range from $20 to $30.

The popular and boisterous *Marco's Supperclub* (☎ 441-7801, 2510 1st Ave) travels the globe with its multiethnic menu, including Jamaican jerk chicken ($15) and eggplant masala ($14); the deep-fried sage leaves ($8) are mandatory. Old-school flair meets cool retro swank at *El Gaucho* (☎ 728-1337, 2505 1st Ave), a modern re-creation of a 1950s supper club, complete with massive steaks, a cigar room, dozens of single-malt scotches and a very stylish clientele. Service is impeccable and an integral part of the show. Dining here is not a meal; it's a thrilling, educational event. À la carte dinners range from $28 to $40; accompanying side dishes are around $5 each.

SEATTLE CENTER (Map 7)

No compilation of Seattle restaurants would be complete without a mention of *Sky City* (☎ 443-2111, 219 4th Ave N), the revolving restaurant atop the Space Needle. Of course the views are tremendous from 500 feet up in the air, but you pay dearly for it. Appetizers cost almost the price of a meal at a top-end restaurant, and dinners range from $27 to $42 per person, or you can get a seafood sampler for $45. The ride up the elevator is free if you have dinner reservations.

QUEEN ANNE (Map 7)
Many of the dining options in Lower Queen Anne, just west of Seattle Center, are geared toward the pre- or postgame crowd attending games at Key Arena. Up on top of the hill, in Upper Queen Anne, restaurants are a bit more upscale, with some very good ethnic restaurants vying for well-heeled customers.

Coffeehouses
Uptown Espresso Bar (☎ 285-3757, 525 Queen Anne Ave N) is the place to meet in Lower Queen Anne. This place is always crowded with filmgoers and refugees from Seattle Center. In Upper Queen Anne, *Caffe Ladro* (☎ 282-1549, 2705 Queen Anne Ave N) is a good spot to read a book. Also try *El Diablo Coffee Company* (☎ 285-0693, 1811 Queen Anne Ave N), where the Latin music and bright walls make this a cheery spot to sip a coffee, devil and all.

Restaurants
Budget In Lower Queen Anne, *Pacific Dessert Company* (☎ 284-8100, 127 Mercer St) is famous in Seattle for its fabulous rich cakes and good coffee. It's a popular after-performance stop for well-dressed operagoers.

In Upper Queen Anne, everyone's favorite breakfast and hangover diner is the *5 Spot* (☎ 285-7768, 1502 Queen Anne Ave N). Try a classic, like the red flannel hash ($8). Avoid the weekends when lines snake out the door, or go early – or go to the 5 Spot for lunch or dinner; this is an excellent place for a quiet meal featuring good American cooking.

Mid-Range In Upper Queen Anne, at Queen Anne Ave N and Boston St, is a clutch of very good ethnic restaurants. *Chinoise Café* (☎ 284-6671, 12 Boston St) is a Pan-Asian restaurant with dishes ranging from Korean barbecue to Japanese sushi to Vietnamese soups. Try the delicious lemongrass stir-fry ($8). Next door, and with outdoor seating, *Orrapin Thai Cuisine* (☎ 283-7118, 10 Boston

St) is the place for excellent Thai curries and noodles. Adding to the ethnic mix, *Banjara* (☎ 282-7752, 2 Boston St) serves up good Indian curry and tandoori dishes and offers all-you-can-eat lunch and dinner buffets.

Popular *Paragon Bar & Grill* (☎ 283-4548, 2125 Queen Anne Ave N) is a bastion of American regional cooking, with a specialty in grilled fish and updated American classics. There's an open fireplace and a lively bar scene. Locals flock to *Queen Anne Café* (☎ 285-2060, 2121 Queen Anne Ave N). This ultra-trendy popular neighborhood spot is open for breakfast, lunch and dinners and serves up traditional comfort food, including sandwiches (around $8) and broiled pork chops ($12).

Top End Lower Queen Anne's fine-dining house is *Kaspar's* (☎ 298-0123, 19 W Harrison St), where fresh Northwest fish and produce are prepared with Continental deftness. The Swiss-born chef-owner is one of Seattle's celebrity chefs. The elegantly understated decor of the dining room adds greatly to the experience, making this an unpretentious place to sip a glass of wine or dine out. Dinners here start at about $20.

A very groovy spot in Upper Queen Anne, *Sapphire Kitchen & Bar* (☎ 281-1931, 1625 Queen Anne Ave N) has a good bar and serves up Spanish-influenced Mediterranean food in a chic dining room with sapphire, red and purple walls. Though the neon sign outside doesn't exactly fit with Queen Anne's style, don't let it turn you off. The Sapphire serves dinner daily and brunch on Sunday.

LAKE UNION (Map 7)
Ringing Lake Union are a number of popular restaurants, most of which offer outdoor seating during fair weather. Over on the west side of the lake, *Adriatica Restaurant* (☎ 285-5000, 1107 Dexter Ave N), at Ward St, sits in an old home overlooking Lake Union at the top of a dizzying flight of stairs. Adriatica offers fantastic views along with its excellent Italian pasta, veal and fish dishes. Meals here average $14 to $22.

PLACES TO EAT

Along the lake's southeastern shores, you'll find longtime favorite ***Chandler's Crabhouse & Fresh Fish Market*** (☎ 223-2722, 901 Fairview Ave N). The location is great – you can watch the boats and seaplanes skimming the lake – and the food is really good. Fish and seafood dishes flirt with international seasonings and preparations just enough to make them exciting but not overbearing. Expect to pay upwards of $20 for a meal at dinner; lunch averages $10 to $15. It's open daily for lunch and dinner and on the weekends for brunch. At the same address, ***Cucina! Cucina! Italian Café*** (☎ 447-2782) can be kind of an annoying singles scene, but the food is pretty good and reasonably priced (entrées average $8 to $14) – stick to the pastas and boutique pizzas – and after a drink, you'll relax into the atmosphere.

Perhaps no restaurant epitomizes old Seattle money as much as ***Canlis*** (☎ 283-3313, 2576 Aurora Ave N), on Hwy 99 on the south side of the Aurora Bridge. Since the 1950s this place overlooking Lake Union has been synonymous with fine dining and, unlike many old-fashioned martini-and-filet-mignon steakhouses, Canlis never went out of style. You'll find fresh fish and seafood, amply cut steaks and excellent service; the piano bar here is another fixture, both very dated and very chic.

On Lake Union's east side is Eastlake, a cool neighborhood that seems far from downtown but is in fact minutes away. Dim lights, good wine and excellent Italian cuisine reign at the delectable ***Serafina*** (☎ 323-0807, 2043 Eastlake Ave E). This is a rich dining experience, both in terms of the full-flavored entrées and the dark, romantic dining room. It gets very busy, so call ahead or be prepared to wait. It's open for lunch weekdays and for dinner daily. In good weather, there's dining on the garden terrace. Up the street, ***Bandoleone*** (☎ 329-7559, 2241 Eastlake Ave E) serves up good Latin food in an inviting and lively atmosphere. You can snack on the small plates (average $10) or go for a full meal (average $20). It is open – for dinner only – daily until 2 am.

CAPITOL HILL (Map 8)
Coffeehouses

Capitol Hill is the center of coffee-shop culture. If you're near the dance clubs on Pine and Pike Sts, head to ***Caffé Vita*** (☎ 325-2647, 1005 E Pike St). The patrons here have fluorescent hair, pierced tongues and plenty of attitude; Vita's open late. Near the bottom of the corridor, ***Bauhaus*** (☎ 625-1600, 301 E Pine) looks like a library (the books are for sale) – wear your best brooding black and have some heavy conversation.

Up on Broadway, you must visit the ***Vivace*** (☎ 860-5869, 321 Broadway E), a tiny espresso stand where you can pay your respects to the Sacred Shrine of Caffeina, Goddess of the Working Day, or sit outside and watch the world go by. ***B&O Espresso*** (☎ 322-5028, 204 Belmont Ave E) is a pleasant spot to write a postcard. If you're looking to nurse a coffee and check your email, you've got a couple of good choices. ***CapitolHill.net*** (☎ 860-6858, 219 Broadway E), upstairs in the Alley Mall, is a quiet spot. The ***Online Coffee Company*** (☎ 328-3713, 1720 Olive Way) also offers beer and wine. This mellow place offers good respite from the chaos of Broadway.

Restaurants

Budget There's no end to good and inexpensive places to eat along Broadway, especially if you like ethnic food. A popular spot for noodles and sushi is the ***HaNa Restaurant*** (☎ 328-1187, 219 Broadway E). ***Siam on Broadway*** (☎ 324-0892, 616 Broadway E) is a favorite for Thai food. For vegetarian meals and fresh juices in a Jetsons-like futuristic interior, go to the ***Gravity Bar*** (☎ 325-7186, 415 Broadway E) in the Broadway Market. The local fave for pizza by the slice ($2) is ***Pagliacci Pizza*** (☎ 324-0730, 426 Broadway E). If you find yourself up late, ***Caffe Minnie's*** (☎ 860-1360, 611 Broadway E) is open 24 hours. If you're looking for a microbrew and a burger, ***Deluxe Bar & Grill*** (☎ 324-9697, 625 Broadway E) is hard to beat.

Just down the hill from the Broadway strip is ***Hamburger Mary's*** (☎ 324-8112, 1525 Olive Way), the local bastion of this San Francisco–inspired burger-and-kitsch emporium. Nearby is one of the best places in town for vegetarian food, the **Green Cat Cafe** (☎ 726-8756, 1514 E Olive Way). It serves up such scrumptious dishes as the Buddha Bowl – rice, veggies and curry noodles – for a mere $5.25.

Near the bottom of the corridor, **Bimbo's Bitchin' Burrito Kitchen** (☎ 329-9978, 506 E Pine St) has more than just a fabulous name. Come here for huge burritos ($5) or for happy hour 4 to 7 pm daily, when drinks are $2. Bimbo's is open until 2 am every day. Near the top of the corridor, **Globe Cafe** (☎ 324-8815, 1531 14th Ave) is mostly known for its poetry readings on Tuesday and Sunday nights, but it's also a good stop for healthful pastries and vegan food.

Mid-Range & Top End Along the Broadway strip, **Café Septieme** (☎ 860-8858, 214 Broadway E) is a trendy, intensely minimalist and arty café with sophisticated yet unfussy homemade grub, including a provolone cheeseburger ($8) or free-range chicken ($15). The **Broadway New American Grill** (☎ 328-7000, 314 Broadway E) mixes a rowdy bar scene with good burgers, ribs and a killer Jamaican jerk chicken ($11). **El Greco** (☎ 328-4604, 219 Broadway E) is a good choice for Mediterranean dishes. If you want to get full and drunk, **La Cocina & Cantina Mexican Restaurant** (☎ 323-1675, 432 Broadway E) has delicious margaritas and an all-you-can-eat Mexican buffet at lunch ($6) and dinner ($9).

Coffee Craze

With the opening of the first Starbucks in Seattle in 1971, Seattle became something of a hub for the coffee craze that overtook the nation. Seattle is cold and rainy; not only did the first few espresso bars give Seattleites a taste for cappuccino and latte, it gave them something warm to hang on to. Soon the entire city was buzzing and jonesing for more. Standards for coffee quality and strength grew, and soon no one put up with anything but the best.

Seattle has a ridiculous amount of coffee shops; every downtown block has at least one, and almost every major building has an espresso cart out front. Even out-of-the-way gas stations and fast-food restaurants offer espresso. In Seattle, if you want a large *regular* coffee (heaven forbid), you ask for 'a large drip,' otherwise they'll look at you funny.

Coffeehouses here have morphed into many things, ranging from the quick-fix kiosk to elegant spaces more appropriate to penning letters or reading novels. Others double as performance spaces for actors, musicians and poets. Somewhere along the way, coffee, it seems, became synonymous with culture.

Noteworthy coffeehouses that offer at least some sustenance in addition to espresso are listed in this chapter. Coffee shops known more for their entertainment or performances are noted in the Entertainment chapter.

Starbucks is by no means the only coffee empire in the region. Its competition includes Seattle's Best Coffee (SBC), Tully's, Torrefazione Italia and a zillion independents. Locals can be fickle and finicky about their tastes, and Starbucks, now that it has achieved such size and notoriety, is both loved and loathed in this town.

'I am *sooo* over coffee.'

PLACES TO EAT

Over on 15th Ave E is another string of good restaurants. A longtime favorite, ***Coastal Kitchen*** (☎ 322-1145, 429 15th Ave E) serves up some of the best food in the neighborhood, with an eclectic mix of Cajun, Mayan and Mexican inspirations. It has a great 'Blunch,' (average $8) served between 8:30 am and 3 pm weekdays. Coastal Kitchen is open 8:30 am to midnight daily. ***Jack's Bistro*** (☎ 324-9625, 405 15th Ave E) is a pleasant low-key diner serving American standards, and it's often easier to get into than the Coastal Kitchen during the breakfast crush. From blocks away you can smell the curry and masala wafting from the kitchen at ***Chutney's Grill*** (☎ 726-1000, 605 15th Ave E). This local restaurant serves up some of the best Indian food in town.

The Pike/Pine corridor is known for its bars, but you can also get good food. Two of Seattle's excellent brewpubs are in this neighborhood. Up at the top of the corridor at Pike and 13th, ***Elysian Brewing Company*** (☎ 860-1920, 1221 E Pike St) is as much a restaurant as a pub, with a full menu of light entrées that strays from the confines of the usual pub fare. The pahjola sandwich ($8) – grilled ahi with wasabi sauce – is an excellent alternative to a burger. At the other end of Pike St at Minor Ave, ***Six Arms Pub & Brewery*** (☎ 223-1698, 300 E Pike St) is a charming old tavern with high ceilings, friendly staff, interesting art and a good selection of sandwiches and burgers. Also on the corridor, ***Satellite Lounge*** (☎ 324-4019, 1118 E Pike St) serves generous portions of standard American food. This clean and friendly place is a good spot for dinner or a cocktail at the bar.

The ***Capitol Club*** (☎ 325-2149, 414 E Pine St) explores an unusual dining niche. This restaurant takes classic North African dishes and updates the sauces and flavors into nouvelle cuisine. Dinners average $15. Seattlelites' favorite spot for Italian food, the no-fuss ***Ristorante Machiavelli*** (☎ 621-7941, 1215 Pine St) specializes in full-flavored Italian cooking without any of the trappings of a high-attitude restaurant. Nearby over on Pike St, ***Tango*** (☎ 583-0133, 1100 Pike St) does a good job with tapas. The unique tapas dishes average $7 and two people would probably want three or four.

THE U DISTRICT (Map 9)
Coffeehouses
Students and strong coffee have always gone together, and along 'the Ave' (University Way NE) in the U District you can find plenty of both. A longtime favorite, ***Café Allegro*** (☎ 633-3030, 4214 University Way NE) launched the Seattle coffee scene. It's tucked in the alley between NE 42nd and NE 43rd Sts, east of University Way. ***Espresso Roma*** (☎ 632-6001, 4201 University Way NE) is the kind of place where you can order a coffee and hang out for four hours. ***Perkengrüven Café*** has two locations on the Ave. The southernmost one (☎ 632-6506, 4112 University Ave NE) is bigger and cleaner. The other (☎ 522-3500, 4736 University Way NE) attracts more of a grunge scene. Up at the northern end of the Ave, ***Grand Illusion Cafe & Espresso*** (☎ 525-2755, 1405 NE 50th Ave) is in the courtyard outside an art movie theater. It's a quiet and nice spot for coffee and conversation.

Restaurants
Budget On the shores of Portage Bay at the southern base of University Ave NE, stop by ***Agua Verde Cafe*** (☎ 545-8570, 1303 NE Boat St). This wonderful little gem overlooks the bay and serves up mouthwatering, garlic-buttery tacos de camarones ($6) and other good Mexican favorites.

Up on the Ave, many cheap eateries are geared toward student tastes and budgets. ***Cafe Allegro at the College Inn*** (☎ 634-2310, 4002 University Way NE), at the College Inn, is a nice spot for a sandwich and offers better food than most quickserve places on the Ave. ***Schultzy's Sausages*** (☎ 548-9461, 4142 University Way) is the place to go for all sorts of grilled sausage sandwiches: It's the 'best of the wurst.' Around the corner, ***Orange King*** (☎ 632-1331, 1411 NE 42nd St) is an old-fashioned greasy spoon, where you can still get a burger and fries for less than $4. For $5 sub sandwiches, head to ***45th St Deli*** (☎ 632-

3359, 4500 University Way NE). Despite the address, its entrance is on 45th St.

A bit farther north along the Ave, the offerings are increasingly ethnic and the quality higher. At ***Thai-ger Room*** (☎ 632-9299, 4228 University Way NE) most dishes cost $6. ***Neelam's*** (☎ 523-5275, 4735 University Way NE) is a favorite for East Indian curries; the all-you-can-eat lunch buffet costs $6. Vegans and vegetarians can find good, cheap Thai food at ***Araya Places*** (☎ 524-4332, 4732 University Way NE). Chinese-food lovers should stop by ***Mandarin Chef*** (☎ 528-7596, 5022 University Way NE), where the portions of Hunan, Szechuan and Mandarin cuisines are huge. ***Tandoor*** (☎ 523-7477, 5024 University Way NE) doesn't look like much on the outside, but the tandoor-roasted meats and other Indian dishes are a delight.

Mid-Range The lively ***Flowers*** (☎ 633-1903, 4247 University Way) serves up a lunchtime vegetarian buffet for $7; dinners include meat choices and average around $10. Thought by many to be the best Indian food place around, where quality is just as important as quantity, ***Cedars Restaurant*** (☎ 527-5247, 4759 Brooklyn Ave NE) serves delicious Middle Eastern and Indian food. À la carte dishes average $9.

Farther north, beyond the Ave action and past Ravenna Park, ***Santa Fe Cafe*** (☎ 524-7736, 2255 NE 65th St) is in a converted storefront and has excellent New Mexican–style food.

WALLINGFORD (Map 10)

In Wallingford, N 45th St stretches past a long strip of inexpensive, mostly ethnic restaurants, giving this charming neighborhood a low-key international feel. Both quality and prices are a step up from what you'll find in the U District, and you'll see a lot fewer students.

Budget

For a switch from the coffee shop routine, the ***Teahouse Kuan Yin*** (☎ 632-2055, 1911 N 45th St) has an impressive selection of black, oolong, green and herbal teas and

paraphernalia to enjoy a pot. It's open 10 am to 11 pm daily; until midnight Friday and Saturday.

None of the restaurants in Wallingford is expensive, but if you're interested in keeping within your budget, you could do worse than heading to one of Seattle's best neighborhood bakeries. ***Boulangerie*** (☎ 634-2211, 2200 N 45th St) is as close as Seattle gets to a real French bakery; the pastries are fantastic. Next door, sit down for breakfast at ***Patty's Eggnest*** (☎ 675-0645, 2202 N 45th St) and enjoy the homey atmosphere.

The most popular stop for breakfast in the outlying neighborhoods, ***Julia's of Wallingford*** (☎ 633-1175, 4401 Wallingford Ave N) is the place to go, especially if your idea of an eye-opener is a stack of pancakes and gallons of coffee. It's also good for lunch or an uncomplicated dinner. If your kind of breakfast is a Bloody Mary and a goat cheese and sun-dried tomato frittata, then stop by the zippy ***Jitterbug Cafe*** (☎ 547-6313, 2114 N 45th St). This is a great spot for lunch or dinner, when the menu is divided between New American and Roman (as from Rome) cooking. Vegetarians can find lots to eat here.

My Brother's Pizza (☎ 547-3663, 2109 N 45th St) is often packed, but there is a takeout window if you just want to order a slice and walk. It has a unique way of serving pizza – upside down and in a bowl.

Mid-Range

India Cuisine (☎ 632-5307, 1718 N 45th St) is a popular tandoor house, though it can be hit and miss – sometimes fantastic, other times not. A better choice for curry and Asian-Indian dishes is ***Mandalay Café*** (☎ 633-0801, 1411 N 45th St) in the yellow house, where the unfussy décor makes room for the excellent menu. For the neighborhood's best Mexican food, go to ***Chile Pepper*** (☎ 545-1790, 1427 N 45th St), where the food always tastes homemade and appropriately fiery. For Southwest Mexican cuisine, ***Beso del Sol*** (☎ 547-8087, 4468 Stone Way N) attracts a lively crowd, especially for the salsa dancing on Friday and Saturday nights. The Italian representative along N 45th Ave is *Simpatico* (☎ 632-1000, 4400 Wallingford Ave N), at Wallingford Center. With its outdoor courtyard, it feels like a real Italian trattoria. You don't find Afghani food on every street corner, and if you'd like to give it a try – it's like a blend of Pakistani and Middle Eastern cooking – then head to *Kabul* (☎ 545-9000, 2301 N 45th St). Get your Japanese fix at *Mushashi's* (☎ 633-0212, 1400 N 45th St), where you can eat cheap by ordering a bento box, or live it up a bit with sashimi and good teriyaki.

With a name like *Bizzarro* (☎ 545-7327, 1307 N 46th St), you'd never guess that this Wallingford hotbed is an excellent neighborhood Italian café. When you learn that it's housed in someone's garage, then the name makes sense. Another strange sight is the large asteroid perched on the rooftop above *The Asteroid Cafe* (☎ 547-2514, 1605 N 45th St). This small café serves up delicious food from South, Central and Northern Italy.

FREMONT (Map 10)
Budget
An institution in this quirky neighborhood, *Still Life in Fremont* (☎ 547-9850, 709 N 35th St) is a great spot to park yourself at a table, drink coffee and nibble on excellent vegetarian food. The soups are especially good. On the other side of Fremont, *Caffé Ladro* (☎ 675-0854, 452 N 36th St) is another nice spot to sip a coffee.

Barlee's Cafe in Fremont (☎ 633-4545, 3410 Fremont Ave N) is the place to go for weekend brunch – the stuff afternoon naps are made of. For excellent Thai noodles, the *Fremont Noodle House* (☎ 547-1550, 3411 Fremont Ave N) is unsurpassed for quality at a very affordable price. For more traditional – and absolutely fabulous – Thai, try *Kwanjai* (☎ 632-3656, 469 N 36th St). Order any of the curries or the salmon *shoo shee* ($8), made with curry, lime and pineapple juice.

Fremont has a great many friendly pubs, where a pint and a burger will run you about $10. The best of the local talent is *Trolleyman Pub* (☎ 548-8000, 3400 Phinney Ave N), the first microbrewery for Seattle's Redhook Ale Brewery. Food choices are simple, mostly soup and sandwiches, but it's a great atmosphere (this was once a trolley barn), and the beer's superb.

A little north of the heart of Fremont is the best place in town for Caribbean food. *Paseo Caribbean Restaurant* (☎ 545-7440, 4225 Fremont Ave N) sits in an easy-to-miss squat white building with a thatch-fringed roof, but it's worth seeking out. Get the jerk pork sandwich at lunch ($6.75) or the jerk chicken dinner ($10). It's closed Sunday and Monday.

Mid-Range
The *Longshoreman's Daughter* (☎ 633-5169, 3510 Fremont Place N) serves bountiful breakfasts, but anytime of day is good. Lunch and dinner feature hearty plates of seasonal vegetables, seafood, meat and excellent garlic mashed potatoes. The place to be in Fremont is the *Triangle Lounge* (☎ 632-0880, 3507 Fremont Place N). Interesting American dishes and outdoor seating make this arrowhead-shaped café a bustling crossroads, though service is often surly. *Kosta's Opa* (☎ 328-3479, 3400 Fremont Ave N), at 34th St N, serves good, inexpensive Greek cooking.

Top End
Fremont's higher-end eateries include the stylish *El Camino* (☎ 632-7303, 607 N 35th St), where the menu is filled with very good regional Mexican dishes. It's open for dinner only. *Pontevecchio* (☎ 633-3989, 710 N 34th St) is the local Italian trattoria, specializing in zesty Sicilian dishes. Entrées average $17. For seafood in this area try *Seattle Catch Seafood Bistro* (☎ 632-6110, 460 N 36th St), a cozy restaurant that grills up the day's catch for $13 to $17. It's open for dinner only.

GREEN LAKE (Map 10)
Hands down the best bakery in town, *Honey Bear Bakery* (☎ 545-7296, 2106 N 55th St) is popular for its giant cinnamon rolls, muffins and cookies. You can also get soups and sandwiches at lunch. The sun streams in the windows here all day, making it a great spot to sit and read a book. Nearby, *Brie & Bordeaux* (☎ 633-3538, 2227 N 56th St) was once

the neighborhood's upscale deli and wine store, but now it includes a friendly bistro where you can get an inexpensive breakfast or lunch and have a mid-range Italian dinner. For something authentically ethnic, try the tangy noodles and stir-fries at **Rasa Malaysia** (☎ 523-8888, 7208 E Green Lake Dr N); they're an exceptional value.

After your run around Green Lake, the place to end up for a beer and a snack is **Six Degrees** (☎ 523-1600, 7900 E Green Lake Dr N). This pub-style bistro is casual by day, but dresses up at night – so does the food.

For fine dining near Green Lake, **Nell's** (☎ 524-4044, 6804 E Green Lake Way N) serves up classic European dishes with Northwest flair. A favorite restaurant, Saleh al Lago, formerly occupied this space, and Nell's has done a good job of filling the void. Dinners here start at $18 and go up to $52 for the chef's five-course tasting menu.

PHINNEY RIDGE (Map 10)

Along the ridge directly west of Green Lake, the quiet neighborhood of Phinney Ridge has a couple of cheap eateries worth mentioning. Constantly collecting accolades for grilling up the best burger in town, **Red Mill Burgers** (☎ 783-6362, 312 N 67th St) also fries up the fattest, yummiest onion rings. There's always a line out the door. Breakfast is heavenly at **Mae's Phinney Ridge Cafe** (☎ 782-1222, 6412 Phinney Ave N), and the tasty milkshakes make it a worthwhile trip any time. Or, have the best of both worlds and go for the 'shake and eggs' breakfast, served until 3 pm daily. This neighborhood's favorite pub, **74th Street Ale House** (☎ 784-2955, 7401 Greenwood Ave N) also serves good food, including a spicy gumbo and good quesadillas. The pub is nonsmoking.

BALLARD (Map 11)

Ballard is known for its waterfront restaurants, but there are also several good places to eat in the charmingly hip historic area.

Budget

When you say the words 'greasy spoon' do they linger on your tongue and make your mouth water? Well then, **Hattie's Hat**

(☎ 784-0175, 5231 Ballard Ave NW) is the place for you. Hattie's serves beer and breakfast all day. It's all about drip coffee here, baby; don't even think about asking for a cappuccino.

Mid-Range

For comfort food with a Scandinavian flair, try **Valdi's Ballard Bistro** (☎ 783-2033, 5410 Ballard Ave NW). Across the street is **Burk's Café** (☎ 782-0091, 5411 Ballard Ave NW). Though you won't mistake redbrick Old Ballard for New Orleans, the Cajun and Creole food here is good enough to make you say 'oh my!' With the atmosphere of an old bordello (owing to the building's history as a brothel), **Madame K's** (☎ 783-9710, 5327 Ballard Ave NW) is an absolutely great place to polish off a bottle of wine and eat some gooey pizza. There's a nice patio out back. For Italian food, the Ballard favorite is **Lombardi's Cucina** (☎ 783-0055, 2200 NW Market St). Lombardi's adheres to a near cultlike devotion to garlic, so be forewarned; the calamari is especially good. This handsome terra-cotta brick-faced building was once a fancy drugstore and soda fountain. Indian-food lovers flock to **India Bistro** (☎ 783-5080, 2301 NW Market St) for the $6 lunch buffet or North Indian specialties, such as the Kashmiri chicken ($9).

OK, so it's a cliché, but **Ray's Boathouse** (☎ 789-3770, 6049 Seaview Ave NW) offers views over the Olympics, nautical decor and an exhaustive fresh fish menu. It offers tourists everything they think of when they ponder Seattle. If you can't get reservations, at least come for a drink on the sundeck. Ray's is about a mile west of the Ballard Locks. Right next door **Anthony's Homeport** (☎ 783-0780, 6135 Seaview Ave NW) boasts much the same menu and views as Ray's. If you can't get into one, try the other.

Across the Ballard Bridge in the Fisherman's Terminal, **Chinook's at Salmon Bay** (☎ 283-4665, 1900 W Nickerson St) is where fish practically leap out of the water and into the kitchen. You can't get fish much fresher than this, and the selection of fish and preparations at this excellent restaurant is huge. A plus is watching the fishing fleet coming in or fishers mending their nets from the massive restaurant windows or the sundeck in summer.

Top End

The most refined restaurant in these parts is *Le Gourmand* (☎ 784-3463, *425 NW Market St*), an excellent French restaurant in an otherwise unprepossessing storefront on the eastern edge of Ballard near Fremont. The dining room is small and exclusive, allowing the chef to prepare everything by hand. Many of the garnishes and herbs are grown in the back garden. Classic French food works well when such care is taken; duck breast, rack of lamb and grilled salmon draped in rich sauces keep people coming back for more. Le Gourmand is a good place for a romantic dinner.

CENTRAL DISTRICT (Map 12)

You'll look a while before you find decent barbecue in Seattle, but the Central District has a couple of places worth checking out. They may not look like much from the outside, but open your mind and your stomach will be happy. *R&L Home of Good Bar-B-Que* (☎ 322-0271, *1816 E Yesler Way*) delivers exactly what its name promises. For traditional, inexpensive Southern-style fare, head for *Catfish Corner* (☎ 323-4330, *2726 E Cherry St*). Catfish strips are the specialty here, and you can accessorize them with all the trimmings, including collards, red beans and rice. *Ms Helen's Soul Food* (☎ 322-6310, *1133 23rd Ave E*) is another favorite for Southern USA specialties such as gumbo, fried catfish and smothered oxtails, followed by peach cobbler. You'll forget industrial fried chicken after tasting the great crusty, spicy chicken at *Ezell's Fried Chicken* (☎ 324-4141, *501 23rd Ave*). Side dishes, like the coleslaw and sweet potato pie, are also good; takeout only. This place boomed after Oprah Winfrey hyped the fried chicken here as some of the best in the country.

For soul food that's upscale but sans attitude, try *Kingfish Cafe* (*Map 8*, ☎ 320-8757, *602 19th Ave E*), bordering Capitol Hill. Co-owned by Sonics guard Gary Payton and run by twin sisters, this place serves up fan-tastic Southern food, from fried chicken to fried green tomatoes and lima bean succotash. It's open for lunch and dinner.

MADISON VALLEY & MADISON PARK (Map 12)

In Madison Valley you can hear the vegetarians howling at the moon. This is it – why go anywhere else? Fervently, almost pentecostally vegetarian, *Café Flora* (☎ 325-9100, *2901 E Madison St*) is a true delight. Even if you normally consider yourself a carnivore, you'll be surprised by how refined the food and atmosphere can be. Unlike at most vegetarian restaurants, the servers here lack dreadlocks. There's lots of seating, including a glass-enclosed atrium. The menu, created weekly, is multicultural and features various kinds of wraps, pizzas, chunky stews and salads. Café Flora is open for lunch and dinner.

Across the street, *Rover's* (☎ 325-7442, *2808 E Madison St*), one of Seattle's most highly regarded restaurants, isn't the kind of top-end restaurant you'd expect to find plunked in a quiet, residential neighborhood. However, the refined interior spaces of Rover's match its high-quality, subtle French cuisine. Specialties are foie gras, fresh fish and seafood made wondrous by the deft additions of Gallic sauces. Local lamb, game and sweetbreads also make appearances on the menu. The pre-fixe menu offers six courses for $65/75 vegetarian/nonvegetarian. Open for dinner only; bring a giant appetite, along with your credit card.

Down in Madison Park, at the end of Madison St just before you hit Lake Washington, is the *Madison Park Café* (☎ 324-2626, *1807 42nd Ave E*). It's a favored, low-priced breakfast and lunch spot in an old converted house. Homemade pastries are very good, as are the frittatas. It's also open for dinner Tuesday to Saturday. Nearby is *Cactus!* (☎ 324-4140, *4220 E Madison St*), which is a popular, not-too-pricey eatery that's half tapas bar and half Southwestern Mexican fine dining. The *Attic Alehouse & Eatery* (☎ 323-3131, *4226 E Madison St*) is a friendly neighborhood pub and a good spot for a beer 'n' burger.

MADRONA (Map 12)

The tiny commercial strip in Madrona has a few great restaurants. *Hi Spot Cafe* (☎ 325-7905, 1410 34th Ave) basks in fame for its incredible cinnamon rolls, Torrefazione coffee and filling breakfasts, including creative omelets served with potatoes. The sandwich-and-salad lunch ($5 to $8) is just as good, and at dinner most entrées stay under $12. *Cafe Soleil* (☎ 325-1126, 1400 34th Ave) is another good, cheap eatery with outdoor tables and friendly service.

Dulces Latin Bistro (☎ 322-5453, 1430 34th Ave) is an elegant little restaurant far from the centers of Seattle gastronomy. But it's worth the excursion to partake of the food and the scene here. The moderately priced, innovative menu reflects a variety of Latin sources, including Italian, Spanish and Central American.

WEST SEATTLE (Map 1)

Nearly everything worth eating in West Seattle is found along a short strip across from Alki Beach or along California Ave SW.

Budget

Alki Bakery (☎ 935-1352, 2738 Alki Ave SW), the blossoming offspring of the busy Alki Café (see below), is worth the line up for a cinnamon roll, fresh cookie and coffee. You can also order takeout sandwiches and salads to eat on the beach.

The competition is fierce over which of these Alki institutions has the best fish-and-chips. *Spud Fish & Chips* (☎ 938-0606, 2666 Alki Ave SW) attracts the tourists, but the locals swear by *Sunfish* (☎ 938-4112, 2800 Alki Ave SW). The best-pizza war wages between Alki's *Pegasus Pizza & Pasta* (☎ 932-4849, 2758 Alki Ave SW) and the off-the-beach *Spiro's Pizza* (☎ 932-5100, 3401 California Ave SW), where the No 6 (artichokes, spinach and feta) will fill your mouth with joy.

Mid-Range

Alki Café (☎ 935-0616, 2726 Alki Ave SW) is one of Seattle's favorite spots for breakfast and brunch; try the fresh baked goods, vegetable-filled omelets or hotcakes. Once the beach crowd goes home, come here for a relaxed dinner of grilled fish, meats or pasta.

Boca (☎ 933-8000, 2516 Alki Ave SW) offers Caribbean- and Latin-style food; the jerked ribs are excellent, and the grilled seabass in banana leaf is a house specialty. Mediterranean and northern African food is the focus at *Phoenicia at Alki* (☎ 935-6550, 2716 Alki Ave SW). The best dishes here are the house specialties, which mix and blend Italian and Moroccan flavors with a bounty of fresh local seafood.

While many restaurants afford views onto Alki Beach and its strutting revelers, most people drive to West Seattle for the view at *Salty's on Alki* (☎ 937-1600, 1936 Harbor Ave SW). This steak and seafood house looks across Elliott Bay onto downtown Seattle; at sunset, the spectacle of lights, shining towers and the rising moon is amazing. The food is secondary, but still quite good.

Carnivores looking to get away from the Alki scene should head to *Jak's Grill* (☎ 935-8260, 2352 California Ave SW). It specializes in huge portions of ribs, chops, steaks and burgers.

Entertainment

Whatever you're into, Seattle's vibrant cultural life has a lot to offer. Shake your groove thing at a dance club downtown, stagger around barhopping in Pioneer Square or dress up with the cocktail set in Belltown. Mix it up with the gay scene on Capitol Hill, slam dance to live music or sip a pint in one of Seattle's excellent pubs. Or you can attend a B flick or foreign film, swoon at the ballet or be enraptured at a live theater performance – it's all here.

Seattle gave birth to Jimi Hendrix; Quincy Jones and Ray Charles began groovin' on Jackson St; garage rock transformed into grunge, and bands like Pearl Jam and Nirvana rocked their ways around the world. Seattle's live performance scene – both large scale and low budget – ranks near the top for large US cities, and open-mic poetry slams decorate the city as much as raindrops.

For a current listing of Seattle's live entertainment offerings, consult the *Seattle Weekly, The Stranger* or the arts sections of the city's daily newspapers. Tickets for most events are available through TicketMaster; see 'Ticket Services.'

COFFEEHOUSES

Seattle often gets the credit for starting the US coffee craze. In the process, Seattle's coffee fanaticism has also served to revitalize the coffeehouse as a social meeting place that offers frequent entertainment in the form of poetry readings, theatrical performances and acoustic music sessions. The following are coffeehouses that are known for more than just food and java. Also see the Places to Eat chapter for other great coffee and tea venues listed by neighborhood.

In Belltown, *Speakeasy Café (Map 6, ☎ 728-9770, 2304 2nd Ave)* is a full-service Internet café with other accoutrements of modern life, like espresso, microbrews and a cigar shop. If you tire of staring at the monitor, take in one of the performances or readings occasionally held here. Having tremendous success in its identity crisis, *Sit & Spin (Map 6, ☎ 441-9484, 2219 4th Ave)* is part coffeehouse, restaurant, bar and laundromat. Live bands play here often, so you can tap your toes while folding your clothes.

Up on Capitol Hill, the *Globe Cafe (Map 8, ☎ 689-8661, 1531 14th Ave)* has frequent musical performances and literary events, including the long-running Red Sky Poetry Theater, which performs on Sunday nights. In the U District, *The Pearl (Map 9, ☎ 547-3326, 4215 University Way NE)* holds poetry readings and open-mic nights. Call to find out what's going on.

PUBS

Maybe it's due to all the rainy days, maybe it's because of the great microbrew selection or maybe it's because Seattleites simply enjoy a pint. Whatever it is, Seattle's got some great pubs. They've been divided here into grand old neighborhood pubs, brewpubs, where beer drinking is a form of art, and Irish pubs, where you can get an earload of Celtic music and a mouthful of Guinness. Most every pub offers something to eat, ranging from simple snacks to full menus.

Neighborhood Pubs

In Belltown, away from the hipster scene, the *Two Bells Tavern (Map 6, ☎ 441-3050, 2313 4th Ave)* is a nice, TV-free pub to sip a beer in and ponder your next move. Also a great place for a meal, the *Belltown Pub (Map 6, ☎ 728-4311, 2322 1st Ave)* offers many local beers and a stylish, low-key atmosphere. Even shy people will inevitably share a conversation while sitting at the bar. Nearby, on the way to Pike Place Market, is one of Seattle's most likeable bars, the *Virginia Inn Tavern (Map 5, ☎ 728-1937, 1937 1st Ave)*. It serves every walk of life in a lively, nonsmoking atmosphere. Lots of draft beers, a nice interior and friendly staff make this a good rendezvous and a great staging area for forays elsewhere.

Up on Queen Anne Hill, *Hilltop Ale House* (Map 7, ☎ 285-3877, 2129 Queen Anne Ave N) is a comfortable neighborhood hangout with good food and beer. Down at the bottom of the hill in Lower Queen Anne, *Floyd's Place Beer & BBQ* (Map 7, ☎ 284-3542, 521 1st Ave N) has just that – finger-licking barbecue and 27 beers on tap.

Over on 15th Ave E in Capitol Hill, *Canterbury Ale & Eats* (Map 8, ☎ 322-3130, 534 15th Ave E) is a British-style pub divided into four small rooms. The bar is always filled with friendly locals sipping one of the many beers on tap. In the U District, the *Blue Moon Tavern* (Map 9, no ☎, 712 NE 45th St) is a dive of an institution made famous by the people who sat here, like Kerouac and Ginsberg. Novelist Tom Robbins did his time here as well.

In Fremont, the *Red Door Ale House* (Map 10, ☎ 547-7521, 3401 Fremont Ave N) is a long-established neighborhood pub. Soon, the pub is going to move one block west to Evanston Ave N, to make way for a new retail development that's due to be completed in 2002. Yes, the Red Door's actual building will be picked up and carried down the street to its new locale, which will reportedly have more restaurant seating and a sundeck. And this is progress?

Up in Phinney Ridge, the nonsmoking *74th Street Ale House* (Map 10, ☎ 784-2955, 7401 Greenwood Ave N) is one of the best pubs in the city for its good menu and friendly vibe. If you're thirsty from too much sunbathing at Green Lake, head to *The Latona* (Map 10, ☎ 525-2238, 6423 Latona NE). It's another nice pub, featuring live jazz on weekends.

Brewpubs

Downtown's only brewpub is the inviting *Rock Bottom Brewery* (Map 2, ☎ 623-3070, 1333 5th Ave), at the base of the Rainier Square Building. A few blocks south of Pioneer Square near Safeco Field, *Pyramid Ale House* (Map 4, ☎ 682-3377, 1201 1st Ave S) has an expansive bar and terrific beers. Tours and tastings are offered here at 2 and 4 pm weekdays and 1, 2 and 4 pm weekends.

In the Pike Place Market, the fun-loving *Pike Place Pub and Brewery* (Map 5, ☎ 622-6044, 1415 1st Ave) offers good pub grub in addition to the handcrafted ales. Two favorite brewpubs are in Capitol Hill, including the *Six Arms Pub & Brewery* (Map 8, ☎ 223-1698, 300 E Pike St), at Minor Ave. A branch of Portland's McMeniman brewpubs, Six Arms is long on cool charm and attracts a good crowd that hunkers in the deep booths or expounds the virtues of the free world at the bar. Up on the other end of E Pike St, *Elysian Brewing Company* (Map 8, ☎ 860-1920, 1221 E Pike St), at 13th Ave, has live music on weekends, plenty of beer and lots of room to drink. It also has a decent menu (see the Places to Eat chapter).

Up in the U District, on the ever-hopping Ave, is the rowdy *Big Time Microbrew & Music* (Map 9, ☎ 545-4509, 4133 University Way NE). Watch out for the students getting wasted for the first time.

Why and how a small neighborhood such as Fremont can support two brewpubs and a number of other bars is best pondered over a glass of ale. *The Trolleyman Pub* (Map 10, ☎ 548-8000, 3400 Phinney Ave N) is Redhook Ale Brewery's main operation,

Macro Amounts of Microbrews

Perhaps it's due to all the water, but Seattle is a bastion of locally microbrewed beers. Most microbreweries started out as tiny craft breweries that produced European-style ales. Many of these small producers initially lacked the capital to offer their brews for sale anywhere but in the brewery building itself, hence the term brewpub – an informal pub with its own on-site brewery. Brewpubs often feature signature beers and ales not available elsewhere. Actually, many of these breweries are no longer so 'micro,' but their operations and quality of beer are still a far cry from Anheuser-Busch or Coors. Most of the brewpubs listed in this chapter offer a taster's selection of the house brews.

ENTERTAINMENT

located in a vintage trolley barn. While the drinkers go to the Trolleyman, partiers go to *Dad Watson's Restaurant & Brewery (Map 10, ☎ 632-6505, 3601 Fremont Ave N)*. This pub lacks old-Seattle charm, but with its British-style brass-and-wood decor, it's a nice place to hang out.

On the way out to Ballard, *Hale's Brewery & Pub (Map 11, ☎ 782-0737, 4301 Leary Way NW)* is a handsome brewpub where there's more focus on the beer than on dining. Bartenders serve up nothing but Hale's own creations from nine taps. There's a full menu and live music is usually featured on weekends.

West Seattle's *Elliott Bay Brewery & Pub (Map 1, ☎ 932-8695, 4720 California Ave SW)* packs them in for darts and excellent beer, including a fine pull of IPA.

Irish Pubs

The *Owl & Thistle (Map 4, ☎ 621-7777, 808 Post Ave)*, tucked away beneath the viaduct on the northern edge of Pioneer Square, has a house Irish band that plays weekdays; weekends offer either rock or touring Celtic bands. Nearby, the more upscale *tir na nog (Map 4, ☎ 264-2700, 801 1st Ave)* specializes in a variety of Scotch and Irish whiskey. Live bands play on weekends. *Kell's Restaurant & Bar (Map 5, ☎ 728-1916, 1916 Post Alley)*, in the Pike Place Market area, has live Irish music Wednesday to Saturday evenings.

In Lower Queen Anne, the lively *TS McHugh's (Map 7, ☎ 282-1910, 21 Mercer St)* gets absolutely packed during events at Seattle Center. In Wallingford, *Murphy's Pub (Map 10, ☎ 634-2110, 1928 N 45th St)* seems to have been transplanted directly from Ireland. There's live Irish music on weekends; the rest of the time the place is filled with dart players. Out in Ballard, *Conor Byrne's (Map 11, ☎ 784-3640, 5140 Ballard Ave NW)* is a traditional Irish pub where the Guinness flows to the tune of live Celtic music on Wednesday and weekends.

BARS

From snazzy cocktail bars to low-down dives, the following are places in Seattle you go primarily to drink – or drink club soda and watch others drink. Some of the city's

---

Sinking the Black

Though many bars have pool tables, the following places specialize in billiards. At *Belltown Billiards (Map 6, ☎ 448-6779, 90 Blanchard St)*, in Belltown, you can also eat a pretty good Italian meal or swill drinks at the bar, but the main draw is playing pool in a swanky location. Not an intentional pool hall, *The Fenix (Map 4, ☎ 467-1111, 315 2nd Ave S)*, upstairs at the Fenix Underground, sort of morphed from a bar into a good place to shoot pool.

Jillian's Billiard Club & Cafe (Map 7, ☎ 223-0300, 731 Westlake Ave N), on the southwest shore of Lake Union, has electronic games, virtual reality gizmos, dartboards and ping-pong tables in addition to its 32 billiard tables. There's also a full-service bar and restaurant. In Fremont, *Ballroom (Map 10, ☎ 634-2575, 456 N 36th St)* is a smoky pool hall and bar that's open 4 pm to 2 am daily.

---

best bars are in restaurants where you can order from a full menu, while others serve only peanuts. This list isn't about the food, however, so here's to all that.

Downtown (Map 2)

Downtown Seattle is a business suit and Nordstrom shopper kind of place, and sometimes it's hard to find a good place to meet for a drink that won't be crowded with stockbrokers and tourists. The bar at *Palomino Euro-Bistro (☎ 623-1300, 1420 5th Ave)*, on the top floor of the City Centre Mall, is very popular with the mostly single, beautiful people. For an elegant cocktail with piano glissandos and stellar views, take the elevator to the swanky *Cloud Room (☎ 682-0100, 1619 9th Ave)*, atop the Camlin Hotel. Over in the Paramount Hotel is the best place to meet for drinks: *Dragonfish Asian Café (☎ 467-7777, 722 Pine St)*. It stirs up wonderful cocktails, such as Lemongrass Lime Rickey (vodka infused with lemongrass) or Dragon's Breath Martini (vodka infused with hot pepper). Also see the Places to Eat chapter.

Known more as a restaurant, the bar at the ***Palace Kitchen*** (☎ 448-2001, 2030 5th Ave) is a great spot to sip a cocktail and have a snack. Way on the other side of Downtown, next to the Alexis Hotel, ***Bookstore Bar & Cafe*** (☎ 382-1506, 1007 1st Ave) is a relaxing spot to kick back with a snifter of cognac and a stogie. The bookshelves are filled with newspapers, magazine and books about beer, wine and cigars. The ***Art Bar*** (☎ 622-4344, 1516 2nd Ave) is a divey place attracting artsy types, who swill wine and discuss epiphany.

Toward Seattle Center, the ***Five Point Cafe*** (☎ 448-9993, 415 Cedar St), in Tillicum Square, has been around since 1929. This is a popular hangout for old-timers as well as bikers and young hipsters. Check out the men's bathroom (if you can) – while standing at the urinal you can get a periscope view of the Space Needle. The Five Point is open 24 hours daily.

Pike Place Market (Map 5)

The various restaurants and pubs around the market provide a good alternative to downtown hotel bars. A favorite for a romantic drink is ***Shea's Lounge*** (☎ 467-9990, 94 Pike St), beside the Chez Shea restaurant (see the Places to Eat chapter). Here you can overlook the market and Puget Sound; there are only a few tables, so come early. The dark, moody ***Alibi Room*** (☎ 623-3180, 85 Pike Place) attracts a smoking, tattooed crowd, but anyone is welcome to enjoy the stiff drinks and views out the back. The ***Pink Door Ristorante*** (☎ 443-3241, 1919 Post Alley) is a pleasant place for a glass of wine; try to catch the live cabaret or jazz offered nightly (also see the Places to Eat chapter).

Belltown (Map 6)

Time was when drinking in Belltown had an edge to it. You went to experience quirky dive bars like the ***Frontier Room*** (☎ 441-3377, 2203 1st Ave), the kind of place you slam your fist on the counter and demand a scotch, just because you can. This old-school bar clings to its gritty roots while the rest of Belltown goes seriously upscale. The same can be said of the ***Lava Lounge*** (☎ 441-5660, 2226 2nd Ave), where the scene changes daily, depending on the crowd or the music playing. The place stays hip mostly by never trying to be, and it's an easy night out swilling beers in one of the Lava's comfy booths.

Now that Belltown has turned uptown, beautiful bartenders serve up beautiful cocktails for the beautiful singles crowd in high heels and Armani suits. Check out this scene at ***Cyclops*** (☎ 441-1677, 2421 1st Ave). With a restaurant on one side and a bar on the other, this place is a happening hangout that maintains its cool with red vinyl seats, lava lamps and friendly staff. ***Axis*** (☎ 441-9600, 2212 1st Ave) attracts gorgeous salivating singles looking to hook up with salivating singles of the opposite sex.

Seattle Center (Map 7)

You'd expect any bar at the Experience Music Project (EMP) to be wildly overpriced, but the ***Liquid Lounge*** (☎ 367-5483, 325 5th Ave N) is a cool spot and the drinks and snacks are reasonably priced. The high ceilings, blue lights and energy of the EMP – as well as the occasional live acts (no cover) – make this a good spot to kick back with a cocktail. For more on the EMP, see the Things to See & Do chapter.

On the border of Belltown, check out ***Tini Bigs Lounge*** (☎ 284-0931, 100 Denny Way), where the gigantic martini list gives the crowd a happy glow.

Queen Anne (Map 7)

In Lower Queen Anne, ***The Mecca Cafe*** (☎ 285-9728, 526 Queen Anne Ave N) is a tiny, dark bar with a diner atmosphere that attracts a loyal, late-night crowd. Nearby,

Sorry Charlies Restaurant & Piano Bar (☎ 283-3245, 529 Queen Anne Ave N) is a fabulous relic of the old-time piano bar. Vocalists of varying ability belt out whatever comes as pianist Howard Bulson's fingers dance along the keyboard; starting 8 pm nightly except Monday.

Up the hill, *Sapphire Kitchen & Bar* (☎ 281-1931, 1625 Queen Anne Ave N) is a top-end Spanish restaurant with a hopping bar scene. In the heart of Upper Queen Anne, *Paragon Bar & Grill* (☎ 283-4548, 2125 Queen Anne Ave N) is a fun place where the in-your-face pickup scene is mellowed by the warm wood, cozy fireplace and strong drinks. Jazz, blues and acoustic live-music acts play here Tuesday, Wednesday, Thursday and Saturday nights.

Capitol Hill (Map 8)

On Broadway at E Thomas St, *Ileen's Sports Bar* (☎ 324-0229, 300 Broadway E) tries really hard to be sporty, but the locals, loyal to the former name of 'Ernie Steele's,' maintain the mix of trendy clientele, alternative music and good, cheap drinks. The smoke and mounted heads of moose and elk don't do much for the sports theme, either. The *Deluxe Bar & Grill* (☎ 324-9697, 625 Broadway E) manages to maintain a somewhat sports-bar atmosphere with vinyl booths, pool tables, constant games on TV and a standard selection of beers and sophisticated diner food (see the Places to Eat chapter). There's a happy hour 3 to 7 pm, and if you didn't get enough the first time around, there's another 11 pm to closing time at 1 am.

Over on 15th Ave E, chose from more than 130 different types of scotch at *Hopscotch* (☎ 322-4191, 332 15th Ave E). It is closed Sunday and Monday. For a beer chaser, hop up the street to *Hopvine* (☎ 328-3120, 507 15th Ave E), where the soft wood, local art and nightly live-music trio make this a comfortable spot.

Down in the Pike/Pine Corridor, *Satellite Lounge* (☎ 324-4019, 1118 E Pike St) serves food, but also has a comfortable bar. *The Comet* (☎ 323-9853, 922 E Pike St) pays sincere homage to the beautiful simplicity of draft beer. An institution on 'the Hill,' The Comet takes no-frills seriously, with cheap pool, cheap beer, bright lights and loyal locals. Dark, smoky *the bad juju lounge* (☎ 709-9951, 1518 11th Ave), where gothic art hangs on the black walls, is a mellow spot for drinks during the week and a packed party scene on weekends. Wear latex, wear leather, wear leopard skin – whichever you choose, you'll fit in. The scene's a little less gritty next door at *Barça* (☎ 325-8263, 1510 11th Ave), where there's lots of space and lights are dim. Barça (pronounced 'bar-**sa**') serves beer and wine only.

Fremont, Wallingford & Green Lake (Map 10)

In Fremont, there's the popular *Triangle Lounge* (☎ 632-0880, 3507 Fremont Pl N), where the neon red 'Prescriptions' sign above the bar doesn't hide the fact that locals come here to get loaded. This triangular bar is a fun place, happily lacking in the snobbery good bars fall prey to when gentrification rolls through. *Bitters Co* (Map 10, ☎ 632-0886, 513 N 36th St) is a wine bar amid a groovy art gallery. Wine connoisseurs should also visit *The Bungalow Wine Bar & Cafe* (Map 10, ☎ 632-0254, 2412 N 45th St), above the Open Books store in Wallingford. It offers a light menu and 2oz tasters of wine (about $4 each). The cozy atmosphere makes it a great spot to do some sipping. A good place to wind up after a saunter around Green Lake, *Six Degrees* (☎ 523-1600, 7900 E Green Lake Dr N) is more of a restaurant, but the large bar has plenty of seats and gets lots of action from neighborhood hipsters, especially on weekends.

LIVE MUSIC

Seattle's gift to the music world, grunge rock, was a passing phase, albeit one of epic proportions. Though the cult of grunge is now generally considered passé, it forced Seattle's club scene into existence. When grunge first made its grumblings in the late 1980s, Seattle had but a few decent venues for bands to play. Medium-size venues sprouted up to fill the void, and suddenly Seattle meant something in the music world.

JOHN ELK III

TED STRESHINSKY

RICHARD CUMMINS

JOHN ELK III

Museums galore (clockwise from top left): Seattle Art Museum, Experience Music Project, Center for Wooden Boats, Museum of Flight

Ways to spend a sunny Saturday – Rudy's Barber Shop on Capitol Hill and the International Fountain

Views of Mt Rainier National Park (clockwise from top left): Paradise Lodge, Dead Horse Trail and Skyline Trail

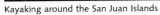

LEE FOSTER

Kayaking around the San Juan Islands

RICHARD CUMMINS

Salmon fishing at Snoqualmie Falls

LEE FOSTER

You drop it, you bought it. Pottery for sale, Orcas Island

The Life & Death of Grunge Music

During the early 1990s, an unprecedented amount of media attention was focused on the Seattle 'grunge rock' phenomenon. Practically every major newspaper and music publication in the world featured something on the topic. *Vogue* (among others) featured photo spreads with supermodels decked out in so-called grunge apparel. The *New York Times* claimed the existence of a secret grunge patois and published a list of ridiculous insider slang terms under the heading, 'Lexicon of Grunge.'

Most Seattle musicians, then and now, consider the media's coverage of their once-obscure music scene laughable. After all, Seattle has always had a thriving local music scene. Pioneering Northwest rock bands like the Kingsmen, the Sonics and Seattle's own legendary Jimi Hendrix helped define rock 'n' roll in the '60s. Local groups like Heart and the Steve Miller Band made it big in the '70s. Blues musician Robert Cray and saxophonist Kenny G gained notoriety in the '80s. None of these artists were represented by the media as being 'Seattle musicians' per se. Not until the city's grunge boom in the '90s did the rest of the world turn to Seattle as the origin of a unique sound.

Bands like Nirvana, Pearl Jam, Soundgarden, Alice in Chains and Screaming Trees achieved tremendous commercial success and sold millions of records worldwide. Seattle became the focus of all the major record labels: Everyone wanted to sign a Seattle band and cash in on the grunge craze. Dozens of bands were offered big-dollar recording contracts, just because they were from Seattle or had a sound similar to that of the handful of grunge bands that had the hits.

But the sound born of the Northwest punk underground was not so easily tamed by corporate America. Most of the bands the record companies were after had developed their music playing rowdy house parties and tiny local rock clubs, rehearsing in basements and garages in the low-rent districts where they lived. Of the many bands that inked major-label contracts, most were dropped within a year. Others broke up as a result of the rigors of touring, songwriting demands and constant partying.

Nirvana lived the quintessential rags-to-riches music story. Working-class kids from Aberdeen, Washington, the band members started out playing parties around Olympia and Seattle. They saved up enough gig money to go into a cheap recording studio and produce a demo. The engineer at the studio liked the tape and passed it on to a friend who owned a small independent record label called Sub Pop. For an estimated $600 Nirvana recorded and mixed the songs for what was to become its debut album, *Bleach*. Its second album, *Nevermind*, sold over 10 million copies.

Nirvana's success brought unwelcome celebrity to lead singer Kurt Cobain. Disillusioned with rock stardom and addicted to heroin, he took his own life in April 1994. The world press converged on Seattle in one final wave to cover the Cobain suicide. Then the media withdrew, apparently disinterested in whatever else Seattle musicians had to offer.

- **Steve Moriarty**
  Seattle musician, formerly of the Seattle rock band 'The Gits'

Nirvana's Kurt Cobain

Today, these live-music venues host a variety of sounds, from world music to folk, jazz to rock 'n' roll. Generally, Seattle clubs do not conform to any one style, and the vibe of a venue often changes nightly, reflecting whatever band is playing. Check for listings in *Seattle Weekly* or in *The Stranger,* whose 'Club Directory' lists phone numbers and addresses for all local venues.

The biggest venues for up-and-coming or alternative bands include the ***Paramount*** *(Map 2, ☎ 682-1414, 911 Pine St),* a recently renovated 3000-seat hall, whose hydraulic seats enable the space to morph into a concert hall, theater or banquet facility. Keep an eye out for what's playing at Belltown's ***Moore Theater*** *(Map 6, ☎ 443-1744, 1932 2nd Ave).* Bands love playing this 1500-seat venue, which makes it an excellent place to see a show. Also in Belltown, the renowned ***Crocodile Cafe*** *(Map 6, ☎ 441-5611, 2200 2nd Ave)* is a springboard for local bands and a real institution of the Seattle alternative-rock scene. 'The Croc' is considered by many to be one of the best live-music clubs in the USA. Near Pike Place Market, ***Showbox*** *(Map 5, ☎ 628-3151, 1426 1st Ave)* hosts everything from indie rock groups to hip-hop swingers. It's a cavernous showroom that reincarnates itself every few years. When bands aren't playing on weekends, DJs take over and the dance party begins.

Near Pioneer Square, the always interesting ***OK Hotel*** *(Map 4, ☎ 621-7903, 212 Alaskan Way S)* caters to various forms of artistic angst: It's as likely to feature slam poetry, bizarre films or performance art as it is live bands. One of the only places ever to have success playing world and reggae music in Seattle is the cozy ***Bohemians Backstage Cafe & Lounge*** *(Map 4, ☎ 447-1514, 111 Yesler Way),* in Pioneer Square. The ***Experience Music Project*** *(EMP, Map 7, ☎ 367-5483, 325 5th Ave N),* at Seattle Center, brought a couple of new venues to town, including Sky Church. This entryway to the museum, jazzed up with a video mosaic and great acoustics, doubles as a concert hall. Smaller acts play in the EMP's 200-seat ***JBL Theater.*** Underage partiers go to ***DV8*** *(Map 7, ☎ 448-0888, 131 Taylor Ave N).* The bar doesn't serve alcohol, so anyone can get in, which attracts a really young crowd. Regardless, keep an eye open because DV8 can get some good bands.

Up on Capitol Hill, one of Seattle's coolest bars, the ***Baltic Room*** *(Map 8, ☎ 625-4444, 1207 Pine St),* oozes sophistication, with ultradim lighting and an excellent mix of live music and DJs spinning jungle, Britpop or dance tunes. Needless to say, the mood changes depending on what's playing, but this is always a hip spot. One of the only true rock clubs in town, the ***Break Room*** *(Map 8, ☎ 860-5155, 1325 E Madison St),* at 14th Ave, features national and local acts, though it's often hit and miss. If you go on a miss night, there's still plenty to do, like play air hockey or pool.

There's also good groovin' goin' on up in Ballard. Lovers of folk, country and acoustic shows can get their fills at the venerable ***Tractor Tavern*** *(Map 11, ☎ 789-3599, 5213 Ballard Ave NW).* Attracting hipsters and weekend warriors, the nearby ***Sunset Tavern*** *(Map 11, ☎ 784-4880, 5433 Ballard Ave NW)* books rock and blues bands. The ***Ballard Firehouse*** *(Map 11, ☎ 784-3516, 5429 Russell Ave NW)* books everything from rock to reggae.

Jazz & Blues Clubs

Pioneer Square is the center for jazz and blues in Seattle. A good place to start is ***New Orleans Creole Restaurant*** *(Map 4, ☎ 622-2563, 114 1st Ave S),* which books Basin St–style jazz, blues and zydeco. Just down the street are a couple of the city's best blues clubs, ***The Central*** *(Map 4, ☎ 622-0209, 207 1st Ave S)* and the seedier ***Larry's Greenfront*** *(Map 4, ☎ 624-7665, 209 1st Ave S).* The ***Old Timer's Café*** *(Map 4, ☎ 623-9800, 620 1st Ave)* also usually has blues.

Downtown, ***Dimitriou's Jazz Alley*** *(Map 2, ☎ 441-9729, 2033 6th Ave),* at Lenora St, is Seattle's most sophisticated and prestigious jazz club, with many national acts passing through. At ***Tula's*** *(Map 6, ☎ 443-4221, 2214 2nd Ave),* in Belltown, you can kick back to the sounds of heart-and-soul jazz musicians, who never made the fame-seeking trip to New York or New Orleans, but so easily could have.

Pioneer Square Party Pass

Designed with the barhopper in mind, this deal gets you in to eight Pioneer Square nightspots for one flat fee. A joint cover fee of $5 (Sunday to Thursday) or $10 (Friday or Saturday) gets you in-and-out privileges at the following clubs: Doc Maynard's Public House; Old Timer's Café; Larry's Greenfront; Bohemians Backstage Cafe & Lounge; The Fenix; Fenix Underground; New Orleans Creole Restaurant; and the Central. If you go between 8 and 9 pm on weekends, the price drops to $8, but remember, pace yourself, you've got a long night ahead of you! Pay the cover at the first club you visit.

Music Festivals

Summer musical festivals include the **Seattle Chamber Music Festival** (☎ 283-8808), held outdoors at Lakeside School (Map 1, 14050 1st Ave NE) in July with a smaller festival at Benaroya Concert Hall in winter. At the University of Washington, the **International Chamber Music Series** (☎ 543-4880, 800-859-5342) is a six-concert series at Meany Hall in autumn and winter. During summer months, open-air performances by nationally known pop and rock music acts are presented by **Summer Nights at the Pier** (☎ 628-0888 for TicketMaster). Concerts are performed at the Waterfront on Piers 62-64.

Children, hipsters and hippies alike will enjoy the **Northwest Folklife Festival** (☎ 684-7300). Held at Seattle Center in May on the Memorial Day long weekend, this is a fun event with music, dance, food and crafts. Check it out at www.nwfolklife.org.

The absolutely best way to kiss the sweetness of Northwest summer goodbye is by rockin' and rollin' to the grooves at **Bumbershoot** (☎ 281-8111). Held in September on the Labor Day long weekend, Bumbershoot brings hundreds of musicians to 25 stages throughout Seattle Center. Previous acts include Ani DiFranco, Indigo Girls, Ben Harper, Savage Garden and Tracy Chapman, to name a few. You can also see live drama performances and comedy and eat plenty of food. Get this year's lineup at www.bumbershoot.com.

DANCE CLUBS

Flexibility reigns in Seattle's clubs; many of Seattle's live-music venues also have DJ nights, which transform them into dance clubs. The gay discos have the hottest dance scene in town, including Re-Bar (see Gay & Lesbian Venues, later), though there are a couple of places that cater to a predominantly straight crowd. On Capitol Hill is the **Vogue** (Map 8, ☎ 443-0673, 1516 11th Ave). At its former location in Belltown it was one of the first clubs where grunge bands like Nirvana and Soundgarden played to slam-dancin' crowds. Today, the Vogue has mostly DJ music, and the atmosphere varies greatly, depending on who's spinning.

The **Fenix Underground** (Map 4, ☎ 467-1111, 315 2nd Ave S) is a popular Pioneer Square club featuring DJs and live music. The club owes its fame in part to owner John Corbett, who played Chris the DJ on TV's Northern Exposure. The frat-boy crowd keeps this place hopping, especially on weekends.

Near Seattle Center, **Polly Esthers** and **Culture Club** (Map 7, ☎ 441-1970, 332 5th Ave N) are two clubs joined by a hallway. These two go seriously retro, with three dance floors and DJs devoted to tunes from the '70s and '80s. On weekends, there's no cover until 9 pm.

GAY & LESBIAN VENUES

Some of Seattle's best bars and dance clubs are considered 'gay bars,' though open-minded drinkers, dancers and lovers of any creed are usually welcome. Gay nightlife centers along the Pike/Pine corridor on Capitol Hill, known simply as 'the corridor.' Almost any bar you go into around town is gay friendly, though the following cater specifically to gay and lesbian clientele. **Wildrose** (Map 8, ☎ 324-9210, 1201 E Pike St), at 11th Ave, is a comfortable lesbian bar. Pool tables, a light menu, Wednesday night karaoke and occasional

Savage Lovin' in Seattle

Born in Chicago in 1964, Dan Savage migrated to Seattle in 1990 and worked as a reporter for Seattle's *The Stranger* since its inception in 1991. The weekly paper became Seattle's outlet for political outrage, its medium for critiquing everything from city planning to music and arts. Dan started writing a sex advice column, *Savage Love*, as a comical and nudging way of waking Seattle up to its sexuality, be it homosexual or heterosexual. By 1993 it was roaring into syndication and started appearing in newspapers all over the USA and Canada. Dan's popularity as a controversial and confrontational tell-all from both sides of the sexual-orientation fence grew, and soon he had a regular spot on National Public Radio, was getting booked for public appearances and getting more 'feedback' mail than he could possibly read.

Though he says *Savage Love* started as a joke, Dan asserts that growing up gay in a primarily heterosexual world makes you think about sexuality and gender in ways other kids don't. 'When sex is what makes you different, you think about it more,' he says. 'In fact, that's the price of admission for gay people – thinking about gender and sexuality.' *Savage Love* brought previously hushed straight and gay sex issues into the wide open; Dan's explicit advice sent shock waves through a world still blushing and tittering over Dr Ruth. *Savage Love* draws criticism from outraged readers, who accuse Dan of intentionally invoking shock value, but *Savage Love* isn't that menacing or deliberate. Instead, it's just one guy's way of taking the taboo out of sex and homosexuality. Dan's take is that being gay or being sexually active shouldn't make you have to shut up.

But Dan's not all sex and dirty talk. Along with his partner Terry (whom he met at Seattle's Re-Bar in the early 1990s), he is a parent. After a long and extensive adoption process, Terry and Dan finally adopted a boy, DJ, in 1998. Savage tells the story in his book, *The Kid: What Happened after my Boyfriend and I Decided to Get Pregnant*. Now, like any other parent, Dan deals with

dirty diapers and balances a relationship, a child and his work. While Terry stays home with DJ, Dan commutes to work every day on the ferry from his home on a Puget Sound island.

What does Dan have to say about Seattle's gay scene? 'There's nothing self-conscious about it, it just is,' he says. Nongay Seattle's open and generally accepting attitude toward homosexuality keeps the gay scene open and generally accepting of nongays. You'll find every member of the sexual gamut in a lesbian venue, for example, women are welcome at gay male bars and so on. 'This is a great town to be gay in, mostly because the straight people are so remarkable,' says Dan. 'Gay people remade straight people, and straight people allowed themselves to be remade.'

live music keep this place jumping. *CC Attle's (Map 8, ☎ 726-0565, 1501 E Madison St)* is a self-proclaimed 'drinkin' bar' and makes a mellow hangout for men. The leather scene rips and roars at *The Cuff (Map 8, ☎ 323-1525, 1533 13th Ave)*, where boys in studded vests glow in the red neon. Though the small dance floor can accommodate a few sweaty bodies, most people come here to shop Cuff's usually juicy meat market. Referred to once as a 'Big, soulless, cha cha palace,' *Neighbours (Map 8, ☎ 324-5358, 1509 Broadway)* parties it up with a mostly male disco scene. Neighbours is in the alley between E Pike or E Pine Sts. Way at the other end of Broadway, the *Elite (Map 8, ☎ 324-4470, 622 Broadway E)* is a small bar that gets crowded mostly with slightly older men.

With its red lights glowing and split-level dance floor pumping, *The Eagle (Map 8, ☎ 621-7591, 314 E Pike St)* attracts mostly men (especially on Hard Core Leather Saturdays), but the dance floor is always hopping with an interesting and enthusiastic crowd.

The multileveled *R Place (Map 8, ☎ 322-8828, 619 E Pine St)* is an easygoing place to sip a microbrew and check out the Capitol Hill scene. The friendly crowd is primarily guys in their mid 20s, but sexual orientation here is secondary to good beer and pool. Oh, my, how beautiful the boys are at *Man Ray (Map 8, ☎ 568-0750, 514 E Pine St)*, across the street from R Place. This video bar, with a totally white interior and blue lighting, draws the upscale male set that shines in the futuristic setting.

Arguably Seattle's best dance club, *Re-Bar (Map 2, ☎ 233-9873, 1114 Howell St)*, at Boren Ave, attracts a lively crowd that comes to boogie on various theme nights. Whether you're gay, lesbian, bi or straight (or still unsure), you'll have fun here on Thursday at the classic Queer Disco, where everyone shakes a little ABBA booty. Saturday nights are devoted to 'ladies who love ladies,' and DJs keep the music going the rest of the week.

Up in Wallingford, *Changes (Map 10, ☎ 545-8363, 2103 N 45th St)* neighborhood pub attracts mostly men.

Pick up *SGN* for more on Seattle's gay and lesbian scene.

THEATER

Seattle has one of the most vibrant theater scenes on the West Coast. The following equity troupes present a range of classical and modern dramatic theater. Check the newspapers for openings; the 'What's Happening' section of the Friday *Seattle Post-Intelligence* has good theater listings.

A Contemporary Theatre (Map 2, ☎ 292-7676, 700 Union St), at Kreielsheimer Place, produces excellent year-round performances. Seattle's best thespians join occasional big-name actors. The box office is open noon to 7 pm Tuesday to Friday. Call to find out what's on or check the Web site at www.acttheatre.org.

In Seattle Center, Seattle's oldest stage, *Seattle Repertory Theatre (Map 7, ☎ 443-2222)* performs in the Bagley Wright Theatre. The Rep produces nine plays per season on its two stages. Its Web site is www.seattlerep.org. Next door, the *Intiman Theatre Company (☎ 269-1900)* performs elaborate dramas at the Intiman Playhouse. Its Web site is at www.intiman.org. The *Seattle Children's Theatre (Map 7, ☎ 441-3322)* offers excellent productions for young theatergoers in the Charlotte Martin and Eve Alvord Theaters.

In Lower Queen Anne, *On the Boards* in the Behnke Center for Contemporary Performance *(Map 7, ☎ 217-9888)*, 1st Ave at W Roy St, performs highly acclaimed original live drama and dance. The *Seattle Theatre Group* performs Broadway and off-Broadway shows, jazz, choral events, dance and silent films at the Paramount (Map 2) and Moore Theaters (Map 6). Call the theaters for showtimes. The stunning *5th Avenue Theatre (Map 2, ☎ 625-1418, 1308 5th Ave)*, designed with a Chinese motif in the 1920s, opened as a vaudeville house, turned into a movie theater and closed in 1979, some thought for good. But an influx of funding and a heritage award saved it in 1980, and now the 5th Ave is Seattle's premier theater for Broadway musical revivals.

Ticket Services

Tickets for most of Seattle's entertainment venues and events, including concerts, comedy, sports and performing arts, are available through TicketMaster (☎ 628-0888, 292-2787), which has ticket centers in several retail chains and some independent stores. Chains include PayLess Drug Stores, Budget Tapes & Discs, Disc Jockey, Tower Records and Wherehouse. Call to charge tickets by phone or to find the location nearest you. Ticket centers are open Monday to Saturday 8 am to 9 pm and Sunday 10 am to 6 pm. If you can buy tickets at the door and there's no risk of the show being sold out, do so; it'll save you the service fee (usually $6 to $10) tacked on by TicketMaster. For last-minute seats, the downtown TicketMaster has its own discount ticket booth (☎ 233-1111) at Westlake Center. Day-of-performance tickets are extra cheap, but you have to pay cash. The booth opens at 10 am daily.

Ticket/Ticket (☎ 324-2744) is another half-price, day-of-performance ticket outlet; however, they won't give information on ticket availability over the phone. There are locations at the Market Information Booth at Pike Place Market and on the upper level of the Broadway Market on Capitol Hill.

Up on Green Lake, **Bathhouse Theatre Company** (Map 10, ☎ 524-9108, 7312 W Green Lake Drive N) takes risks with modern adaptations of classics and original contemporary dramas. **Empty Space Theatre** (Map 10, ☎ 547-7500, 3509 Fremont Ave) presents off-beat shows and readings. Downtown, **The Annex Theatre** (Map 2, ☎ 728-0933, 1916 4th Ave) also produces alternative productions. Tickets for all the above venues are available through TicketMaster (see 'Ticket Services').

Both the **Cornish College of the Arts** (Map 8, ☎ 323-1486, 710 E Roy St), on Capitol Hill, and the **University of Washington School of Drama** (Map 9, ☎ 543-4880) churn out impressive student productions.

CLASSICAL MUSIC, OPERA & DANCE

Under maestro Gerard Schwartz, the **Seattle Symphony** (☎ 215-4747, 200 University St) has earned its reputation as the heart of the Seattle classical music scene. The symphony has presented several successful series since Schwartz came aboard in 1984 and has released a number of recordings to critical acclaim. Worth noting is the symphony's Discover Music Series – concerts designed to introduce children to various aspects of classical music. The symphony performs at the new Benaroya Concert Hall (Map 2), 2nd Ave at University St downtown. Its Web site is www.seattlesymphony.org.

Also performing at Benaroya, the only professional chamber orchestra in the Northwest, Seattle's **Northwest Chamber Orchestra** (☎ 343-0045) focuses on chamber music of the 17th to 20th centuries. The orchestra performs at various venues throughout the city, including Benaroya Concert Hall. Call or check listings in local newspapers for schedule and venue information. (See Live Music, earlier, for chamber-music festivals.)

The **Seattle Opera** (☎ 389-7676) has only gotten stronger under the directorship of Speight Jenkins. The company features a program of four or five full-scale operas every season, including a summer Wagner's Ring cycle that draws sellout crowds. Performances are held at the Opera House in Seattle Center (Map 7). Its Web site is www.seattleopera.org. Also performing at the Opera House is the **Pacific Northwest Ballet** (☎ 441-9411), the foremost dance company in the Northwest. Check out the performance schedule at www.pnb.org.

The **Seattle Men's Chorus** (☎ 323-2992) is one of the nation's most active gay choral groups, with nearly three dozen engagements throughout the year. Its Christmas concert is a popular holiday sellout. Check it out at its Web site, www.seattlemenschorus.org. At the University of Washington's Meany Hall, keep an eye out for the **World Dance Series** (☎ 543-4880, 800-859-5342), where six major works usually blow audiences away. Various dance performances also come to the Paramount and Moore Theaters (see Live Music, earlier).

CINEMAS

Although suburban multiscreen cinema complexes are common enough in Seattle, there are still a number of small independent theaters that go out of their way to feature the unusual and obscure. At opposite ends of Capitol Hill are two of the best art and foreign-film cinemas, the *Egyptian (Map 8, ☎ 323-4978, 805 E Pine St)* and the *Harvard Exit (Map 8, ☎ 323-8986, 807 E Roy St)*. Cineasts will like the offbeat fare at the *Grand Illusion Cinema (Map 9, ☎ 523-3935, 1403 NE 50th St)* in the U District.

Some first-run houses tend toward foreign and smaller independent films. The following theaters offer first-run art and foreign films alongside mainstream smash hits: *Broadway Market Cinemas (Map 8, ☎ 323-0231)*, in the Broadway Market on Capitol Hill; the *Varsity Theater (Map 9, ☎ 632-3131, 4329 University Way NE)*, in the U District; and the *Metro Cinemas (Map 9, ☎ 633-0055, 45th Ave)*, also near the university. For a full listing of movie theaters, times and locations, check *The Stranger* or *Seattle Weekly*.

Film Festivals

The biggest event of the year for filmgoers is the *Seattle International Film Festival (☎ 464-5830)*, a three-week-long extravaganza of films from around the world, including many American debuts. The festival is usually held in late May and early June, with most showings at the Egyptian and the Harvard Exit. Check out the festival Web site at www.seattlefilm.com. In October, the popular *Seattle Lesbian & Gay Film Festival (☎ 323-4274)* shows the world's best new gay films at the Egyptian and Harvard Exit, as well as various theaters around town.

COMEDY CLUBS

Seattle's main venue for stand-up comedy is *Comedy Underground (Map 4, ☎ 628-0303, 628-0888, 222 S Main St)*, near Pioneer Square. If you can make a crowd chuckle, stop by Monday for open-mic night. Comedy shows happen at 8 pm daily, with late shows 10 pm Friday and Saturday. Check it out at www.comedyunderground.com. If you've never seen theater sports, take in a show at the

Market Theater (Theater Sports) (Map 5, ☎ 781-9273, 1428 Post Alley), below Pike Place Market. Theater sports combines improvisation with competition, which usually results in a wild evening of audience-inspired madness. Shows are at 10:30 pm Friday and Saturday; tickets cost $10. There's also a show at 7 pm Sunday; $5. It's a good idea to call ahead and reserve, or you can join the line from 9:30 pm.

SPECTATOR SPORTS

There was a time when Seattle's professional baseball team was nothing but an annoying itch on the upper right shoulder of the USA, but not anymore. The *Seattle Mariners (☎ 628-3555)* won a division title in 1995 and promptly moved into the shiny new $417-million open-air Safeco Field. In 2000, the M's (as they are fondly referred to) missed a World Series berth by a hair, but snagged even more love from their devoted fans. The season runs April to October, and games are played at 7:05 or 7:35 pm weeknights; 1:05 or 6:05 pm Saturday; and 1:35 pm Sunday. There are also occasional midday games during the week. Call the hot line or check out their Web site at www.mariners.org.

The Northwest's only National Football League (NFL) franchise, the *Seattle Seahawks (☎ 425-827-9777)* have enjoyed both roaring success and dismal slumps, one of which prompted former owners to put the team on the selling block, which left Seattlelites fearing its relocation. In 1997 Microsoft cofounder Paul Allen saved the day by purchasing the Seahawks franchise, with the stipulation that the Hawks get a new stadium (see 'Paul Allen: Seattle's Co-Owner' in the Things to See & Do chapter). With that, the Hawks' former home, the Kingdome, quickly became a pile of rubble. It's now a busy construction zone as the new 72,000-seat stadium takes shape. During construction, the Hawks play at UW's Husky Stadium, until the as-yet-unnamed stadium opens in late summer 2002. Tickets range from $15 to $68. Check out the progress at www.seahawks.com.

Seattle's National Basketball Association (NBA) franchise, the *Seattle SuperSonics (☎ 283-3865)*, provides plenty of excitement at Key Arena in Seattle Center. The Sonics' season runs November to late April. Tickets range from a reasonable $9 to a whopping $120. Games start at 7 pm. The Sonics' Web site is www.nba.com/sonics. If you've never experienced professional women's basketball, you've got to check out the Women's National Basketball Association's ***Seattle Storm*** *(☎ 283-3865)*. The Storm play April to September at Key Arena, and game time is usually 7 pm. Tickets range from $8 to $27. Check out more at www.wnba.com/storm.

Also playing at Key Area, the ***Seattle Thunderbirds*** *(☎ 448-7825)* rip around the ice in the Western Hockey League (WHL) from September to March. The games are lively and well attended, and tickets are very reasonable, ranging from $10 to $22.

Soccer's no stranger in Seattle either. The A-League ***Seattle Sounders*** *(☎ 622-3415)* currently play at Memorial Stadium at Seattle Center, but will move to the new Seahawks Stadium upon its completion. The soccer season runs May to mid-September; tickets range from $10 to $15. Get more information at www.seattlesounders.com.

The University of Washington Huskies teams are another Seattle obsession. The Huskies football team plays at Husky Stadium and the men and women's basketball teams play at the Edmundson Pavilion, both of which are on campus. The women's basketball team draws huge crowds. For information about all spectator sports at UW, call ☎ 543-2200 or check out the Web site at www.gohuskies.com.

You can also buy tickets for all the above teams through TicketMaster outlets (☎ 628-0888) or Pacific Northwest Ticket Service (☎ 232-0150).

Shopping

Downtown dominates Seattle's retail scene with glamorous malls that in themselves are works of art. But take a look in the corners of Pioneer Square for splendid art and antique shops, or in the many nooks and crannies of Pike Place Market for everything from embroidered tea towels to lollypop condoms. Make the Waterfront your stop for obligatory souvenirs, become a gear junkie at one of many outdoor outfitters. Several of the outlying neighborhoods display quirky local wares, and Seattle lives up to its literary reputation with an excellent selection of general and specialty bookstores.

Most city stores, especially the ones geared toward tourists, are open every day (though some close on Sunday), typically 9 or 10 am to 6 pm. Malls and department stores keep later hours, often staying open until 8 or 9 pm.

Remember that an 8.8% sales tax is added to all purchases, except food to be prepared for consumption. The sales tax is not (like the European VAT or Canadian GST) refundable to tourists.

WHERE TO SHOP
Downtown (Map 2)

The main shopping area in Seattle is downtown between 3rd and 6th Aves and between University and Stewart Sts. Everything is here, from the Banana Republic store in the old Coliseum Theater on 5th Ave and Pike St, to the ridiculously huge Northwest-based Niketown (☎ 447-6453) at 1500 6th Ave.

There are two principal department stores downtown. Born and raised in Seattle, **Nordstrom** (☎ 628-2111), Pine St between 5th and 6th Aves, occupies a giant space in the former Frederick and Nelson Building. Closer to Pike Place Market, Nordstrom Rack (☎ 448-8522), 1601 2nd Ave, offers closeouts and returns from the parent store. The **Bon Marche** (☎ 344-2121), 3rd Ave at Pine St, is Seattle's oldest and largest department store.

There are plenty of malls downtown. The decorative boutique mall **Westlake Center** (☎ 467-3044), 4th Ave at Pine St, is one of the megamall Rowse developments that are cropping up in big US cities. Here you'll find shops like Jessica McClintock (☎ 467-1048), Crabtree & Evelyn (☎ 682-6776) and the Galleries of Neiman Marcus (☎ 447-0901). There are some local stores as well, including an outlet of Fireworks (☎ 682-6462), which offers inexpensive funky-arty gifts from regional craftspeople.

The fancy **City Centre Mall** (☎ 223-8999), 5th Ave between Pike and Union Sts, has a higher class of tenant, including Barney's New York (☎ 622-6300), Ann Taylor (☎ 623-4818) and FAO Schwarz (☎ 442-9500). The treasure in here is the local company Design Concern (☎ 623-4444), which has a creative selection of upscale office tools and toys, watches, soaps and local jewelry.

Rainier Square (☎ 373-7119), between 4th and 5th Aves and Union and University Sts, is a mall where you'll find it all. Upscale clothing stores include Brooks Brothers (☎ 624-4400) and Oregon's famed Northwest Pendleton (☎ 682-4430), which sells its trademark plaid wool shirts and blankets. The cool Channel 9 Store (☎ 682-8198) is filled with educational videos and games,

while Fox's Gem Shop (☎ 623-2528) displays its Tiffany collection and Louis Vuitton (☎ 749-0711) oozes with luxury leather goods.

Seattle's newest boutique mall, **Pacific Place** (☎ 405-2655), 600 Pine St between 6th and 7th Aves, ranks at the top. Clothiers include J Crew (☎ 652-9788), Club Monaco (☎ 264-8001) and J Peterman (☎ 264-1560). The large stores of Pottery Barn (☎ 621-0276) and Williams-Sonoma (☎ 621-7405) are fun to look around in. Take a moment to gape in the window at Tiffany & Co. The mall's top level features a movie theater, a pub and a couple of restaurants.

Pike Place Market (Map 5)

No visit to Seattle is complete without several hours of wandering the market. For the compulsive browser, amateur chef, hungry traveler on a budget or student of the human condition, Seattle has no greater attraction than Pike Place Market.

This is shopping central in Seattle: Dozens of market food stalls hawk everything from geoduck clams to fennel root to harissa. (For suggestions on food stalls, see the Places to Eat chapter.) Everything pertaining to food is also available in the market. Don't miss the excellent cookware store, Sur La Table (☎ 448-2244), 84 Pine St, next door to the Seattle Garden Center (☎ 448-0431), which stocks a vibrant collection of seeds, bulbs and gardening books.

The North Arcade of the market is mostly given over to craftspeople, who sell their own goods from tables and benches; this is a good place to pick up something uniquely Seattle. Beneath the market is a maze of little shops selling everything from comic books to crystals. If you enjoy browsing, you can spend hours here: the shops just don't end. Check out MJ Feet's Birkenstock Store (☎ 624-2929), 1514 Pike Place, for the latest in hippie footwear. The Great Wind Up (☎ 621-9370) has every wind-up toy and gizmo known to humankind, and then some. Feeling enchanted? Stop by Market Magic Shop (☎ 624-4271) to buy magic and conjuring supplies. Other market purveyors are listed throughout this chapter.

WHAT TO BUY
Books

Bookworms in Seattle come crawling out at the least suggestion of literary splendor. While you can find giant chain bookstores in Seattle, you never need shop there; the representation of local general and specialty booksellers is excellent, and the community of supportive bibliophiles keeps them going strong.

General One of the best general bookstores in the Northwest is the Elliott Bay Book Company (Map 4, ☎ 624-6600), 101 S Main St. This rambling bookstore takes up an entire block of historic storefronts in Pioneer Square. The interior, all exposed red brick and high ceilings, is absolutely stuffed full of new books and browsing customers. Downstairs is a popular café. Elliott Bay is the local leader in author appearances, with some writer appearing at a reading or signing almost nightly.

On Capitol Hill, the best general bookstore is Bailey/Coy Books (Map 8, ☎ 323-8842), 414 Broadway E, with a good gay and lesbian section. Up on 15th St, another independent bookstore is Pages (Map 8, ☎ 324-1000), 432 15th Ave E.

In the U District, the University Bookstore (Map 9, ☎ 634-3400), 4326 University Way NE, is a vast all-purpose bookstore that serves the University of Washington. It has another outlet downtown (Map 2, ☎ 545-9230), 1225 4th Ave.

The Fremont Place Book Co (Map 10, ☎ 547-5970) 621 N 35th St, is a friendly shop with a small but interesting collection. Up on the hill, Queen Anne Avenue Books (Map 7, ☎ 283-5624), 1629 Queen Anne Ave N, is another good neighborhood bookstore.

Specialty Seattle has some great theme bookstores. Around Pioneer Square Flora & Fauna Books (Map 4, ☎ 623-4727), 121 1st Ave S, is good for books on natural history and local field guides. Seattle Mystery Bookshop (Map 4, ☎ 587-5737),

117 Cherry St, is a specialty store for page-turners and whodunits. Around Pike Place Market, Peter Miller Architecture & Design Books (Map 5, ☎ 441-4114), 1930 1st Ave, specializes in architecture books. At the Pike St entry to the market, Left Bank Books (☎ 622-0195) serves the reading needs of the political hard left. On Capitol Hill, Beyond the Closet Books (Map 8, ☎ 322-4609), 1501 Belmont Ave, is the city's gay-focused bookstore. Open Books (Map 10, ☎ 633-0811), 2414 N 45th St in Wallingford, is devoted totally to poetry; call to ask about readings and events. Nearby, Astrology et al (Map 10, ☎ 548-1095), 1711 N 45th St, sells everything from horoscope guides to tarot cards.

For outdoor activities guides, the Mountaineers (Map 7, ☎ 284-6310), 300 3rd Ave in lower Queen Anne, has one of the best selections anywhere. In addition to books, it also has CDs, videos, maps and technical manuals.

Near the University District, All For Kids (Map 9, ☎ 526-2768), 2900 NE Blakely, has one of the largest selections of children's books in town, and it also stocks a lot of children's music. Another bookstore with a good children's selection is the Secret Garden Bookshop (Map 11, ☎ 789-5006), 2214 NW Market St, up in Ballard.

Travelers will want to make a pilgrimage to Wide World Books & Maps (Map 10, ☎ 634-3453), 4411 Wallingford Ave N. In addition to a great selection of travel guides, this pleasant store offers a full array of travel accessories and a staff of seasoned globetrotters. Watch for frequent slideshows and author events. Marco Polo (Map 8, ☎ 860-3736), 713 Broadway E, is a small intimate travel bookstore up on Capitol Hill. Downtown, Rand McNally (Map 2, ☎ 264-6277), 1218 4th Ave, has a full selection of travel guides and maps. The source for maps is Metsker Maps (Map 4, ☎ 623-8747), 702 1st Ave, near Pioneer Square.

For books in Japanese, on Japanese culture (in both English and Japanese) and Japanese works translated into English, go to Kinokuniya (Map 4, ☎ 587-2477), 519 6th Ave S, above Uwajimaya in the International District. On Capitol Hill, Multilingual Books & Tapes (Map 8, ☎ 328-7922), 1205 E Pike St, sells materials in 100 different languages.

Used On Capitol Hill, Twice Sold Tales (Map 8, ☎ 324-2421), 905 E John St, is a rambling used-book store that stays open very late and never closes on Friday. Dinosaur heads and rockets stick out of the walls, and you'll likely see one of the store's eight cats roaming the rafters. Look for the bubble machine outside. Also on Capitol Hill, Pistil Books & News (Map 8, ☎ 325-5401), 1010 E Pike St, has both new and used books and magazines.

Two great used-book stores are in the U District. Magus Books (Map 9, ☎ 633-1800), 1408 NE 42nd St, specializes in scholarly books, and University Used & Rare Books (Map 9, ☎ 632-3738), 4213 University Way NE, is the place to look for tomes long out of print – you'll have good luck finding them here.

Periodicals

Seattle has several excellent newsstands. In Pike Place Market, Read All About It (☎ 624-0140) is right across from DeLaurenti's. Up on Broadway, Steve's Broadway News (Map 8, ☎ 324-7323), 204 Broadway E, is the place to go for magazines and foreign newspapers; or visit its twin Steve's Fremont News (Map 10, ☎ 633-0731), on Fremont Ave N in Fremont. The university's newsstand of choice is Bulldog News & Espresso (Map 9, ☎ 632-6397), 4208 University Way NE. Terminals offer Internet access at 50¢ for 10 minutes. The small monitors are no good for Web surfing, but if you want to check your email, they work just fine.

Antiques

Little antique shops pop up all around the city, though the highest concentration is found around Pioneer Square. Pioneer Square Antique Mall (Map 4, ☎ 624-1164), 601 1st Ave, is a warren of little shops right across from the pergola; it's actually part of the Seattle 'underground' (see 'A Town

Underground' in the Things to See & Do chapter) and can be somewhat claustrophobic. Find all manner of antiques and collectibles at Jackson Street Gallery (Map 4, ☎ 447-1012), 108 S Jackson St. Jean Williams Antiques (Map 4, ☎ 622-1110), 115 S Jackson St, sells English and French period antiques, while Elliott Bay Antiques (Map 4, ☎ 340-0770), 165 S Jackson St, features Asian furniture and art.

A charming store for small antiques, including jewelry, toys and dishes, is Antiques at Pike Place (☎ 441-9643), 92 Stewart St. Up in Fremont, weed through the junk at the Fremont Antique Mall (Map 10, ☎ 548-9140), 3419 Fremont Ave N – you just might find something you can't live without.

If you're trying to retrofit fixtures into an older home, check out the selection of doors, sinks, hardware and plumbing fixtures at Seattle Building Salvage (Map 6, ☎ 448-3453), 202 Bell St in Belltown.

Art

The Seattle area is known for its Pilchuck school of glassblowing art. Glasshouse Studio (☎ 682-9939), 311 Occidental Ave S, is the city's oldest glassblowing studio – stop by to watch the artists in action. The Foster/White Gallery (Map 4, ☎ 622-2833), 123 S Jackson St, features glassworks, paintings and sculpture by mainstream Northwest artists.

The Stonington Gallery (☎ 405-4040), 119 S Jackson St, focuses on intricate arts by coastal Native artists from Washington to Alaska. Other Northwest Coast Indian and Inuit art and artifacts, including baskets and jewelry, are sold at Legacy Ltd Gallery (Map 2, ☎ 624-6350), 1003 1st Ave. Affordable and authentic Native American crafts are available at Traditions & Beyond (Map 4, ☎ 621-0655), 113 Cherry St. Part of its proceeds go to Native programs and education.

For something totally different, check out StreetLife Gallery (Map 6, ☎ 956-8046),

Glassmaster Dale Chihuly

This modern master of glassmaking – claimed by *Fine Art* magazine to be to glass what Steven Spielberg is to film – was born in Tacoma in 1941. After an education in design and fine arts, Chihuly won a Fulbright scholarship to study the art of glassmaking on the island of Murano, the renowned glassmaking center near Venice.

Chihuly returned to the Seattle area in 1971 to found the Pilchuck Glass School; this studio is credited with transforming glass – previously used mostly for utilitarian or decorative purposes – into a medium of transcendent artistic expression. Chihuly's blown-glass sculptures defy the everyday experience of glass: infused with lush color, sensual textures and a physicality that is at once massive and delicate, these pieces extend the very notion of 'glassness' into new realms of recognition.

The Seattle area is home to a number of Chihuly installations, and many local art galleries display his works (as well as the works of other glass artists – Seattle is a hotbed of glass artistry). Get a sense of Chihuly's craft in the 2nd-floor atrium of City Centre Mall, which contains several glass sculptures. Anyone serious about Chihuly's work should make the trip down to Tacoma to see his massive installation in the Union Station Federal Courthouse and the smaller works at the Tacoma Art Museum (see Puget Sound in the Excursions chapter).

Chihuly lives and works at his 25,000-sq-foot studio on Lake Union, called the Boathouse. A car accident left him blind in one eye (he wears a trademark eye patch); ever since, he has lacked the necessary depth perception to continue solo glassblowing. Chihuly now oversees a team of glassblowers who perform the principal construction of his works.

Today, Chihuly's art is represented in over 125 museums around the world. Some of his recent major works include the *Chandeliers* series (1992), the *Chihuly Over Venice* project (1995) and set designs for the Seattle Opera's *Pelléas et Mélisande* (1993).

2301 2nd Ave, a studio and exhibition space for homeless artists.

At Seattle Center, the Northwest Craft Center (Map 7, ☎ 728-1555) is mostly dedicated to ceramics by regional craftspeople. Fireworks Fine Crafts Gallery (Map 4, ☎ 682-8707), 210 1st Ave S, is a wonderful mixture of funky handmade jewelry, furniture, pottery and you name it. This is a good place to actually buy something artsy without spending your annual income. Another relatively inexpensive place to look for local arts and crafts is Phoenix Rising Gallery (Map 5, ☎ 728-2332), 2030 Western Ave, near Pike Place Market. For funky jewelry and 'functional art' by local artists check out Frank and Dunya (Map 10, ☎ 547-6760), 3418 Fremont Ave N.

Cameras & Photo Supplies

The foremost selection of film and photographic supplies in Seattle is Cameras West (Map 2, ☎ 622-0066), 1908 4th Ave, right downtown. For one-hour photo developing, Kits Cameras (Map 2, ☎ 682-3221), 806 3rd Ave, also has a branch at Westlake Center.

Music

Seattle has some good specialty stores for recordings but, oddly, no locally owned comprehensive source for mainstream or classical music. For that, you need to go to Tower Records (Map 7, ☎ 283-4456), 500 Mercer St, near Seattle Center. Locally based Cellophane Square can special order anything. Visit its shop in the U District (Map 9, ☎ 634-2280), 4538 University Way NE.

Whether you're looking for recordings of Coltrane or the Duke, you'll have a good shot of finding them at Bud's Jazz Records (Map 4, ☎ 628-0445), 102 S Jackson St. Bud specializes in vintage vinyl recordings of early and hard-to-find jazz. Another good source for rare records of all sorts is Fallout Records & Comics (Map 8, ☎ 323-2662), 1504 Olive Way on Capitol Hill.

When grunge music was born in Seattle, Sub Pop was the record label that endured the arduous but oh-so-worthwhile labor pains, giving birth to its beautiful grungy

baby. Its retail outlet, the Sub Pop Mega Mart (☎ 652-4356), in the Sanitary Market Building at the Pike Place Market, still sells recordings of new local bands. Up on Capitol Hill, The Orpheum (Map 8, ☎ 322-6370), 618 Broadway, is another source for cutting-edge local and alternative music.

In Belltown, Singles Going Steady (Map 6, ☎ 441-7396), 2219 2nd Ave, specializes in hardcore punk, hip-hop and ska.

Souvenirs & Fun Shops

There's a good selection of locally made crafts, food products and regional wines to choose from in Seattle. For the full gamut of souvenirs, you need simply to stroll up and down the boardwalk along the Waterfront. You may wish to begin your shopping foray at the landmark Ye Olde Curiosity Shop (☎ 682-5844), on Pier 54, where you'll find an ample supply of Seattle souvenirs. If you're looking for something more authentically Northwest, head to Made in Washington (☎ 467-0788), 1530 Post Alley, in Pike Place Market or in Westlake Center downtown.

One of the coolest shops in Pike Place Market, Tenzing Momo (☎ 623-9837), in the Economy Market Building, is a unique natural apothecary, with shelves of glass bottles filled with herbs and tinctures to cure any ail.

In Fremont, Deluxe Junk (Map 10, ☎ 634-2733), 3518 Fremont Place N, carries an interesting collection of, well, junk. If you're

How much carry-on luggage am I allowed ?

DEBRA MILLER

SHOPPING

looking to fit in with the crowd on Capitol Hill, Urban Outfitters (Map 8, ☎ 322-1800), 401 Broadway E, in the Broadway Market sells clothing geared toward young folks looking to score points on the hip scale.

Erotica

If you're looking for the weird and wonderful, or just the weird, stop by the Pink Zone (Map 8, ☎ 325-0050), 211 Broadway, where you can choose from a good selection of naughty greeting cards, unusual condoms, leather-studded G-strings and tame sex toys. Also on Capitol Hill, the delightful Toys in Babeland (Map 8, ☎ 328-2914), 707 E Pike St, is a sex-toy store for women (looking for a glass dildo? You've come to the right spot). Lovers of sweet things should check out Wallingford's Erotic Bakery (Map 10, ☎ 545-6969), 2323 N 45th St, where erection confections and other exotic desserts are made to order. Ask for a business card so you can mail it home and shock a loved one.

Second-Hand Clothes

Looking for groovy stuff but don't want to pay a lot? Capitol Hill is the place to go. Crossroads Trading Co (Map 8, ☎ 328-5867), 325 Broadway E, and nearby Red Light (Map 8, ☎ 329-2200), 312 Broadway E, both sell a good collection of second-hand clothes. Red Light also has a U District location (Map 9, ☎ 545-4044), 4560 University Way NE.

Outdoor Gear

The state-of-the-art REI (Map 7, ☎ 323-8333), 222 Yale Ave N, is right by I-5 south of Lake Union. This outdoor recreation megastore has become a tourist destination: the store has its own climbing wall; you can check out the rainproofing of various brands of gear by entering a special rainstorm shower; or road-test hiking boots on a simulated mountain trail. You can get almost every kind of outdoor equipment and gear here, from hiking boots to kayaks, from pitons to bicycle tires. REI rents all forms of ski packages, climbing gear and camping equipment – call for daily/weekly rates (for more on REI, see the Activities chapter).

Near REI, Feathered Friends (Map 7, ☎ 292-2210), 119 Yale Ave N, stocks high-end climbing equipment, made-to-order sleeping bags and backcountry ski gear. Patrick's Fly Shop (Map 7, ☎ 323-3302), 2237 Eastlake Ave E, near Lake Union, has been around as long as anyone can remember. It offers workshops on fly-fishing, sells equipment and gladly gives advice.

For hardcore camping, climbing and hiking equipment, go to The North Face (Map 2, ☎ 622-4111), 1023 1st Ave, downtown toward the Waterfront. Nearby is Warshal's Sporting Goods (Map 2, ☎ 624-7304), 1000 1st Ave, an old-fashioned hunting and fishing store with an excellent selection of camping and outdoor gear.

The fashionable outdoor clothing at Patagonia (Map 6, ☎ 622-9700), 2100 1st Ave in Belltown, may seem to be only for the very adventurous, but experience a sodden winter in Seattle and you'll understand why this is where the locals shop for rain gear and outdoor apparel. A unique store in Fremont, Second Bounce (Map 10, ☎ 545-8810), 315 N 36th St, sells used outdoor gear, such as clothing, boots, backpacks and camping gear. This is a good way to save some money if you've decided on an impromptu hiking trip, but you don't have the gear with you.

Bicycles

Seattle's largest bicycle dealer is Gregg's Greenlake Cycle (Map 10, ☎ 523-1822), 7007 Woodlawn Ave NE near Green Lake. It has a huge stock of all kinds of bikes and accessories. Elliott Bay Bicycles (Map 6, ☎ 441-8144), 2116 Western Ave in Belltown, aims more at pro or hardcore cyclists who are prepared to slap down big bucks for bikes. On Capitol Hill, Velo Stores (Map 8, ☎ 325-3292), 1533 11th Ave, has a good selection of road and mountain bikes, along with a helpful staff.

Recycled Cycles (Map 9, ☎ 547-4491), 1007 NE Boat St, at the bottom of the U District along Lake Union, sells used and consignment bikes. It also has a wide selection of parts including cranks, forks, pedals, tires and tubes.

Food & Drink

Specialty Foods Perhaps the gift that says I ♥ Seattle the most is a whole salmon or other fresh seafood from the fish markets. All the markets will prepare fish for transport on the plane ride home, or you can just call and have them take care of the overnight shipping. In Pike Place Market, try Jack's Fish Spot (☎ 467-0514) or Pike Place Fish (☎ 682-7181, 800-542-7732). At the Fishermen's Terminal, on the south side of the Ballard Bridge, Wild Salmon Fish Market (☎ 283-3366, 888-222-3474), 1900 W Nickerson St, sells the freshest salmon and shellfish in town. The market will ship fresh fish at very reasonable prices.

Even if you don't have a kitchen handy, shopping for food is great fun in Pike Place Market; you can channel your shopping urges into buying local jams or syrups, hunting for obscure spices and condiments or picking out a bottle of local wine for drinking later. De-Laurenti's (☎ 454-7155) is a mandatory market stop for the Italian chef or Continental food enthusiast. Not only is there a stunning selection of cheeses, sausages, hams and pastas, but there's also the largest selection of capers, olive oils and anchovies that you're likely to find this side of Genoa. The wine selection is also quite broad.

Other ethnic stores in the market include The Souk (☎ 441-1666), for Middle Eastern and North African comestibles, and El Mercado Latino (☎ 623-3240), which has a wide array of chilis and other products needed to make authentic Caribbean and Central American foods. Just below the market, The Spanish Table (☎ 682-2827), 1427 Western Ave, stocks excellent ingredients from Spain and Portugal.

In the International District, Uwajimaya (Map 4, ☎ 624-6248), 519 6th Ave S, is a wonderful supermarket filled with everything needed to prepare Japanese and other Asian foods, including many different kinds of fish, meats, fruits and vegetables. Cooking vessels, hard-to-find spices and other flavorings and even the necessary cookbooks can be found at the market as well.

If you've got a sweet tooth to satisfy, try the confection truffles at Dilettante Chocolates (Map 8, ☎ 329-6463), 416 Broadway E.

Wine If a present of regional wine seems an appropriate gift, check out Pike & Western Wine Shop (Map 5, ☎ 441-1307), 1934 Pike Place at the northern end of Pike Place Market. Its selection and friendly service make this a great place to get introduced to the wines of the Northwest. Market Cellar Winery (☎ 622-1880), 1419 1st Ave at the southern end of the market, makes its own wine and sells do-it-yourself home brew kits.

Another source for regional wines is Seattle Cellars, Ltd (Map 6, ☎ 256-0850), 2505 2nd Ave. In Wallingford, there's no snobbery at City Cellars (Map 10, ☎ 632-7238), 1710 N 45th St, which has great wines at reasonable prices.

Excursions

One of the hardest things about writing a city guide is resisting the urge to write about all the great things *surrounding* the city! Well, here in this small chapter, you'll get a glimpse of what Seattle's surrounding areas have to offer.

You could spend an afternoon in the high-tech mega-burbs of the Eastside or take a ferry across Puget Sound to one of the rugged green islands for lunch. Rent a car and drive south to the incredible Mt St Helens National Volcanic Monument or Mt Rainier National Park, or explore the capital city of Olympia. Plan a cycling tour of the San Juan Islands or catch the *Clipper* over to Victoria, Canada's uniquely British harborside town. Seattle is an excellent launchpad for whatever excursion you plan to make.

THE EASTSIDE

Across Lake Washington are the suburbs of Bellevue, Kirkland, Redmond and Woodinville – collectively known as the Eastside. At one time these were mostly bedroom communities for Seattle; however, with the arrival of high-tech firms, the Eastside no longer rests on Seattle's pillow. Life focuses on the shopping centers: If you ask someone what there is to do on the Eastside, they will almost invariably answer, 'Well, there's the malls…'

For suburban centers, the Eastside cities are pretty nice. Lake Washington borders both Bellevue and Kirkland, with Lake Sammamish bringing up the rear to the east. Much of the area has a manicured, well-kept look that implies the soaring prosperity. Incomes on the Eastside are roughly double those in Seattle proper. You'd have no problem buying a BMW or a Jag here, and housing costs are simply astonishing: The average house price in Kirkland is $280,000, while on the west edge of Bellevue the average house price is $430,000.

The superheated economy on the Eastside can be explained in a few words: Microsoft, AT&T, Nintendo, Apex and AVT.

However, these high- and bio-tech firms are just the tip of the iceberg; in 1996, 547 technology firms were located along the I-405 corridor between Renton and Bothell.

If you're traveling to Seattle on business, chances are good that you'll be spending some time on the Eastside. Don't despair: While there's nothing remarkable about Eastside cultural offerings, these fast-growing suburbs are pleasant, parks are plentiful and the restaurants are good.

Getting There & Away To reach Bellevue from downtown Seattle, take I-90 to I-405 northbound. Exit at NE 8th St. If you're on public transport, take bus No 226 from the downtown bus tunnel to the Bellevue Transit Center, 108th Ave NE atat NE 6th St. When traveling from Downtown to anywhere on the Eastside, you cross a zone and must pay a two-zone fare. During peak hours (6 to 9 am and 3 to 6 pm weekdays) the fare is $2/50¢ adults/seniors and youths; off-peak hours $1.25/50¢.

To reach Kirkland from downtown, take Hwy 520, the Evergreen Point Bridge. It's the most notoriously gridlocked of all Seattle bridges, and there's nothing to be done but get on and wait your turn. You can either exit onto Hwy 908 and take surface streets north up to Kirkland or take I-405 up to exit 18 and turn back to the west toward Lake Washington. By bus, take route No 255 from the downtown bus tunnel.

Redmond is directly east of Kirkland on either Hwy 908 (NE 85th St becoming NE Redmond Way) or Hwy 520. Marymoor Park is off Hwy 520 at W Lake Sammamish Parkway NE. Take bus Nos 251 or 254 from downtown Seattle. To get to Marymoor Park, take bus No 256, get off at the Redmond Park & Ride and transfer onto bus No 249.

Woodinville is 14 miles north of Bellevue off I-405. From downtown Seattle, take bus No 307.

Bellevue

Bellevue was long the suburb that Seattleites loved to disdain. However, the mass immigration to the Seattle area has boosted the population of this city on the eastern shores of Lake Washington to the point that Bellevue is now Washington's fifth-largest city, an upscale burg with high-cost housing and attractive parks. If you're used to suburbs being low-rise, you'll be surprised at the high-flying Bellevue skyline.

If you're looking for the civic heart and soul of Bellevue, look no further than **Bellevue Square**, Bellevue Way NE at NE 8th St, the shopping mall that sets the tone for downtown and the surrounding communities. Over 200 stores are here, including Nordstrom, Bon Marche and Northwest Discovery, a craft, jewelry and gift shop with items from local artisans. Even if you don't need to go shopping, the **Bellevue Art Museum** (☎ 425-454-3322), 510 Bellevue Way NE, in a brand new building across from the mall, has changing exhibits of contemporary Northwest art and is worth a stop. It's open 10 am to 5 pm Tuesday and Saturday, noon to 8 pm Wednesday to Friday, and noon to 5 pm Sunday. Admission is $7/5 adults/students and seniors.

Trails lead through **Bellevue Botanical Gardens**, a 36-acre public garden (☎ 425-451-3755), Main St at 124th Ave NE, which focuses on rhododendrons, some of which are huge and very old, along with other native plants. At the visitors center is a gift shop and a botanical library. A former orchard, it also features a Japanese garden, a wetlands garden and a rock garden. The gardens are open daily from dawn to dusk. Admission is free.

The **Rosalie Whyel Museum of Doll Art** is a large collection of historical and collectible dolls from around the world. The museum (☎ 425-455-1116), 1116 108th Ave NE near the junction with NE 12th St, is purposely built in a larger than usual scale to make the whole enterprise seem to the visitor like a dollhouse. The museum is open 10 am to 5 pm Monday to Saturday, and 1 to 5 pm Sunday. Admission is $7/6/5 for adults/seniors/children five to 17.

Places to Stay Most hotels in and around Bellevue are designed with the expense-account traveler in mind. However, there's still some value at **Eastgate Motel** (☎ 425-746-4100, 800-628-8578, 14632 SE Eastgate Way), with rooms at $50/55. Some kitchens are available.

Otherwise, Bellevue is a pricey place to stay. The large suites at **Embassy Suites Hotel Bellevue** (☎ 425-644-2500, 3225 158th Ave SE) have a microwave and fridge, two telephones, two TVs and voice mail. There's also a pool and exercise facilities to keep you in shape. Suites run from $119 to $239.

Right in the heart of downtown, **Hyatt Regency Bellevue** (☎ 425-462-1234, 800-233-1234, 900 Bellevue Way NE) sets the standard for business-class lodgings, with luxury rooms and all the facilities you'll ever need. Rooms go for $190 to $265; suites are from $425. At the upscale **DoubleTree Hotel Bellevue** (☎ 425-455-1300, 800-222-8733, 300 112th Ave SE), rooms are large and well furnished and begin at $169/184, with suites from $295.

Places to Eat Bellevue's not exactly the cuisine capital of western Washington, and by and large the selections and certainly the views are better at nearby Kirkland. But there are a few notable spots besides the mall food courts and hotel restaurants.

An object of local marvel, **Dixie's Barbecue** (☎ 425-828-2460, 11522 Northup Way) is a homespun barbecue joint operating out of a former automotive garage. The owner will menace you with 'The Man' sauce until – despite his warnings to the contrary – you try it on your dinner (it's not all *that* hot). **Pogacha** (☎ 425-455-5670, 119 106th Ave NE) is a bakery and café that prepares Croatian-style pizza breads, for which the restaurant is named. You can also get other basic Mediterranean-style entrées here at a good price.

Bellevue's favorite Japanese restaurant is **I Love Sushi** (☎ 425-454-5706, 11818 NE 8th St). Despite the somewhat eye-rolling name, the sushi, sashimi and tempura are very good. On the top of the Key Bank Building, **Spazzo Mediterranean Grill**

EXCURSIONS

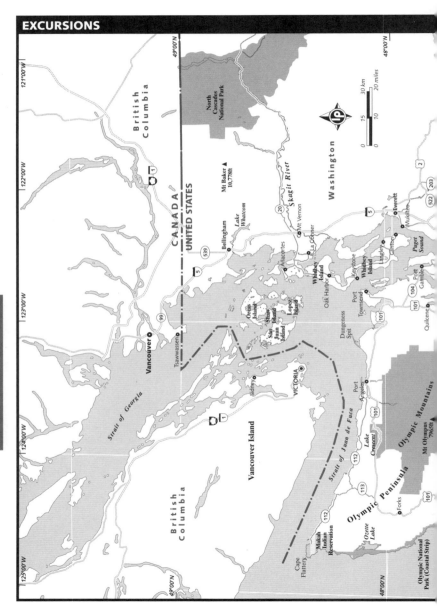

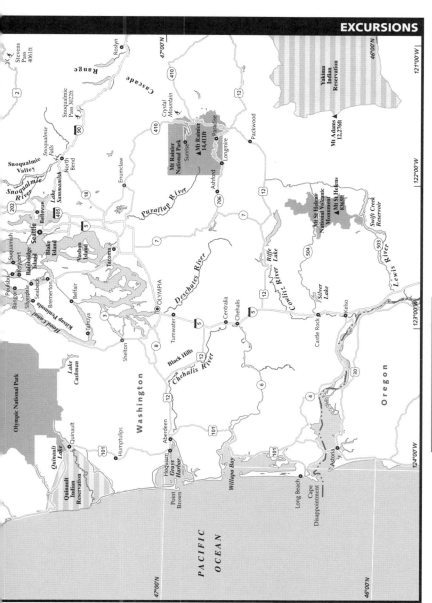

(☎ 425-454-8255, 10655 NE 4th St) serves a variety of pan-Mediterranean dishes in a lively dining room with good views. Choose your cuisine: Italian, Spanish, Greek, Turkish or North African. Or, don't decide and just order from the tapas menu. *Tosoni's* (☎ 425-644-1668, 14320 NE 20th St) serves up even better Mediterranean food, though the location's not so noteworthy. This humble strip-mall denizen is a favorite of locals, who are used to fine things coming in unlikely packages.

Daniel's Broiler (☎ 425-462-4662, 10500 NE 8th St), on the 21st floor of the Bank of America Building (adjacent to the Hyatt Regency), is an excellent place to eat a steak. Dinners are pricey, but the views over Lake Washington to the Seattle skyline are spectacular.

Kirkland

North of Bellevue on I-405, Kirkland is known for its lakefront business district, marinas and antique shopping malls. This is by far the most pleasant of the Eastside neighborhoods, and some of the best public access to Lake Washington is along Lake Ave W. Here you'll also find a number of waterfront restaurants, some with docks for customers arriving by private boat.

This is also the only neighborhood on the Eastside where you might want to park and walk around just for the fun of it. The center of Kirkland is Central Way NE at Lake St S; Lake Washington glimmers just yards away beyond the shops and the restaurants, giving the neighborhood a maritime feeling.

You'll know you're in Kirkland when you see the famed statue of a cow with a howling coyote on its back (longtime Seattle-watchers may remember when this life-size sculpture adorned Occidental Square in the Pioneer Square area). Lining the streets are high-end furniture, art and home-decor stores. If you missed Sur La Table in Pike Place Market, be sure to stop in at the Kirkland store.

After walking through the galleries and boutiques along Lake St S and Central Way NE, drop on over to **Marina Park**, the largest public pier on Lake Washington, and watch the yachting and sailing crowd trim their sails and sun their bodies. Farther up the hill the **Kirkland Antique Gallery** (☎ 425-828-4993), 151 3rd St, has more than 90 different dealers under one roof. Another good place to dawdle is the **Kirkland Arts Center** (☎ 425-822-7161), 620 Market St. Housed in one of the oldest buildings on the Eastside (from 1891), the center offers art classes and has ongoing shows of local artists. Visitors can enroll in weekend workshops or six- to eight-week courses in drawing, painting, printmaking and sculpture. For a list of upcoming courses, check out the Web site at www.kirklandartscenter.org.

Places to Stay Right off Hwy 520, *La Quinta Inn Kirkland* (☎ 425-828-6585, 800-531-5900, 10530 NE Northup Way), is a modern motor hotel with rooms at $89/99 and suites at $119.

The Eastside's nicest hotel, *The Woodmark Hotel on Lake Washington* (☎ 425-822-3700, 800-822-3700, 1200 Carillon Point), sits right on Lake Washington, just south of downtown Kirkland. Most rooms overlook the marina and downtown Seattle. Rooms are spacious, art-filled and exquisitely furnished. Rates begin at $200, with suites from $310.

Places to Eat When it comes to food, Kirkland is definitely where you want to be at mealtime on the Eastside. It's not just that the food is better here than elsewhere – and it is – but depending on where you choose to eat, you'll have wonderful views over Lake Washington and the Seattle skyline, an especially magical combination at sunset.

A Hale's Ales brewpub, *Kirkland Roaster & Alehouse* (☎ 425-325-8486, 111 Central Way), is at ground zero in Kirkland, and you could do far worse than abandon yourself to the delicious burgers, ribs and salads. And of course, the beer is some of the best in the Northwest.

Most Kirkland restaurants are decidedly upscale. Right on the water, *Anthony's Homeport* (☎ 425-822-0225, 135 Lake St), one of the Eastside's best restaurants, offers excellent-quality seafood. Seafood is also the specialty at *Third Floor Fish Café* (☎ 425-822-3553, 205 Lake St).

Trade views for French cuisine and walk up the road to **Bistro Provençal** (☎ 425-827-3300, 212 Central Way), the Eastside's premier French restaurant. All of your French favorites are here, including rack of lamb, duck breast and a dazzling wine list.

For Italian food, **Calabria Ristorante Italiano** (☎ 425-822-7350, 132 Lake St) offers Italian classics, and the strip-mall location will feel quite homey after a glass of wine.

North over the Kirkland ridge, Market St drops down onto Juanita Bay. One of Seattle's first great Italian restaurants, **Cafe Juanita** (☎ 425-823-1505, 9702 NE 120th Place), is tucked away on a backstreet. This is still one of the best places to partake of upscale Italian cuisine.

Redmond

East of Kirkland is Redmond, a sprawling suburb and the center of Seattle's high-tech industry. Computer giant Microsoft dominates life here, along with dozens of other technology-related companies. A zillion service industries have sprung up to serve their mighty masters.

Besides shopping and working in high tech, there's not much else to Redmond, except **Marymoor Park**. One of greater Seattle's best, this park caps the northern shores of Lake Sammamish. It's extremely popular as a picnic destination, though what might be of more interest to a traveler is the velodrome (see the Activities chapter) and the rock climbing walls. The park is also the beginning of the Sammamish River Trail, an 11-mile track that runs past Chateau Ste Michelle (see Woodinville, later) and links up with the Burke-Gilman Trail at Kenmore's Log Boom Park.

Places to Eat Redmond is home to all those Microsoft techno-brats, whose idea of dinner is eating candy in front of their monitors. As the M&M joke goes, eat one of each color and you've had a balanced meal. Those who rise from their desks graze at the Microsoft cafeterias (which are not open to the public).

If you find yourself hungry in Redmond, **Shilla Asian Grill & Sushi Bar** (☎ 425-882-3272, 2300 8th Ave) has good Japanese and

Korean entrées. **Big Time – The Uncommon Pizzeria** (☎ 425-885-6425, 7824 Leary Way) is the local favorite for boutique pizza. For Italian and Mediterranean dishes, **Il Bacio** (☎ 425-869-8885, 16564 Cleveland St) is where the locals go.

Woodinville

Woodinville has managed to escape much of the suburban sprawl of the other Eastside communities, though it has seen its share. It's home to two popular wineries and now a brewpub, all of which do an amazing job of self-promotion. This is a popular day trip for Seattleites, especially when the wineries sponsor summer concerts. **Chateau Ste Michelle** (☎ 425-488-1133), at 14111 NE 145th St, is one of Washington's first wineries (though most of their wine production is in the Yakima area). This historic 87-acre estate, originally home to a pioneer lumber baron, lends itself easily to picnics and jazz music concerts in the summer. It is open for wine-tasting from 10 am to 4:30 pm daily. Across the street, Washington State's oldest producer of premium wines, **Columbia Winery** (☎ 425-488-2776), 14030 NE 145th St, has more wine-tasting daily from 10 am to 7 pm; tours are available on weekends, less frequently on weekdays. Columbia hosts blues concerts in the summer.

Redhook Ale Brewery (☎ 425-482-3232), 14300 NE 145th St, is one of Washington's first microbreweries. Its Woodinville brewery, pub and restaurant, the **Forecasters Public House** (☎ 425-483-3232, 14300 NE 145th St), offers several afternoon tours daily and is an

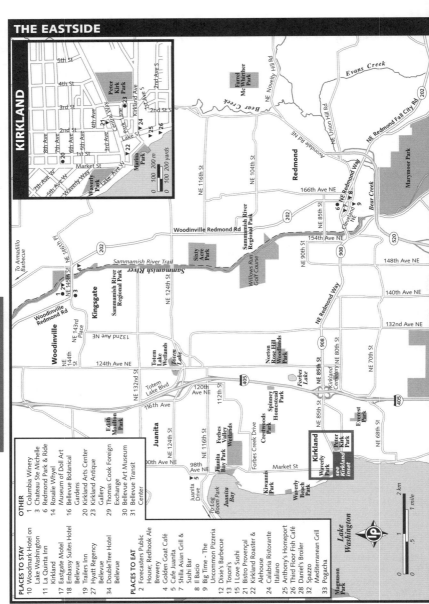

THE EASTSIDE

KIRKLAND

EXCURSIONS

PLACES TO STAY
10 Woodmark Hotel on Lake Washington
11 La Quinta Inn Kirkland
17 Eastgate Motel
18 Embassy Suites Hotel Bellevue
19 Trailers Inn
27 Hyatt Regency Bellevue
34 DoubleTree Hotel Bellevue

OTHER
1 Columbia Winery
3 Chateau Ste Michelle
6 Redmond Park & Ride
14 Rosalie Whyel Museum of Doll Art
16 Bellevue Botanical Gardens
20 Kirkland Arts Center
23 Kirkland Antique Gallery
29 Thomas Cook Foreign Exchange
30 Bellevue Art Museum
31 Bellevue Transit Center

PLACES TO EAT
2 Forecasters Public House; Redhook Ale Brewery
4 Golden Goat Café
5 Cafe Juanita
7 Shila Asian Grill & Sushi Bar
8 Il Bacio
9 Big Time - The Uncommon Pizzeria
12 Dixie's Barbecue
13 Tosoni's
15 I Love Sushi
21 Bistro Provençal
22 Kirkland Roaster & Alehouse
24 Calabria Ristorante Italiano
25 Anthony's Homeport
26 Third Floor Fish Café
28 Daniel's Broiler
32 Spazzo
33 Pogacha

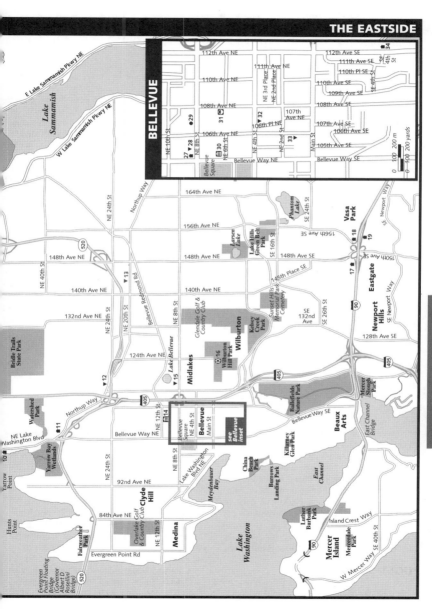

THE EASTSIDE

BELLEVUE

EXCURSIONS

excellent spot for a meal and a beer. Another good Redmond eatery is the popular *Armadillo Barbecue (☎ 425-481-1417, 13109 NE 175th St)*, which serves up Texas-style barbecue ribs and chicken. The *Golden Goat Café (☎ 425-483-6791, 14471 Woodinville-Redmond Rd NE)* has good Italian fare.

SNOQUALMIE VALLEY
East of the Eastside, the Snoqualmie Valley has long been a quiet backwater of dairy farms, orchards and produce gardens. Although suburbs are quickly taking over the valley, there's still enough of a rural, small-town ambience to make for a pleasant drive or bike ride. Snoqualmie is also a popular ski and snowboard resort (see the Activities chapter).

To get there follow I-90 east from Seattle. Exit at North Bend (31 miles), and get onto Hwy 202, which follows the Snoqualmie River north. North Bend is *Twin Peaks* country, if you recall David Lynch's creepy hit TV series from the early 1990s. *Mar T's Cafe* in North Bend was the diner with the famous cherry pie and cups of joe; it's still a good place for lunch or a slice of pie. The *Salish Lodge and Spa (☎ 425-888-2556, 800-826-6124)* is a beautiful resort that sits atop 268-foot **Snoqualmie Falls**. Many of the scenes in the TV series were filmed in the lodge. Rooms start at $329 a night. Visitors can look at the falls from the lodge's dining room, or be more athletic and hike to the base along a winding trail.

Up the road, the little town of **Snoqualmie** has a number of antique stores and shops, including a store devoted to Northwest wines. The Snoqualmie and Tolt Rivers meet at John McDonald Park in **Carnation**, a great place for a picnic, a swim or a hike along the rivers. Carnation was once the center of the valley's dairy industry, and there are still a number of farms here. Stop by roadside stands for a basket of fruit or vegetables. Farther north, **Duvall** is far enough from Seattle to retain its rural small-town atmosphere. Wander Main St and check out the small shops and nurseries.

PUGET SOUND
Puget Sound is a great area to explore by ferry, and an outing on the sound makes a relaxing day trip, whether you're going by car or bike or just on foot. Most of the ferry trips depend on Washington State Ferries (☎ 206-464-6400, 800-843-3779). Ferry schedules are available at the main office at Pier 52 or at www.wsdot.wa.gov/ferries.

Vehicle ferries to Bainbridge Island and Bremerton board at the Washington State Ferries main terminal at Pier 52 in Seattle, on Alaskan Way at Marion St. Ferries run frequently throughout the day (the number depends on the season). Walk-on passengers pay $4.50 for the roundtrip. Cyclists pay an extra 70¢. The fare for a car and driver is $8, or $10 during peak hours. Commuter-oriented passenger-only ferries to Bremerton and Vashon Island leave Pier 50, just south of the main ferry terminal, on weekdays only. The one-way fare is $3.70. Car ferries also traverse the sound from the Fauntleroy Dock in West Seattle to Vashon Island. Fares cost $4.50 for walk-on passengers, $8/10 for car and driver.

To get to the Kitsap Peninsula and the Hood Canal, take the ferry to Bainbridge Island, which is linked to the peninsula by the Agate Pass Bridge. A public bus travels to Poulsbo from the Bainbridge ferry dock. You can also reach Kitsap Peninsula by crossing the Tacoma Narrows bridge from Tacoma.

Bainbridge Island
The most popular ferry trip for tourists is between Seattle and Winslow, Bainbridge Island's biggest town. Winslow has an array of shops and restaurants within an easy walk of the ferry dock.

The **Bainbridge Island Winery** (☎ 206-842-9463) near Winslow is a good destination for cyclists or wine-lovers who don't mind a short walk (it's just north of town on Hwy 305). It's open for tastings from noon to 5 pm Wednesday to Sunday. If you want to rent a bike on the island, call BI Cycle (☎ 206-842-6413), 195 Winslow Way. Rentals cost $5/25 per hour/day. Island information is available from the **Bainbridge Island Chamber of Commerce** (☎ 206-842-3700), 590 Winslow Way E, just up the road from the ferry terminal.

A visit to Bainbridge must include a visit to *Cafe Nola (☎ 206-842-3822, 101 Winslow Way)*. The *Steamliner Diner (☎ 206-842-8595,*

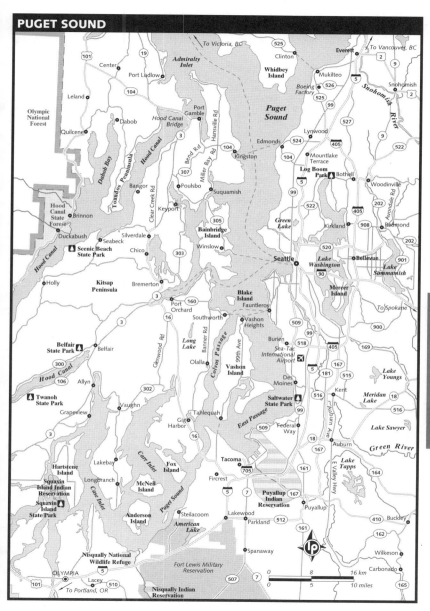

PUGET SOUND

397 Winslow Way E) has good home-style cooking, and there are local microbrews to quaff at the ***Harbour Public House*** *(☎ 206-842-0969, 231 Parfitt Way).*

Vashon Island

More rural and countercultural than Bainbridge Island to the north, Vashon has resisted suburbanization – a rare accomplishment in Puget Sound. Much of the island is covered with farms and gardens, and its little towns double as commercial hubs and artists' enclaves. The island also provides unencumbered vistas of the Cascades, from Mt Rainier in the south to Mt Baker in the north. Vashon is a good island to explore by bicycle or car, lazily stopping to pick berries or fruit at a 'u-pick' garden or orchard. Plan a hike in one of the county parks.

Budget travelers will be glad for the ***HI Seattle/Vashon AYH Ranch*** *(☎ 206-463-2592, 12119 SW Cove St),* a great hostel with bunk beds available in the summer for $10 to $15; during the winter they operate as a hotel with private single/double rooms for $30/50.

Vashon is just big enough to offer several good places to eat. ***Emily's Cafe and Juice Bar*** *(☎ 206-463-6460),* on Vashon Hwy SW at Bank Rd SW, offers light vegetarian fare. The ***Back Bay Inn*** *(☎ 206-463-5355, 24007 Vashon Hwy SW)* serves up local cuisine in a delightful inn.

From Pier 50 in Seattle, a passenger-only ferry leaves eight times daily for Vashon Island. However, the ferry deposits you in the north of the island, distant from the centers of Vashon commerce and culture, so you'll need to bring a bike or have a lift arranged. From Fauntleroy in West Seattle, a car ferry leaves almost 40 times daily for Vashon.

If you're traveling from Seattle by car, you can turn a visit to Vashon into a loop trip by taking the Tahlequah ferry from the southern end of the island to Tacoma, returning to Seattle via the mainland's I-5.

Blake Island

Blake Island is a state park and can only be approached by boat. This made it a safe place to host the 1993 APEC conference, where President Clinton met with 14 Asian leaders. The most popular facility on the island is **Tillicum Village** (☎ 206-443-1244), which features the **Northwest Coast Indian Cultural Center & Restaurant**. Boat tours depart from Pier 55 in Seattle (see Organized Tours in the Getting Around chapter). The package includes a traditional Indian salmon bake, dancing and a film about Northwest Native Americans. After the meal, there's time for a short hike or a bit of shopping. Tours last four hours and depart daily from May to mid-October; the rest of the year they are held only on weekends. The cost of the tour is $65 for adults, $59 for seniors and $25 for children five to 12.

Kitsap Peninsula & Hood Canal

The Kitsap Peninsula is flanked on the east by Puget Sound and on the west by Hood Canal. Parts of the peninsula are very suburban and are largely bedroom communities linked to Seattle by ferry. The US military also has major holdings on Kitsap, with the Naval Shipyard at Bremerton, the Naval Undersea Warfare Center in Keyport and Bangor Naval Submarine Base.

Many of the peninsula's older towns are now hubs for massive housing developments. **Poulsbo**, once known as a Norwegian-dominated fishing village, is now a traffic and strip-mall nightmare, although the old waterfront area is still nice, if rather touristy. **Port Gamble** is an old mill town that lost its main industry years ago. The old Victorian homes and storefronts, after being allowed to molder, were preserved as a National Historic Site. There's a good museum here, and exploring the quiet old tree-lined streets is like traveling back in time.

The **state parks** with beaches at Belfair and Tahuya on the south shores, and Scenic Beach State Park near Seabeck, farther north, make pleasant stops.

Also worth visiting is the **Suquamish Museum & Tribal Center** (☎ 360-598-3311) near Suquamish. The museum screens a film about the area's Native American inhabitants and also has artifacts and interpretive displays. It is open 10 am to 5 pm daily. Admission costs $4/3/2 adults/seniors/children.

The **Hood Canal** is a narrow, 75-mile-long channel that divides the Olympic and Kitsap Peninsulas. The waters of the canal can get quite warm in summer, making the southeastern shores a popular place for weekend homes. Major rivers flow into the Hood Canal from the Olympic Mountains, usually keeping the waters pure and not too saline – perfect for oysters. Oyster farming was a major industry on Hood Canal until recent frequent red tides left the shellfish unsafe to eat. Red tides come from an excess of dinoflagellates in salt water, which produce toxins that contaminate crustaceans, bivalves and the people who eat them.

Bremerton

Bremerton is the largest town on the Kitsap Peninsula and is Puget Sound's principal naval base. The main attraction here is the **Naval Museum** (☎ 360-479-7447), 130 Washington Ave, and USS *Turner Joy* (☎ 360-792-2457), 300 Washington Beach Ave. This historic US Naval destroyer is berthed at the waterfront park, right next to the ferry terminal. Self-guided tours are available daily in summer and from Thursday to Sunday in winter. The museum is open 10 am to 5 pm Monday to Saturday and 1 to 5 pm Sunday from May through September; closed Monday the rest of the year.

After you have explored Bremerton's harbor, take the small passenger ferry to **Port Orchard**, a charming little town that's become an antiques capital. You can have lunch under the wooden arcades that line the downtown bayfront.

TACOMA

Tacoma was known for years as a beleaguered mill town with the world's largest wooden dome stadium and a boarded-up, though architecturally notable, downtown. People who still speak ill of this Puget Sound city probably haven't been there recently, or they didn't bother to look beyond the shopping malls. In the 1980s, while no one was paying much attention, artists who found Seattle too expensive moved their studios south, and community activists renovated old theater buildings and other once-grand downtown structures. An influx of new residents who find Tacoma's housing prices a lot more bearable than Seattle's has enlivened this town whose location can't be beat. Backed up against the foothills of Mt Rainier, Tacoma faces onto the fjords of the Puget Sound and the jagged peaks of the Olympic Mountains.

One of Tacoma's biggest attractions, **Point Defiance Zoo & Aquarium** (☎ 253-591-5337) is part of the large, dramatically situated Point Defiance Park; the aquarium is especially notable. It's open 10 am to 5 pm daily. Admission costs $7.25/6.75/5.50 adults/seniors/youths. **Washington State History Museum** (☎ 253-272-3500, 888-238-4373), 1911 Pacific Ave, is the state's leading history museum. The primary exhibit is 'Hall of Washington History,' a chronological examination of the state's past. The museum is open 10 am to 4 pm weekdays (until 8 pm Thursday), 11 am to 5 pm Saturday and noon to 5 pm Sunday. Admission costs $7/6.25/5 adults/seniors/students; free 5 to 8 pm Thursday.

Artist Dale Chihuly is a Tacoma native whose blown glass is on display at several public showcases. The **Tacoma Art Museum** (☎ 253-272-4258), at 12th St and Pacific Ave, has a permanent display of some of Chihuly's more intimate works. The museum is open 10 am to 5 pm Tuesday to Saturday (until 8 pm Thursday) and noon to 5 pm Sunday; closed Monday. Admission costs $5/4 adults/seniors and students. The handsome, domed **Union Station**, at Pacific Ave at 19th St, was renovated into the architecturally stunning **Union Station Federal Courthouse**. The beautifully refurbished waiting room is dominated by several massive works by Chihuly, including a translucent, three-story cluster of sensuous, deep-blue grapes hanging from the rotunda. (See 'Glassmaster Dale Chihuly' in the Shopping chapter.)

Tacoma is about half an hour south of Seattle on I-5. Both Greyhound and Amtrak make several trips daily between Seattle and Tacoma. Tacoma's Greyhound depot (☎ 253-383-4621) is at 1319 Pacific Ave. The Amtrak station (☎ 253-627-8141) is at 1001 Puyallup Ave.

OLYMPIA

Olympia, the Washington State capital, is a small, cozy city that runs on politics but has a surprisingly hip, alternative side. No small part of Olympia's progressive side is driven by **Evergreen State College**, an innovative public university with 3100 students. It was founded in 1971 at the height of the student movements that began in the '60s. When you find that Olympia offers better music, cinema and coffee than you might expect, thank Evergreen. In addition to being a pleasant place, Olympia makes a good base from which to explore the Olympic Penin-sula, the Pacific Coast beaches and Mt Rainier National Park.

Olympia was the epicenter of the 2001 earthquake, which delivered quite a massive blow to the lovely Washington State **Legislative Building**, rendering it closed for business until at least 2004. While the building's 287-foot dome (the fourth largest in the world) and giant Louis Tiffany chandelier hanging in the rotunda remain intact, the rest of the building suffered severe damage. For more information, stop by the **State Capitol Visitor Center** (☎ 360-586-3460) at 14th Ave and Capitol Way. It's open 8 am to 5 pm week-

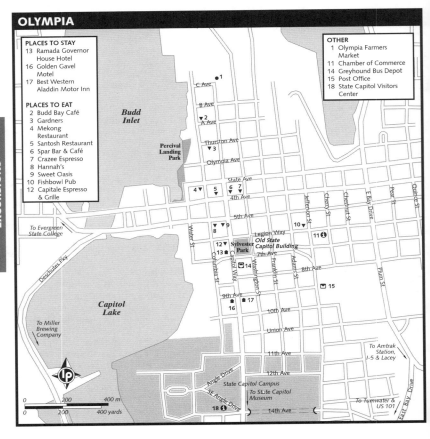

OLYMPIA

PLACES TO STAY
13 Ramada Governor House Hotel
16 Golden Gavel Motel
17 Best Western Aladdin Motor Inn

PLACES TO EAT
2 Budd Bay Café
3 Gardners
4 Mekong Restaurant
5 Santosh Restaurant
6 Spar Bar & Café
7 Crazee Espresso
8 Hannah's
9 Sweet Oasis
10 Fishbowl Pub
12 Capitale Espresso & Grille

OTHER
1 Olympia Farmers Market
11 Chamber of Commerce
14 Greyhound Bus Depot
15 Post Office
18 State Capitol Visitors Center

days year-round and 10 am to 4 pm weekends from late May to September.

The **State Capitol Museum** (☎ 360-753-2580), 211 W 21st Ave, has exhibits depicting Olympia's early days and is open 10 am to 4 pm Tuesday to Friday. Political junkies should take the free self-guided tour of the **Old State Capitol Building** at 600 S Washington St, which served as the state's legislature from 1901 to 1928.

Olympia's downtown area is an enjoyable place to wander around. **Percival Landing Park**, along the harborfront, has boardwalks where you can commune with the local seals and watch sailors readying their boats. Another one of the city's pleasures, the **Olympia Farmers Market** (☎ 360-352-9096), 700 Capitol Way, offers fresh local produce, crafts and snacks and operates from 10 am to 3 pm Thursday through Sunday from May through September; the market is open weekends only in April and October through December.

Both Amtrak and Greyhound make regular runs to Olympia from Seattle. By car, Olympia is 1½ hours south of Seattle on I-5.

Brewery Tours Olympia was long famous for its namesake beer, formerly brewed in nearby Tumwater. The brewery was taken over by Miller. The Miller Brewing Company (☎ 360-754-5177) offers free brewery tours from 9 am to 4:30 pm daily except Sunday. To get to the brewery, take I-5 south to exit 103. It's off the side of the highway and literally the only thing around. (By the way, Olympia beer is now brewed in Texas.)

Places to Stay & Eat The *Golden Gavel Motel* (☎ 360-352-8533, 909 Capitol Way S), is one of the least expensive places to stay in Olympia; single/doubles are $50/54. Across the street, the *Best Western Aladdin Motor Inn* (☎ 360-352-7200, 900 Capitol Way S), is where many state representatives stay while the legislature is in session; $60/69. The *Ramada Governor House Hotel* (☎ 360-352-7700, 800-272-6232, 621 Capitol Way S), is Olympia's fanciest lodging, with a heated pool, guest laundry, fitness center, restaurant and convention facilities; room prices range from $140 to $270.

There's no better place for a traditional breakfast than the old-fashioned, wood-paneled *Spar Bar & Café* (☎ 360-357-6444, 114 4th Ave E). It's a diner, cigar shop, newsstand and bar combo that hasn't changed since the 1930s.

The *Mekong Restaurant* (☎ 360-352-9620, 125 Columbia St NW), is the local favorite for Thai food, while *Capitale Espresso & Grille* (☎ 360-352-8007, 609 Capitol Way S), offers a selection of spicy – though somewhat pricey – Italian pastas. *Santosh Restaurant* (☎ 360-943-3442, 116 4th Ave E) serves an Indian buffet at lunch ($6) and dinner ($10). For inexpensive Mediterranean food, try *Sweet Oasis* (☎ 360-956-0470, 507 Capitol Way).

Gardners (☎ 360-786-8466, 111 Thurston Ave) serves the city's best seafood, pasta and steaks. If you're looking for a table with a view, go to the *Budd Bay Café* (☎ 360-357-6963, 525 Columbia St NW), right above the marina on Percival Landing. Seafood dinners are between $16 and $20.

In Olympia's coffeehouses you're more likely to spot local artists, students and stylishly disenfranchised youth than lobbyists; saunter down 4th Ave to find fistfuls of trendy coffee shops. For late-night espressos and post-concert discussions, the place to go is *Crazee Espresso* (☎ 360-357-7781, 124 4th Ave E). The *Fishbowl Pub* (☎ 360-943-3650, 515 Jefferson St SE) serves its own Fish Tale ales. *Hannah's* (☎ 360-357-9890, 123 5th Ave SW) is the place to go to play pool and eat a burger.

SAN JUAN ISLANDS

The San Juan archipelago contains 457 islands sprawled across 750 sq miles of Pacific waters in the area where Puget Sound and the straits of Juan de Fuca and Georgia meet. Only about 200 of these islands are named and only a handful are inhabited. Washington State Ferries provides service to the four largest islands – San Juan, Orcas, Shaw and Lopez – while others are accessible only by private boat or plane.

Until about 20 years ago the islands were considered inaccessible and backward. Their patchwork fields, forests, lakes, sheep pastures and fishing boats setting sail from tiny rock-lined harbors were ignored by all

EXCURSIONS

but the fishers and farmers inhabiting the islands. Today, however, tourism is the mainstay of local economies: The islands are a major holiday destination without enough lodging to handle the crowds during the summer high season. And yet, despite the inevitable adulteration that commercialization brings, the islands retain their bucolic charm and make for a restful retreat.

While many people come to the San Juan Islands for rest and recuperation, outdoor activities are also a popular reason to visit. Bicycling is a major obsession. The islands are small, largely flat, and laced with deserted roads, making this a great getaway for cyclists. Sea kayaking is another favorite sport. The rocky coast and relatively protected waters make for a perfect environment to explore by kayak. Wildlife along the coastline – seabirds, seals and sea lions, otters and even orcas – is also abundant. Most marinas have sailboats for rent. Whale-watching trips are also popular excursions.

Most beaches are privately owned, so don't count on lying on the beach unless your resort owns some sandy oceanfront. Hiking is restricted to the parks, notably Moran State Park on Orcas Island.

Lodging frequently fills up during the summer, so don't even think about heading out without reservations during July and August – you may end up having to take the last ferry back to the mainland. Most reservations are made months ahead, and the most attractive places to stay are often booked even further in advance. Accommodations are also expensive: You'll be pressed to find accommodations for less than $100 a night during the summer.

If you're having trouble finding rooms, or want someone else to do the hunting, contact All Island Reservations (☎ 360-378-6977). For information about the San Juans in general, contact the San Juan Islands Visitor Information Center (☎ 360-468-3663), PO Box 65, Lopez, WA 98261.

Getting There & Away Two airlines fly from Seattle to the San Juans. Harbor Air Lines (☎ 800-359-3220) offers flights from Sea-Tac Airport to Friday Harbor Municipal Airport on San Juan Island and to Eastsound Airport on Orcas Island. Kenmore Air (☎ 360-486-1257, 800-543-9595) flies to Lopez, Orcas and San Juan Islands on seaplanes from Lake Union.

The majority of people who visit the San Juans arrive on Washington State Ferries (☎ 206-464-6400, 800-808-7977 in Washington, 800-843-3779 automated information). From the mainland, car ferries leave from Anacortes and depart for the four busiest islands; not all ferries go to all islands, so read the ferry schedule carefully. Travel time to Lopez, the closest island, takes 45 minutes; to the most distant port, Friday Harbor on San Juan, it's 1¼ hours. Ticket prices vary depending on destination, but some examples include: From Anacortes to Lopez Island $6.80/21.25 walk-on passenger/car and driver; to San Juan Island (Friday Harbor) $6.80/28.25; to Shaw Island or Orcas Island $6.80/25.00. Get to Anacortes by following I-5 north of Seattle for about 65 miles to exit 230. Take the exit and drive 20 miles west on Hwy 20 to the Anacortes Ferry Terminal.

Between the islands, transport is by inter-island ferries, which travel a circular route exclusively between the four main islands. Inter-island travel is $11.25 for car & driver. Ferries also depart from Anacortes and the San Juans for Sidney, BC, on Vancouver Island. The trip takes about three hours, with westbound stops at San Juan and Orcas Islands; eastbound, the ferry stops at San Juan only. The fare to Sidney is $11/41.

In summer the passenger-only *Victoria Clipper* (☎ 360-448-5000, 800-888-2535) travels twice-daily from Seattle to Friday Harbor on San Juan Island and to Rosario Resort & Spa on Orcas Island before continuing on to Victoria, BC. The two-hour journey costs $66 one-way, $109 roundtrip in high season. In winter a weekend-only service goes from Seattle to the San Juans, but with no continuation on to Victoria. Additionally, in the summer privately owned passenger-only ferries depart from Bellingham, Port Townsend and Victoria, BC, bound for the San Juans.

There is no public transport on the San Juan Islands. However, most motels and inns will pick up registered guests at the ferry if they are notified in advance. Lopez, Orcas and San Juan Islands each have a taxi service, and in summer the erratic Orcas Tortas bus (no ☎) can sometimes be hailed between Orcas Landing, West Sound, Eastsound and Moran State Park. Rental cars are available in Friday Harbor, and bike-rental shops are almost more common than cafés.

Lopez Island

Lopez is the most agricultural of the San Juan Islands and the closest to the mainland and has resisted the commercialization of its farmland better than the other islands. Here, pastures are for grazing sheep or hay-making – they aren't merely the aesthetic property of quaint country inns and B&Bs. If you want quiet, pastoral charm and don't need organized fun, Lopez is hard to beat.

Fields and pastures stretch across the island's central plateau, and the island gets rockier toward the south; near MacKaye Harbor, the stony fields and cliff-lined bay look for all the world like the Hebrides.

Places to Stay Built to resemble a Victorian mansion, the *Edenwild Inn* (☎ 360-468-3238) in Lopez Village is the most eye-catching building on the island, with lovely formal gardens, a wide porch and gables. Rooms run from $88 to $175.

On the other side of the island, the *Inn at Swifts Bay* (☎ 360-468-3636) is east on Port Stanley Rd (look for mailbox No 856 and the banners hanging from the decks). This graceful inn offers a hot tub, easy beach access and 3 acres of surrounding woods for solitude. Rooms run $95 to $185. Standing stalwart and white at the edge of a shallow bay, the *MacKaye Harbor Inn* (☎ 360-468-2253, 949 MacKaye Harbor Rd), is near the south end of the island. The inn, once a 1920s sea captain's home, provides bicycles, rowboats and kayaks for guests. Rooms cost $115 to $175. The *Islander Lopez Resort* (☎ 360-468-2233, 800-736-3434, 2864 Fisherman Bay Rd), south of Lopez Village, is as close to a bona fide motel as you'll find in the San Juans, with rooms from $80 to $260. Across from the units is a bar and restaurant that gives onto a marina.

If you want to camp, *Spencer Spit State Park* (☎ 360-468-2251, 800-452-5687 for Reservations Northwest), is just 5 miles southeast of the ferry landing on Baker View Rd.

Places to Eat Nearly all the places to eat on Lopez are in Lopez Village; in fact, they practically constitute the village. The *Love Dog Cafe* (☎ 360-468-2150) is open all day; you can sit on the verandah below the grape arbor and watch the boats in the harbor. The most noted restaurant on Lopez is the *Bay Cafe* (☎ 360-468-3700), which occupies an old storefront. Inventive ethnic seafood dishes headline the menu. Currently, they serve dinner only, although that may change.

Shaw Island

Shaw Island is the smallest of the San Juan Islands that gets ferry service, and it has the fewest facilities for travelers. However, there are good reasons to disembark at Shaw, especially if you're on two wheels. The lack of an organized tourist industry means that the island's roads are mostly free of traffic. The rolling hills are covered with sheep, whose

EXCURSIONS

wool plays a large part in Shaw's major cottage industries – spinning and knitting.

The one thing that nearly everyone notes about the ferry landing at Shaw is the fact that it is operated by Franciscan nuns. The nuns also operate the small general store and sell gas at the tiny marina near the ferry landing.

The **campground** (☎ 360-378-1842) at South Beach County Park is really the only place to stay. There are a dozen campsites, with pit toilets only, costing $12 a night.

Orcas Island

Orcas is the largest of the San Juan Islands, and in terms of rugged physical beauty, it is probably the most fetching. **Mt Constitution** is, at 2407 feet, the highest point in the San Juans, but it is only one of several forested peaks around which the rest of the island folds in steep valleys. Along the rocky coast, narrow cliff-lined inlets serve as harbors for small pleasure boats.

In some ways Orcas Island is the most exclusive of the San Juans: The rocky promontories and isolated harbors look good in real estate brochures, so retirement homes, resort communities and weekend manses take the place of agriculture.

Orcas Island offers a wide array of tourist attractions, including **Moran State Park**, the San Juans' largest and a favorite of hikers. There's really not a town here – Eastsound, however charming, is just a collection of businesses at a crossroads. Life revolves around the resorts, which are scattered around the island.

Places to Stay For years, the place for upscale visitors has been **Rosario Resort & Spa** (☎ 360-376-2222, 800-562-8820) on Rosario Way, 4 miles south of Eastsound off the Horseshoe Hwy. The Rosario mansion, built in the early 20th century, is the centerpiece of a resort complex that includes almost 130 modern rooms, tennis courts, swimming pools, elaborate tiled spa facilities in the basement, two fine restaurants and a marina. Accommodations run from $200 to $360, depending on room type and views.

Doe Bay Resort & Retreat (☎ 360-376-2291, 376-4755) is on the island's easternmost shore, 18 miles east of Eastsound off the

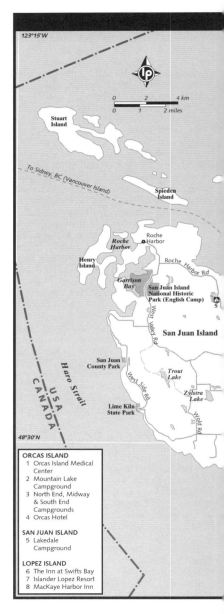

ORCAS ISLAND
1 Orcas Island Medical Center
2 Mountain Lake Campground
3 North End, Midway & South End Campgrounds
4 Orcas Hotel

SAN JUAN ISLAND
5 Lakedale Campground

LOPEZ ISLAND
6 The Inn at Swifts Bay
7 Islander Lopez Resort
8 MacKaye Harbor Inn

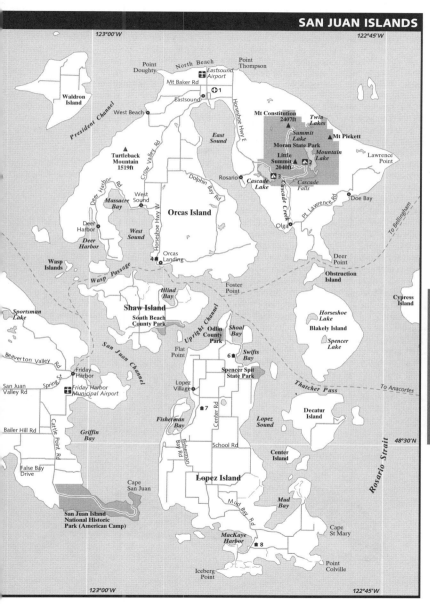

SAN JUAN ISLANDS

123°00'W

122°45'W

Waldron
Island

Point
Doughty

North Beach

Point
Thompson

Eastsound
Airport

Mt Baker Rd

Eastsound

1

Eastsound

West Beach

President Channel

Mt Constitution
2407ft

Twin
Lakes

Summit
Lake

Mt Pickett

East
Sound

Moran State Park

Horseshoe Hwy E

Mountain
Lake

Lawrence
Point

Crow Valley Rd

Turtleback
Mountain
1519ft

Little
Summit
2040ft

2

Deer Harbor Rd

Dolphin Bay Rd

Rosario

Cascade
Lake

3

Cascade
Falls

Doe Bay

West
Sound

Cascade Creek

To Bellingham

Massacre
Bay

Orcas Island

Pt Lawrence Rd

Deer
Harbor

West
Sound

Olga

Deer
Harbor

Horseshoe Hwy W

Deer
Point

Wasp
Islands

Orcas
Landing

4

Obstruction
Island

Wasp Passage

Foster
Point

Cypress
Island

Blind
Bay

Shaw Island

Horseshoe
Lake

Sportsman
Lake

South Beach
County Park

Blakely Island

Upright Channel

Odlin
County
Park

Shoal
Bay

Spencer
Lake

San Juan Channel

Flat
Point

Swifts
Bay

6

Beaverton Valley Rd

Friday
Harbor

Spencer Spit
State Park

Thatcher Pass

To Anacortes

San Juan
Valley Rd

Spring St

Friday Harbor
Municipal Airport

Lopez
Village

Center Rd

Decatur
Island

Bailer Hill Rd

Cattle Point Rd

7

Fisherman
Bay

Fisherman Bay Rd

Lopez
Sound

Center
Island

Griffin
Bay

School Rd

48°30'N

False Bay
Drive

Rosario Strait

Cape
San Juan

Lopez Island

Mud
Bay

San Juan Island
National Historic
Park (American Camp)

Mud Bay Rd

Cape
St Mary

MacKaye
Harbor

8

Point
Colville

Iceberg
Point

123°00'W

122°45'W

EXCURSIONS

Horseshoe Hwy on Pt Lawrence Rd. This slightly shabby, comfortable and welcoming vacation spot is by far the least expensive and most 'alternative' lodging in the San Juans. There are campsites, dorm and hostel rooms ($16), a tree house and various levels of cabins. Cabin rates begin at $59 a night. Don't miss the clothing-optional outdoor hot tub.

At Orcas Landing the historic refurbished *Orcas Hotel* (☎ 360-376-4300) offers a dozen rooms ($79 to $189), some with private facilities. This handsome inn with wraparound porches and great views also has an espresso bar, restaurant and lounge.

Deer Harbor, west of Orcas Landing, is one of the island's most beautiful harbors. The *Resort at Deer Harbor* (☎ 360-376-4420) seems to own – and rent out – pretty much every building in this little hamlet. There's a wide array of accommodations ranging from cottages ($189 to $259) to motel-style bungalows to small houses right on the water ($239 to $299). The resort also offers a swimming pool, boat rentals, bike rentals and a small restaurant and market.

In Eastsound the *Outlook Inn* (☎ 360-376-2200) on Horseshoe Hwy has both modern motel rooms and rooms in a refurbished Victorian hotel ($84, $140 or $245). Just next door the *Eastsound Landmark Inn* (☎ 360-376-2423) is a modern place that has spacious suites with full kitchens, fireplaces and balconies; suites are $150 to $175, depending on the view.

Moran State Park (☎ 360-376-2326), to the southeast of Eastsound on the Horseshoe Hwy, is the largest camping area in the San Juans. Choose from four different lakeside *campgrounds;* sites are $12.

Places to Eat Most restaurants – except those at Rosario Resort – are in Eastsound. *La Famiglia Ristorante* (☎ 360-376-2335), on Prune Alley, features good, nicely priced Italian favorites, while *Bilbo's Festivo* (☎ 360-376-4728), off North Beach Rd, has Mexican and Southwestern cuisine. For highbrow cuisine go to *Christina's* (☎ 360-376-4904), along Horseshoe Hwy in Eastsound. Fresh seafood is the major item on the highly eclectic, rather French-by-Northwest menu.

San Juan Island

Most visitors find that San Juan, of all the islands, offers the most hospitable blend of sophisticated amenities, rural landscapes and bustling harbors. A large part of the island's draw is Friday Harbor – with a population of 1930, it's the only real town in all the San Juan Islands. Even so, it's small enough to navigate on foot. Most of the hotels and restaurants are either on or just off the main drag, Spring St, which runs uphill half a block over from the ferry landing. But follow any of the streets out of Friday Harbor and you're soon on a central plateau where small farms, dairies and lakes fill the verdant landscape.

The only other community of any size is Roche Harbor, on a beautiful bay to the northwest. This used to be the center of a lime-processing operation run by John McMillan, an attorney from Tacoma. The imposing complex included lime kilns, a grand hotel, a private estate, workers' cottages, a small railway, a company store, a chapel and a shipping wharf. The lime factory closed in the 1950s and the extensive buildings are now part of the Roche Harbor Resort.

The magnificent orca whale

Places to Stay In Friday Harbor, the newly remodeled *Friday's B&B* (☎ 360-378-5848, 800-352-2632, 35 1st St)* has rooms with fireplaces and Jacuzzis or outdoor hot tubs for $90 to $215. Slightly less in price, the *San Juan Inn* (☎ 360-378-2070, 800-742-8210, 50 Spring St)* is another historic hotel that has been updated with modern conveniences without losing its Victorian charm.

On the hill just above town, *Blair House B&B* (☎ 360-378-5907, 345 Blair Ave)* is a woodsy, 1909 home offering five rooms with shared or private bath ($85 to $150) and a cottage ($175).

As the plural name intimates, the *Inns at Friday Harbor* (☎ 360-378-4000, 800-752-5752)* is in fact two different lodgings separated by two blocks. The first, at 410 Spring St, is an older, well-maintained motel with a pool (rooms start at $118), while the second, at 680 Spring St, is a more modern complex with suite-style rooms (starting at $146).

The most exclusive and whimsically elegant lodging in Friday Harbor is the *Friday Harbor House* (☎ 360-378-8455, 130 West St)*. It's a modern boutique hotel with great views over the harbor; all rooms have a fireplace, Jacuzzi tub and other upscale niceties. Rooms run $200 to $300, including breakfast.

Roche Harbor Resort (☎ 360-378-2155, 800-451-8910)*, in Roche Harbor, is just about the nicest place to stay in all the San Juans. You can still spend the night at the imposing old Hotel de Haro on the resort's grounds, which has wide, ivy-covered verandahs and formal gardens. Rooms at this landmark inn start at $85. A number of refurbished workers' cottages, just a few yards from the swimming pool and playground, fill a grassy meadow above the harbor ($220). Modern condominiums are discreetly tucked behind a stand of trees. In addition to the lodgings, there's a marina with boat rentals, restaurant, lounge and – on the dock – an old general store. You can even land your private jet on the airstrip.

If you're camping, the versatile *Lakedale Campground* (☎ 360-378-2350, 2627 Roche Harbor Rd)*, has 115 tent sites, 15 sites reserved for cyclists and 19 RV sites (no hookups), plus three tent cabins.

Places to Eat Near the waterfront, *Front St Ale House & San Juan Brewing Company* (☎ 360-378-2337, 1 Front St)* is the island's only brewery, serving up British-style beers in a real pub atmosphere. The food's good, too: Traditional British favorites like steak-and-kidney pie and bangers and mash keep good company with standbys such as chili, chowder and hamburgers. The *Springtree Cafe* (☎ 360-378-4848, 310 Spring St)* offers casual bistro-style dining in a spare but comfortable café. The menu tends toward seafood and vegetarian dishes. The intimate dining room at the *Friday Harbor House* (☎ 360-378-8455, 130 West St)* has a fireplace and great views. The menu is small but tempting, with seasonal Northwest cuisine in the $15 to $20 range.

MT RAINIER NATIONAL PARK

Mt Rainier, at 14,411 feet, is the Cascades' highest peak. With its 26 glaciers, it's the most heavily glaciated peak in the USA outside of Alaska. Seattleites simply call it 'the mountain,' as it is so visible from Seattle windows and looks simply magical on sunny days. Although it looks closer, Rainier is actually 95 miles southeast of the city (about a 2½-hour drive). Rainier is more than a mountain; it's a Northwest icon loved both for its majestic simplicity and its solid natural power as one of the great Cascade volcanoes.

The Mt Rainier National Park (☎ 360-569-2211) attracts hikers, climbers, campers and drivers. Hiking trails range from wildflower nature walks to 10-day round-the-mountain loops. Climbing to the top of Mt Rainier is a major undertaking and should only be attempted with a guide. Before any overnight backpacking trip it's necessary to stop by an NPS ranger station or visitors center and obtain a backcountry permit.

Park entrance fees are $10 per car and $5 for pedestrians, motorcyclists and cyclists. For information on the park, call or write to the superintendent's office (☎ 360-569-2211) at Mt Rainier National Park, Ashford, WA 98304. Information can also be obtained at any of the visitors centers found at park entrances and at Longmire and Sunrise.

EXCURSIONS

There are four entrances to the park, but Hwy 706, near Ashford, and Hwy 410 from Enumclaw are the easiest for short excursions from Seattle. All roads except the Hwy 706 Nisqually entrance to Paradise close down in the winter.

Paradise

The main entrance road, Hwy 706 (also known as the Nisqually-Longmire Rd), comes in through the town of Ashford, near the park's southwest corner, and follows the Nisqually River into the park. This route leads up to the Paradise Viewpoint and to the Paradise Inn (see Places to Stay, later). Paradise is especially known for its alpine wildflower meadows, which are laced with hiking trails. Follow the Skyline Trail on foot for a good view of the **Nisqually Glacier**. All other roads to the park close down in the winter, but this route is plowed as far as Paradise, which then becomes the setting-off point for cross-country skiers and snowshoers.

Sunrise

Some of the best views of Mt Rainier – with **Emmons Glacier** sliding down its face, Little Tahoma Peak in the foreground and the craggy Goat Rocks Wilderness Area off to the southeast – are from Sunrise. Sunrise's open meadows are scattered with trees and linked by hiking trails. Since it's on the mountain's east side, the Sunrise area benefits from Mt Rainier's rain shadow and receives less precipitation than the damp west side. It doesn't take long for hikers to become enraptured with Sunrise, which usually means you have to deal with crowds. Try to hike on a weekday and hit the trail early in the morning. Park naturalists lead a 1½-mile hike each Sunday afternoon on a **Sunrise Goat Watch** from the Sourdough Ridge to explore the mountain goat's habitat. Get to Sunrise by following Hwy 410 east from Enumclaw.

Places to Stay

There are two lodges in the park. The grand ***Paradise Inn*** is a fantastic old log lodge on the mountain's south flank. Huge fireplaces anchor each end of the lobby,

massive timbers hold up the ceiling and comfortable leather sofas and chairs face onto windows with views of the peak. It's open mid-May to mid-September only. ***Longmire National Park Inn*** is smaller and cozier, and is open year-round, which makes it convenient for cross-country skiers. For reservations at either lodge, call ☎ 360-569-2275.

Plenty of accommodations can be found at Ashford, Packwood and Enumclaw. There are also two campgrounds near Longmire and one near Sunrise; for information on all the park's campgrounds, call ☎ 360-569-2211, ext 2304.

Getting There & Away

There's no public transportation to Mt Rainier, but Gray Line (☎ 206-626-5208, 800-426-7532) runs bus tours of the park. The 10-hour tour departs from the Convention Center in Seattle at 8 am daily May through September and costs $50. It also offers an overnight trip for $160, including accommodations.

For a fun, truly Northwest adventure from Seattle, Barefoot Backpacker (☎ 206-320-0505), 2115 E Mercer St, runs an overnight camping trip to both Mt Rainier and Mt St Helens. The trip costs $100 per person but includes all meals, park fees and camping gear. Trips leave from the HI Seattle hostel and from the Green Tortoise hostel.

MT ST HELENS NATIONAL VOLCANIC MONUMENT

While a trip to Mt St Helens from Seattle makes for a long day, the sights here are absolutely unique. For anyone interested in geology and natural history, this trip is well worth the expenditure of time.

For most people in the Pacific Northwest, the events of May 18, 1980, are welded into memory. Mt St Helens erupted with the force of 21,000 atomic bombs, leveling hundreds of square miles of forest and spreading volcanic ash across the Pacific Northwest and as far northeast as Saskatchewan. After the smoke cleared, Mt St Helens, once a comely and symmetrical 9677-foot mountain covered with glaciers, had blown 1300 feet off its peak, and a mile-wide crater yawned on its north side. Spirit Lake, once a resort destination below the peak, was totally clogged with fallen timber and debris and the rivers that flowed off the mountain were flooded with mud and ash. In 1982, 172 sq miles around the mountain were included in the Mt St Helens National Volcanic Monument.

There are two main entry routes into the region; however, only the attractions on Hwy 504, on the northwest side of the mountain would make sensible day trips from Seattle. To get there, take I-5 to exit 49 near Castle Rock, which is 150 miles (a little over two hours) south of Seattle, and follow the signs. The trip takes about three hours total.

In Castle Rock the Mt St Helens Visitor Center (☎ 360-274-2100), 3029 Spirit Lake Hwy, has lots of free information on the mountain. It also has impressive exhibits about the Cascade volcanoes and post-eruption ecology. From the visitors center, follow the Spirit Lake Hwy and you'll encounter some rest areas and viewpoints, all with exhibits telling more of the Mt St Helens tale. An $6 entry fee (per person, payable at the visitors center) gets you access to all US Forest Service attractions. The center is open 9 am to 5 pm daily in summer; 9 am to 4 pm daily in winter.

Along Hwy 504, other attractions include the **Hoffstadt Bluff Red Area Viewpoint**, a **forest center**, which, run by forestry giant Weyerhauser, shows a rather pro-forestry view on how trees were salvaged after the volcano's blast. The next big stop is the impressive **Coldwater Ridge Visitor Center** (☎ 360-274-2131), open 9 am to 5 pm daily in summer and 9 am to 4 pm in winter, though there's talk of it closing in winter altogether. The **Johnson Ridge Observatory** (☎ 360-274-2140) tops off the Hwy 504 attractions, and offers views into the crater.

If you're looking to hike Mt St Helens, you'll need to get a $15 permit ahead of time from the monument headquarters (☎ 360-247-3900). The climb takes about four hours up and two hours down, though the difficulty changes depending on the

weather. Be sure to check on conditions before heading up.

If you don't have a car, consider joining the Barefoot Backpacker (☎ 206-320-0505) overnight camping trip to both Mt Rainier and Mt St Helens. (See Getting There & Away under Mt Rainier, earlier.)

VICTORIA

The capital of British Columbia, Canada, Victoria is just a short ferry ride across the Strait of Juan de Fuca from Seattle, making this Seattle's most popular day trip. Most people travel to Victoria just to take in the much-vaunted English atmosphere of this harborside city. Certainly, Victoria is charming and eminently worthy of a visit; however, its Englishness is a fairly thin veneer laid on for the tourists.

Victoria's downtown faces onto the Inner Harbour, which is busy with ferries, sailboats and small passenger ships. This is where the *Victoria Clipper* from Seattle docks. Flanking downtown across the harbor are the **Parliament Buildings**, which are especially lovely when lit at night. Call ☎ 250-387-3046 for information on free tours. The acclaimed **Royal British Columbia Museum** (☎ 250-387-3701, 953-4629 for recorded information), 675 Belleville St, is well worth a few hours or even half a day of your time. It is open 9 am to 5 pm daily. Admission costs C$8/5 adults/senior, students and children.

Thirteen miles north of Victoria are the **Butchart Gardens**, 800 Benvenuto Ave, 50 acres of formal gardens linked by winding paths. The gardens feature frequent concerts and fireworks displays; in summer they are illuminated. The gardens open at 9 am daily; closing times vary by season. From mid-June to October admission costs C$16.50/8.25/2 adults/youth/children. Admission drops to between C$8 and C$13 for adults the rest of the year.

Victoria is also a good shopping destination. Shops selling British woolens, Northwest Indian art, outdoor gear and souvenirs line the streets.

Along the Inner Harbour, you'll find the **Visitor Info Centre** (☎ 250-953-2033) at 812 Wharf St.

EXCURSIONS

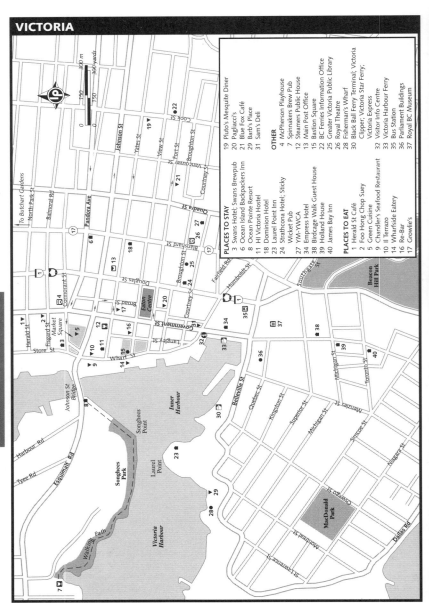

VICTORIA

PLACES TO STAY
3   Swans Hotel; Swans Brewpub
6   Ocean Island Backpackers Inn
8   Ocean Pointe Resort
11 HI Victoria Hostel
18 Dominion Hotel
23 Laurel Point Inn
24 Strathcona Hotel; Sticky
    Wicket Pub
27 Empress Hotel
34 Holland House
38 Birdcage Walk Guest House
39 Holland House
40 James Bay Inn

PLACES TO EAT
1   Herald St Café
2   Foo Hong Chop Suey
5   Green Cuisine
9   Chandler's Seafood Restaurant
10 Il Terrazo
14 Wharfside Eatery
16 Re-Bar
17 Growlie's

19 Pluto's Mesquite Diner
20 Pagliacci's
21 Blue Fox Café
29 Barb's Place
31 Sam's Deli

OTHER
4   McPherson Playhouse
7   Spinnakers Brew Pub
12 Steamers Public House
13 Main Post Office
15 Bastion Square
22 Greater Victoria Public Library
25 BC Ferries Information Office
26 Royal Theatre
28 Fisherman's Wharf
30 Black Ball Ferry Terminal; Victoria
    Clipper; Victoria Star Ferry;
    Victoria Express
32 Visitor Info Centre
33 Victoria Harbour Ferry
35 Bus Station
36 Parliament Buildings
37 Royal BC Museum

Places to Stay

You'll have trouble finding reasonably priced rooms from mid-May through September. Tourism Victoria's room-reservation service (☎ 800-663-3883) may be able to help.

Victoria is a hosteler's dream town, with accommodations to suit every age and taste. **Ocean Island Backpackers Inn** (☎ 250-385-1785, 888-888-4180, 791 Pandora Ave) enjoys a great location in central Victoria. Full of life and art, this big old building features about 155 beds and a spacious kitchen. Dorm rooms cost C$20 and private rooms are C$40. The **HI Victoria Hostel** (☎ 250-385-4511, 888-883-0099, 516 Yates St) also sits near the Inner Harbour and all the major sights. Dorm rooms cost C$16.50/20.50 members/non-members; a few private rooms cost C$37 to C$44. Reservations are a must. The **YM-YWCA** (☎ 250-386-7511, 880 Courtney St) are both in the same building, but the residence is only for women. A dorm bunk with bedding costs C$20. Private single rooms cost C$38.50.

Birdcage Walk Guest House (☎ 250-389-0804, 877-389-0804, 505 Government St) offers five guest rooms with private bathrooms in a historic home for C$100 to C$150. Nearby, the delightful **Holland House Inn** (☎ 250-384-6644, 800-335-3466, 595 Michigan St) rents 16 rooms for C$145 and up.

The **Strathcona Hotel** (☎ 250-383-7137, 800-663-7476, 919 Douglas St) charges C$79/99 and up. It's a bustling place with several popular bars and a restaurant.

A few blocks from the Inner Harbour, **James Bay Inn** (☎ 250-384-7151, 800-836-2649, 270 Government St) is a favorite spot. Rooms start at C$106. The renovated **Dominion Hotel** (☎ 250-384-4136, 800-663-6101, 759 Yates St) offers charming rooms that start at C$119/129. **Swans Hotel** (☎ 250-361-3310, 800-668-7926, 506 Pandora Ave) is in a gem of a downtown building near the waterfront. Studio suites start at C$159. **Laurel Point Inn** (☎ 250-386-8721, 800-663-7667, 680 Montreal St) guards the entrance to the Inner Harbour. Amenities include saunas, an indoor pool, balconies and good views; rates start at C$190.

Across the Inner Harbour, and with tremendous views, the **Ocean Pointe Resort** (☎ 250-360-2999, 800-667-4677, 45 Songhees Rd) combines luxury-class rooms (starting at C$159) with spa and sports facilities.

The **Empress Hotel** (☎ 250-348-8111, 800-441-1414, 721 Government St) is practically synonymous with Victoria. Built in 1908 and surrounded by lovely gardens, the Empress attracts lots of honeymooners, bus-tour groups and well-heeled travelers. Rates are all over the map, depending on season and demand, but plan on paying about C$239 for a room facing the city, more for a harbor view.

Places to Eat

Victoria is a great dining town, offering everything from tea rooms and pubs to cutting-edge Pacific Rim cuisine. **Growlie's** (☎ 250-383-2654, 615 Yates St) features 10 varieties of eggs Benedict. Another favorite breakfast spot is the **Blue Fox Café** (☎ 250-380-1683, 101-919 Fort St).

Right in the thick of things, **Sam's Deli** (☎ 250-382-8424, 805 Government St) offers reasonable prices, with C$6 sandwiches big enough for two. **Pluto's Mesquite Diner** (☎ 250-385-4747, 1150 Cook St), a few blocks from downtown in a converted gas station, serves breakfast until 2 pm and a variety of yummy burgers, quesadillas and Mexican platters (C$7 to C$11) for lunch and dinner.

At Market Square, at the corner of Johnson and Wharf Sts, **Green Cuisine** (☎ 250-385-1809, 560 Johnson St) boasts a delicious vegetarian buffet. In Chinatown, the small and basic **Foo Hong Chop Suey** (☎ 250-386-9553, 564 Fisgard St) serves good, simple Cantonese food (C$5 to C$8). **Barb's Place** (☎ 250-384-6515, 310 St Lawrence St), housed in a shack on Fisherman's Wharf, offers fish and chips starting at about C$7.

The wildly popular **Re-Bar** (☎ 250-360-2401, 50 Bastion Square) is a happening spot offering an eclectic, international menu (heavily vegetarian, with most dishes C$7 to C$12) and an on-site bakery. For pasta, **Pagliacci's** (☎ 250-386-1662, 1011 Broad St) features a clever movie-theme menu, with dishes starting at C$11. Live music acts play Sunday through Wednesday evenings.

EXCURSIONS

You can dine on the patio at the **Wharf-side Eatery** (☎ *250-360-1808, 1208 Wharf St*), which specializes in fresh seafood (C$20 to C$25) but also serves pizza and burgers. Bustling and popular, **Il Terrazzo** (☎ *250-361-0028, 555 Johnson St*) is the best place in town for Italian pastas, grilled meats and tempting pizza. Most main dishes cost C$8 to C$16 for lunch (served daily except Sunday) and C$15 to C$30 for dinner.

Treat yourself at the **Herald St Café** (☎ *250-381-1441, 546 Herald St*), where delicious pastas go for C$9 to C$12 at lunch and C$15 to C$19 at dinner. It also offers vegetarian dishes, great desserts and about 350 wine selections. The well-established **Chandler's Seafood Restaurant** (☎ *250-385-3474, 1250 Wharf St*) specializes in ocean fare, with dinner prices starting at C$15.

Entertainment
For some of the best beer in all of BC, go to **Spinnakers Brew Pub** (☎ *250-386-2739, 308 Catherine St*), where they've also got a great deck with views of the Inner Harbour. **Swans Brewpub** (☎ *250-361-3310, 506 Pandora Ave*) takes up half the main floor of Swans Hotel.

It doesn't make its own beer, but the **Sticky Wicket Pub** (☎ *250-383-7137, 919 Douglas St*), in the Strathcona Hotel, has good food and beer plus a rooftop patio with beach volleyball courts. For live local bands, head to **Steamers Public House** (☎ *250-381-4340, 570 Yates St*).

Victoria's big venues for theater and music are the McPherson Playhouse (☎ 250-686-6121), 3 Centennial Square, and the elegant Royal Theatre (☎ 250-386-6121), 805 Broughton St. You can watch ballet, dance and music performances by the Victoria Symphony (☎ 250-385-6515) and the Pacific Opera Victoria (☎ 250-386-6121).

Getting There & Away
The only boat leaving downtown Seattle for Victoria is the *Victoria Clipper* (☎ 206-448-5000, 800-888-2535). It departs from Pier 69 (2701 Alaskan Way) bound for Victoria at 8:30 am daily during winter months, with additional boats at 7:30, 8 am and 3:30 pm in

Traveling to Canada
The border between Canada and the USA has tightened considerably in the past few years, even for citizens of these countries. By law, you are required to carry a passport. However, you may be asked to produce only a driver's license or nothing at all.

Visitors from most Western countries do not need visas for Canada, but there are exceptions. Visitor visas, which are free, are granted for a period of six months and are extendable for a fee. You must apply for an extension at a Canadian Immigration Centre.

US currency is accepted in Canada for most purchases so it may not be necessary to exchange money if you're only making a short side trip from the USA. You won't get US$ back for change, though – transactions are converted to US$ at the current exchange rate (around US$1=C$1.52), and the equivalent change is given in Canadian dollars. Keep in mind that banks in the USA will change Canadian bills, but not coins – it's a good idea to use them up before heading back to the USA.

high season (mid-May to mid-September). This is a passenger-only ferry; adult fare for the two- to three-hour trip is $62.50 one-way, $125 roundtrip in high season; children are half price.

A car ferry used to depart from Pier 48 in Seattle to Victoria but no longer. Anyone wishing to bring a car to Victoria must do so with Washington State Ferries (☎ 206-464-6400, 800-843-3779 in Washington). Ferries depart from Anacortes (also the departure point for the San Juan Islands), about 85 miles north of Seattle off I-5, and arrive at Sidney, BC, which is about 30 minutes from downtown Victoria. Vehicle reservations are optional (but recommended) for the service between Anacortes and Sidney; reservations are mandatory on trips from Orcas Island and Friday Harbor on San Juan Island. Call the reservation line at ☎ 360-376-2134 or 378-4777. Travelers to Victoria should bring proper identification and be prepared to go through Canadian customs upon arrival in British Columbia.

If you're flying to Victoria, you have a couple of fun and very scenic options. Kenmore Air (☎ 425-486-1257, 800-543-9595) flies seaplanes from Seattle's Lake Union to Victoria's Inner Harbour for $183 roundtrip. Helijet Airways (☎ 800-665-4354) flies helicopters from Boeing Field (near Sea-Tac) to Victoria for $224. Regular commercial flights are available from Sea-Tac on Air BC and Horizon Air (see the Getting There & Away chapter).

Thanks

We owe thanks to readers of the previous edition who wrote to us with their observations and updates:

Eric Carlson, Linda Carlson, Richard Felber, MJ Glassco, the International Bicycle Fund, Mike Jacobs, Mary Lou Krause, Gordon & Sandra McHarrie, George F Nassif, Oliver Niederhoff, Michelle Ryan, Tony Stewart, Adam Stott, Alexander Sybrandi and Isabella Willinger

LONELY PLANET

You already know that Lonely Planet produces more than this one guidebook, but you might not be aware of the other products we have on this region. Here is a selection of titles which you may want to check out as well:

Pacific Northwest
ISBN 0 86442 534 1
US$24.95 • UK£14.99

Vancouver
ISBN 0 86442 659 3
US$14.95 • UK£8.99

British Columbia
ISBN 1 86450 220 7
US$16.99 • UK£10.99

Canada
ISBN 0 86442 752 2
US$24.95 • UK£14.99

Hiking in the USA
ISBN 0 86442 600 3
US$24.99 • UK£14.99

USA phrasebook
ISBN 1 86450 182 0
US$6.99 • UK£4.50

Available wherever books are sold.

Lonely Planet Guides by Region

Lonely Planet is known worldwide for publishing practical, reliable and no-nonsense travel information in our guides and on our Web site. The Lonely Planet list covers just about every accessible part of the world. Currently there are 16 series: Travel guides, Shoestring guides, Condensed guides, Phrasebooks, Read This First, Healthy Travel, Walking guides, Cycling guides, Watching Wildlife guides, Pisces Diving & Snorkeling guides, City Maps, Road Atlases, Out to Eat, World Food, Journeys travel literature and Pictorials.

AFRICA Africa on a shoestring • Botswana • Cairo • Cairo City Map • Cape Town • Cape Town City Map • East Africa • Egypt • Egyptian Arabic phrasebook • Ethiopia, Eritrea & Djibouti • Ethiopian Amharic phrasebook • The Gambia & Senegal • Healthy Travel Africa • Kenya • Malawi • Morocco • Moroccan Arabic phrasebook • Mozambique • Namibia • Read This First: Africa • South Africa, Lesotho & Swaziland • Southern Africa • Southern Africa Road Atlas • Swahili phrasebook • Tanzania, Zanzibar & Pemba • Trekking in East Africa • Tunisia • Watching Wildlife East Africa • Watching Wildlife Southern Africa • West Africa • World Food Morocco • Zambia • Zimbabwe, Botswana & Namibia
Travel Literature: Mali Blues: Traveling to an African Beat • The Rainbird: A Central African Journey • Songs to an African Sunset: A Zimbabwean Story

AUSTRALIA & THE PACIFIC Aboriginal Australia & the Torres Strait Islands • Auckland • Australia • Australian phrasebook • Australia Road Atlas • Cycling Australia • Cycling New Zealand • Fiji • Fijian phrasebook • Healthy Travel Australia, NZ and the Pacific • Islands of Australia's Great Barrier Reef • Melbourne • Melbourne City Map • Micronesia • New Caledonia • New South Wales • New Zealand • Northern Territory • Outback Australia • Out to Eat – Melbourne • Out to Eat – Sydney • Papua New Guinea • Pidgin phrasebook • Queensland • Rarotonga & the Cook Islands • Samoa • Solomon Islands • South Australia • South Pacific • South Pacific phrasebook • Sydney • Sydney City Map • Sydney Condensed • Tahiti & French Polynesia • Tasmania • Tonga • Tramping in New Zealand • Vanuatu • Victoria • Walking in Australia • Watching Wildlife Australia • Western Australia
Travel Literature: Islands in the Clouds: Travel in the Highlands of New Guinea • Kiwi Tracks: A New Zealand Journey • Sean & David's Long Drive

CENTRAL AMERICA & THE CARIBBEAN Bahamas, Turks & Caicos • Baja California • Belize, Guatemala & Yucatán • Bermuda • Central America on a shoestring • Costa Rica • Costa Rica Spanish phrasebook • Cuba • Cycling Cuba • Dominican Republic & Haiti • Eastern Caribbean • Guatemala • Havana • Healthy Travel Central & South America • Jamaica • Mexico • Mexico City • Panama • Puerto Rico • Read This First: Central & South America • Virgin Islands • World Food Caribbean • World Food Mexico • Yucatán
Travel Literature: Green Dreams: Travels in Central America

EUROPE Amsterdam • Amsterdam City Map • Amsterdam Condensed • Andalucía • Athens • Austria • Baltic States phrasebook • Barcelona • Barcelona City Map • Belgium & Luxembourg • Berlin • Berlin City Map • Britain • British phrasebook • Brussels, Bruges & Antwerp • Brussels City Map • Budapest • Budapest City Map • Canary Islands • Catalunya & the Costa Brava • Central Europe • Central Europe phrasebook • Copenhagen • Corfu & the Ionians • Corsica • Crete • Crete Condensed • Croatia • Cycling Britain • Cycling France • Cyprus • Czech & Slovak Republics • Czech phrasebook • Denmark • Dublin • Dublin City Map • Dublin Condensed • Eastern Europe • Eastern Europe phrasebook • Edinburgh • Edinburgh City Map • England • Estonia, Latvia & Lithuania • Europe on a shoestring • Europe phrasebook • Finland • Florence • Florence City Map • France • Frankfurt City Map • Frankfurt Condensed • French phrasebook • Georgia, Armenia & Azerbaijan • Germany • German phrasebook • Greece • Greek Islands • Greek phrasebook • Hungary • Iceland, Greenland & the Faroe Islands • Ireland • Italian phrasebook • Italy • Kraków • Lisbon • The Loire • London • London City Map • London Condensed • Madrid • Madrid City Map • Malta • Mediterranean Europe • Milan, Turin & Genoa • Moscow • Munich • Netherlands • Normandy • Norway • Out to Eat – London • Out to Eat – Paris • Paris • Paris City Map • Paris Condensed • Poland • Polish phrasebook • Portugal • Portuguese phrasebook • Prague • Prague City Map • Provence & the Côte d'Azur • Read This First: Europe • Rhodes & the Dodecanese • Romania & Moldova • Rome • Rome City Map • Rome Condensed • Russia, Ukraine & Belarus • Russian phrasebook • Scandinavia & Baltic Europe • Scandinavian phrasebook • Scotland • Sicily • Slovenia • South-West France • Spain • Spanish phrasebook • Stockholm • St Petersburg • St Petersburg City Map • Sweden • Switzerland • Tuscany • Ukrainian phrasebook • Venice • Vienna • Wales • Walking in Britain • Walking in France • Walking in Ireland • Walking in Italy • Walking in Scotland • Walking in Spain • Walking in Switzerland • Western Europe • World Food France • World Food Greece • World Food Ireland • World Food Italy • World Food Spain **Travel Literature:** After Yugoslavia • Love and War in the Apennines • The Olive Grove: Travels in Greece • On the Shores of the Mediterranean • Round Ireland in Low Gear • A Small Place in Italy

Mail Order

Lonely Planet products are distributed worldwide. They are also available by mail order from Lonely Planet, so if you have difficulty finding a title please write to us. North and South American residents should write to 150 Linden St, Oakland, CA 94607, USA; European and African residents should write to 10a Spring Place, London NW5 3BH, UK; and residents of other countries to Locked Bag 1, Footscray, Victoria 3011, Australia.

INDIAN SUBCONTINENT & THE INDIAN OCEAN Bangladesh • Bengali phrasebook • Bhutan • Delhi • Goa • Healthy Travel Asia & India • Hindi & Urdu phrasebook • India • India & Bangladesh City Map • Indian Himalaya • Karakoram Highway • Kathmandu City Map • Kerala • Madagascar • Maldives • Mauritius, Réunion & Seychelles • Mumbai (Bombay) • Nepal • Nepali phrasebook • North India • Pakistan • Rajasthan • Read This First: Asia & India • South India • Sri Lanka • Sri Lanka phrasebook • Tibet • Tibetan phrasebook • Trekking in the Indian Himalaya • Trekking in the Karakoram & Hindukush • Trekking in the Nepal Himalaya • World Food India **Travel Literature:** The Age of Kali: Indian Travels and Encounters • Hello Goodnight: A Life of Goa • In Rajasthan • Maverick in Madagascar • A Season in Heaven: True Tales from the Road to Kathmandu • Shopping for Buddhas • A Short Walk in the Hindu Kush • Slowly Down the Ganges

MIDDLE EAST & CENTRAL ASIA Bahrain, Kuwait & Qatar • Central Asia • Central Asia phrasebook • Dubai • Farsi (Persian) phrasebook • Hebrew phrasebook • Iran • Israel & the Palestinian Territories • Istanbul • Istanbul City Map • Istanbul to Cairo • Istanbul to Kathmandu • Jerusalem • Jerusalem City Map • Jordan • Lebanon • Middle East • Oman & the United Arab Emirates • Syria • Turkey • Turkish phrasebook • World Food Turkey • Yemen **Travel Literature**: Black on Black: Iran Revisited • Breaking Ranks: Turbulent Travels in the Promised Land • The Gates of Damascus • Kingdom of the Film Stars: Journey into Jordan

NORTH AMERICA Alaska • Boston • Boston City Map • Boston Condensed • British Columbia • California & Nevada • California Condensed • Canada • Chicago • Chicago City Map • Chicago Condensed • Florida • Georgia & the Carolinas • Great Lakes • Hawaii • Hiking in Alaska • Hiking in the USA • Honolulu & Oahu City Map • Las Vegas • Los Angeles • Los Angeles City Map • Louisiana & the Deep South • Miami • Miami City Map • Montréal • New England • New Orleans • New Orleans City Map • New York City • New York City City Map • New York City Condensed • New York, New Jersey & Pennsylvania • Oahu • Out to Eat – San Francisco • Pacific Northwest • Rocky Mountains • San Diego & Tijuana • San Francisco • San Francisco City Map • Seattle • Seattle City Map • Southwest • Texas • Toronto • USA • USA phrasebook • Vancouver • Vancouver City Map • Virginia & the Capital Region • Washington, DC • Washington, DC City Map • World Food New Orleans **Travel Literature:** Caught Inside: A Surfer's Year on the California Coast • Drive Thru America

NORTH-EAST ASIA Beijing • Beijing City Map • Cantonese phrasebook • China • Hiking in Japan • Hong Kong & Macau • Hong Kong City Map • Hong Kong Condensed • Japan • Japanese phrasebook • Korea • Korean phrasebook • Kyoto • Mandarin phrasebook • Mongolia • Mongolian phrasebook • Seoul • Shanghai • South-West China • Taiwan • Tokyo • World Food Hong Kong • World Food Japan **Travel Literature:** In Xanadu: A Quest • Lost Japan

SOUTH AMERICA Argentina, Uruguay & Paraguay • Bolivia • Brazil • Brazilian phrasebook • Buenos Aires • Buenos Aires City Map • Chile & Easter Island • Colombia • Ecuador & the Galápagos Islands • Healthy Travel Central & South America • Latin American Spanish phrasebook • Peru • Quechua phrasebook • Read This First: Central & South America • Rio de Janeiro • Rio de Janeiro City Map • Santiago de Chile • South America on a shoestring • Trekking in the Patagonian Andes • Venezuela **Travel Literature:** Full Circle: A South American Journey

SOUTH-EAST ASIA Bali & Lombok • Bangkok • Bangkok City Map • Burmese phrasebook • Cambodia • Cycling Vietnam, Laos & Cambodia • East Timor phrasebook • Hanoi • Healthy Travel Asia & India • Hill Tribes phrasebook • Ho Chi Minh City (Saigon) • Indonesia • Indonesian phrasebook • Indonesia's Eastern Islands • Java • Lao phrasebook • Laos • Malay phrasebook • Malaysia, Singapore & Brunei • Myanmar (Burma) • Philippines • Pilipino (Tagalog) phrasebook • Read This First: Asia & India • Singapore • Singapore City Map • South-East Asia on a shoestring • South-East Asia phrasebook • Thailand • Thailand's Islands & Beaches • Thailand, Vietnam, Laos & Cambodia Road Atlas • Thai phrasebook • Vietnam • Vietnamese phrasebook • World Food Indonesia • World Food Thailand • World Food Vietnam

ALSO AVAILABLE: Antarctica • The Arctic • The Blue Man: Tales of Travel, Love and Coffee • Brief Encounters: Stories of Love, Sex & Travel • Buddhist Stupas in Asia: The Shape of Perfection • Chasing Rickshaws • The Last Grain Race • Lonely Planet…On the Edge: Adventurous Escapades from Around the World • Lonely Planet Unpacked • Lonely Planet Unpacked Again • Not the Only Planet: Science Fiction Travel Stories • Ports of Call: A Journey by Sea • Sacred India • Travel Photography: A Guide to Taking Better Pictures • Travel with Children • Tuvalu: Portrait of an Island Nation

Index

Text

A

accommodations 129–36.
  See also Places to Stay
  index
  B&Bs 129, 134, 135
  camping 129
  hostels 38, 130, 132
  hotels 130–6
activities 119–28. *See also*
  individual activities
African Americans 28, 32, 45,
  116
AIDS/HIV 36, 48
air travel 56–60
  airlines 58
  glossary 57
  museum 117–8
  tickets 56, 57
airport 63–4
  accommodations near 136
  customs 39–40
  security 47
  transportation to/from 64
Alaska Building 74
Alexie, Sherman 31
Alki Beach Park 118, 125
Alki Trail 120
Allen, Paul 19, 20, 93, 94,
  167
Ameripass 60–1
Amtrak 61
antiques 171–2, 180, 187
Apex Mountain Resort 126
aquariums
  Point Defiance Zoo &
    Aquarium 187
  Seattle Aquarium 89–90
architecture 31–2
  books 46
  tours 72, 73–5, **74**
Arctic Building 73
art. *See also* museums
  galleries 28, 104, 172–3,
  180

native 28–9, 77
public 29, 76, 106, 107–8
Art Institute of Seattle 51
Asian Americans 28, 83
ATMs 41

B

B&Bs. *See* accommodations
Bainbridge Island 71, 184,
  186
Bainbridge Island Winery 184
Ballard 71, 111–3, **Map 11**
  entertainment 158, 162
  restaurants 153–4
  transportation 113
Bank of America Tower 32,
  73
Barry, Lynda 31
bars 158–60
baseball 82, 167
basketball 167–8
Bathhouse Theatre 110
beaches 111, 116, 117, 118,
  125
beer. *See* bars; brewpubs &
  breweries; microbrews;
  pubs
Bellevue 177, 180
Bellevue Art Museum 177
Bellevue Botanical Gardens
  177
Belltown 90–2, **Map 6**
  accommodations 132–3
  coffeehouses 145
  entertainment 156, 158,
    159, 162
  restaurants 144–6
  transportation 91–2
Benaroya Concert Hall 74
Betty Bowen Park 97
bicycles 45, 67, 71, 119–21,
  174, 190
Big White Ski Resort 126
billiards 158

Binns, Archie 30
birds 25
Blake Island 186
blues clubs 162
boats. *See* cruises; ferries
body art 99
Boeing 9, 18–9, 27, 117
Boeing, William 18
books 45–6. *See also*
  libraries; literature
bookstores 170–1
Bremerton 187
brewpubs & breweries
  157–8, 181, 189
British Columbia
  ski resorts 126–7
  traveling to 200
  Victoria 197–201, **198**
Broadway 98, 100
Burke, Thomas 120
Burke Museum 103–4
Burke-Gilman Trail 67, 71,
  119–20
buses 60–1, 64, 68–9
business district 76
business hours 53
Butchart Gardens 197

C

camera stores. *See* photography
camping. *See* accommodations
Canada. *See* British Columbia
Capitol Hill 70–1, 98, 100–1,
  Map 8
  accommodations 135
  coffeehouses 148
  entertainment 156, 157,
    160, 162, 163, 165,
    166, 167
  restaurants 148–50
  transportation 101
Carl English Jr Botanical
  Gardens 112

Bold indicates maps.

Places to Stay

Bold indicates maps.

Places to Eat

Boxed Text

Seattle Map Section

MAP 1 SEATTLE

PLACES TO EAT
4 Salty's on Alki
6 Pegasus Pizza &
   Pasta; Boca; Spud
   Fish & Chips;
   Phoenicia at Alki; Alki
   Café; Alki Bakery;
   Sunfish
7 Jak's Grill
8 Spiro's Pizza

OTHER
1 Lakeside School
2 Underwater Sports
3 Sierra Club
5 Alki Point Lighthouse
9 Elliott Bay Brewery & Pub
10 West Seattle
   Municipal Golf
   Course
11 Thriftway Market
12 Museum of Flight
13 Fauntleroy Ferry
   Terminal
14 Vashon Island Ferrry
   Terminal

Saint Edward
State Park

Big Finn
Hill Co.
Park

Dewey
Park

Bitter
Lake

Jackson Park
Golf Course

NE 145th St

130th St NW

NE 125th St

Lake
City

Inverness

Magnuson
Park

Bitter
Lake

Carkeek
Park

Haller
Lake

105th St

Northgate

N 80th St

Meadow
Point

Golden
Gardens
Park

North
Beach

Ballard
NW Market St

NW
65th St

Green
Lake

Woodland
Park

N 50th St

NE 45th St

University
of Washington

Lake
Washington

Discovery
Park

West Point

Shilshole
Bay

Fremont

MAP 11

MAP 10

MAP 9

Evergreen Point
Floating Bridge
(Governor Albert
D Rosellini Bridge)

Queen
Anne

Lake
Union

Washington
Park Arboretum

Capitol
Hill

Seattle
Center

Downtown

Seattle
University

Madrona

Lake
Washington

MAP 7

MAP 8

MAP 6

MAP 2

Puget
Sound

Elliott
Bay

Duwamish Head

MAP 5

MAP 4

Mercer
Island

Alki
Beach
Park

Alki

Alki
Point

SW Admiral Way

Harbor
Island

Harbor

West Seattle Fwy

Alaskan Fwy

Colman
Park

Mount
Baker
Park

Beacon
Hill

West
Seattie

SW Alaska St

Camp
Long

Georgetown

Jefferson
Park Golf
Course

Columbia

Bailey
Peninsula

Seward
Park

South Seattle
Community
College

Duwamish River

Ranier
Valley

Lake
Washington

Point Williams

Lincoln
Park

SW Roxbury St

Brace
Point

To Southworth
Ferry Terminal

Vashon Island

Route 16

Routes 26, 28, 39, 42

Metro Tunnel { 5 a.m. - 7 p.m. M-F
10 a.m. - 6 p.m. Sat }

Tunnel Stations

Tunnel Entrance

Accessible Entrance

Metro Customer Service

Ride Free Area (6 a.m. to 7 p.m.)

Waterfront Streetcar & Stations

Seattle Center Monorail

Accessible Route

Footpath from Ferry to Tunnel

Stair Access

Parks

King County METRO

CUSTOMER ASSISTANCE

All phone numbers, unless otherwise noted, are in the 206 area code.

Rider Information	553-3000	Accessible Service	263-3113	Ridematch/Vanpool	625-4500
TTY Users	684-1739	TTY Users	263-3116	TTY Users	684-1855
Customer Service	553-3060	Lost and Found	553-3090	Community Transit	800-562-1375
TTY Users	684-2029	Pass Sales	624-PASS	Pierce Transit	800-562-8109
BUS-TIME	287-8463	Ferry Service	464-6400	Sound Transit	888-889-6368

Make your connection with Metro Online — http://transit.metrokc.gov/

King County
Metro Transit
©2001

MAP 4 PIONEER SQUARE & INTERNATIONAL DISTRICT

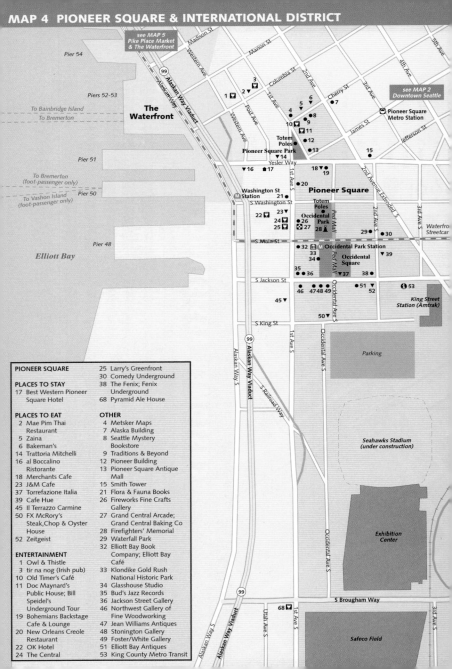

see MAP 5
Pike Place Market
& The Waterfront

see MAP 2
Downtown Seattle

The
Waterfront

Pioneer Square
Metro Station

Pier 54

Piers 52-53

To Bainbridge Island
To Bremerton

Pier 51

To Bremerton
(foot-passenger only)

To Vashon Island
(foot-passenger only)

Pier 50

Pier 48

Elliott Bay

Totem
Poles

Pioneer Square Park

Yesler Way

Washington St
Station

S Washington St

Pioneer Square

Totem
Poles

Occidental
Park

S Main St

Occidental Park Station

Occidental
Square

S Jackson St

Waterfront
Streetcar

King Street
Station (Amtrak)

S King St

Parking

Seahawks Stadium
(under construction)

Exhibition
Center

Safeco Field

S Brougham Way

PIONEER SQUARE

PLACES TO STAY
17 Best Western Pioneer
Square Hotel

PLACES TO EAT
2 Mae Pim Thai
Restaurant
5 Zaina
6 Bakeman's
14 Trattoria Mitchelli
16 al Boccalino
Ristorante
18 Merchants Cafe
23 J&M Cafe
37 Torrefazione Italia
39 Cafe Hue
45 Il Terrazzo Carmine
50 FX McRory's
Steak,Chop & Oyster
House
52 Zeitgeist

ENTERTAINMENT
1 Owl & Thistle
3 tir na nog (Irish pub)
10 Old Timer's Café
11 Doc Maynard's
Public House; Bill
Speidel's
Underground Tour
19 Bohemians Backstage
Cafe & Lounge
20 New Orleans Creole
Restaurant
22 OK Hotel
24 The Central

25 Larry's Greenfront
30 Comedy Underground
38 The Fenix; Fenix
Underground
68 Pyramid Ale House

OTHER
4 Metsker Maps
7 Alaska Building
8 Seattle Mystery
Bookstore
9 Traditions & Beyond
12 Pioneer Building
13 Pioneer Square Antique
Mall
15 Smith Tower
21 Flora & Fauna Books
26 Fireworks Fine Crafts
Gallery
27 Grand Central Arcade;
Grand Central Baking Co
28 Firefighters' Memorial
29 Waterfall Park
32 Elliott Bay Book
Company; Elliott Bay
Café
33 Klondike Gold Rush
National Historic Park
34 Glasshouse Studio
35 Bud's Jazz Records
36 Jackson Street Gallery
46 Northwest Gallery of
Fine Woodworking
47 Jean Williams Antiques
48 Stonington Gallery
49 Foster/White Gallery
51 Elliott Bay Antiques
53 King County Metro Transit

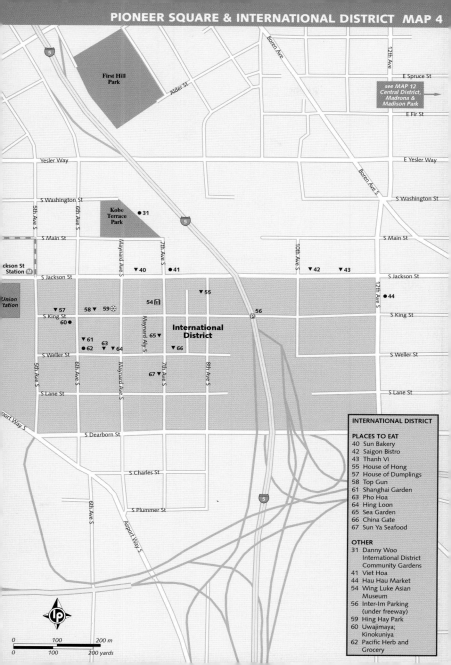

5

First Hill
Park

Alder St

Boren Ave

12th Ave

E Spruce St

see MAP 12
Central District,
Madrona &
Madison Park

E Fir St

Yesler Way

E Yesler Way

Boren Ave S

S Washington St

S Washington St

5th Ave S

6th Ave S

Kobe
Terrace
Park

● 31

5

10th Ave S

S Main St

S Main St

Maynard Ave S

7th Ave S

ackson St
tation Ⓜ

S Jackson St

▼ 40

● 41

S Jackson St

12th Ave S

Union
tation

▼ 57

58 ▼ 59 ❀

54 🏛

▼ 55

● 44

S King St

● 60

56 🅿

S King St

S Weller St

▼ 61
● 62

63
▼ ▼ 64

International
District

65 ▼

▼ 66

Maynard Aly S

S Weller St

7th Ave S

8th Ave S

67 ▼

S Lane St

5th Ave S

6th Ave S

Maynard Ave S

S Lane St

port Way S

S Dearborn St

S Charles St

6th Ave S

Airport Way S

S Plummer St

5

0   100   200 m
0   100   200 yards

Ⓛⓟ

MAP 5 PIKE PLACE MARKET & THE WATERFRONT

PLACES TO STAY
6 Hotel Edgewater
18 Pensione Nichols
23 Inn at the Market;
   Campagne; Café Campagne
42 HI - Seattle

PLACES TO EAT
1 Old Spaghetti Factory
11 Anthony's Pier 66; Bell
   Street Diner
13 Cutter's Bayhouse
14 Etta's Seafood
17 Le Pichet
36 Il Bistro
39 Steamer's Seafood Cafe
41 Typhoon!
43 Wolfgang Puck Café
45 Elliott's Oyster House
48 Ivar's Acres of Clams

ENTERTAINMENT
15 Virginia Inn Tavern
19 Kell's Restaurant & Bar
34 Showbox

OTHER
2 Seattle Trade & Technology
   Center
3 Spirit of Puget Sound
   Harbor Cruises
4 Port of Seattle
5 Victoria Clipper (Ferry to
   San Juan Islands)
7 Art Institute of Seattle
8 Port of Seattle Cruise
   Terminal
9 Bell Harbor International
   Conference Center
10 Odyssey Maritime Discovery
   Center
12 Phoenix Rising Gallery

16 Peter Miller Architecture &
   Design Books
20 North End Building: Pink
   Door Ristorante; Pike &
   Western Wine Shop
21 Soames Dunn Building
22 Stewart House: Antiques at
   Pike Place
24 Seattle Garden Center; Sur
   La Table
25 North Arcade; Blazing
   Saddles
26 Triangle Building
27 Sanitary Market Building
28 Market Heritage Center
29 Market Parking
30 Main Arcade: Vyvyn's
   Lazonga
31 Pedestrian Elevator
32 Corner Market Building:
   Chez Shea; Shea's Lounge
33 Market Information Booth;
   Ticket/Ticket
35 Economy Market Building:
   Market Theater (Theater
   Sports); Alibi Room
37 South Arcade: Pike Place
   Pub & Brewery
38 Pike Place Market Medical
   Clinic
40 Seattle Aquarium;
   Omnidome Theatre
46 Argosy Cruises; Tillicum
   Village Tours
47 Ye Olde Curiosity Shop
49 Washington State Ferries
   (Ferry to Bainbridge Island
   and Bremerton)
50 Washington State Ferries
   (Ferry to Vashon Island and
   Bremerton)

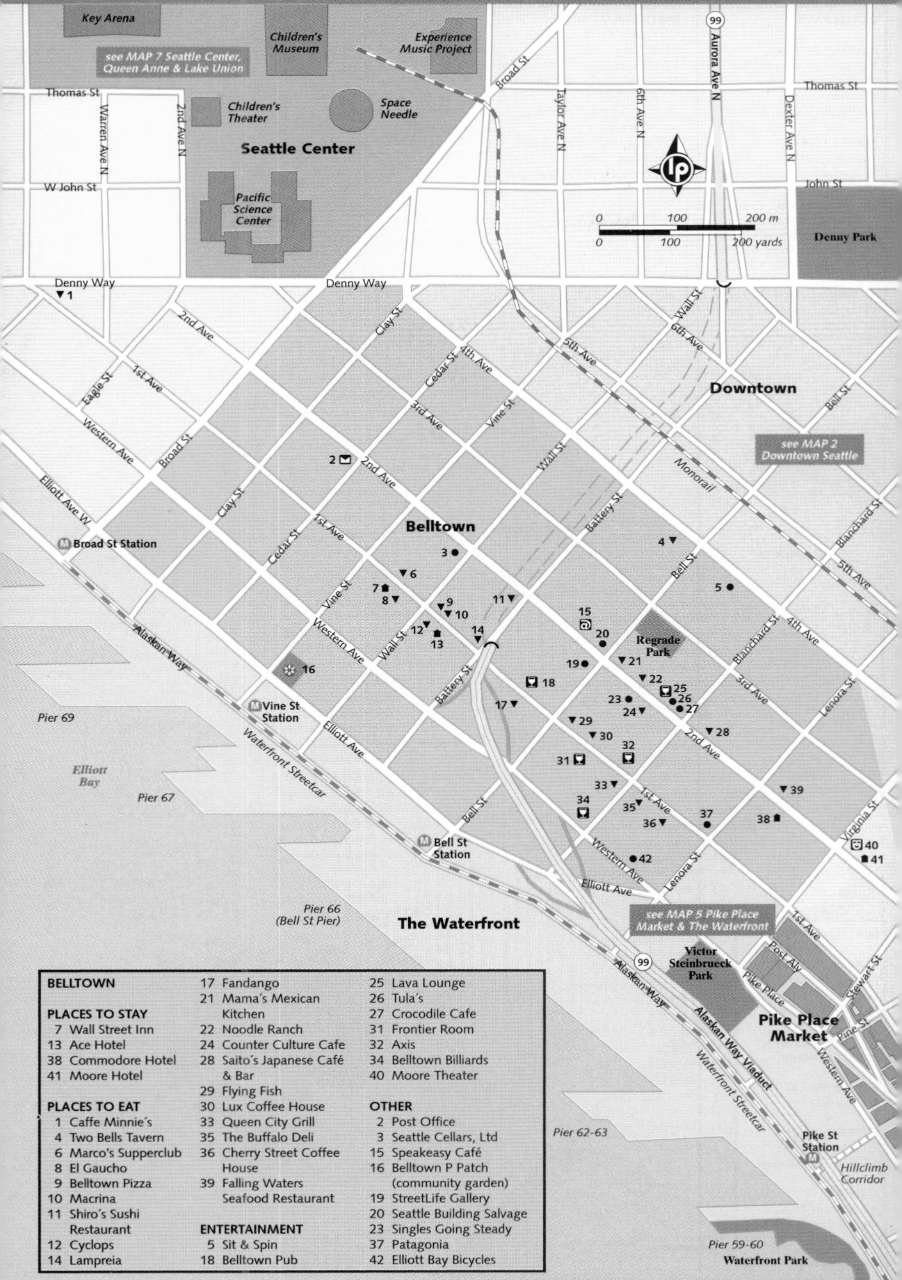

MAP 6 BELLTOWN

Key Arena

see MAP 7 Seattle Center, Queen Anne & Lake Union

Children's Museum

Experience Music Project

Aurora Ave N

99

Thomas St

Thomas St

Warren Ave N

2nd Ave

Children's Theater

Space Needle

Taylor Ave N

6th Ave N

Dexter Ave N

John St

Seattle Center

W John St

Pacific Science Center

Denny Park

Denny Way

▼ 1

Denny Way

Denny Way

Wall St

Downtown

Bell St

2nd Ave

1st Ave

Eagle St

Clay St

Cedar St

4th Ave

3rd Ave

Vine St

5th Ave

6th Ave

see MAP 2 Downtown Seattle

Western Ave

Broad St

2 ⌂

2nd Ave

Wall St

Monorail

Battery St

4 ▼

Elliott Ave W

Clay St

Belltown

3 ●

5 ●

Bell St

5th Ave

M Broad St Station

Cedar St

1st Ave

7 ▼ ▼ 6
8 ▼

▼ 9
12 ▼ ▼ 10
13 ▼

14
▼

11 ▼

15
⌂
20 ●

Regrade Park

21 ▼

Blanchard St

4th Ave

Lenora St

Alaskan Way

Vine St

Western Ave

Wall St

16 ✳

18 ▢

19 ●

22 ▼
25
⌂ 26 ▼
23 ● 27 ▼
24 ●

3rd Ave

M Vine St Station

Battery St

Elliott Ave

17 ▼

▼ 29
30 ▼

28 ▼

2nd Ave

Pier 69

Waterfront Streetcar

31 ▢

32
▢

34 ▼
35 ▼
36 ▼

33 ▼

1st Ave

38 ▼

▼ 39

Elliott Bay

Pier 67

37 ●

Virginia St

40 ▢
41 ▢

M Bell St Station

▼ 42

Lenora St

Western Ave

Pier 66 (Bell St Pier)

The Waterfront

Elliott Ave

see MAP 5 Pike Place Market & The Waterfront

99

Victor Steinbrueck Park

Pike Place Market

Post Aly

Pike Pl

Stewart St

Alaskan Way

Waterfront Streetcar

Pier 62-63

Pike St Station M

Western Ave

Hillclimb Corridor

Pier 59-60

Waterfront Park

Alaskan Way Viaduct

0   100   200 m
0   100   200 yards

MAP 7 SEATTLE CENTER, QUEEN ANNE & LAKE UNION

QUEEN ANNE

PLACES TO STAY
18 Queen Anne Hill B&B
35 MarQueen Hotel
37 Hampton Inn
47 Inn at Queen Anne

PLACES TO EAT
3 Caffe Ladro
4 Banjara
5 Orrapin Thai Cuisine
6 Chinoise Café
8 Paragon Bar & Grill
9 Queen Anne Café
17 El Diablo Coffee Company
21 Sapphire Kitchen & Bar
22 5 Spot
41 Pacific Dessert Company
43 Uptown Espresso Bar
51 Kaspar's

ENTERTAINMENT
7 Hilltop Ale House
34 Behnke Center for
      Contemporary Performance
39 Sorry Charlies Restaurant &
      Piano Bar
40 T.S. McHugh's
44 Mecca Cafe
45 Floyd's Place Beer & BBQ
46 Uptown Cinemas
52 Polly Esther's/Culture Club

OTHER
15 Thriftway Market
16 Queen Anne Pool
19 Queen Anne Library
20 Queen Anne Avenue Books
36 Larry's Market
38 Tower Records
48 Post Office
50 The Mountaineers

SEATTLE CENTER

PLACES TO STAY
54 Vagabond Inn
57 Best Western
      Executive Inn
58 Seattle Inn
59 Travelodge by the
      Space Needle

PLACES TO EAT
55 Sky City

ENTERTAINMENT
56 DV8
63 Tiny Bigs Lounge

OTHER
42 Intiman Theatre
49 Northwest Craft
      Center
53 AAA

Aurora Bridge
(George Washington
Memorial Bridge)

see MAP 10
Fremont,
Wallingford
& Green Lake

Queen Anne Drive

Smith St
W Smith St

McGraw St
W McGraw St

Lynn St
W Boston St   Boston St
W Crockett St   Crockett St
Newton St

W Howe St

see MAP 11 Ballard &
Discovery Park

W Blaine St

Queen Anne

W Garfield St   Hayes St
W Galer St   Garfield St
                     Galer St

W Lee St
Betty Bowen Park
W Comstock St
W Highland Drive   Highland Drive
Kerry Park
W Prospect St   Prospect St
W Kinnear Place   Ward St
Kinnear Park   Aloha St
W Olympic Place   Valley St
W Mercer place   Roy St
W Roy St   Mercer St
Elliott Bay Park
W Republican St
W Harrison St   Harrison St

Elliott Bay   Thomas St
Myrtle Edwards Park   W Thomas St
                     W John St
                     Denny Way

Seattle Repertory Theater
Opera House
International Fountain
Memorial Stadium
Key Arena
Children's Museum
Experience Music Project
Seattle Center
Children's Theatre
Space Needle
Pacific Science Center

Belltown
see MAP 6 Belltown

0   200   400 m
0   200   400 yards

Western Ave
Denny Way
5th Ave Monorail
Battery

1st Ave W, 2nd Ave W, 3rd Ave W, 4th Ave W, 5th Ave W, 6th Ave W, 7th Ave W, 8th Ave W, 9th Ave W, 10th Ave W
1st Ave N, 2nd Ave N, 3rd Ave N, 4th Ave N, 5th Ave N, 6th Ave N
Queen Anne Ave N
Warren Ave N
Nob Hill Ave N
Bigelow Ave N
Taylor Ave N
Dexter Ave N
Aurora Ave N
Westlake Ave N
Waverly Place N
Elliott Ave W
Alaskan Way W
Broad St

Gas Works Park

E Hamlin St

see MAP 12
Central District,
Madrona &
Madison Park

Roanoke Park

E Roanoke St

520

Delmar Drive E

Fuhrman Ave E

E Louisa St

E Interlaken Blvd

● 2

E Lynn St

▼ 12
■ 13

E Boston St

▼ 14

E Newton St

● 10

● 11

Lake Union

Eastlake

Lakeview Cemetery

☆ *Louisa Boren Lookout*

I 5

see MAP 8
Capitol Hill

St Mark's Cathedral

● 26

■ 27

Volunteer Park

● 25

E Highland Drive

Reservoir

● 23

● 24

E Prospect St

Capitol Hill

▼ 32

E Aloha St

■ 33

● 29

Tashkent Park

● 30

E Roy St

● 31

E Mercer St

Mercer St

E Republican St

Harrison St

E Harrison St

Thomas St

Cascade Playground

E Thomas St

John St

● 61

E John St

● 62

E Denny Way

Lincoln Reservoir

Denny Way

Downtown

see MAP 2
Downtown Seattle

E Howell St

Seattle Central Community College

E Olive St

LAKE UNION

PLACES TO STAY

13 Eastlake Inn
26 Tugboat Challenger Bunk & Breakfast
27 Silver Cloud Inn Lake Union
29 Courtyard Marriott
33 Marriott Residence Inn
60 Holiday Inn Express

PLACES TO EAT

1 Canlis
12 Bandoleone
27 Serafina
28 Adriatica Restaurant
32 Cucina! Cucina! Italian Café; Chandler's Crabhouse & Fresh Fish Market

OTHER

2 Patrick's Fly Shop
10 Northwest Outdoor Center
11 Sailing in Seattle
23 Argosy Cruises
24 Kenmore Air Seaplane Terminal
25 Moss Bay Rowing & Kayak Center
30 Jillian's Billiard Club & Cafe
31 Center for Wooden Boats
61 REI
62 Feathered Friends
64 Adjacent; Against; Upon Sculpture

MAP 8 CAPITOL HILL

PLACES TO STAY
5 Mildred's B&B
6 Bacon Mansion B&B
7 Shafer Baillie Mansion
8 Salisbury House B&B
47 Hill House B&B
53 Capitol Hill Inn B&B
55 Gaslight Inn B&B

PLACES TO EAT
12 Deluxe Bar & Grill
13 Siam on Broadway
16 Caffe Minnie's
17 Chutney's Grill
20 Kingfish Cafe
23 La Cocina & Cantina Mexican Restaurant
24 Pagliacci Pizza
29 Coastal Kitchen
31 Jack's Bistro
33 Broadway New American Grill
35 Vivace
38 HaNa Restaurant
40 El Greco
41 Café Septieme
42 B&O Espresso
43 Online Coffee Company
50 Green Cat Cafe
52 Hamburger Mary's
56 Capitol Club
57 Bimbo's Bitchin Burrito Kitchen
62 Ristorante Machiavelli
63 Bauhaus
73 Tango
80 Caffé Vita
84 Satellite Lounge

ENTERTAINMENT
11 The Harvard Exit
15 Elite
18 Canterbury Ale & Eats
21 Hopvine
32 Hopscotch
37 Ileen's Sports Bar (formerly Ernie Steele's)
58 Man Ray
64 R Place
65 The Egyptian
67 the bad juju lounge
68 Vogue
69 Barca
70 The Cuff
71 Globe Cafe
72 CC Attle's
74 Six Arms Pub & Brewery
75 The Eagle
78 Neighbours
79 The Comet
82 Wildrose
86 Elysian Brewing Company
87 Break Room

Louisa Boren Lookout

E Garfield St

16th Ave E

Grandview Place E

E Galer St

E Garfield St

Lakeview Cemetery

Volunteer Park

Reservoir

Federal Ave E

E Galer St

10th Ave E

E Highland Drive

Broadway E

E Prospect St

E Highland Drive

Harvard Ave E

E Aloha St

E Highland Drive

19th Ave E

18th Ave E

see MAP 12 Central District, Madrona & Madison Park

17th Ave E

16th Ave E

E Aloha St

E Roy St

E Mercer St

15th Ave E

14th Ave E

13th Ave E

12th Ave E

11th Ave E

Federal Ave E

10th Ave E

Broadway E

Harvard Ave E

Boylston Ave E

Belmont Ave E

Summit Ave E

Tashkent Park

Belmont Ave E

Lakeview Blvd E

E Roy St

E Mercer St

see MAP 7 Seattle Center, Queen Anne & Lake Union

Capitol Hill

Downtown

Lincoln Reservoir

Bobby Morris Playfield

Seattle Central Community College

Washington Convention & Trade Center

see MAP 12 Central District, Madrona & Madison Park

see MAP 2 Downtown Seattle

Streets:
19th Ave E
18th Ave E
17th Ave E
16th Ave E
15th Ave E
14th Ave E / 14th Ave
13th Ave E / 13th Ave
12th Ave E / 12th Ave
11th Ave
10th Ave E / 10th Ave
Federal Ave E
Broadway E
Harvard Ave E / Harvard Ave
Boylston Ave E / Boylston Ave
Belmont Ave E / Belmont Ave
Summit Ave E / Summit Ave
Bellevue Ave E / Bellevue Ave
E Republican St
E Harrison St
E Thomas St
E Denny Way
E Howell St
E Olive St
E John St
E Pine St
E Pike St
E Union St
Crawford Place
Olive Way
Howell St
S Madison St

OTHER
1 St Mark's Cathedral
2 Volunteer Park Conservatory
3 Water Tower Observation Deck
4 Seattle Asian Art Museum
9 Cornish College of the Arts
10 Marco Polo
14 The Orpheum
22 Pages
25 Council Travel
26 Dilettante Chocolates
27 Broadway Market; Ticket/Ticket; Cinemas; Urban Outfitters; Gravity
28 Bailey/Coy Books
30 Rainbow Natural Grocery
34 Crossroads Trading Co
36 Red Light
39 Alley Mall; Capitolhill.net
44 Pink Zone
45 Steve's Broadway News
46 Twice Sold Tales
48 Post Office
49 Kinko's
51 Fallout Records & Comics
54 12th Ave Laundry
59 Rudy's Barber Shop
60 Madison Market
61 Baltic Room
66 Velo Stores
76 Beyond the Closet Books
77 Toys in Babeland
81 Pistil Books & News
83 Superstar
85 Multilingual Books & Tapes

MAP 9 THE U DISTRICT

PLACES TO STAY
13 Chambered Nautilus B&B Inn
14 Silver Cloud Inn
20 University Plaza Hotel
24 Best Western University Tower (Meany Tower Hotel)
26 Seattle University Travelodge
43 University Inn
49 College Inn; Cafe Allegro at the College Inn

PLACES TO EAT
1 Santa Fe Cafe
3 Tandoor
4 Mandarin Chef
6 Cedars Restaurant
7 Grand Illusion Cafe & Espresso
9 Neelam's
11 Perkengruven Café
12 Araya Places
25 45th Street Deli
36 Espresso Roma
38 Thai-ger Room
39 Café Allegro
42 Orange King
46 Shultzy's Sausages
47 Perkengruven Café
54 Agua Verde Cafe

ENTERTAINMENT
8 Grand Illusion Cinema
21 Blue Moon Tavern
22 Metro Cinemas
27 Varsity Theater
30 U of W School of Drama
34 The Pearl
44 Big Time Microbrew & Music
45 Playhouse Theater
48 UW Arts Ticket Office

OTHER
2 Minds' Eye Tattoo
5 Anchor Tattoo
10 University Maytag Laundry
15 Ti Cycles
16 All For Kids
17 Red Light
18 Cellophane Square
19 Wizards of the Coast Game Center
23 City Greens Market
28 STA Travel
29 University Bookstore
31 Al Young Bike & Ski
33 Council Travel
35 University Used & Rare Books
37 Post Office
40 Bulldog News & Espresso
41 Magus Books
50 UW Visitors Center
51 Ranier Vista
52 Drumheller Fountain
53 Recycled Cycles

Calvary Catholic Cemetery

University Village Mall

Burke-Gilman Trail

University View Place N

NE Blakeley St

Ravenna Park

Cowen Park

U District

see MAP 10
Fremont,
Wallingford &
Green Lake

University Way NE
Brooklyn Ave NE
Roosevelt Way NE
NE Ravenna Blvd

NE 35th St
NE 55th St
NE 54th St
NE 53rd St
25th Ave NE
24th Ave NE
23rd Ave NE
Ravenna Ave NE
21st Ave NE
20th Ave NE
19th Ave NE
18th Ave NE
17th Ave NE
16th Ave NE
15th Ave NE
12th Ave NE

NE 70th St
NE 68th St
NE 65th St
NE 62nd St
26th Ave NE
NE 60th St

NE 63rd St
N Naomi Place
NE 58th St

NE 70th St
NE 69th St
NE 68th St
NE 67th St
NE 66th St
8th Ave NE
Weedin Place NE
NE 65th St
NE 64th St
NE 63rd St
NE 62nd St
NE 59th St
NE 58th St
NE 57th St
NE 56th St
NE 53rd St
NE 50th St
NE 47th St
Roosevelt Way NE
NE Ravenna Blvd
NE 5th Ave

NE 52nd St
NE 50th St

34th Ave NE
35th Ave NE
NE 52nd St
NE 50th St
NE 48th St
NE 47th St

22nd Ave NE

21st Ave NE
20th Ave NE
19th Ave NE
18th Ave NE
17th Ave NE
16th Ave NE
15th Ave NE

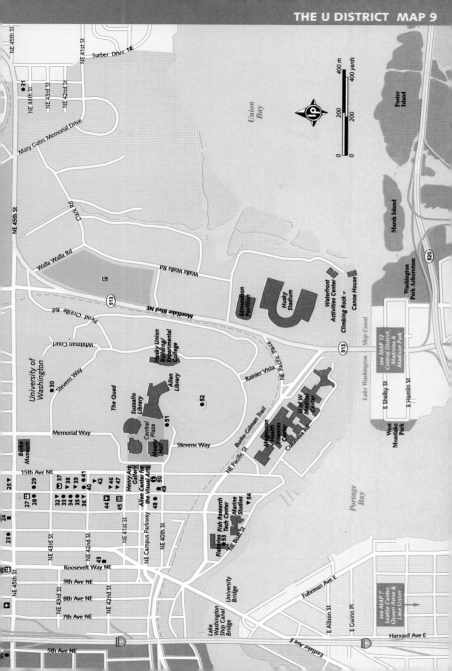

400 m
400 yards

NE 45th St
Surber Drive NE
NE 44th St
● 31
NE 43rd St
NE 42nd St

Union Bay

Foster Island

Mary Gates Memorial Drive

NE 45th St

Clark Rd

Walla Walla Rd

513

Pend Oreille Rd

Mondlake Blvd NE

Walla Walla Rd

Marsh Island

520

Washington Park Arboretum

Edmundson Pavilion
Husky Stadium
Waterfront Activities Center
Climbing Rock
Canoe House

Ship Canal

University of Washington

Whitman Court

Stevens Way

● 30

The Quad

Husky Union Building/ Experimental College

Suzzallo Library
Allen Library
● 52

Central Plaza
Meany Hall
▼ 51

Memorial Way

Rainier Vista
NE Pacific Place

513

see MAP 12
Central District, Madrona & Madison Park

Lake Washington

E Shelby St
E Hamlin St

Burke-Gilman Trail

NE Pacific St

Stevens Way

UW Health Sciences Center
U of W Medical Center
Columbia Rd

West Montlake Park

Burke Museum

15th Ave NE

25 ▼
27 田 ● 37
28 ● ● 29
● 38
32 ▶ ▼ 39
33 ● ● 41
34 ● 42
35 ● 40 ●
36 ● ▼ 46
       ▼ 47
Henry Art Gallery
Allen Center for the Visual Arts
44 ▣ ● 50
45 ▣ 49 ●
        48 ●

Portage Bay

24 ▼
23 ●

NE 43rd St
NE 42nd St
NE Campus Parkway
NE 41st St
NE 40th St

● 43

Roosevelt Way NE
9th Ave NE
8th Ave NE
7th Ave NE

NE 45th St
NE 43rd St

5th Ave NE

Fisheries
Fish Research Tech Center
Marine Studies
● 53
NE Boat St
▼ 54

University Bridge
Lake Washington Ship Canal Bridge

Eastlake Ave E

Fuhrman Ave E

E Allison St
E Gwinn Pl

Harvard Ave E

see MAP 7
Seattle Center, Queen Anne & Lake Union

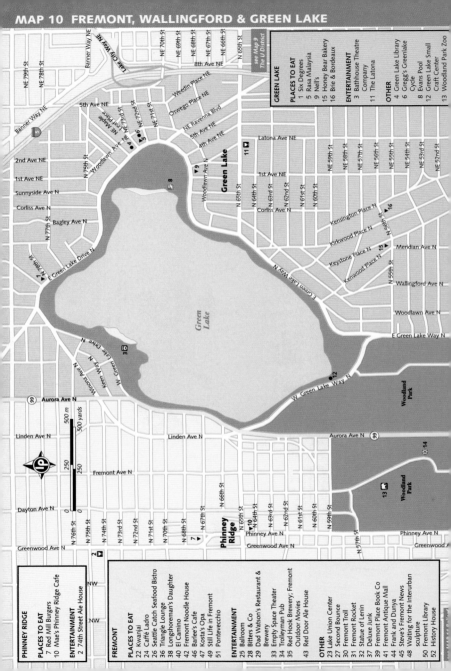

MAP 10 FREMONT, WALLINGFORD & GREEN LAKE

GREEN LAKE

PLACES TO EAT
1 Six Degrees
5 Rasa Malaysia
9 Nell's
15 Honey Bear Bakery
16 Brie & Bordeaux

ENTERTAINMENT
3 Bathhouse Theatre Company
11 The Latona

OTHER
4 Green Lake Library
6 Gregg's Greenlake Cycle
8 Evans Pool
12 Green Lake Small Craft Center
13 Woodland Park Zoo

see Map 9 The U District

PHINNEY RIDGE

PLACES TO EAT
7 Red Mill Burgers
10 Mae's Phinney Ridge Cafe

ENTERTAINMENT
2 74th Street Ale House

FREMONT

PLACES TO EAT
22 Kwanjai
24 Caffé Ladro
26 Seattle Catch Seafood Bistro
36 Triangle Lounge
38 Longshoreman's Daughter
40 El Camino
42 Fremont Noodle House
46 Barlee's Cafe
47 Kosta's Opa
49 Still Life in Fremont
51 Pontevecchio

ENTERTAINMENT
25 Ballroom
28 Bitters & Co
29 Dad Watson's Restaurant & Brewery
33 Empty Space Theater
34 Trolleyman Pub
35 Red Hook Brewery; Fremont Outdoor Movies
43 Red Door Ale House

OTHER
23 Lake Union Center
27 Second Bounce
30 Fremont Troll
31 Fremont Rocket
32 Statue of Lenin
37 Deluxe Junk
39 Fremont Place Book Co
41 Fremont Antique Mall
44 Frank and Dunya
45 Steve's Fremont News
48 Waiting for the Interurban sculpture
50 Fremont Library
51 History House

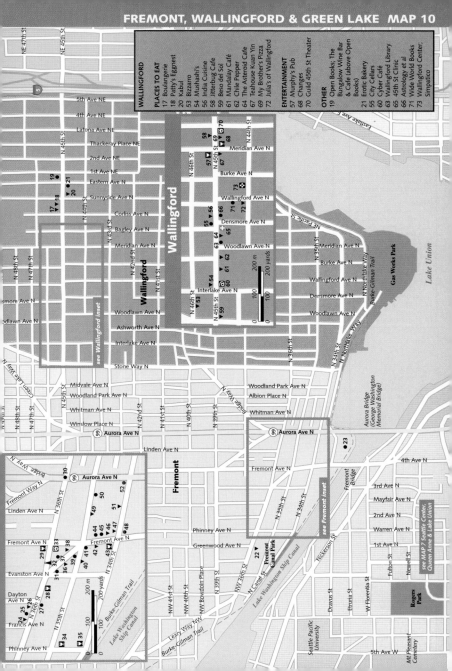

MAP 11 BALLARD & DISCOVERY PARK

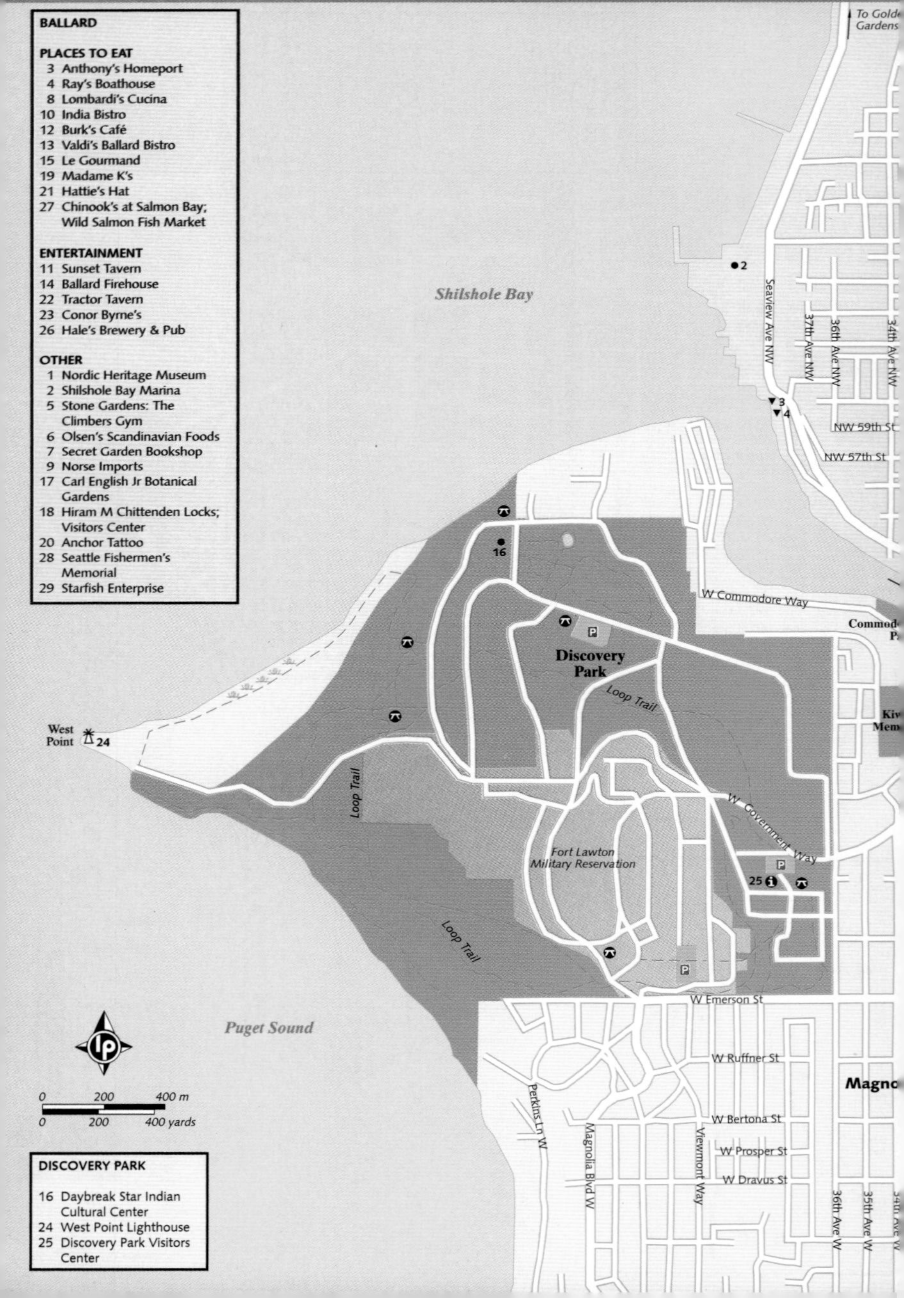

Shilshole Bay

To Golden
Gardens

● 2

Seaview Ave NW
37th Ave NW
36th Ave NW
34th Ave NW

▼ 3
▼ 4

NW 59th St

NW 57th St

● 16

W Commodore Way

Commodo
Pa

**Discovery
Park**

Loop Trail

Kiwa
Memo

*West
Point* ⚓ 24

Loop Trail

W Government Way

25 ℹ

Loop Trail

*Fort Lawton
Military Reservation*

Puget Sound

W Emerson St

Magno

W Ruffner St

W Bertona St

W Prosper St

W Dravus St

Perkins Ln W
Magnolia Blvd W
Viewmont Way
36th Ave W
35th Ave W
34th Ave

0   200   400 m
0   200   400 yards

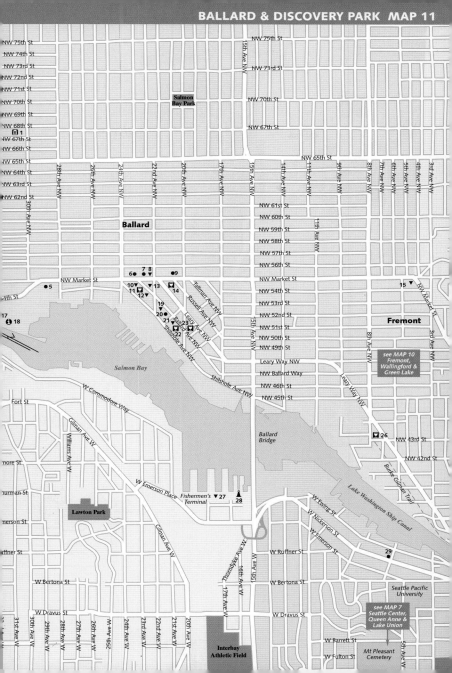

NW 75th St
NW 74th St
NW 73rd St
NW 72nd St
NW 71st St
NW 70th St
NW 69th St
NW 68th St
NW 67th St
NW 66th St
NW 65th St
NW 64th St
NW 63rd St
NW 62nd St

30th Ave NW
28th Ave NW
26th Ave NW
24th Ave NW
22nd Ave NW
20th Ave NW
17th Ave NW
15th Ave NW

NW 75th St
NW 73rd St
NW 70th St
NW 67th St

15th Ave NW

14th Ave NW
11th Ave NW
9th Ave NW
8th Ave NW
7th Ave NW
6th Ave NW
5th Ave NW
4th Ave NW
3rd Ave NW

Salmon
Bay Park

NW 65th St

Ballard

NW 61st St
NW 60th St
NW 59th St
NW 58th St
NW 57th St
NW 56th St

NW Market St

11th Ave NW

6● 7 8●
●9

NW Market St

●5

NW 54th St
NW 53rd St
NW 52nd St
NW 51st St
NW 50th St
NW 49th St

15th

NW Market St

15● ▼

Fremont

4th St

10▼
11 ▢ 13
12▼

▢
14

17
18

19
20●
21●
22
23

Tallman Ave NW
Russell Ave NW
Leary Ave NW
Shilshole Ave NW

Leary Way NW

8th Ave NW

3rd Ave NW

see MAP 10
Fremont,
Wallingford &
Green Lake

Salmon Bay

Shilshole Ave NW

Leary Way NW

NW Ballard Way
NW 46th St
NW 45th St

NW 43rd St
NW 42nd St

▢ 26

Fort St

W Commodore Way

Burke Gilman Trail

more St

Gilman Ave W
Williams Ave W

Ballard
Bridge

Lake Washington Ship Canal

thurman St

emerson St

Lawton Park

W Emerson Place

Fishermen's ▼ 27
Terminal

Cilman Ave W

28

29●

ruffner St

W Ruffner St

W Nickerson St
W Ewing St
W Emerson St

Seattle Pacific
University

W Bertona St

W Bertona St

see MAP 7
Seattle Center,
Queen Anne &
Lake Union

W Dravus St

W Dravus St

31st Ave W
30th Ave W
29th Ave W
28th Ave W
27th Ave W
26th Ave W
25th Ave W
24th Ave W
23rd Ave W
22nd Ave W
21st Ave W
20th Ave W

17th Ave W

16th Ave W

15th Ave W

W Barrett St

W Fulton St

Mt Pleasant
Cemetery

5th Ave W

Interbay
Athletic Field

Thorndyke Ave W

MAP 12 CENTRAL DISTRICT, MADRONA & MADISON PARK

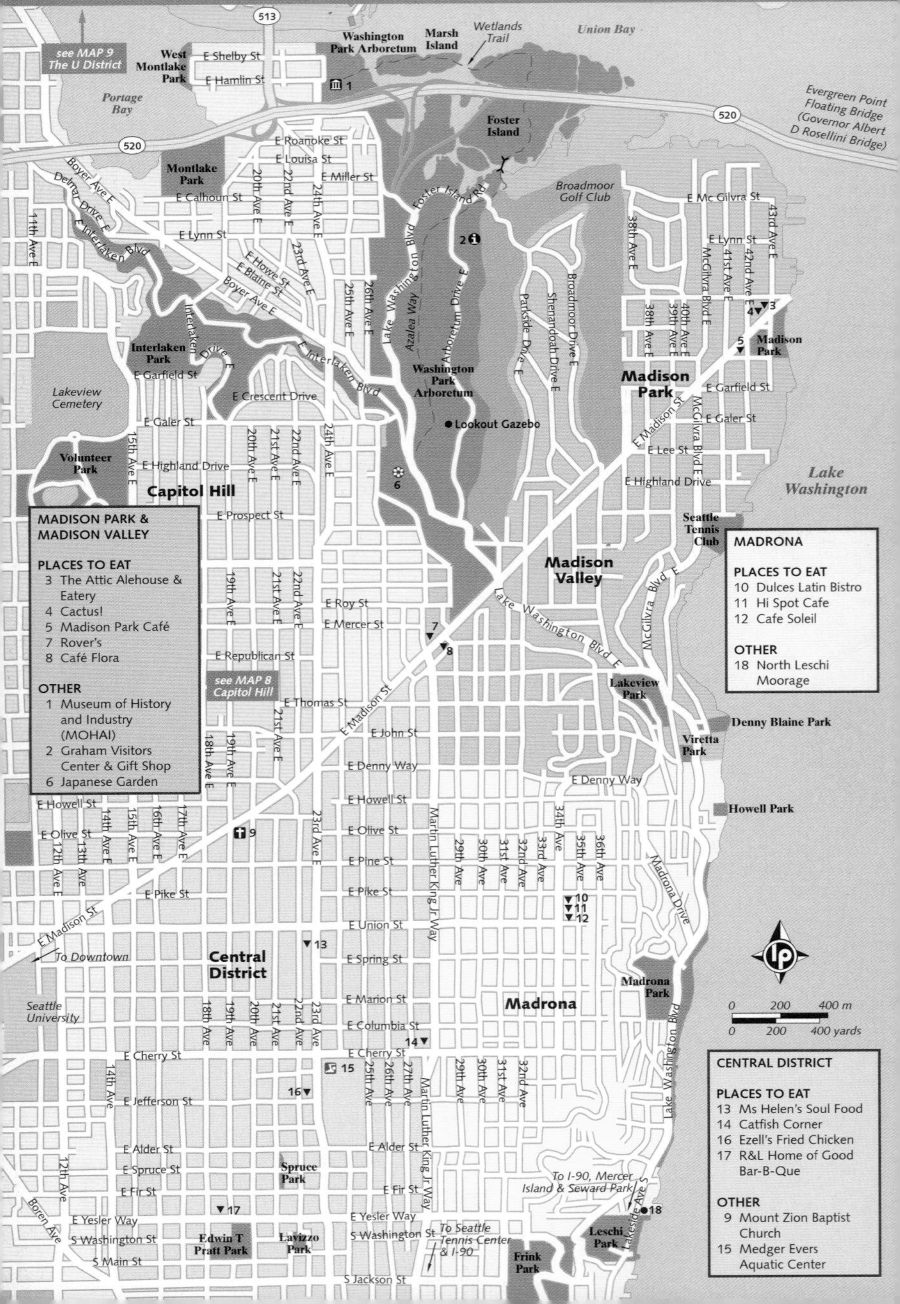

see MAP 9
The U District

West
Montlake
Park

E Shelby St
E Hamlin St

Washington
Park Arboretum

Marsh
Island

Wetlands
Trail

Union Bay

513

Portage
Bay

520

Montlake
Park

E Roanoke St
E Louisa St

E Miller St

E Calhoun St

20th Ave E
22nd Ave E
24th Ave E

Foster Island Rd

Foster
Island

Broadmoor
Golf Club

Evergreen Point
Floating Bridge
(Governor Albert
D Rosellini Bridge)

520

E Mc Gilvra St

38th Ave E
39th Ave E
40th Ave E

E Lynn St

McGilvra Blvd E
41st Ave E
42nd Ave E
43rd Ave E

Boyer Ave E
Delmar Drive E
Interlaken Blvd

E Lynn St

E Hazel St
E Blaine St

Interlaken Drive E

Azalea Way

Arboretum Drive E

Parkside Drive E
Shenandoah Drive E
Broadmoor Drive E

Lake Washington Blvd

Boyer Ave E

E Howe St

25th Ave E
26th Ave E

Interlaken Blvd

Interlaken
Park

11th Ave E

E Garfield St

Lakeview
Cemetery

E Galer St

E Crescent Drive

Washington
Park
Arboretum

Madison
Park

Madison
Park

4

3

5

Madison Park

E Garfield St

E Galer St

Lake
Washington

Volunteer
Park

15th Ave E

E Highland Drive

20th Ave E
21st Ave E
22nd Ave E
24th Ave E

Capitol Hill

E Prospect St

Lookout Gazebo

6

E Lee St
E Highland Drive

E Madison St

McGilvra Blvd E

Seattle
Tennis
Club

E Roy St

E Mercer St

19th Ave E
21st Ave E

Madison
Valley

Lakeview
Park

7

8

E Republican St

see MAP 8
Capitol Hill

E Thomas St

E John St

18th Ave E
19th Ave E
21st Ave E
23rd Ave E

E Denny Way

E Denny Way

Viretta
Park

Madrona Blvd E

Denny Blaine Park

Howell Park

E Howell St

E Olive St

9

E Olive St
E 12th Ave
E Olive St

4th Ave E
13th Ave E
15th Ave E
16th Ave E
17th Ave E

E Pine St

E Pike St

E Pine St

E Pike St

Martin Luther King Jr Way

29th Ave E
30th Ave E
31st Ave E
32nd Ave E
33rd Ave E

34th Ave E

36th Ave E

10
11
12

E Union St

E Madison St

To Downtown

13

Central
District

E Spring St

E Marion St

Madrona

18th Ave E
19th Ave E
20th Ave E
22nd Ave E
23rd Ave E

E Columbia St

14

E Cherry St

Madrona
Park

E Madison St

Seattle
University

4th Ave E
12th Ave E

E Cherry St

15

25th Ave E
26th Ave E

29th Ave E
30th Ave E
31st Ave E
32nd Ave E

E Jefferson St

16

Martin Luther King Jr Way

Leschi
Park

Lake Washington Blvd

S McClellan St

E Alder St

E Spruce St

E Fir St

E Alder St

Spruce
Park

E Fir St

17

E Yesler Way

S Washington St

S Main St

Edwin T
Pratt Park

Lavizzo
Park

E Yesler Way

S Washington St

To Seattle
Tennis Center
& I-90

To I-90, Mercer
Island & Seward Park

Frink
Park

18

Leschi
Park

S Jackson St

0   200   400 m
0   200   400 yards

close to a colorful Seattle bus stop

orful cherry trees in bloom in the arboretum

MAP LEGEND

ROUTES

City	Regional	
	Freeway	Pedestrian Mall
	Toll Freeway	Steps
	Primary Road	Tunnel
	Secondary Road	Lane
	Tertiary Road	Trail
	Dirt Road	Walking Tour

TRANSPORTATION

Train	Bus Route
Metro	Ferry

ROUTE SHIELDS

Interstate Freeway — 5
State Highway — 2
US Highway — 101
Trans-Canada Highway — 1

HYDROGRAPHY

River; Creek — Spring; Rapids
Canal — Waterfalls
Lake — Dry; Salt Lake

BOUNDARIES

International — County
State — Disputed

AREAS

Beach	Cemetery	Golf Course	Market
Building	Forest	Park	Reservation
Campus	Garden; Zoo	Plaza	Swamp

POPULATION SYMBOLS

NATIONAL CAPITAL ... National Capital	**Large City** ... Large City	Small City ... Small City
STATE CAPITAL ... State Capital	**Medium City** ... Medium City	Town; Village ... Town; Village

MAP SYMBOLS

Place to Stay — Place to Eat — Point of Interest

Airport Runway	Church	Museum	Skiing - Downhill
Airport	Cinema	Observatory	Stately Home
Archeological Site; Ruin	Dive Site	Park	Surfing
Bank	Embassy; Consulate	Parking Area	Synagogue
Baseball Diamond	Footbridge	Pass	Tao Temple
Battlefield	Gas Station	Picnic Area	Taxi
Bike Trail	Hospital	Police Station	Telephone
Border Crossing	Information	Pool	Theater
Buddhist Temple	Internet Access	Post Office	Toilet - Public
Bus Station; Terminal	Lighthouse	Pub; Bar	Tomb
Cable Car; Chairlift	Lookout	RV Park	Trailhead
Campground	Mine	Shelter	Tram Stop
Castle	Mission	Shipwreck	Transportation
Cathedral	Monument	Shopping Mall	Volcano
Cave	Mountain	Skiing - Cross Country	Winery

Note: Not all symbols displayed above appear in this book.

LONELY PLANET OFFICES

Australia
Locked Bag 1, Footscray, Victoria 3011
☎ 03 8379 8000 fax 03 8379 8111
email talk2us@lonelyplanet.com.au

UK
10a Spring Place, London NW5 3BH
☎ 020 7428 4800 fax 020 7428 4828
email go@lonelyplanet.co.uk

USA
150 Linden Street, Oakland, CA 94607
☎ 510 893 8555, TOLL FREE 800 275 8555
fax 510 893 8572
email info@lonelyplanet.com

France
1 rue du Dahomey, 75011 Paris
☎ 01 55 25 33 00 fax 01 55 25 33 01
email bip@lonelyplanet.fr
www.lonelyplanet.fr

World Wide Web: www.lonelyplanet.com *or* AOL keyword: lp
Lonely Planet Images: lpi@lonelyplanet.com.au